Principles
and
Techniques
of
Appraisal Review

Compiled and Edited by

THE NATIONAL ASSOCIATION OF

REVIEW APPRAISERS

Published by

Todd Publishing, P.O. Box 246, St. Paul, Minnessota 55102

Published in the United States of America by Todd
Publishing, St. Paul, Minnesota 55102.

First Printing, 1980

Library of Congress Catalog Card Number: 79-92760

International Standard Book Number: 0-935988-18-1

Preface

"Principles and Techniques of Appraisal Review" is a response to the need for a collection of information specifically designed for the Review Appraiser. This book, developed by the National Association of Review Appraisers, deals with the professional field of Appraisal Review.

Acknowledgements

We would like to express our sincere thanks and appreciation to Walter S. Hanni, CRA, Real Estate Consultant, San Francisco, California, and Board Member of the National Association of Review Appraisers (N.A.R.A.); and to Robert G. Johnson, CRA, Executive Director of N.A.R.A., for their special contribution to the making of this text. And thanks to all of the authors: Stephen Bye, CRA; Robert L. Clark, CRA; James T. Coe, CRA; B. L. "Bill" Dunaway, CRA; Marion E. Everhart, CRA; Julius A. Gilliam, CRA; Morgan Gilreath, Jr., CRA; Vigdor Grossman, Melvin Gruenhagen, CRA; Walter S. Hanni, CRA; Hubert Hitchcock, CRA; Samuel L. "Les" King, CRA; Marc Andrew Louargand, CRA; Claude R. Moore, Jr., CRA; and Norman G. Schmuhl, CRA; for the donation of their time and experience.

Also, we would like to extend our thanks to many others who have helped us in putting this book together.

National Association of Review
Appraisers' Educational Committee

INTRODUCTION

Real estate appraisals have been reviewed by someone ever since the first appraisal was made, owing to the fact that the appraisals have been made in almost all cases for someone other than the Appraiser himself to make a decision to buy, sell, encumber, dispose of, tax, litigate, manage, or for some other real estate related reason. Because real estate is the major source of wealth in nearly every economy, the accuracy and validity of the appraisal is of the utmost importance — thus the need for competent qualified Reviewers.

The employer, client, or person the appraisal is prepared for or whomever has reason to peruse the report is a Reviewer, in effect, and as such must be convinced, beyond any reasonable doubt, as to the reasonableness and adequacy of the conclusions of the Appraiser. The layman perusing the report, who does not have the necessary professional education and background, does not usually have the technical ability to make that important decision.

Over the past half century or so, this branch of the appraisal profession has grown in stature and the need for it has increased in equal degree to the increase in growth and technical ability of the appraisal profession itself. While much has been written on the principles and techniques of appraising — there have been many books and monographs written on its various categories and phases, including innumerable articles in the various trade journals — research and investigations of bibliographies reveal few articles and no formal publications as such on Appraisal Review.

Reviewing is a vital process and adjunct to the appraisal process. The establishment in 1975 of the National Association of Review

Appraisers has, as a major objective, sought to rectify this situation in this highly specialized field. The rapid growth it has experienced is an obvious indication that this specialized field of Review Appraising is an area that was long overdue in being represented on an individual professional basis. The Association recognizes all the existing appraisal organizations and it is not the intent to duplicate, but rather to complement and augment their services to the real estate profession as a whole.

The National Association of Review Appraisers, in response to this obvious need and to satisfy its dedicated objectives, has conducted Professional Developmental Seminars on Appraisal Review across the United States and in international areas since 1976. These educational seminars have been the forerunners for the official publication which was introduced in 1978 — the "N.A.R.A. Appraisal Review Journal."

The absence of any formal publication on Appraisal Review has instigated the publication of this handbook. Its aim is to present a coordinated practical study of Reviewing that can be used as an authoritative source of information on modern Appraisal Review.

"Principles and Techniques of Appraisal Review" has been divided into three parts. Part I covers, in general, the Reviewer's role, duties, function, processes and methods, decisions, recommendations, and qualifications. In Part II, specific review and analysis procedures for the various categories and types of appraisals are explained. Part III of this volume is comprised of the Appendix which includes examples of various types of reviews and forms used in Reviewing.

The National Association of Review Appraisers wishes to express its gratitude to the many contributors to this handbook for the conscientious efforts and fine presentations. Additional thanks are extended to the numerous members, other individuals, organizations, and N.A.R.A. Executive Director, Robert G. Johnson, CRA, who have made this publication possible.

Walter S. Hanni, CRA, MAI
Chairman
Education and Textbook Committee
National Association of Review Appraisers

Contents

PART I

The Reviewer

CHAPTER ONE

Duties and Functions

of the

Review Appraiser

WALTER S. HANNI, CRA, MAI

Walter S. Hanni, CRA, MAI, is a private Real Estate Appraisal Consultant in San Francisco, California. He has been Chief Appraiser and Chief Review Appraiser for the U.S. Army Corps of Engineers, San Francisco District, and was Chief of Real Estate for the Federal Public Housing Administration, San Francisco Regional Office, and Chief Real Property Officer, Department of Housing and Urban Development, San Francisco Regional Office, prior to retirement.

Duties and Functions

of the

Review Appraiser

INTRODUCTION

The duty and function of the Reviewing Appraiser has been an extremely important one in the profession of appraising. It is an area that has taken on added importance as the appraisal profession has advanced through the years from the days of "windshield appraising" to the modern sophisticated approaches to value used today. Thus, the Reviewer has an important place in the over-all valuation picture.

Appraisals have been reviewed ever since appraisals have been originated, by someone in some form or another. However, until more recent times these reviews were accomplished by non-professional individuals who were not experienced as Appraisers, with no consideration being given to the "appraisal process".

The past procedures were inadequate to meet the administrators' or clients' requirements and to protect the expenditure or guarantee of funds no matter what the purpose of the appraisal may have been.

Governmental institutions followed by financial institutions have been in the forefront which has changed this post situation. From this has evolved the present highly functionalized duties and responsibilities of the Reviewing Appraiser as I will discuss herein.

DUTIES AND FUNCTIONS OF THE REVIEW APPRAISER

Why are Appraisal Reviewers Necessary

To start with, why are appraisal Reviewers used or why is it necessary to review appraisals, assuming they are made by competent, qualified Appraisers, probably designated by one of the professional organizations; this, on the surface, appears to be an "unnecessary function". What I mean is — then why is the Review Appraiser necessary or required? There are some very good reasons why.

To Justify the Expenditure of Funds:
The administrator of the organization, whether it be a public body who is responsible to the "taxpayers", or the private body with responsibility to the stockholders or whomsoever, has a responsibility to conserve funds and justify, without any reasonable doubt, any expenditure or loan guarantee as to value received. The review procedure in effect is the additional "hedge" or "buffer". In other words, it was appraised by a professional and reviewed by a professional for added "safety".

Correction of Errors, Omissions or Commissions:
We must also keep in mind that Appraisers, in both fee and staff, are human like all of us; subject to mathematical error, misunderstanding of the assignment, rendering an estimate of value based upon a wrong premise, unclear rationale or many other faults. The Reviewer is absolutely necessary to clarify and correct these deficiencies. In other words, as the "technical intermediary", to secure a report from the Appraiser that fully convinces the decision-making officers of the validity of the estimate.

Mandatory Requirement:
Some organizations or agencies have a mandatory requirement that all or certain categories of appraisals be reviewed and approved by a professional Reviewer — in other words, regulatory requirements.

Bolster Appraisers Conclusions:
There is also a well-grounded theory that two professional conclusions are better than one. In effect, the second

professional, the Reviewer, could be considered almost a "joist Appraiser." He has corroborated the Appraiser's conclusion and thus adds additional weight thereto.

Technical Check for Administrators:
The administrator may also not have any direct control over the Appraiser. He has need for the services and advice of knowledgeable and technically reliable people under his control and who are conversant with his own organization's requirements — in other words, the appraisal may have been furnished from a second or third source over which he had no control in the hiring of or the specifications for performance.

As a Check on Quality Performance:
He may also perform another function, in larger appraisal organizations, as a "training vehicle" or check on "quality performance" of staff Appraisers and/or fee Appraisers regularly hired. This could also be true in a small private organization.

Failure of Appraiser to do Thorough Job:
Failure on the part of the prime Appraiser to do a thorough job is probably one of the major reasons for the need of the Review Appraiser. The written work is oftentime ambiguous. The Appraiser has sometimes, without realizing it, failed to include in his written narrative report the thinking or "rationale" which led him to a particular conclusion or estimate. It thus may leave many unanswered questions in the mind of his client or the Reviewer. Many mistakes made in appraisals go back to failure to recognize and theoretically perform the old "kindergarten" appraisal process. Also, the sufficiency and quality of data presented by the Appraiser is of ultimate importance.

Good Review Appraisers and Poor Review Appraisers:
Let's also admit that there are good Review Appraisers and poor Review Appraisers. The fact that poor ones do exist does not obviate the necessity for, nor the importance of, the Review Appraiser.

Another Important Function:
If the Appraiser knows, beforehand, that his appraisal is going to be professionally reviewed, he just might be more careful in the production of his finished product than if it were being reviewed by someone who is not fully knowledgeable of appraisal

techniques and procedures. I have found this to be very true and helpful in the reviewing function. This has often made the difference between submission of an unsatisfactory report and an approvable report.

Compatibility of the Administrative Function and the Review Function

In effect, the reviewing Appraiser is the organizational representative who gives technical organization approval regarding appraisal and valuation matters; his position is specialized and necessary. It implicates the specialized appraisal techniques, the rendering of sound judgement, and the making of unbiased decisions. While the reviewing Appraiser is a representation of the management organization, he must also, to a high degree, be "autonomous", not in any way subject to "directed" reviews or decisions to meet the particular desires of management — let us say to make a "project fly." However, this also does not mean that the Reviewer must be "inflexible." As a part of the management organization, in the course of, and as part of, the review function, conferences with management echelons concerned with a project are often desirable and essential. He should be fully oriented as to the requirements, problems and objectives of the organization, as well as the particular project itself — economics, engineering and other matters.

The appraisal is one of the "cogs" in the overall wheel — the reviewing Appraiser functions as the valuation interpreter and advisor to management in this respect.

I think the most important observation I can make concerning the review appraisal function is:

> "The Appraisal Review is the last defense between the valuation opinion and consummation of the acquisition or whatever the purpose may be."

Reviewer's Function to Approve, Not Disapprove

It is not the Reviewer's function to disapprove, as such, but more to attempt to secure an approvable, and justified valuation, within a measurable degree of value probability, of the property in question and which solves the intended purpose of the appraisal requirement.

SUMMARY

The Review Appraiser has an important function and duty to his employer and is an essential element in the overall valuation procedure, and his duties and functions are:

1. Responsibility to assure just compensation
2. Clarify and correct appraisal deficiencies.
3. Perform mandatory reviewing requirements.
4. Corroborate and bolster Appraiser's conclusions.
5. Perform professional technical assistance to his employer.
6. Appraisal quality and performance evaluation — function as a training vehicle.
7. Secure proper performance from the Appraiser in accordance with the appraisal contract and instructions.
8. Professionally monitoring of the Appraiser.
9. Documentation of the review performed.
10. Gives final organization approval regarding appraisal and valuation matters.
11. Operate in an autonomous position not subject to direct reviews.
12. Must confer with management on valuation matters and be fully oriented as to the requirements, problems and objectives of the organization he represents.
13. Reviewer's function to secure an approvable and justified valuation.

Appraisal Review is the last defense before acceptance of the final valuation.

CHAPTER TWO

Relationship of

Review Appraiser

and Appraiser

WALTER S. HANNI, CRA, MAI

Walter S. Hanni, CRA, MAI, is a private Real Estate Appraisal Consultant in San Francisco, California. He has been Chief Appraiser and Chief Review Appraiser for the U.S. Army Corps of Engineers, San Francisco District, and was Chief of Real Estate for the Federal Public Housing Administration, San Francisco Regional Office, and Chief Real Property Officer, Department of Housing and Urban Development, San Francisco Regional Office, prior to retirement.

Relationship of

Review Appraiser

and Appraiser

INTRODUCTION

Appraisals have been reviewed by someone ever since the first appraisal was made, since they have usually been made for someone other than the Appraiser himself. This is therefore not something new on the appraisal scene.

In connection with reviewing, several questions have been raised: one question is why is it necessary to review appraisals, assuming they are made by competent qualified Appraisers designated by one of the professional organizations. The question has also been raised by some Appraisers as to the competency of the Reviewer — he being less experienced than I am. There has also been charges made that the Reviewer is just a "nit-picker" and has to find something wrong just to justify his job. There are charges by some Appraisers that no matter what value I justify, it won't be approved unless it is the pre-determined amount that they can make a "deal on."

These questions and charges have already been discussed to a limited extent in previous chapters; however, there is one question which I wish to raise, since it has been often asked of me — "What is the relationship or should there be a relationship between the Reviewer and the Appraiser?"

Each has a place in the overall reviewing picture; each has a definite place in the process spectrum; each has certain responsibilities and duties, and with the word "rights" being bandied about these days in connection with almost everything. I would thus like to point out the major points or factors in order that we may get a clearer perspective of what this relationship really should be.

There are different theories about the appraisal process and, as a result, it has been exceedingly difficult to distinguish between unsound valuations, made by honest-intentional Appraisers, and actually fraudulent valuations. This, in effect, is one of the Reviewer's functions.

It is also impossible, in many cases at least, for the ordinary laymen to distinguish between a good and a bad appraisal. This again is where the Reviewer's function is required and is a necessity in the entire appraisal spectrum procedure in order to secure appraisals which are adequately substantiated and justified; to satisfy the contractual requirements; to justify the expenditure of public and private funds and to meet the varied sophisticated requirements for which appraisals are made in our society.

First, I would like to point out and clarify the responsibilities of the Reviewer.

Responsibilities and Relationship of the Reviewer — Objective of Reviewer

The major objective of the Reviewer is not merely to approve or disapprove an appraisal, but more to secure an approvable appraisal. In other words, his functional objective is not merely to peruse the report and neither approve it or disapprove it, depending upon whether he liked the final value conclusion or not. His position is one that goes beyond that. He must professionally, objectively, make a determination that the Appraiser has complied with the contractual requirements, in all respects, and be soundly and substantially justified in his valuation. And if in the Reviewer's opinion he has not, it is his responsibility to attempt to secure the necessary justification, substantiation, corrections, additional data, fulfillment of omissions or commissions or whatever, in his professional and technical judgement, is required to make the report submitted satisfactory.

Clarify and Correct Deficiencies

The Reviewer, having the objective to secure an approvable appraisal, has the responsibility to secure clarification of any points in the appraisal which, in his opinion, have not been adequately or clearly explained by the Appraiser, as well as any other deficiencies or omissions which, in his opinion, are essential or not in compliance with the initial specifications and instructions furnished to the Appraiser; also, to secure correction of any computational or other errors which he may find in the report. In his review, the Reviewer must not be a "nit-picker" — just finding something wrong, inconsequential as it might be.

It is also his responsibility to advise the Appraiser of these items or factors which he may not have been adequately advised upon or have been inadequately explained in his initial contract specifications as to the requirements he was supposed to perform under his contract. What I mean is that some of these things may not have been clearly set forth to the Appraiser in his initial assignment, which should have been.

Clarify Contract Specifications and Requirements

The Reviewer should be in a position to clarify the Contract Specifications and requirements for the Appraiser. The Reviewer should be in this pre-reviewing position as early in the appraisal process as possible. He should be involved at the time the original contract negotiations are conducted with the Appraiser, as well as be available during the Course of Preparation of the appraisal to clarify and instruct the Appraiser as to exactly what is expected and to answer any questions the Appraiser may have. He should also furnish the Appraiser with any available data or information which may assist the Appraiser in the performance of his assignment. — This is important.

The Appraiser must also realize this and should call upon the Reviewer in connection with any questions he may have in the course of the performance of his assignment. If the Appraiser does not do this, he is delinquent in performance of his assignment.

In the course of my reviewing, many of the omissions or commissions which have been made by the Appraiser were directly attributable to either inadequate specifications and instructions or were misunderstood. In many cases the Appraiser had a question, unsure of how he should proceed, but failed to ask, thinking if it is wrong I will hear about it later. However, time and effort will be saved on the part of both, if these questions can be resolved before completion of the appraisal. This can save a great deal of time and effort upon the Reviewer and the Appraiser. Our mutual objective is to secure an appraisal which is mutually acceptable.

Act as Go-Between
Another function or duty of the Reviewer is to act as a "go-between" for the Appraiser and the client. He is the man in the middle, with the responsibility to interpret for the Appraiser, clearly, what the principal or client requires of the Appraiser. It is up to the Reviewer to determine what the principal really wants or requires. Sometimes the principal thinks he wants some particular type of value or other specification when really he requires something else. It is the Reviewer's duty to interpret or advise the principal in this respect, and make such clear to the Appraiser as well as the client.

Availability for Professional Counsel
It is the responsibility of the Reviewer to be available during the course of preparation of the appraisal and to be available to the Appraiser for professional counsel. The Reviewer is supposed to be a fully qualified technical professional in his field. Often, "two heads" can be better than one in solving a problem. He can often assist the Appraiser in making a determination as to what course to follow. This can also eliminate many future disagreements at the time of the review. The Appraiser should also be aware of this and take whatever advantage there may be in such mutual discussion.

The Reviewer is Not the Appraiser
The Reviewer must always remember that he is not the Appraiser. This is sometimes difficult for some Reviewers to do. He must be cognizant that he is not assigned to do the appraisal; this has already been accomplished. He must place himself in the position of "interpreter" rather than "performer". He must not attempt to "second guess" the Appraiser. His function is to make a determination as to whether or not the Appraiser has adequately substantiated and justified the valuation conclusion reached. If the Appraiser has adequately done this, it makes no difference whether or not he has reached the valuation conclusion the principal or Reviewer would like to have or had a pre-conceived opinion of what it should or could have been if he

were doing the appraisal himself. This is the Appraiser's prerogative — not the Reviewer's.

Follow Sound Principles and Practices
The Reviewer is in effect reviewing the appraisal process and in so doing, must at all times follow sound appraisal principles and practices that have been tried and accepted in the appraisal field. In this respect, the Reviewer must also be careful that he does not become a theorist lost in philosophy, methodology and theory. He must always remember that while there is theory and accepted principles and practices in appraising, it is still an inexact science, and therefore, must also be reviewed as such. He must never attempt to substitute his judgement for that of the Appraiser, unless the Appraiser's judgement is obviously not well substantiated and in error.

When there is a fine line of distinction, the benefit of doubt should be granted the Appraiser unless it is beyond reasonable doubt. As the saying goes, he must "never lose sight of the doughnut because of the hole."

No Right to Change Appraiser's Conclusions
It is a cardinal reviewing rule, which the Reviewer must always adhere to, that he has no authority to change an Appraiser's conclusions or any part thereof without the Appraiser's permission. Any changes, corrections, additions or deletions, should always be documented in writing, by the Appraiser, and included as part of the appraisal and the reviewing report.

This does not mean that minor mathematical, typographical or other such discrepancies cannot be changed as long as they do not materially change the report and its conclusions or context; however, unless these changes are obvious, the Reviewer should at least obtain verbal approval from the appraiser and document it as such. Such documentation should always be referred to in his reviewing document.

Clarifying Versus Influencing the Appraiser
There can be a "fine line" between the Reviewer's securing clarification or substantiation of a particular factor or conclusion, reached by the Appraiser, and the outright attempt to influence the Appraiser to change his appraisal. While the Reviewer may not agree with the Appraiser, in some respects, he must not attempt to influence or *force* the Appraiser to change his conclusion by veiled threats, or other means, to satisfy his own

whims or thinking. This does not mean that the Reviewer has no right to disagree with the Appraiser. He has that prerogative to disagree and can disapprove the report, providing such can be fully justified and substantiated. He can also appraise the property himself or secure a second appraisal, but "influencing" should not be used by the Reviewer.

Responsibilities and Relationship of the Appraiser — Objective of the Appraiser

The major objective of the Appraiser must be to comply with his appraisal contractual requirements in every respect and to satisfy his client's objective insofar as it is within his professional prerogative to do so.

To furnish a report that is adequate, fully substantiated and justified in all respects, and that no reasonable question can be raised that the valuation estimated is not a sound and reasonable indication of the properties "probable" market value — is his major objective and responsibility.

In essence, the Appraiser's objective and responsibility should be to do a thorough professional job which cannot be attacked from a professionally technical aspect in any respect. This is his basic responsibility as a professional Appraiser irrespective of his professional designations obtained or how good he may think he is professionally — the Appraiser does have the responsibility to produce an appraisal report which will satisfy all the requirements of the professional Reviewer who is qualified to make such a review. These factors include the following:

Correct Interpretation of What Client Requires
There are all kinds of Interpretations of Value. The client often does not know what he wants. He may think so, but upon the Appraiser's further explanation and questioning, that is not what he really wants or needs to solve his valuation problem. The Appraiser has the responsibility to thoroughly understand the purpose, requirements, specifications, and objectives of the organization obtaining the appraisal and/or advising and clarifying what is required before he commences the assignment.

Right to Defend his Conclusions and Also Welcome Critique
As previously mentioned, the assumption must be made that the Appraiser is honest and well qualified or you would not have hired him to do the job.

The Appraiser, therefore, as a qualified professional, must be given or have the right to defend his conclusions. If you as the Reviewer think he may be wrong, in some aspects, he must be given the chance to defend and submit additional justification for any aspect or factor of his appraisal which you as the Reviewer or client do not completely agree with. Even after he has submitted his further explanation or justification, he has the right to stand upon his professional conclusion.

On the other hand, it is also the Appraiser's duty as a professional to welcome critique of his product and make whatever changes or additional justification that may rightly be in order to explain any of his determinations or conclusions.

This should be done without additional fee unless the original concept or requirement of the assignment has been materially changed.

Always Attempt to Work with Rather than Against Client or Reviewer

The Appraiser has a duty to work with the individual who has employed him. This does not mean that he in any way should compromise his professional integrity to estimate a value which in any way would violate his moral or professional ethics by coming up with a value just to satisfy a client's desires; however, he should refuse the job in the first place or after preliminary investigation that the client's desires are not reasonably professionally justifiable and meeting the Appraiser's ethical standards.

The Appraiser and the Reviewer or client must mutually support and complement each other.

Consult with Reviewer and/or Client

The Appraiser should consult with the Reviewer or client before and during the course of the appraisal process. Any questions which arise during the course of the appraisal should be clarified, rather than postponing it until after the appraisal is concluded, expecting that if it is wrong or I have misinterpreted the problem, they will tell me so and I can rectify it then. This will not resolve but only perpetuate the problem.

The Reviewer should be there for professional counsel to clarify. If there is no one to do this, then you also cannot blame the Appraiser.

Amount of Fee Immaterial

The amount of fee the Appraiser has accepted is immaterial with respect to the magnitude the job finally turns out to be. For an Appraiser to "shortcut" the final appraisal submission because it turned out to be more work than he originally estimated is unconscionable. Also, to refuse to further substantiate or do additional work on a report based upon the fee obtained is also no defense, unless additional work, over and beyond the original contract requirements is demanded.

Report Writing an Important Element

Probably one of the greatest weaknesses of Appraisers is the inability to communicate their findings without any question of doubt. Report writing is truly an art, and with semantics, the problem in our language what it is, this is understandable; however, we must accept this and the Appraiser should make every attempt to project or clarify what is in his "mind" into the written word, which is also clearly understandable to his client, even if it takes more work. On the other hand, you cannot expect him to be a "magician" and we as Reviewers must make every attempt to read or review "between the lines" to understand what the Appraiser is attempting to convey — this is not easy.

Failure to do a Thorough Job

This is a common charge attributable to "so called" poor appraising and in many cases is uncalled for. Since the Appraiser did not come up with what you thought you wanted, one can always claim this, rightly or wrongly.

If the Appraiser has fully substantiated and justified his findings in all respects, to the best of his professional ability, and has attempted to convince you that he has done so, this is all that can be expected of the Appraiser whether you agree with him or not.

Confidentiality

When an Appraiser has prepared an appraisal for a particular client, he has an inherent right that his conclusions or any part thereof is kept confidential between himself and the particular client and not given or used by second or third parties without his permission. I am not speaking from the standpoint of what legal entities may require or rule, but merely from the standpoint of what is morally, professionally and ethically right; what, in my opinion, are his rights. Clients and Reviewers should make every effort to protect this justifiable right in every way legally permissible.

SUMMARY

Appraisals have been reviewed ever since appraisals have been made. It has been exceedingly difficult, especially for the laymen, to distinguish between a good and bad appraisal or between a good appraisal and a fraudulent one. This is where the technical Review Appraiser's expertise is required.

Both the Reviewer and the Appraiser have a particular place in the overall appraisal — reviewing spectrum — and each has certain rights.

The objective of the Reviewer is to secure an approvable appraisal report and the objective of the Appraiser is to satisfy his contractual requirements and present a professional piece of work to satisfy his client's objectives. Each of the two have specific commitments within the scope of their technical responsibilities.

The crux of the entire question of their relationship is that they must work together and not against each other with the ultimate objective to produce a finished product that adequately substantiates and justifies the purpose intended.

CHAPTER THREE

Requirements and Methods of the Reviewing Appraiser

WALTER S. HANNI, CRA, MAI

Walter S. Hanni, CRA, MAI, is a private Real Estate Appraisal Consultant in San Francisco, California. He has been Chief Appraiser and Chief Review Appraiser for the U.S. Army Corps of Engineers, San Francisco District, and was Chief of Real Estate for the Federal Public Housing Administration, San Francisco Regional Office, and Chief Real Property Officer, Department of Housing and Urban Development, San Francisco Regional Office, prior to retirement.

Requirements and Methods

of the

Reviewing Appraiser

INTRODUCTION

The reviewing of appraisals in their various forms and types has been a regulatory requirement of most Federal Agencies, many other public agencies and other corporate and financial organizations for many years.

In the distant past, this function was performed by individuals who were not professionally or technically qualified. Whether or not the appraisal met contractual requirements, accepted appraisal principles and practices, complete substantiation and justification of conclusions reached, professional competency and ethical procedures of the Appraiser, the resolution of divergencies between two appraisals and other technical matters were completely overlooked or not considered as being consequential, because of the Reviewer's incompetence to make such professional determinations. This is still done in some instances today.

Through the years, especially in the last 25 years, appraisal reviewing has developed into a highly technical sub-art of the appraisal profession with experienced, professional Appraisers performing this function. The National Association of Review Appraisers was established to organize and assist those in this specialized reviewing field. It is my objective in presenting this subject, to further assist those involved in this important function and their mission as Reviewing Appraisers.

The Reviewing Appraiser has certain responsibilities to himself, as a professional in his field of endeavor; to his employer from whom he receives his compensation; to the Appraiser, whose work he is reviewing; and, to the publc in general, who may be ultimately paying the "bill" for the services rendered.

There are also certain requirements which the Reviewer is obligated to do. Also, there are certain established methods or procedures through which the reviewing process is accomplished. These and other functions will be discussed in this chapter.

From practice and experience there are certain methods of reviewing procedures which have been developed by those experienced in the "field", and which are recommended to be followed in "most" situations of appraisal reviewing.

There have been many requirements or regulations to be followed in the course of review appraising, as well as forms used in the procedure. These will vary with every organization and the appraisal purpose involved, and I might add that there are many others. While I cannot refer to all of the many varied requirements or forms used, I will attempt to give you some insight or reference to some of these areas on appraisal reviewing.

There are certain factors or conditional requirements prior to the actual preparation of the required appraisal, which the Reviewer should have some control over in order to not only perform his responsibilities, but also to assist the performance of his function and to secure the objective of his principle — which is to secure an approvable appraisal report.

There are certain accepted processes or procedures, which have been developed through the recent years of appraisal reviewing, which are generally accepted in the reviewing profession. These are general concepts as such. However, they are the ones which we in the profession have used in the past to be most effective and indicative of our professional capability. They are also those procedures which are generally accepted in our professional field as being sound, and meeting our objective as Reviewing Appraisers.

PART I

RESPONSIBILITIES AND REQUIREMENTS OF THE REVIEWING APPRAISER

When we speak of responsibilities and requirements of the Reviewing Appraiser, we are actually speaking of several or numerous different functions.

Scope

The Review Appraiser, in effect, is the person responsible for appraisal quality control and the decisions upon which his employer relies for his valuation decisions or whatever his purpose may be. This quality control, as such, is not solely dependent upon the actual review of the final product — it goes back before the production of the appraisal itself. There are certain important factors which are conducive to producing the "product" which we require and which will facilitate our review.

Selection of the Appraiser
A good system of selecting the best qualified Appraiser for the particular type of properties is the various geographical areas covered by the Appraiser.

Qualifying the Appraiser, as such, as to his ability to perform the assignment, is a subject within itself, which will not be discussed herein.

Appraisal Contract Specifications
Appraisal contract specifications and instructions, which are not only all encompassing, but which are already set forth and are understandable to the Appraiser as to the appraisal requirements are of extreme importance. The Reviewing Appraiser should have a part not only in preparing these specifications, but in administering them with the Appraiser and with the organization he represents.

An example of such a comprehensive contract specification is shown in Exhibit (1).

Skimpy or "brief" specifications, in my opinion, are of no value. It has been my experience in contracting for appraisals, that many of the misunderstandings or shortcomings in appraisal reports are directly the result of inadequate specifications and instructions to the appraiser as to what the principle wants.

Exhibit 1

SPECIFICATIONS AND INSTRUCTIONS
FOR PREPARATION OF APPRAISAL REPORT

1. **Format.** The report shall be bound in book-fashion, in the left margin, in a durable cover with a typewritten or printed label on the face thereof, identifying the appraised property, the project number and name of the Local Authority. The paper used shall be good grade bond (the heavier, the better in order to withstand repeated usage), of a size 8½″ x 11″. All pages shall be numbered consecutively from the beginning of the report to the end, including maps, plans, photographs and exhibits, and each important heading and subheading shall be shown in the Table of Contents.

2. **Outline**

  a. In order to facilitate professional review, easy reading, proper grouping and uniformity, the text shall be divided into three parts: Part I; Part II, A and B; Part III. The report shall contain brief tabulations (schedules) of computative, comparable and/or supporting data with brief explanations thereof, and with references to fuller records or more extensive computations of discussions which are included as exhibits in Part III.

  b. The outline, *Instructions and Description of Contents* below specifies the general pattern for Appraisal Reports using accepted appraisal principles and practices, and represents as a *minimum* the essentials which should be included. Any other data, information, approaches, etc., among other things which may be considered necessary or essential, should be included in the report. This outline may vary, dependent upon the type of property under appraisal and/or different parcels involved. Additional data may be recited with respect to the property or properties involved, as considered necessary, in an appropriate place within this outline. Any items omitted as being not applicable (such as information or valuation of improvements on vacant land) should be shown in the report with the statement "Not Applicable," and the justification or reason for its omission.

3. **Instructions and Description of Contents**

Part I — Introduction

1. **Title Page**

  This shall include:

  a. Project Number
  b. Location of Property (Name and Street Address or other location identification)
  c. Date of the Report
  4. For Whom Prepared
  e. Name of Appraiser

2. **Letter of Transmittal**

   The purpose of this is to transmit the Report. It shall be addressed to the individual or Local Authority who requested the services, and should contain:

   a. Location of Property Appraised
   b. Statement of Interest being Appraised and Purpose of the Appraisal
   c. Statement that a Valuation Investigation and Analysis was made, giving the name of the individuals making such investigation and the dates thereof.
   d. Total Valuation Estimate
   e. Date as of which the Valuation Estimate applies
   *f. Signature of Appraiser (Seal if applicable)

3. **Table of Contents**

   This shall be arranged in accordance with the topical headings and sub-headings with corresponding page numbers.

4. **Photograph of Area**

   A large size photograph of the location and/or general area shall be included; preferable, an aerial photograph, if such is available, with the specific property outlined thereon.

5. **Statement of Limiting Conditions**

   This shall include statements as to the following contingent and limiting conditions:

   a. That the Title is marketable (There can be no "market value" of property that is not marketable).
   b. That no responsibility is answered by the Appraiser for legal matters, especially those affecting Title to the property (This may be qualified if legal advice has been obtained and included in the report concerning certain matters).
   c. That the Legal Description furnished him is correct.
   d. That certain opinions, estimates or other data furnished him by others (and were properly identified) are correct.
   e. Any other limiting conditions or assumptions (completely spelled out).

6. **Summary**

   This summary of important conclusions is, in fact, a resume of the essential highlights of the report and its purpose is to offer an immediate and convenient reference, in brief, which shall include the following:

   a. Parcel Number
   b. Owner's Name
   c. Highest and Best Use
   d. Type of Property
   e. Present Zoning

*Certificate of Value may also be included in Letter of Transmittal if so desired.

    f.   Type of Improvements (if vacant, so indicate)
    g. Parcel Area (Square Feet)
    h. Breakdown of Valuation of each Parcel
        (1) Land
        (2) Indicated value per S.F. or acre as applicable
        (3) Improvements
        (4) Severance or other damages
        (5) Total Value
    i.   Salvage Value of Improvements

The above may be in tabulation or chart form on folding sheets if necessary.

7. References

List sources of data incorporated in the report; that is, records, documents, persons consulted and technical specialists utilized.

Part II — Analysis and Conclusions

This section comprises the analysis, valuation estimates and conclusions of the Appraiser and is divided into two parts: Part A, General Data, which is applicable to all the properties included in the appraisal, and Part B, which comprises the data and valuation information applicable to the property in particular. Where more than one parcel is involved, the information shall be included for each parcel separately as the parcel appraisal. Where certain items may be applicable to all parcels, it should be set out separately ahead of the parcel appraisals and so indicated as being applicable to all parcels involved.

Part A. General Data — (Applicable to all properties in project area)

8. Purpose of Appraisal

This should detail the purpose for which the appraisal is made and define each of the values required.

9. Legal Description

There should be recited here, a description by subdivision name, square or block and lot number, metes and bounds or such other description as will properly identify the property appraised. The Legal Description may be an exhibit in Part III; if so, state here, especially for long descriptions. Where there are a number of parcels involved, the description of each parcel should be included in Part B under each individual parcel valuation data.

10. City and Area Data

Detailed information relative to the social, economic and political background of the city and area or region should be included in this section of the report and discussed to the extent that it affects the value of the property being appraised. Major employment in the area, employment centers and relation of same to property being appraised.

11. Neighborhood Data

Under this item there shall be included a detailed discussion of all data., mostly social and economic, as they pertain to the neighborhood in which the appraised property is located. Among other factors which should be included, the following should be discussed:

a. Life Stage of Neighborhood
b. Population Trend
c. Per Cent of Home Ownerships
d. Vocations, Wage Levels and Rent Levels
e. Conformity of Development
f. Vacancy in Residential and Commercial Units
g. Prestige and/or Pride of Ownership
h. Restriction and Zoning
i. New Construction Activity
j. Per Cent of Vacant Land
k. Encroachment — Changing Use
l. Availability of Housing

The above factors will all be discussed in detail and the Appraiser's opinion as to their effect upon the market value of the appraised property.

12. Utilities

Under this item detailed information shall be given on the availability, source and adequacy to serve the property on all utilities. Location and distance from the property on all utilities should be indicated. Where a particular utility, such as sewers, is not available to the site, it should be so indicated. The availability and effect upon the valuation of the property should be fully discussed.

a. Water
b. Gas
c. Electricity
d. Sanitary Sewer
e. Storm Sewer
f. Other (Specify such as steam for heat)

13. Street Improvements
Under this item, access, or lack thereof, to the property should be fully discussed. A brief description of the character and type of street improvements bounding the site as well as in the surrounding area should be included as well as the street or road net to major thoroughfare in the area. Where streets are not improved or not in at all, it should be so stated.

14. Transportation

The availability and distance to the nearest local public transportation should be stated. The type, cost, adequacy and frequency of schedules should be indicated. Information as to other transportation generally serving the city and area should also be indicated.

15. Amenities

The location, distance from the appraised property and adequacy of miscellaneous facilities should be discussed in detail, including their relationship and effect upon market value of the property.

a. Schools
b. Markets and Stores
c. Churches
d. Parks
e. Playgrounds
f. Public Libraries
g. Other Community Facilities (Specify)

16. Favorable and Unfavorable Factors

Under this item, the various factors which are favorable to the property should be enumerated and discussed. Any hazards or nuisances which affect the property, such as obnoxious facilities, smoke, smell, noise, traffic, etc., should be thoroughly discussed, indicating their location and relationship to the property as well as its effect upon market value.

17. Real Estate Market Conditions

Market activity and level of the current real estate market conditions including supply and demand factors affecting the area as well as the specific type of property and future indicated trends shall be discussed in detail and the extent to which they affect the value of the property being appraised.

Part B. Property Data and Valuation

This section shall comprise the parcel appraisal valuation portion of the report with the data being applicable to the specific property or properties being appraised. The information and data concerning each parcel will be set out separately and be so identified by parcel number, "tabbed" for easy reference. Detail narrative discussion of each item should be included.

18. Property Data

A narrative description of the land, all improvements and other factors shall be included.

a. *Ownership* Name and address of owners of record.
b. *Area* — This item shall include the shape, dimensions and land area in both square feet and acreage as well as comparative effects of size or shape from a market value standpoint. A plat of the parcel should be included in this section.
c. *Size* — Under this item, a narrative discussion should include type of soil and soil bearing capacity, topography, grading or fill requirements, drainage, easements, rights-of-way, canals, streams, and any other characteristics which affect the parcel's value should be included.
d. *Improvements* — Describe each structure and each utility or outside improvement, structural and construction details, number and type of units, age and size of buildings, condition along with a discussion of functional in utility and analysis of layout. A plat of the building should be included.

e. *Equipment* — Under this item, include a narrative descriptive analy-sis of the mechanical equipment installed in each structure includ-ing lighting, heating, air conditioning, water supply, plumbing, fire protection, power, stoves, refrigerators, blowers, ventilation. This discussion should include the type and purpose of the equipment, physical condition, adequacy or inadequacy, obsolescence, etc.

f. *Assessed Value and Annual Tax Load* — Include the current assess-ment of land and improvements separately and dollar amount of Real Estate Taxes and Tax Rate. In this discussion, the Appraiser should reflect his opinion as to the effect of this tax burden upon the marketability of the property. Special assessments should be separately set out and discussed. The Appraiser should determine if the site area or any portion thereof is subject to special assessments. The nature of same and the total amount yet due on each parcel should be so indicated. Inasmuch as special assessments are to be paid in full by the seller at the time of closing, the valuation of par-cels involved with assessments should be made as though the prop-erties were free and clear of all assessments and the Appraiser should so indicate in his report. The Appraiser is therefore cau-tioned that comparable sales used should be carefully analyzed for such assessments and adjusted accordingly on a comparative basis with subject property.

g. *Zoning* — Indicate the existing zoning for subject property or prop-erties including a definition and the restrictions of such zoning, including height limitations, parking requirements, etc. It should also be indicated if the property is presently operating at a variance to the existing zoning. The Appraiser should discuss the effect of such zoning related to the highest and best use upon the market-ability of the property being appraised and whether or not any pro-spective change in zoning is indicated or probable.

h. *Property History* — The history of the property's use, mainly in recent years, should be discussed. The date acquired by the present owner, price paid and whether such was considered a "market sale" at the time of acquisition. Where the Appraiser's current estimate of market value is substantially at variance with the price paid by the present owner, the reason and justification for such difference should be fully discussed and the adjustments which were made to bring this previous sale up to present date. The attitude of the owner towards sale of the property as well as the possibility or prob-ability of condemnation shall also be included herein.

i. *Photographs of Property or Parcel* — A photograph or photographs of different views at least 3" x 5" in size shall be included for each parcel at the beginning of the parcel valuation of each parcel.

19. Analysis of Highest and Best Use

This section should contain a narrative discussion of the Appraiser's con-clusions concerning the highest and best use and reasons therefore. If the property is presently developed to its highest and best use, it should be so stated and, if not, the Appraiser should indicate his opinion as to what the use should be and for which there is a market, along with his justifications and reasoning. This should also be related to the existing and/or prospective zoning of the property.

20. Land Value

This should include the Appraiser's opinion of the value of the land, supported and justified fully by sales and offerings of comparable, or most nearly comparable, lands having like optimum uses. Differences shall be carefully analyzed and weighed for location, size, shape, date of sale, zoning, utility and any other pertinent factors, each being clearly stated and explained as to the various adjustments made and how it indicates the value of the land being appraised. *This must be fully justified and substantiated.*

21. **Estimate of Value by Summation Approach**

This is the Appraiser's estimate of the market value of the property as indicated by cost in the form of computative data, arranged in the following sequence, stating sources and justification of costs or prices used and for each type of depreciation.

    a.   Estimated cost of all improvements and equipment new in today's market.
    b.   Estimated accrued depreciation of all kinds.
    c.   The subtraction of b from a above.
    d.   The addition of the Land Value, Item 19 above, to c above.

The use of flat percentage figures (age-method) for estimating depreciation is not considered acceptable without full substantiation and justification for any percentage used. The breakdown method of observed depreciation should be used wherein application of the following factors of depreciation are fully treated and substantiated:

    a.   Estimate of Rehabilitation Cost.
    b.   Estimate of General Deterioration.
    c.   Estimate of Curable Functional Obsolescence.
    d.   Estimate of Incurable Functional Obsolescence.
    e.   Estimate of Economic Obsolescence — justified by market data.

The land value portion of this approach should be justified upon the basis of Section 19 above. Where this approach is not applicable, the Appraiser should so indicate with the reasons therefore.

22. **Estimate of Value as Indicated by Income Approach**

    a.   This is the Appraiser's estimate of the property's value based upon an analysis of the present worth of the future potential benefits of the property measured by the net income which a fully informed person is warranted in assuming the property will produce during its remaining useful life, which is then capitalized at a justified rate to reflect its current value from a prudent investment standpoint (particularly in the case of income or investment real estate). This approach is arranged in the form of computative data to show the following, along with whatever else may be considered pertinent, and to include factual data and justification to support each figure and factor used.

        (1) Estimated Gross Income — Derived from rental analysis of unit rates being paid for similar competitive accommodations.
        (2) Vacancy and Credit Losses — From experience records and the market.
        (3) Effective Gross Income
        (4) Operating expenses, itemized under three subheads to show:

        (a) Operating Costs
        (b) Reserves for Replacements
        (c) Fixed Charges (Taxes, Insurance, etc.)
    (5) Net Income (3 less 4)
    (6) Capitalization of Net Income shall be at the rate prevailing for this type property and location. It shall reflect current market conditions and trends, interest rates, return that will attract equity capital, reliability of constant stream and all other factors which may influence the rates applicable to the particular property. The capitalization rate and technique used shall be justified by narrative explanation supported by sources of rates and factors used.

b.   Where properties are vacant and unimproved and are suitable under their optimum use for income development, the "residual approach" to value must be fully explored and set out in his report. Under this approach technique, by the development of a hypothetical improvement upon the site, the computative analysis and capitalization will result in a "residual" value to the land. This approach, if used, and the computation used shall be fully justified and substantiated in all respects.

c.   Where vacant land has a potential use developed for subdivision purposes, the Appraiser must also include the "Development Method", which technique reflects the value of the land if it were subdivided and sold, subtracting all development costs, profit, etc., resulting in a residual value to the land in its present unimproved condition. Under this approach, all development costs used, income from the sale of finished lots, profit and other items must be fully substantiated and justified as well as the proper interest and discount for the time element involved. A sketch plat of the proposed subdivision will also be included in this section. In connection with this approach, it is often necessary that the Appraiser secure the services of technical engineering specialists to develop a proposed plan of development and engineering cost estimate. In such cases, the Engineer's Report should be referred to in this section of the appraisal and a copy of his report included in Section III, Addendum.

Where any form of the Income Approach is not utilized, the Appraiser should so indicate with the reasons therefore.

23. **Estimate of Value as Indicated by Comparative Method (Market Approach)**

This shall recite the Appraiser's opinion of the property's value as substantiated by records of sales and offerings of comparable properties. All recent sales should be listed and reflected in this valuation or omission explained. Differences shall be weighed for location, size, shape, date of sale, zoning, utility and such other factors as may be pertinent shall be clearly stated and explained in relation to its comparability and reflection of the value of subject property. Where there are no directly comparable or recent sales of properties, it may be necessary for the Appraiser to utilize older sales, less comparable properties or go farther afield to secure an adequate number of sales to justify value and thus more extensive adjustments are necessary. A statement that there are no recent comparable sales in the area will not be acceptable.

24. Correlation and Interpretation of Estimate and Conclusion of Value

Under this item, the Appraiser shall include a narrative discussion wherein he has interpreted all the foregoing valuation estimates as well as all other pertinent factors affecting value, with his reasons why one or more of the conclusions of value reached is most indicative of the market value of the property. The scope of this final correlation is dependent upon the purpose of the appraisal and the complexity of the appraisal problem as well as the adequacy or inadequacy of pertinent data as well as the processing procedures and reasonableness thereof, which have been carried out. This will be thoroughly discussed in order that his reasoning and conclusions are beyond question. The unit basis of value for land (re square feet, acre, lot, etc.) and for buildings (square feet) should be included for the convenience of the reviewer in relating the value of subject land and improvements to historical transactions.

25. Salvage Value of Improvements

The Appraiser shall include the salvage value or value for removal off-site for each of the structures on each parcel separately in the parcel valuation. This is required in the event the owners elect to retain the improvements, this amount will be deducted from the market value of the property. In the event the improvements on a parcel have a minus value and are a detriment to the highest and best use of the property, their removal or demolition cost should be estimated and deducted from the market value of the parcel.

26. Severance Damage

If any of the properties are partial takings of an ownership, severance damage must be fully described and discussed. If it is the Appraiser's opinion that there is none, it should be so stated with the reasons therefore. The method of estimation and the valuation therefore must be fully discussed and supported by justifiable evidence or persuasive argument.

27. Plottage or Assemblage Value

Where a project site is comprised of a number of smaller parcels and it is indicated in the market that after acquistion of these smaller parcels by the Local Authority, the combined assemblage of smaller parcels will have a greater per square foot value than the smaller parcels, before assemblage, the Appraiser should so indicate and include a detailed discussion of this factor with his estimate supported by market data sales clearly justifying this plottage value.

28. Certification of Appraiser

If the Appraiser so desires, this certification may be included in the letter of transmittal; however, as a minimum, it shall include the following statements:

a. That the Appraiser has no undisclosed interest in the property, or contemplated.

    b.   That the Appraiser's employment and his compensation are not contingent upon the valuation found.

    c.   That he has personally and thoroughly inspected the property.

    d.   That according to the best of his knowledge, everything contained in the report is true and that no important facts have been withheld or overlooked.

    e.   That the appraisal has been made in accordance with the standards of practice or code of ethics of the professional group or association in which he may hold membership.

    f.   That the values required of the described property are a certain number of dollars as of a certain date.

    g.   Signature of the Appraiser.

Part III — Addenda

Under this section shall be included all exhibits, charts, plats, plans, graphs, maps, photographs, reports, documents, specifications, detailed estimates, etc., which may be referred to in his report or are used to further substantiate his findings or are considered pertinent thereto. All exhibits must be presented in a neat, attractive and convenient manner. All charts, maps, graphs, etc., must be prepared in a professional and workmanlike manner.

29. Vicinage Map

An adequate sized City or area map, the scale of which will readily identify the site location and other important facilities, as required or necessary. The site area should be shown in red and so indicated in the map legend.

30. Comparative Data Map

The site area should be shown in red and all sales numbered and shown in yellow. If feasible, this map may be combined with the Vicinage Map.

31. Detail of Comparative Data

A sales analysis sheet shall be included for each sale and will include, among other things that may be necessary, the following:

    a.   Photograph of the Property
    b.   Grantor
    c.   Grantee
    d.   Date of Sale
    e.   Recording Data
    f.   Type of Transfer
    f.   Amount of Internal Revenue Stamp
    h.   Source of Information
    i.   Verified Sales Price
    j.   By Whom Verified
    k.   Breakdown of Sales Price
        (1) Amount to Land
        (2) Amount to Improvements
    l.   Terms of Sale
    m.   Improvements at Time of Sale
    n.   Use of Property

o. Zoning
p. Description — Location of Property
q. Assessment Data
r. Remarks — Including Comparison Adjustments

*32. **Plot Plans**

*33. **Floor Plans**

34. **Other Pertinent Exhibits — Charts, Graphs, Historical Income and Expense Data, Detailed Estimates, Abstracts of Leases, etc.**

35. **Special Reports — Prepared by Technical Specialists hired by the Appraiser in connection with the Appraisal.**

36. **Qualifications of Contract Appraiser**

The Appraiser shall include a statement of his diversified qualifications as evidence that he is qualified to make such an appraisal. This should include facts about his education, technical training, type and years of experience, trade and professional organizations of which he is a member, courts in which he has appeared as an expert witness, individuals and organizations for whom he has made appraisals and important and similar assignments.

General

1. **Parcel** — The term parcel, as used herein, means any tract or contiguous tracts of land the apparent title to which is held by the same person or persons, regardless of whether such tract or tracts consist of platted lots or are otherwise normally divided. The Appraiser shall collaborate with the Local Authority in numbering each parcel in order that such numbering will be the same as those used in the project Surveys, Title Reports, and other land documentation.

2. **Review of Reports** — It should be undestood by the Appraiser that the appraisal reports are subject to careful, professional review by the Public Housing Administration. Therefore, they must be fully detailed, narrative type reports with all items and factors clearly set forth, and full substantiated and justified in every respect and in such a manner that there will be no doubt in the Reviewer's mind as to his conclusions. All deficiencies or items which, in the Reviewer's opinion, require further substantiation or justification must be performed by the Appraiser in the form of a supplemental report at the Appraiser's own expense in accordance with the Appraisal Contract.

*All Plats and Plans may be bound as facing pages opposite the description, tabulation or discussions they concern.

Responsibility To The Appraiser

Effective and expeditious contract approval, review and approval of the appraisal, including payment of the fee is imperative. Any delays in these aspects can result in reviewing problems as well as cause discussion between the parties involved. It is also important that any definitive instructions for special considerations and conditions be made known to the Appraiser prior to entering into any contract for appraisal.

It is also imperative that the principle requiring the appraisal furnish the Appraiser with everything he has and knows about the property, and gives the Appraiser what he needs to know in order to do the job which is expected of him. Don't hold back any data on the property — let him decide on how important it is to reach a decision of market value. On numerous occasions I have seen where information was withheld from the Appraiser, which could have made a difference on the conclusions reached, on the assumption that "let him find it out on his own, this is what we are hiring him for". This is a very erroneous attitude, since many times such information may not be readily obtainable by the Appraiser and could make some material difference in his conclusion were it known to him.

The reviewing process should insure that staff review Appraisers thoroughly document inquiries made of Appraisers regarding items of major importance to evaluating the adequacy of the report.

On the other hand, give the Appraiser the latitude to present his best "professional work" without restricting him to "rules and regulations" which may restrict him from presenting his professional opinion — as he sees it. Allow the Appraiser to have at least some degree of flexibility, and to use his initiative unless it violates the purpose and objective upon which the appraisal is being made. The Reviewer must always remember that he is dealing with a professional who also has certain rights to express his professional conclusions.

Professional Counseling

Another important factor in the process of review appraising is that the Review Appraiser be available for professional counsel to the contract Appraiser, whereby questions which arise prior to, or during the course of preparation of an appraisal may be resolved or clarified — rather than after the fact. It has been my experience that such close corroboration between the parties involved is extremely important in expediting the over-all valuation procedure and approval of the appraisal. If agreement can be reached on questionable matters, approaches or other factors of an appraisal in advance of the review, it will reduce any questions which may be raised during the course of the reviewing process and also make the Reviewer's job less of a problem.

Review Appraiser, Not The Negotiator
The Reviewing Appraiser should confine himself to the task of reviewing the appraisal itself and not becoming directly involved in the negotiation settlement. He should be an unbiased party in the over-all transaction, merely giving his opinion as the validity of the market value as appraised. This does not mean that he should ignore any other appraisals presented by the parties involved. In the event an appraisal is presented by the party opposing his principle, this should be considered along with the appraisal he has already reviewed and should be reviewed and given the same credence as a second appraisal. However, he must always maintain his position, and function as the "advisor" on valuation methods to the negotiators rather than the advocating participant. This does not mean, however, that the Reviewer cannot operate in a quasi-advisory capacity in the course of negotiations, and he should do so.

It was never intended that the Review Appraiser should have any kind of veto power over negotiations or condemnation settlements. This is a matter which should be resolved by the negotiation and legal elements, rather than the Reviewer.

Reviewer, Not The Appraiser
One important "rule" that should always be remembered is that the Reviewer is not the Appraiser. It is not anticipated, nor part of his prerogative, that he will substitute his judgement for that of the Appraiser unless the judgement of the Appraiser is irrefutably erroneous and the Reviewer can adequately justify this conclusion.

From my observations, this is a "weakness" of many "inexperienced" Review Appraisers. They attempt to do the appraisal and substitute their judgement, rather than strictly perform a review of the appraisal that has been made. They often attempt to substitute a value coinciding with their pre-conceived conclusions, rather than reviewing that which the Appraiser has arrived at in an "unbiased" professional manner.

The Reviewer is the "interpreter", not the "performer", which I think is the best interpretation of his duty.

Reviewer As Expert Witness

The use of the Reviewing Appraiser as an expert witnes is, in my opinion, not recommended because frequently they are subject to the accusation of being "advocates" for their principle. Also, they did not actually make the appraisal and cannot testify as though they had made the appraisal. However, they can be called upon and may testify as to their "opinion" of the Appraiser's conclusions if they have made a detailed analysis and field review of the Appraiser's report, if they are called upon to do so. They can't testify to the value as though they were the appraiser, unless they have actually made a "full scale" appraisal themselves. They are then the Appraiser, not the Reviewer.

Practical Reviewing

Sometimes reviewing incompetence takes the form of the "theorist" who is lost in appraisal philosophy, or the "technician" who is incapable of essential analysis and mature judgement which is required to make that "weighted" decision as a professional Reviewing Appraiser. The Reviewer has to be "practical" and "realistic" in all respects. Theory and philosophy are important — but they must be kept in their place and not go "overboard". We must always respect and keep in mind the competence and ability of those whose appraisals we are reviewing; usually they are well experienced, competent, and not amateurs.

Reviewer Documentation

It is extremely important that, in the course of the reviewing process, the staff Reviewing Appraisers thoroughly document their actions during the course of their review. This will facilitate any inquiries which may subsequently be made in respect to the Appraiser's conclusion concerning any items of major importance to evaluating the adequacy and validity of the report.

For a Reviewing Appraiser to not document his findings, on at least any major appraisal, is not considered to be professionally acceptable or ethical.

APPRAISAL REVIEWING METHODS AND PROCESSES USED IN REVIEWING

Scope

There are normally two major methods through which the appraisal review function is usually accomplished and some variations thereof.

The First Method — Single/Individual Review
I call this the "one shot method", whereby the appraisal is delivered to the principle and is reviewed in its entirety by a single Reviewer or process and does not proceed beyond that point. The Reviewer may or may not be remote from the property or the Appriaser. However, under this method no further review is made other than in the instance of a multiple or joint review which may actually take other factors into consideration, in addition to the actual value of the property itself, or other considerations.

This method of review is usually made by smaller or local organizations and many financial institutions. The individual Reviewer performing this function usually has full approval or disapproval authority.

The Second Method — The Echelon Or Sometimes Called
The Cumulative Process Or Method
I often call this "the shot gun method", since it involves more than one professional opinion or review. Under this method the appraisal report is reviewed in whole or in part at several different levels or echelons. The final review is usually made by a Reviewer who is remote from the property, project and the Appraiser. This is the type of review which is often performed by larger organizations, many governmental agencies, and larger organizations with field offices, regional offices and central offices. In many instances, each echelon has to perform a review of some sort and make their own determinations and recommendations.

Under this method, one or the other of the echelons may be delegated the major reviewing authority and the others merely corroborate or disagree with the conclusions. The basis for major approval authority is sometimes based upon the "dollar amount" of the property or the "size of the project". Other echelons not having major approval authority may only make a "cursory" or concurrence type of appraisal review.

Multiple Person Reviews
In some instances, the review at a particular echelon may be done by more than one individual. Where there are large appraisal work loads, an initial review may be made by a "technician" who merely checks clerical, mathematical, or possibly a check list of essential contractual items covered. This is normally followed by a more detailed technical review by a professional Reviewer.

In this procedure, the individual who finally signs the reviewing statement and recommendation is the "responsible Reviewer". He should verify and corroborate any determinations made by others which he has relied upon to formulate his opinion conclusions.

Two Step Method
The review process can also be accomplished in more than "one step" or by one Reviewer. This is often done in many agencies whereby they have a "Senior Reviewing Appraiser" who reviews all staff and/or contract appraisals and who prepares a detailed review and analysis of all reports which is later reviewed and approved by a "Chief" Reviewing Appraiser in the same element of the organization. This is done to further assure or "fireproof" the conclusions.

Recordation of Review Made
The review record should be in writing of some form and should always be signed by the Reviewer authorized to do so, and in many cases it is concurred by someone in higher authority or other management or organizational elements. This is dependent upon the policy requirements and procedures of the organization and does not detract from or reduce the initial Reviewer's primary responsibility to perform his function as a Reviewer.

Review Record: The review record may be in any of the following forms.

Signature or Concurrence Type
This is the type which is often used on the form type of appraisals. This merely states that I have reviewed the subject report and it is approved or disapproved — or even merely the

word approved. In the case where such an appraisal is not approved, there may or may not be justification for its disapproval. It may be left unsigned and a second appraisal obtained, or it may be disapproved with a justifying statement. However, for the record, if the appraisal is not approvable, some statement and justification for the action taken should be made in writing and placed in the records of the organization.

Check Sheet Or Form Type Review
This is sometimes called the "positive" type review — detailing and recording by a "check sheet" or other type of form all the actions or steps taken in the course of the review. This form may be quite elaborate or short, depending upon the circumstances and the type of appraisal being reviewed.

This form can also be used as a "quality control guide", depending upon the "ability" and "quality" of appraisals prepared by both staff and fee Appraisers — in other words, a "training vehicle".

In connection with this type of review, see the following examples of Appraisal Review Forms:

Exhibit 2. U.S. Department of Interior — Reviewer's Appraisal Analysis — U.S.D.I. — Bureau of Land Management Form Type Review — 9300-11 (with approval to use)

Exhibit 3. General Services Administration Form GSA 1305

Exception Type Review
This type of review is a short form narrative review and records only exceptions taken by Reviewers, recording these exceptions and the actions taken regarding them and agreement for approval or disapproval. The reasoning taken is usually in a short memorandum of no more than one page or so. This type of review is more than a mere approval or disapproval — concurrence type review, but is less than a detailed narrative, formal type review.

Combination Form Type Review
This combines the check sheet type review, two above, with the exception type review, three above. The advantage of this type over the strictly check sheet type of review is that it gives the Reviewer an opportunity for further elaboration upon the

EXHIBIT 2

UNITED STATES DEPARTMENT OF THE INTERIOR BUREAU OF LAND MANAGEMENT			Serial Number		Type of Case
REVIEWER'S APPRAISAL ANALYSIS			Name of Applicant		
Appraiser			Legal Description		
CONTRACT					
Fee $		Time Allowed			
Number		Date	Type of Property		
DATE					
Appraisal	REVIEW		Size		Appraised Value $
	Field	Office			

INSTRUCTIONS: Items 1 through 44 are provided as an aid in answering major questions (H). Explain all negative answers (J).

Comment fully on inadequacies and recommendations.
A — Adequate — meets Departmental Standards.
I — Inadequate — does not meet Departmental Standards. Revisions or clarification necessary.

Check (✔) appropriate box. If not applicable, place (0) in box "A".

ITEM	A	I	ITEM	A	I
A. FORM AND PRESENTATION			**C. COST APPROACH (CON.)**		
1. Conformance to Departmental Standards			26. Land value		
(inclusion and sequence of all significant			a. adequate sales and offerings		
items)			b. date and condition of each sale or offering		
2. Purpose–definition of value			c. sales verification		
3. Legal description			d. adjustments to current market		
4. Certification–standard clauses, signature,			e. similarities and differences with subject		
and date			property—explained, weighted, justified		
5. Owner given opportunity to accompany			f. logical conclusion based on fact		
appraiser			27. Land value added ☐ yes ☐ no		
6. Maps showing subject and comparables,			28. Summation value		
plats, and photos					
7. Statement of limiting conditions			**D. INCOME APPROACH**		
8. Rights being appraised			29. Gross annual rent by comparison		
9. Area, neighborhood data			30. Vacancy and credit loss		
10. Property description, condition, and adaptable			31. Expenses and fixed charges		
use			32. Net annual income from rent		
11. Taxes, assessments, and rates			a. attributable to whole property		
12. Highest and best use			b. attributable to improvement		
a. for land			c. attributable to land		
b. for total property			33. Method of capitalization		
13. Approaches to be used			34. Capitalization rate–justified		
			35. Value		
B. MARKET APPROACH					
14. Adequate sales and offerings			**E. CORRELATION AND VALUE**		
15. Last sale of subject property analyzed			36. Correlation of estimates		
16. Date and condition of each sale or offering			37. Approach that is controlling		
17. Sales verification			38. Value conclusion		
18. Adjustment to current market					
19. Similarities and differences with subject			**F. FAIR RENTAL**		
property—explained, weighted, justified			39. Logical relationship to comparables		
20. Contributing value of minerals, timber,			40. Differences factually justified		
etc.			41. Does estimate reflect contemplated lease		
21. Value indicated and justified based on			provisions? ☐ yes ☐ no		
fact					
			G. EMINENT DOMAIN		
C. COST APPROACH			42. Plats submitted showing relation of par-		
22. Cost estimates			tial take to whole property		
23. Depreciation–physical			43. Damages and/or benefits justified and prop-		
24. Depreciation–functional			erly measured		
25. Depreciation–economical			44. Damages separately stated		

(Continue on reverse)   Form 9300–11 (June 1975)

ITEM	YES	NO	ITEM	YES	NO
H. OVERALL EFFECTIVENESS			**H. OVERALL EFFECTIVENESS (CON.)**		
45. Is the appraisal problem clearly stated?			51. Do you recommend the report:		
46. Is the property accurately delineated and			a. as a basis for contemplated action?		
described?			b. without further clarification?		
47. Is the best and most profitable use of the			**I. APPLICABLE TO FEE APPRAISERS ONLY**		
property stated, and used for basis of			52. Do you recommend the report for fee pay-		
value?			ment?		
48. Is supporting data accurate?			53. Does the appraiser's panel rating seem		
49. Is conclusion logically and factually			appropriate?		
related to supporting data?			54. Would you recommend this appraiser for		
50. Are all essential items included?			other similar assignments?		

J. REVIEWER'S COMMENTS *(Use Additional Sheets if Necessary)*

EXHIBIT 3

REVIEWER'S APPRAISAL ANALYSIS (For use by Staff Appraiser in Reviewing Appraisal Reports)	PURPOSE OF APPRAISAL		
	☐ IN-LEASE ☐ ACQUISITION ☐ TRANSFER ☐ OUT-LEASE ☐ DISPOSAL ☐		

APPRAISER	FEE $	TYPE OF PROPERTY
CONTRACT NO.	CONTRACT DATE	TIME ALLOWED	NAME AND ADDRESS OF PROPERTY
EFFECTIVE DATE OF REPORT	DATE REVIEWED	

REVIEWER	APPRAISED VALUE $	CASE NO.

INSTRUCTIONS

Items 1 through 45 are provided as an aid in answering Major Questions in Part VII.
Explain all negative answers on reverse (Part VIII). Comment fully on inadequacies and recommendations.

E - Excellent - Meets or exceeds specifications.
A - Adequate - Meets minimum needs. Clarification may be desirable.
I - Inadequate - Does not meet needs. Revision or clarification necessary.

ITEM	E	A	I		ITEM	E	A	I
I. FORM AND PRESENTATION				**III. ANALYSIS AND TECHNIQUE (con.)**	**E. MARKET APPROACH**			
1 CONFORMANCE TO GSA SPECIFICATIONS (As to format, inclusion and sequence of all significant items)					30. LIST OF SALES AND OFFERINGS			
2. AREA, CITY, NEIGHBORHOOD DATA					31. SAME LIST ADJUSTED TO CURRENT MARKET			
3. LEGAL DESCRIPTION INCLUDED? ☐ YES ☐ NO					32. SPECIAL CONDITIONS TO EACH SALE			
4. PROPERTY DESCRIPTION, CONDITION, AND ADAPTABLE USE					33. RELATION OF SALE OR OFFERING TO SUBJECT PROPERTY - SIMILARITIES AND DIFFERENCES WEIGHTED			
5. INSURANCE AND TAX LOAD: PLANS, PHOTOS AND MAPS					34. VALUE INDICATED AND JUSTIFICATION			
6. CERTIFICATION - STANDARD CLAUSES, SIGNATURE AND DATE				**IV. MACHINERY AND EQUIPMENT**	35. DESCRIPTION AND CONDITION			
					36. ANALYSIS OF UTILITY			
II. DELINEATION OF ASSIGN.					37. VALUE FOR IN-PLACE USE (If applicable)			
7. PURPOSE, INCLUDING DEFINITION OF VALUE					38. VALUE FOR OFF-SITE USE " "			
8. HIGHEST AND BEST USE - FOR LAND - FOR TOTAL PROPERTY				**V. FAIR RENTAL**	39. FAIR RENTAL ESTIMATE			
9. STATEMENT OF LIMITING CONDITIONS					40. LOGICAL RELATIONSHIP TO COMPARABLES .			
A. LAND VALUE BY COMPARISON					41. BASED ON INTEREST PLUS CAPITAL RECAPTURE (If applicable)			
10. ADEQUATE LISTINGS					42. DOES ESTIMATE REFLECT CONTEMPLATED LEASE PROVISIONS? ☐ YES ☐ NO			
11. DATE AND CONDITIONS OF EACH SALE				**VI. CORRELATION AND VALUE**	43. CORRELATION OF ESTIMATES			
12. SAME LIST ADJUSTED TO CURRENT MARKET					44. THE APPROACH THAT IS CONTROLLING: _____			
13. SIMILARITIES AND DIFFERENCES WITH SUBJECT PROPERTY					45. VALUE CONCLUSION			
14. LOGICAL CONCLUSION						YES	NO	
15. MAP SHOWING COMPARABLES					46. IS THE APPRAISAL PROBLEM CLEARLY STATED?			
B. LAND RESIDUAL TECHNIQUE (If used)					47. IS THE PROPERTY ACCURATELY DELINEATED AND DESCRIBED?			
16. LOGICAL CONCLUSION				**VII. OVERALL EFFECTIVENESS**	48. IS THE BEST AND MOST PROFITABLE USE OF THE PROPERTY STATED, AND USED FOR BASIS OF VALUE?			
C. COST APPROACH					49. IS SUPPORTING DATA ACCURATE?			
17. COST ESTIMATES					50. IS CONCLUSION LOGICALLY RELATED TO SUPPORTING DATA?			
18. DEPRECIATION - PHYSICAL					51. ARE ALL ESSENTIAL ITEMS INCLUDED?			
19. DEPRECIATION - FUNCTIONAL					**IS THE REPORT RECOMMENDED:**			
20. DEPRECIATION - ECONOMIC					52. AS A BASIS FOR CONTEMPLATED ACTION?			
21. LAND VALUE ADDED? ☐ YES ☐ NO					53. WITHOUT FURTHER CLARIFICATION?			
22. SUMMATION VALUE					54. FOR FEE PAYMENT?			
D. INCOME APPROACH					**AS EVIDENCED BY THIS REPORT:**			
23. GROSS ANNUAL RENT BY COMPARISON					55. DOES THE APPRAISER'S PANEL RATING SEEM APPROPRIATE?			
24. VACANCY AND CREDIT LOSS					56. WOULD YOU RECOMMEND THIS APPRAISER FOR OTHER SIMILAR ASSIGNMENTS?			
25. EXPENSE AND FIXED CHARGES INCLUDING RESERVES FOR REPLACEMENT								
26. NET ANNUAL INCOME FROM RENT								
27. METHOD OF CAPITALIZATION								
28. CAPITALIZATION RATE - JUSTIFIED								
29. VALUE								

GENERAL SERVICES ADMINISTRATION (Continue on reverse) GSA FORM NOV 67 1305

VIII. REVIEWER'S COMMENTS

deficiencies found, action taken, and concluding recommendations. Also, an actual field review can be incorporated in this type of review which can be made in any form applicable to the particular situation.

An example of this type form is as follows. (Exhibits 4 and 5)

EXHIBIT 4

APPRAISAL REVIEW AND ANALYSIS FORM

Project _____

Location _____

VALUATION		Date of Review	_____
Land....................	$ _____	Appraiser	_____
Improvements	_____	Report Date of Appraisal	_____
Other Damages	_____		
Salvage Value of Improvements	_____	Effective Date	_____
		No. of Parcels	_____
TOTAL APPRAISED VALUE:.................	$ _____	Type of Property	_____
		Highest and Best Use	_____

AREA:

Acres: _____

Sq. Ft.: _____

Land only
Per Sq. Ft. _____
Per Acre $ _____

RATINGS

E = Excellent
A = Adequate
I = Inadequate
O = Omitted
N = Not Needed

	E	A	I	O	N
I. FORMAT AND PRESENTATION					
1. Conformance to HUD Contract and Appraisal Specs.					
2. Appearance and Arrangement					
3. Letter of Transmittal					
4. Table of Contents					
5. Summary of Important Facts					
6. Photographs of Area and Property					
7. Vicinage Maps, Plats, Plans, Charts, etc.					
8. Other Exhibits					
9. Supporting Reports of Technical Specialists					
10. Certification of Appraiser					
11. Limiting Conditions and Assumptions					
12. References and Sources of Information					
II. DELINEATION OF ASSIGNMENT					
13. Purpose of Appraisal					
14. Definition of Value					
15. Address of Property					
16. Classification of Property					

EXHIBIT 4 (Continued)

III. ANALYSIS AND TECHNIQUE	E	A	I	O	N
A. General:					
17. City and Area Data					
18. Neighborhood Data					
19. Measurement of Economic Background					
20. Real Estate Market Conditions					
21. Utilities					
22. Street Improvements					
23. Transportation					
24. Amenities					
25. Favorable and Unfavorable Factors					
B. Property Data:					
26. Ownership					
27. Property History					
28. Previous Sale Price					
a. Justification for difference with Appraised Value					
29. Area					
30. Improvements					
a. Age and Condition					
b. Structural and Construction Detail					
c. Installed Equipment					
d. Use and Functional Detail					
31. Zoning					
32. Assessed Value and Annual Tax Load					
33. Adequacy of Property Data					
C. Analysis of Highest and Best Use:					
34. Discussion and Analysis					
35. Reasonableness of Conclusion – Justified					
D. Land Valuation by Comparison					
36. Adequate Listings and Sales					
37. Map Showing Location of Subject and Sales					
38. Date and Conditions of Each Sale					
39. Adjustments to Current Market					
40. Adjustments and Comparisons with Subject Property					
41. Reasonableness of Conclusions					
42. Per Square Foot and/or Per Acre Indication					
E. Land Residual Technique:					
43. Adequacy of Substantiation					
44. Execution of Technique					
45. Reasonableness of Conclusion					

EXHIBIT 4 (Continued)

	E	A	I	O	N
F. Cost Approach to Value:					
46. Cost Estimates Used					
47. Justification of Cost Factors					
48. Reasonableness of Estimates					
49. Adequacy of Improvements (Over and Under)					
50. Remaining Economic Life					
51. Estimate of Accrued Depreciation					
a. Physical					
b. Functional					
c. Economic					
52. Estimate of Rehabilitation Cost					
53. Land Value Added (Market Approach)					
54. Summation Value					
55. Reasonableness of Conclusion					
56. Salvage Value of Improvements					
G. Income Approach to Value:					
57. Gross Annual Rent by Comparison					
58. Vacancy and Credit Loss					
59. Operating Expenses					
60. Effective Gross Income					
61. Reserves for Replacements					
62. Allowances for Future Depreciation					
63. Fixed Charges					
64. Net Annual Income					
65. Method of Capitalization					
66. Capitalization Rate – Justified					
67. Reasonableness of Capital Value Estimate					
H. Building Residual Approach:					
68. Adequacy of Substantiation					
69. Execution of Technique					
70. Reasonableness of Conclusion					
I. Development Technique Approach:					
71. Improved Lot Valuation (Market Approach)					
72. Development Costs – Substantiated					
73. Overhead and Profit					
74. Adjustment for Development Time Factor					
75. Plat of Subdivision					
76. Consistency with Zoning and Highest and Best Use					
77. Residual Value to Land					
78. Reasonableness of Conclusion					
J. Estimate of Value by Comparative – Market Approach					
79. Adequacy of Sales and Offerings					
80. Special Conditions of Sales Considered					

EXHIBIT 4 (Continued)

		E	A	I	O	N
	81. Adjusted to Current Market					
	82. Comparison to Subject property – Similarities and Differences Weighed					
	83. Supply and Demand for Comparable Properties					
	84. Over or Under Improvement Adjustment					
	85. Reasonableness of Value Indication					
	K. Severance or Other Damages:					
	86. Justification Therefor					
	87. Technique Used (Before and After)					
	88. Execution of Technique					
	89. Reasonableness of Conclusions					
	L. Plottage or Assemblage Value:					
	90. Justification Therefor					
	91. Market Support					
	92. Reasonableness of Conclusions					
IV.	CORRELATION AND CONCLUSIONS OF VALUE					
	93. Summary of Pertinent Factors					
	94. Correlation of Estimates					
	95. The Approach That is Controlling					
	96. Value Conclusion – Justified					
	97. Soundness of Reasoning					
V.	OVERALL EFFECTIVENESS					
	98. Appraisal Problem Clearly Stated					
	99. Property Accurately Delineated and Described					
	100. Highest and Best Use Justified					
	101. Accuracy of Supporting Data					
	102. Accuracy of Mathematical Computations					
	103. All Essential Items Included					
	104. Proper Approaches Used					
	105. Techniques Expertly Executed					
	106. Parcel Valuations are Compatible					
	107. Reasonableness of Final Conclusions					

VI.   FIELD REVIEW OF APPRAISAL

In addition to the normal office review of this appraisal, a field review

_____ Was Made

_____ Was Not Made

during which the property, supporting data, and other pertinent factors were viewed and given careful consideration by the reviewer.

VII.   REVIEWER'S COMMENTS (Reference by Item Number)

N.A.R.A. Form #5102

NATIONAL ASSOCIATION OF REVIEW APPRAISERS
Suite 410
Midwest Federal Building
St. Paul, Minnesota 55101

EXHIBIT 5

PARCEL VALUATIONS - SUMMARY SHEET

Parcel No.	Owner	Land	Improvements	Other Damages	Total
TOTAL					

RECOMMENDATIONS

_____ Approval of this appraisal for a total amount of $_____
is recommended. (If qualified approval, state conditions.)

_____ Approval of this appraisal is not recommended at this time and
securing of an additional appraisal is recommended.

Comments:

_____ Payment of the appraisal fee is recommended.

Comments:

This review has been prepared in accordance with the Code of Ethics of the National Association of Review Appraisers. The recommendations, as indicated above, are the result of the careful review and analysis that have been made and represents my considered professional opinion of this appraisal.

Reviewed by: _____   Date _____

Review Concurred by: _____   Date _____

N.A.R.A. Form #5103

NATIONAL ASSOCIATION OF REVIEW APPRAISERS
Suite 410
Midwest Federal Building
St. Paul, Minnesota 55101

Detailed Formal Type Narrative Review
This is a fully detailed narrative type of review which covers the major factors in an appraisal, indicating what the Appraiser covered, the adequacy or inadequacy of his justification and substantiation of each item, and the Reviewer's acceptance or rejection of each item. It also recites the steps which were taken to rectify any deficiencies, omissions or commissions and the results of these items, thus giving any subsequent Reviewers or management a concise analysis of the important factors which affect the valuation as well as the purpose and needs upon which the appraisal was premised. These factors include economics, highest and best use, various approaches used, sales data and analysis, and the numerous other factors which are covered under the basic appraisal process as well as the particular characteristics of the project being appraised and the particular requirements of the organization for which the appraisal is being prepared.

An example of an outline for this type of review is shown in Exhibit 6, "Outline For Detailed Review & Analysis", designed by Walter S. Hanni, CRA.

Some actual examples of detailed narrative appraisal reviews — approvals — disapprovals are shown under Chapter VII "Reviewer's Final Decision Or Recommendations" by Walter S. Hanni, CRA.

This type of review is the ultimate type of review, in my opinion, and is only made on full detailed narrative appraisal reports or substantial properties for important acquisition or disposal purposes and on those which may involve controversial, litigation or eminent domain proceedings.

Minimum Review Requirements

At a minimum, the review process should include an initial review for appraisal content and technique and where considered essential or feasible, a field review of subject property including relevant market and economic data.

During either of these steps, the Reviewer may request supplemental data for clarification, further substantiation or corrections from the Appraiser, which is then made a part of the original report and *must* be included as part of the field review.

Where a field review is made, it is advisable, if possible, to have the Appraiser accompany the Reviewer — much more can be

EXHIBIT 6

OUTLINE FOR DETAILED REVIEW AND ANALYSIS

SUBJECT: Appraisal Review and Analysis

TO: _____

_____

In compliance with your request and in accordance with my authority, I have

carefully reviewed the attached appraisal report which covers _____ .

Subject report as of _____

was prepared by _____ .

I have reviewed the subject report from the standpoint of meeting established specifications and requirements, as well as conforming to acceptable professional appraisal practices and techniques; scope of the appraisal investigation; factual data considered; reasoning and logic of the appraisal process and reasonableness of the valuation conclusion of _____ .

I.   **FORM AND PRESENTATION:**

II.   **DELINEATION OF ASSIGNMENT:**

III.   **ANALYSIS TECHNIQUES AND DATA UTILIZED:**
   A. *Factural Data Considered*
   B. *Factual Errors or Omissions:*
   C. *Reasoning and Logic of Appraisal Process Utilized:*
   D. *Reconciliation and Reasonableness of Conclusion Reached:*
   E. *Adequacy of Report:*

IV.   **APPRAISER'S QUALIFICATIONS:**

V.   **FIELD REVIEW:**

VI.   **APPRAISER DISCUSSION** (Conference);

VII.   **SITE REPORT VALUATION:**

VIII.   **OFFER TO SELL:**

IX.   **REVIEWER'S CONCLUSIONS AND RECOMMENDATIONS:**

X.   **CONTRACT DATA:**
   1. Contract number:
   2. Date of Contract:
   3. Time Element:
   4. Date Received:
   5. Appraisal Fee:

BY _____

CONCURRED _____

accomplished and questions resolved on the spot rather than "second hand".

Telephone discussions between the Reviewer and the Appraiser are also advisable for clarification and should be followed by supplemental data from the Appraiser.

The appraisal review is normally not completed until all supplemental data has been obtained and reviewed. In some cases, a review can be completed subject to receiving the requested data which has previously been agreed upon and corroborated between the parties.

Other Data Utilized By The Reviewer

There is considerable data which the Reviewer may have in his own "data plant" in the organization files, other reliable sources, previous planning reports or subject site or vicinage sites, his own knowledge and experience in the area which can be beneficially used by the Reviewer in the course of his review. This is important, especially if there is any question about any of the factors or decisions reached in the Appraiser's report and can also be used to "bolster" the Appraiser's conclusions or estimates, or vice-versa — if the appraisal is weak — let us say.

It is perfectly permissible to use whatever information he may have to further substantiate or refute any conclusions reached, providing that he can fully substantiate and justify his opinions with factual data.

When A Second Appraisal Is Obtained

The procedure which I normally use when it is necessary to secure a second appraisal is to separately review the second appraisal, independently (as was done on the first appraisal) in its entirety and then prepare a separate or consolidated — joint reviewing statement of both appraisals. The result of this is an over-all reviewing conclusion and recommendation including my own discussions with each Appraiser and my field review of each appraisal, plus my own field review conclusions.

An example of such a two appraisal review is shown in Part III, Exhibit 3.

Field Review Requirements

Any major appraisal, especially if there is any question involved, should be field reviewed. There are many in the professional reviewing field that maintain that *all* appraisal reports must be reviewed — let me say that this is the "ideal". However, the ideal is not always possible and I feel that we must be realistic about this. It is my considered opinion and experience as a Reviewer, that it is not necessary or practical to field review every appraisal report made.

There are several rules or "criteria" which apply to this theory or principle.

1. *If you have a small Review or Appraisal* work load and a small geographical area of coverage — not involving a lot of travel time — such may be entirely feasible and should be done in every case.

2. *Volume, time and expense* are important factors. However, these should not eliminate the requirements for review where such is considered required or essential.

3. *Necessity is another factor* why to field review an appraisal which is approvable in all respects, just for the trip.

4. *Cost is another factor* — It costs additional funds and time to review an appraisal. This can be an important factor where there is a "high volume" of reviews being performed. It may be impossible to review every appraisal and only "spot" review particular ones or those which appear to be "out of line" or as a "performance" check.

5. *Realistic* — To, let's say, field review every V.A. or similar appraisal would not be practical — spot checks and field reviews — yes — or for a reason — yes.

6. *Depending upon policy* — It may be that all appraisals involving large monetary amounts or over certain limits must be or should be field reviewed. It is my opinion that all multiple-ownership projects and large monetary acquisitions should "automatically" be field reviewed, even though the valuations appear to be realistic.

7. *Selective Basis* — It is my opinion that the best "general" basis for field review from the Reviewer's personal stand-

point is the selective basis. Those which the Reviewer, from his review, feels that a field review is necesary or essential to satisfy his conclusions or those that are required for some special reason or another; or certain conditions are known in advance which will create problems such as serious negotiating problems, controversial problems involving highest and best use, transitional use, improvement value, etc., should be field reviewed to make a determination in the Reviewer's mind as to the validity and justification of the Appraiser's conclusion.

Securing Supplemental Data From The Appraiser

In the innumerable appraisals I have reviewed, which include mostly those by qualified and designated Appraisers, as well as some which were not, I can only think of a few instances of where an Appraiser was uncooperative and refused to furnish supplemental data which I considered necessary. Usually, Appraisers I have dealt with have been very cooperative, have accepted any reviewing comments or suggestions that I made and attempted, to the best of their ability, to satisfy any questions which I raised concerning their reports.

True — I may not have always agreed with the Appraisers, as to their explanations or justification submitted in supplement, that it really answered the questions which I raised. However, they performed satisfactorily — perhaps to the best of their ability and within their professional prerogative.

Judgement

Appraising is not an exact science, and therefore cannot be reviewed as such. Many factors in appraising are "judgement factors" and must be accepted to a "reasonable degree" by the Reviewer. Although all factors must be justified and substantiated to the "fullest degree possible" by factual data. However, we must still accept the fact that appraising is not an exact science — and therefore cannot be reviewed as such.

Rule Of Thumb Checks

Rule of thumb checks are of extreme importance to the Review Appraiser. While these are not infallible, if the Appraiser varies widely from them, they can raise a signal to the Reviewer. As an example, where "motels" of a certain size category are selling for "let's say" five times their income and the Appraiser concludes a value which "let's say" is ten times — then maybe we should investigate his conclusion more closely unless the Appraiser has adequately indicated and substantiated the wide divergence in his report.

Echelon Reviewer's Securing Of Additional Data

In the case of the echelon reviewing system, the Reviewer at a higher echelon who takes exception to a report should go directly to the Appraiser for additional data and not back to the previous Reviewer. Once a review is completed at a particular echelon, in my opinion, that is completed staff action. However, an information copy of any disagreements should be sent to the lower echelon.

SUMMARY

In summarization of this chapter, I would like to point out the following important points which were discussed.

1. Reviewing has been a regulatory requirement by most Federal Agencies, many other public and private agencies for many years.
2. Over the past 25 years or so, appraisal reviewing has developed into a highly technical sub-art of the appraisal profession, being performed by experienced reviewing professions.
3. There are certain requirements to which the Reviewer has obligations.
4. There are certain established methods or procedures under which the review process is performed.
5. There have been many requirements or regulations to be followed in review appraising, as well as varied forms or types used in reviewing.
6. The objective is to secure an approvable appraisal report.
7. Selection of the most competent qualified appraiser to do the job is an initial step.
8. Detailed appraisal contract specifications and instructions to the Appraiser are of major importance.
9. Professional counseling to the Appraiser, prior to and during the course of preparation of the appraisal, is of the utmost importance.

10. The Review Appraiser should never act as the negotiator, except on an "advisory" basis.
11. The Reviewer must always remember that he is not the Appraiser — rather, he is the "interpreter, not the performer".
12. The Reviewer does not "normally" act as an expert witness.
13. The Reviewer must always be practical and realistic.
14. The Reviewing Appraiser should always document his findings in some form.
15. The appraisal review is normally functioned under one of the following methods:
    a. Single review
    b. Echelon review
    c. Multiple person review (variation of a.)
    d. Two-step method (variation of b.)
16. Recordation of the review may be in any of the following forms:
    a. Signature of concurrence type
    b. Check sheet or form type review
    c. Exception type
    d. Combination form type review
    e. Detailed narrative type review
17. Other data available may be utilized by the Reviewer in the course of his review.
18. Where a second appraisal is obtained, the second should be individually reviewed and then a "joint" review and recommendation of both made.
19. Field review is not always considered essential or required. There is certain criteria which governs this theory or principle.
20. Securing supplemental data from the Appraiser or the settlement of questionable items can usally be obtained.
21. Appraising is not an exact science and therefore cannot be reviewed as such.
22. Rule of thumb checks are often useful to the Appraiser.
23. An "upper echelon" Reviewer should not go back to the previous Reviewer but rather go back to the Appraiser himself for additional data.

CHAPTER FOUR

Appraisal Purpose

and the

Reviewer

MARC ANDREW LOUARGAND, CRA

Marc Andrew Louargand is an Assistant Professor of Finance/Real Estate, and Insurance at the School of Business and Economics, California State University at North Bridge. He holds an M.B.A. in Urban Land Economics from UCLA and is currently completing a Ph.D. in Land Economics at UCLA.

Professor Louargand is a Certified Review Appraiser and a member of the American Real Estate and Urban Economics Association.

Appraisal Purpose

and the

Reviewer

> *"While assuring appraisal quality is a prime*
> *obligation of the Review Appraiser,*
> *understanding the overall objectives of his or*
> *her client or company, can many times be*
> *equally important."*
> *Otto Tronowsky, CRA, Past President National*
> *Association of Review Appraisers*

INTRODUCTION

Appraisal reports often follow a standardized format which have
been developed to demonstrate that the Appraiser has
considered all of the factors which may be pertinent to the value
conclusion. The Reviewer must be cognizant of the problem
which may arise due to the report format being more
standardized or general than the nature of the appraisal problem
itself.

The Reviewer must hold, foremost in the review process, a
conceptualization of the purpose or objective which motivated
the report, as well as a framework of analysis which is designed
on the specific characteristics of the problem at hand.

This chapter presents two ways of looking at the review

process. The first is an informal typology of the various motivations and objectives inherent in the appraisal process, and is based on my experience in the field. This approach attempts to point out some of the common analytic pitfalls associated with different types of appraisal situations.

The second idea involves a more formal treatment of the nature of the risk faced by real estate investors, and is an extension of the first idea. The analysis of the specific nature of risk is not a new idea in the literature of investments but, to my knowledge, it has not been treated before in the manner presented here. Before elaborating on these ideas, however, some definition of terms is in order.

Scope of the Appraisal Process

The historical distinction between appraisals as an estimate of the fair market value and the feasibility study as a more comprehensive analysis of the financial and market viability of a proposed project or major acquisition has become increasingly blurred in recent years. The majority of the appraisal assignments I have encountered in recent years have included elements of feasibility analysis or full scale feasibility studies contained within appraisals of proposed developments and acquistions.

During this period which saw the typical appraisal report take on added complexity, another trend has been quite pronounced. Namely, the increasing participation in the market by institutions and organizations who are generally involved in large scale real estate investments. As this group is currently the focus of appraisal review activity, and as the group is more than likely to be involved with projects which require feasibility type analysis as well as traditional appraisals, the focus of this chapter will be on this expanded definition of the appraisal process. Therefore, the term appraisal report will be considered to include the concept of feasibility analysis. In the same vein, the terms Appraiser and Analyst will be used interchangeably throughout the chapter.

TYPES OF APPRAISAL REPORTS AND
CONCERNS OF THE REVIEWER

A list of the various types of appraisal reports a Reviewer might encounter would be too cumbersome to deal with in the scope of this chapter. Instead, a typology is offered below which groups appraisal activity according to the overall purpose which is served by the investigation. While by no means exhaustive, such a typology might include four categories: Financial Reporting, Financial Decision-Making, Litigation, and Investment Decision-Making.

Working within this typology the Reviewer must ascertain that the special nature of any given appraisal assignment has been treated successfully. Included below are a series of points the Reviewer should keep in mind when dealing with the various types of reports.

Financial Reporting

Reports are often generated to comply with requests or requirements of regulatory agencies such as the Securities and Exchange Commission, State Commissioners of Corporations, and State Departments of Real Estate. For example, blind pool syndicates and real estate investment trusts are often required to file independent appraisals of their property acquisitions. Requirements of the SEC may lead to reports being generated during the course of mergers and acquisitions by publicly-held companies.

In the case of regulatory reports, the Reviewer must make certain that the content and format of the report meet regulatory requirements. Such agencies are notorious for developing reporting formats which could baffle the mind of Solomon and try the patience of Job. Despite this problem, the Reviewer is responsible for insuring that the client is not deterred or delayed from its objective by errors of form. It is not safe to assume that the Analyst has met the proper guidelines: the Reviewer must determine that this has been done.

It has been my experience that some public agencies request data which is far different from that found in the standard report format. The Reviewer must determine that all of the data requested, if available, has been supplied.

The analytic processes and conclusions in regulatory reports flow from objectives which are quite unlike those of an investor. Regulatory agencies are charged with protection of the public; directly, by preventing misrepresentation; and indirectly, by monitoring the behavior of organizations and their principals. The Reviewer should keep these objectives in mind when evaluating such a report. It is the Reviewer's ethical responsibility to determine that financial and fiscal relationships contrary to public policy are not represented in a misleading manner. It is also the Reviewer's responsibility to determine that the data and analysis presented in the report are legitimate and straightforward and that the conclusions are not presented in such a way as to lessen any unfavorable aspect.

Internal reporting by firms is a fast developing area of appraisal practice. There is a growing movement to report corporate assets at market value rather than at book value in quarterly and annual financial statements. Internal reporting standards are hopelessly archaic in much of the corporate sector. Recent trends toward market value reporting presage a major change in reporting techniques and a major involvement in corporate finance for the Appraiser. The Reviewer should be familiar with the guidelines of the accounting industry when examining such reports, but should also be prepared to append his or her own judgments about the proper format for these reports. This is a new area of appraisal practice and part of the Reviewer's responsibility is to see that realistic and proper guidelines are developed.

Perhaps the most important benefit of this movement will be to help the corporate sector to develop optimal holding techniques for real property assets. Book value reporting techniques have led to widespread sub-optimization. Market value appraisals of corporate assets should examine the financial implications of all the available techniques of financing and tenure in the corporate context.

The other major concern in these reports should be an allegiance to the corporate objectives and motivations for holding real property. Manufacturing and service firms hold real property as an intermediate good in the production process; therefore, their needs are different from those of the developer or investor. Rates of return, probability of loss, and alternative use analyses must be dealt with in the corporate context first, and in the market context second.

Financial Decision-Making

Internal use of appraisals, pricing studies, and market surveys is becoming the norm for large development organizations, as well as for non-real estate companies whose activities put them in the real estate market as a sideline.

Some typical independent reports commissioned by a large developer would include market pricing analyses, estimation of proper rent schedules, analysis of capital structure and selection of optimum financing techniques. The Analyst plays a role in all of these activities and must often look beyond the standard analysis used in estimating fair market value. Internal reports of this nature are, by definition, unlike standard format appraisals. The Reviewer should be certain that the Analyst has taken into account the specific circumstances of the client organization and has incorporated them into the analysis and conclusions. The individual capital structure, operating efficiencies, tax situation, and marketing capabilities of the organization are clearly influential in the decision-making process and should be allowed for in the analysis.

In the case of acquisitions and mergers, the acquiring firm often needs to determine the value of newly acquired assets and then must make decisions regarding their retention, disposition, or financial restructuring. Real property holdings of this type are subject to strategies which are not those of the ordinary investor. Again, the analysis must be cast in the organizational context and should speak to the unique characteristics of the situation and the organization. Perhaps the greatest service that the Analyst and the Receiver can provide such a client is the ability to combine the insights gained from standard format work with those engendered by the specific context of the assignment. I have often seen the fruits of this service in the form of highly profitable alternatives which grew out of the analysis.

Litigation

The number of possible types of analysis required in litigation is limited only by the range of litigious behavior in our society. There are civil actions regarding historical values, partial damages, adherence to contractual terms, and many others. Governments enter the picture through condemnation, property and income tax disputes, and many other areas.

The legal arena is one which often requires that the analysis be carried out under a set of suppositions which are highly artificial and potentially misleading.

This is one area in which the Reviewer's role is critically important, yet often goes unfilled. Attorneys for litigants often rely on an Analyst's report without having it reviewed by a competent professional. There are two aspects of the litigation appraisal process which are extremely important. First, the Analyst is expected to uncover data, analyze it, arrive at conclusions, and present the supporting arguments skillfully and forcefully. It is a fact, however, that any three Analysts can, and often do, arrive at three different conclusions. Second, the litigation process is an adversary one, and the attorney must expect that the conclusions of any given Analyst are subject to disputation.

Because of this situation, the Reviewer should be involved in this process on two fronts. First, as in any review situation, he or she should render a judgement regarding the validity and suitability of the analysis. Second, and perhaps more important, the Reviewer should be able to provide the attorney with a concise statement on the likely alternatives to the analysis which might be presented, an outline of their rationale, and an independent opinion as to their relative merits. This is not to say that the Analyst or Reviewer should forsake independence, but that the Reviewer should provide a comprehensive analysis of the potential viewpoints which may be at odds with the Analyst's

Investment Decision-Making

The realm of investment decision-making with respect to real property assets encompasses the greatest variety of appraisal and analysis. Investors, both individual and institutional, require analysis to make purchase and sale decisions. Developers require feasibility studies, both market and economic. Developers also frequently look for advice on development configuration, staging, expected absorption rates, and many other forms of input to the investment decision.

Another type of investor, the lender, typically makes *no* investment decision regarding real estate without some form of analysis by the Appraiser. The lender's viewpoint is radically different from the developer's, even though they look at the same transaction or development. The needs of the lender require different assumptions about the market, the local economy, and the viability of any given product.

Rather than attempt to discuss all of these potential appraisal situations, I would like to extend the informal typology presented so far by introducing a more formal technique which involves characterizing the nature and extent of risk faced by the investor in order to determine the proper elements of appraisal analysis.

Risk is the basic concept of investment analysis, and can be separated into various categories depending on its nature. The Reviewer, by reference to the specific nature of the risk in any given investment, can then determine if the analysis speaks directly to the relevant factors which influence the riskiness of the investment and by extension, the expected rates of return and the project's present value.

Specifically, the Analyst and the Reviewer need to be concerned with *market risk, financial risk,* and the *degree of risk concentration.* Due to the number of possible combinations of these three factors and their possible categorizations, the information about them is presented in matrix form in the following tables.

Table 1 and Table 2 depict the combination of Market and Financial risk levels and the Degree of Risk Concentration in several types of real estate development. Table 1 deals with lender participants in such projects, while Table 2 deals with investor participants of several types in the same projects.

As used in the tables, the definition of Market and Financial Risk vary somewhat. In the case of lender participants, Market Risk is defined as the probability of loss under conditions of lack of marketability of the proposed project. In the case of lenders, the concept of loss is assumed to be synonymous with default. Each type of lender represented in the table has a characteristic risk exposure in each type of project which is described as low or high to indicate the probability of such a loss due to lack of marketability.

In the case of investors, the probability of loss due to market risk is based on a concept of loss which ranges from sub-optimal returns to default and total loss of investment. Market Risk is the first entry in each of the boxes found in the tables.

Financial Risk is defined as the probability of loss due to instability in the financial condition of the principal or the inability or failure of the principal to perform as expected. In the case of lenders, loss is assumed to be synonymous with default, while an investor's loss could range from sub-optimal returns to default and total loss. Financial Risk is the second entry in each of the boxes found in the tables.

The degree of concentration of both types of risk is expressed as a composite ranging from Concentrated to Dispersed. This is essentially the number of eggs in one basket argument. Concentrated risk would indicate that the investor or lender's participation rides on a single entity and that entity's response to market and financial conditions. Dispersed risk would indicate that the participant can rely on a large number of actors, each subject to varying degrees of financial risk or market risk. The

Table 1

LENDER PARTICIPANT

KEY	
Market Risk	
Financial Risk	
Degree of Risk Concentration	

PROPERTY TYPE	CONSTRUCTION LENDER	TAKEOUT LENDER	SWING LENDER
Single Family Homes	High, High, Concentrated	Low, Low Dispersed	High, High, Concentrated
Condominiums	High, High, Concentrated	Low, Low, Dispersed	High, High, Concentrated
Apartments	Low, High, Concentrated	High, Medium, Concentrated	High, High, Concentrated
Office Buildings	Low, High, Concentrated	High, Low, Concentrated	High, High, Concentrated
Office Buildings w/Major Tenants Committed	Low, Medium, Dispersed	Low, Low, Dispersed	Low, High, Dispersed
Retail Commercial	Low, High, Concentrated	High, Low, Concentrated	High, High, Concentrated
Retail Commercial w/Major Tenants Committed	Low, Medium, Dispersed	Low, Low, Dispersed	Low, High, Dispersed
Industrial	Low, High, Concentrated	High, Low, Concentrated	High, High, Concentrated
Industrial w/Major Tenants Committed	Low, Medium, Dispersed	Low, Low, Dispersed	Low, High, Concentrated

Table 2

EQUITY PARTICIPANT

KEY
Market Risk
Financial Risk
Degree of Risk Concentration

PROPERTY TYPE	DEVELOPER	JOINT-VENTURE PARTNERS		LAND LEASE HOLDERS	
		INVESTOR	SUBORDINATED LANDOWNER/ PARTNER	UNSUBORDINATED	SUBORDINATED
Single Family Homes	High, Variable Concentrated	High, High Concentrated	Same as Investor	Low, High Concentrated	High, High Concentrated
Condominiums	High, Variable Concentrated	High, High Concentrated	Same as Investor	Low, High Concentrated	High, High Concentrated
Apartments	High, Variable Concentrated	High, High Concentrated	Same as Investor	Low, High Concentrated	High, High Concentrated
Office Buildings	High, Variable Concentrated	High, High Concentrated	Same as Investor	Low, High Concentrated	High, High Concentrated
Offices w/Major Tenants Committed	Low, Medium Dispersed	Low, Medium Dispersed	Same as Investor	Low, Medium Dispersed	Low, Medium Dispersed
Retail Commercial	High, Variable Concentrated	High, High Concentrated	Same as Investor	Low, High Concentrated	High, High Concentrated
Retail Commercial w/Major Tenants Committed	Low, Medium Dispersed	Low, Medium Dispersed	Same as Investor	Low, Medium Dispersed	Low, Medium Dispersed
Industrial	High, Variable Concentrated	High, Dispersed	Same as Investor	Low, High Concentrated	High, High Concentrated
Industrial w/Major Tenants Committed	Low, Medium Dispersed	Low, Medium Dispersed	Same as Investor	Low, Medium Dispersed	Low, Medium Dispersed

Degree of Risk Concentration is the last entry in each of the boxes.

A comprehensive example would be: from Table 1, a comparison of two lenders' risk exposure in two projects, a condominium development and an apartment building. In the case of the condominium, the construction lender faces high market risk because the construction loan typically remains in force until the units are sold and individual escrows are closed (with a commensurate reduction in construction loan principal). The construction lender faces a high financial risk because the stability of the loan during the construction and sales process is dependent on the financial health and business vitality of the developer. For the same reason, the construction lender's risk is concentrated in the developer and dependent on his ability to run a healthy business, successfully complete construction, and sell the units.

By contrast, the condominium takeout lender's position is one of relatively low market risk since funds are not advanced until the units are sold, and financial risk is spread across the individual buyers and their personal financial condition which is subject to scrutiny at the time of advancing the takeout. Also, the risk is dispersed in the financial side by the above, and to some degree on the market side since the lender can expect that individual unit owners will have different tenure horizons so that a defaulted unit can be introduced into an orderly market flow.

In the case of apartment buildings, the construction lender faces a relatively low market risk so long as the takeout is conditional only upon the issuance of a certificate of occupancy. In recent years, however, it has become increasingly common for takeout lenders to require a fixed percentage of accomplished rent-up before advancing the takeout. In this case, both construction and takeout lenders share the market risk. The characterizations in Table 1 do not assume such arrangements. The financial risk to the construction lender is high since the conditions are the same as in the condominium project with respect to the lender's reliance on the strength and ability of the developer. By the same token, the lender's risk is concentrated in the developer.

The apartment takeout lender faces a high market risk in the absence of a rent-up clause, since there is some probability of funding a loan on an empty apartment building with uncertain rental prospects. It is assumed that the financial risk to this lender is moderate since the lender has the opportunity to make a careful scrutiny of the project and the developer at the time of the loan commitment. The risk is concentrated since the lender can look only to the owner/developer whose performance under the loan is subject to factors extraneous to the encumbered property.

Due to the differing nature of the exposure to market and financial risk, as well as the different degrees of concentration of risk, as well as the different degrees of concentration of risk, each type of project and each type of participant requires careful analysis of certain critical points before making a decision. The nature of these critical points changes with the level and concentration of each type of risk. Following is a brief discussion of these critical points under the various risk conditions:

HIGH FINANCIAL RISK: The analysis should contain a heavy component which is borrower or investor specific, as well as project specific. Projected absorption rates, project cash flow projections, developer track records, and the financial and operating history of comparable projects should be major features of the analysis.

HIGH MARKET RISK: The analysis should be project specific, relying heavily on analysis of market feasibility, pricing schedules and their competitiveness, projected absorption rates, project compatibility with the existing market, and potential resale behavior.

CONCENTRATED RISK: The critical points here are project and/or investor specific. The emphasis in analysis of high market risk and high financial risk situations is also equally relevant to a situation of high concentration.

DISPERSED RISK: Evaluation of dispersed risk situations needs to be heavily market specific rather than project specific. Near term and intermediate term economic trends which will impact nationally or localy on the relevant buyer or borrower group need to be analyzed carefully and expanded beyond the standard brief introductory sections of the typical appraisal/feasibility report. In the case of dispersion achieved through the lease guarantee of a regional or national tenant, the analysis should include careful review of the tenant's financial statements. The study of trends in the tenant's industry is also recommended. In the more general case, careful attention must be paid to industry-wide or regional demand and supply analysis for the product in question, be it homes or storefronts. Many lenders and investors have lost substantial investments in projects which were "perfect" from the standpoint of the strength of the developer and the marketability of the product because they failed to apprehend the near-term future for the market in its entirety.

Low Market Risk and Low Financial Risk

For any number of reasons, a specific investment may enjoy low market risk, low financial risk, or both. It is the Reviewer's task to be certain that such a characterization is legitimate, and that the Analyst's report or the Reviewer's evaluation contain a discussion of the reasons for, and a justification of that characterization.

CONCLUSION

It is the Reviewer's role to provide insight and evaluation. Merely checking off the contents of a report against a standard format worksheet does not fulfill the demands of this role. Rather, the Reviewer must think carefully about the particular nature of the appraisal assignment and the motivations and objectives of the client organization.

The Reviewer must determine that the report does, in fact, speak to these particular circumstances to the same degree that it meets general standards of value analysis.

Beyond the level of objectives and motivations, one of the Reviewer's most powerful tools is the ability to analyze the nature and extent of risk faced by the client organization. Only by fully understanding the risk can the Reviewer determine if the report answers relevant questions and examines the critical variables.

While the standardized report format has done much to spread professional standards throughout the industry, it can be dangerously misleading in the absence of careful consideration of all of the specifics of the appraisal situation.

CHAPTER FIVE

Legal Problems Encountered

by the

Review Appraiser

SAMUEL L. "LES" KING, CRA

Samuel L. "Les" King is currently serving as Assistant Attorney General of Texas (Counsel to Parks and Wildlife Department).

For the past eighteen years, Mr. King has devoted the majority of his time in the public and private sectors of law to the fields of Eminent Domain and Real Property.

Mr. King, who is a Certified Review Appraiser, has had final review responsibility for all appraisals made for or on behalf of the Parks and Wildlife Department of Texas.

Legal Problems Encountered

by the

Review Appraiser

From the time of our birth until our death, we, individually, are prospective owners of some real property right. The property right may be limited to that of a tenant, but it carries with it the implied warranty to have a livable place to reside (*Kamarth v. Bennett*, 21 Tex. Sup. Ct. J. 315, April 14, 1978).[1] During our lives, if we acquire any of the "bundle of sticks" rights of real property ownership, we are confronted with valuation problems arising from the taxing abilities of the Federal, State, and local governmental bodies, the requirements of financial institutions, the necessity of nsurance safeguards and the individual's desire to buy, sell or trade in real property. We are affected by real property valuation problems arising from the governmental and quasi-governmental bodies' rights of eminent domain, exercise of police powers, utility rate making process, etc.; and on our death, the real property valuation problems continue with the probate courts, the State and Federal Estate Tax sectors, and then the valuation problems are handed to our heirs and devisees in Inheritance Tax procedures.

Thus, we are a nation of property rights and, as we grow, the need to make proper determinations of the value of those property rights becomes more important. The expert's opinion of value, the reasonable judgment call, must be based upon factual information that is acceptable to those legal principles and concepts governing property valuation and ownership.

It is not the duty of the Review Appraiser to make an appraisal of the property and reach a conclusion of market value. It is his duty to analyze the appraisal based upon the factual information it contains and determine whether or not the judgment calls made by the Appraiser are in fact supported by the admissible evidence contained in the report.

The Review Appraiser's function is, in many respects, analogous to that of an appellate judge. His function increases in importance as more of the valuation questions are finally resolved in judicial or quasi-judicial proceedings.

The Review Appraiser must now approach every appraisal from the viewpoint that it has the probability of appearing in some form of litigation. (*See,* Jordan, *Modern Texas Discovery* (1st Ed. 1974).[2]His burden has expanded to include a basic understanding of the legal problems involved in ownership, as well as the ability to evaluate the procedures used and the conclusion reached by the Appraiser.

There is an astounding number of valuation cases reported involving valuation questions brought about by erroneous description of the property appraised. Generally, the sufficiency of the description of the property in deeds determines the sufficiency of the description of lands in a court proceeding involving valuation, and similar rules of evidence apply. If the ambiguity in a description was patent, parole or extrinsic evidence would not be admissible to explain the defect. *State v. Egger,* 347 S.W. 2d 630 (Tex. Civ. App. — Austin 1961, no writ).[3]

Description of the land sought to be appraised should be such that a surveyor could go upon the land and mark out the property in question. *Wooten v. State,* 142 Tex. 238, 177 S.W. 2d 56 1944).[4] If the description is so defective that the property appraised cannot be properly identified, then the jurisdiction of the judicial body does not attach and the entire matter must have a new beginning. *See, Miers v. Housing Authority of City of Dallas,* 268 S.W. 2d 325 (Tex. Civ. App. — El Paso 1953, writ ref'd. n.r.e.).[5]

Only in those situations where the discrepancies of description can be eliminated without material prejudice to the owner of the property and without injecting entirely new matter, will the valuation proceedings be allowed to stand. *State v. Nelson,* 160 Tex. 515, 334 S.W. 2d 788 (1960).[6]

The appraisal report should not be approved if it does not include the proper legal description, preferably by metes and bounds or by reference to an approved plot of record, of the property valued. It is good review procedure to require a survey plat of the property appraised, showing the location of improvements, easements, means of access, areas of restricted or controlled areas that are of record, elevations, contours, flood plain areas, visible encroachments and other environ affecting value.

The term "owner" embraces the fee simple owner, the tenant for life, a lessee, a condition subsequent and any other person who has an interest in the property. *See, Houston North Shore Ry. Co. v. Tyrell,* 128 Tex. 248, 98 S.W.2d 786 (1936);[7] *Forth Worth and Denver Railway Company v. Judd,* 4 S.W.2d 1032 (Tex. Civ. App. — Amarillo 1928, writ dism'd); 2 A.L.R. 785; 95 A.L.R. 1090.[8]

The term "land" or "real estate" includes everything embraced by the term when used in its legal sense. "It indicates not only the soil but everything attached to it, whether attached through the course of nature — or by the hand of men — ." *McGee Irrigating Ditch Co. v. Hudson,* 85 Tex. 587, 22 S.W. 967 (1893);[9] *Brazos River C. and Reclamation District v. Adkisson,* 173 S.W.2d 294 (Tex. Civ. App. — Eastland 1943, writ ref'd).[10] It includes "every estate or use capable of segregation and ownership such as incorporeal hereditaments and other rights and privileges incidental to the land and necessary to complete title". *Houston North Shore Ry. Co. v. Tyrell, supra.*[11]

Valuation problems have been presented to the court involving riparian rights, ocean beach water rights, irrigation rights, water volumes, severance of surface fee from mineral fees, oil and gas in place, mineral leases, dirt and rock for fill, life estate, remainder estates, air and space, lessor and lessee, conditions subsequent and the right to overflow land, etc., etc., etc. The "bundle of sticks" is big!

Who owns what "stick" out of the "bundle of sticks"? Which "stick" is to be appraised and what effect does the ownership of other "sticks" have upon the "stick" appraised?

In *Gossett v. State,* 417 S.W.2d 730 (Tex. Civ. App. — Eastland 1967, writ ref'd n.r.e.),[12] the court was presented with the question of unity of ownership. The facts in that situation are interesting for there was little question regarding the problem of unity of use or the question of highest and best use.

Three brothers owned an equal undivided interest in the parent tract of land. Its highest and best use was for a shopping center site. They sub-divided the tract into three equal tracts retaining an equal undivided interest in each tract. Subsequently, they formed a corporation in which they had equal shares. They conveyed the middle tract to the corporation (Tract 2). Later, one of the brothers sold his interest out of Tract 3 to one of the brothers, but Tract 1 remained in the undivided joint ownership of the three brothers.

The problem of valuation arose in a condemnation proceeding where a portion of Tract 1 was to be taken. The court held that Tract 1 was to be appraised separately from the other two tracts, since there *was no unity of ownership.*

No testimony regarding the valuation of Tracts 2 and 3 was permitted in evidence even though it was admitted that the highest and best use of the tracts remained the same and that the three tracts were being used as a unit.

The majority opinions hold that where separate but contiguous tracts are jointed by unity of use and unity of ownership, they will be treated as a single unit for valuation purposes. *McLennan County v. Stanford,* 350 S.W.2d 208 (Tex. Civ. App. — Waco 1961, no writ);[13] *See also, Calverty v. City of Denton,* 755 S.W.2d 522 (Tex. Civ. App. — Fort Worth 1964, writ ref'd n.r.e.).[14]

Where there is a single ownership and a clear and undisputed unity of use, the courts have held that valuation of the tracts, whether two or more, as a unit was proper even though the tracts were not contiguous. *State v. South Main Baptist Church,* 361 S.W.2d 898 (Tex. Civ. App. — Houston 1962, writ ref'd n.r.e.).[15]

The foregoing is not intended as a treatise on the problems incurred in the answer to the question of unity of ownership. There are many variations of the problem; for example, in *State v. Lock,* 468 S.W.2d 560 (Tex. Civ. App. — Beaumont 1971, writ ref'd n.r.e.),[16] the appellate court reversed the trial court in a situation where there was a single ownership of two tracts with unity of use. The two tracts were not contiguous, but were severed by an existing State highway. Deep water was available on one tract, but not on the other. For years, the water had been pumped under the highway from one tract (Tract A), to the other (Tract B). The appellate court found that the right to pipe the water under and across the highway right-of-way was a *permissive* use and not a legal right, so, therefore, the evidence regarding the increased valuation to Tract B, because of the availability of water, was not permitted and its admission was reversible error. However, in *Creighton v. State,* 366 S.W.2d 840 (Tex. Civ. App. — Eastland 1963, writ ref'd n.r.e.),[17] the court indicated that if the right to cross the right-of-way was a *legal* right and not a *permissive* right, then the tracts, whether two or more, would be properly valued as a unit.

These examples are intended only to highlight the single ownership valuation problems presented to the Appraiser and to the "Review Appraiser". A completely different problem of valuation is presented in the situation of single tract but ownership of different estates.

The majority rule appears to be that the values of the component estates cannot be added together in such a manner as to exceed the value of the whole. In *Urban Renewal Agency v. Trammel,* 407 S.W.2d 773 (Tex. 1966),[18] the Supreme Court held that the trial court had erred by submitting apportionment issues in such a manner as to allow or encourage the jury to work backwards from the value of the respective estates of a lessor and lessee to arrive at the total value of the land.

The Appraiser's breakdown of market value must comply with the issues to be submitted by the court. Otherwise, his opinion of market value will be struck. *State v. Meyer,* 403 S.W.2d 366 (Tex. 1966).[19] Thus, in those instances of multiple estates, the Review Appraiser should require the appraisal report to establish an opinion of value of the whole property and then, secondly, establishment of an opinion of value of each component part. *See, Urban Renewal Agency v. Trammel, supra.*[20]

The Review Appraiser must check the accuracy of the appraisal process used on each estate and be sure that the valuations reached "are in conformity with good appraisal techniques".

It is good review procedure to require supporting information regarding the legal description of the property to be appraised. Complete title or ownership analysis is a necessity.

The Appraiser and the Review Appraiser should make inquiry regarding rights of parties in possession, any apparent encroachments, regulatory controls, such as zoning, required agency permits and other restrictive controls that would not normally be a part of the deed records.

In Texas, and many other states, the extra territorial rights granted to the cities and municipalities by statute are increasing in importance in their relationship to valuation matters. The awareness of the Review Appraiser to these factors cannot be overemphasized.

The costs incurred by a proper and complete survey showing all the environs of the property and an accurate legal opinion regarding the title of the property is usually a minor expense in the appraisal process; but, they are exactly that, they are a part of the appraisal process.

The discussion has, thus far, dealt with legal problems in the appraisal process prior to exercising the valuation techniques and procedures. Regardless of the estate to be appraised, the conclusion sought is the same; i.e., what is the market value of the estate appraised? Regardless for whom and for what reason, whether for loan, sale, hazard insurance, tax or other reasons, the purpose of the appraisal Reviewer is the same; to find support in the appraisal for the market value of the estate appraised.

The appraisal process is based upon the consideration and analysis of many factors including the effect that the political, social, economic and legal environments have upon the actions of the buyer and seller. The courts have recognized the importance of these in the appraisal process and state that as a general rule the Appraiser or witness has " . . . the right to introduce evidence of anything which would tend to affect the value of the land in the eyes of a prospective purchaser or which tends to make it more or less valuable to the owner . . . " *South Texas Electric Cooperative, Inc. v. Ermis*, 396 S.W.2d 955 (Tex. Civ. App. — Corpus Christi 1955, no writ).[21] It is the responsibility of the Review Appraiser to make sure that the Appraiser has considered these factors and made the proper analysis regarding their effect on market value.

There is no hard and fast rule that can be established that will assure the admission of value testimony in every instance. The courts take the viewpoint that the trial judge has the responsibility of the final decision and it is in his discretion whether or not the testimony will be admitted.[22] *Bruner v. State*, 391 S.W.2d 149 (Tex. Civ. App. — Forth Worth 1965, writ ref'd n.r.e.).[22] If, however, " . . . it appears reasonably probable to the trial judge that the *wants* and *needs* of the *particular community* may result, within a reasonable time, in the lifting of restrictions, he should admit [the] testimony . . . " (Emphasis added.) *City of Austin v. Cannizzo*, 153 Tex. 324, 267 S.W.2d 808 (1954).[23]

In order to determine the "wants" and "needs" of the "particular community" and reach a conclusion of their effect upon market value, it is necessary for the Appraiser to give a comprehensive, descriptive analysis of the area showing the growth factors (population and social trends, etc.), the economic influences (employment opportunities, average purchasing power, etc.), types of business activity (manufacturing, retail, financial, etc.), school, recreation facilities, changing land uses, utility and land patterns, population shifts and the various types of civic factors.

The appellate courts recognize that a wide range of factors must be considered. *City of Abilene v. Blackburn*, 447 S.W.2d 474 (Tex. Civ. App. — Eastland 1969, writ ref'd n.r.e.)[24]. The activity in the market, the public improvements regarding accessibility, the facts and circumstances connected with location and the quality and character of the land and area are factors influencing value considered by the courts to be admissible. *See, City of Corpus Christi v. Polasek*, 404 S.W.2d 826 (Tex. Civ. App. — Corpus Christi 1966, no writ)[25] *State v. Willey*, 351 S.W.2d 900 (Tex. Civ. App.—Waco 1961, no writ);[26] *State v. Cartwright*, 351 S.W.2d 905 (Tex. Civ. App. — Waco 1961, writ ref'd n.r.e.)[27]; *Floyd County v. Clements*, 150 S.W.2d 447 (Tex. Civ. App. — Amarillo 1941, writ dism'd jdgmt. cor.)[28]; *City of Ft. Worth v. Charbonneau*, 166 S.W. 387 (Tex. Civ. App. — Forth Worth 1914, writ dism'd).[29].

In every valuation problem the definition of "market value" remains the same; i.e., the price the property (estate) will bring when offered for sale by one who desires to sell, but is not obligated to sell, and is bought by one who desires to buy, but is under no necessity of buying, taking into consideration the *uses* to which the property is adaptable in the reasonable foreseeable future. *City of Austin v. Cannizzo,supra.*[30]

It is easy for the Review Appraiser to become so enmeshed in the techniques and procedures of appraising that we fail to analyze the factual reasoning that the Appraiser has employed on which to base his judgment. We can lose sight of the ultimate conclusion to be reached. It is important that we keep the nuances of the definition "market value" in mind.

"Market value" includes consideration of the highest and best use and is not limited to the use to which the owner is putting it at the time of valuation. *City of Tyler v. Ginn*, 225 S.W.2d 997 (Tex. Civ. App. — Texarkana 1949, writ dism'd w.o.j.), 148 Tex. 604, 227 S.W.2d 1022 (1050).[31] While it is proper to consider the evidence of the adaptabilities of the property for agricultural, mining, grazing and timber purposes, they should be considered only so far as they materially affect or throw light on the crucial inquiry; i.e., market value. *City of Cushing v. Buckles*, 134 Okla. 206, 273 Pac. 346 (1928).[32] However, an Appraiser may not prove the uses as separate items and then add the separate items of value to obtain the valuation of the whole. *U.S. v. Phillips*, 50 F. Supp. 454 (N.D. Ga. 1943).[33]

Where the items of use considered are irreconcilable, widely divergent and totally inconsistent with each other, the consideration of them jointly is improper. *United States v. Certain Lands, Etc.*, 51 F. Supp. 66 (S.D. N.Y. 1943).[34] The "adaptability for uses in the reasonable foreseeable future" excludes speculative and mere possible or imaginary uses. *Morton Butler Timber Co. v. U.S.*, 395 S.W.2d 426 (Tex. Civ. App. — Tyler 1965, writ ref'd n.r.e.).[36]

The best test regarding "highest and best use" would be to apply the discount for "risk" that a buyer spending his own hard cash would apply. The Appraiser must show in his appraisal that the "uses" which he considered would actually command a market price for such purposes. *A. D. Graham & Co. v. Pennsylvania Turnpike Comm.*, 347 Pa. 622, 33 Atl.2d 22 (1943);[37] *United States v. Rayno*, 136 F.2d 376 (1st Cir. 1943).[38] In *Brewer v. Blue Mountain Consolidated Water Co.*, 126 Pa. Super. 553, 191 Atl. 408 (1937),[39] the court admitted testimony regarding "uses" by taking into consideration other evidence showing "demand." While the Review Appraiser should not substitute his judgment for that of the Appraiser, he should require sufficient factual information developed from the marketplace, by which to test the opinion of "highest and best use."

As a Review Appraiser and as an attorney, I ask the Appraiser to include in his consideration the present use and any transitional uses before he establishes the "highest and best use." In support of his opinion, I ask that he consider an analysis of the neighborhood and area, impact of the present social and economic atmosphere, anticipation of future markets, availability of capital, project earnings, the stability of the local or area economy, the property rights involved, adaptability of the property to the use, demand for the use, adaptability of present or future improvements to the land uses and trends in government controls and regulations affecting the proposed use.

One final admonition, it is within the discretion of the trial court to permit evidence of the supporting testimony regarding highest and best use and the majority of courts seem to say that if it will enable the court and jury to determine market value, it will be admitted. *See, South Texas Electric Cooperative, Inc. v. Ermis, supra;*[40] *City of Austin v. Cannizzo, supra.*[41] The one thing the courts seem to agree on is that an "illegal use" cannot be considered in making a determination of market value. However, if the consistency of the standards used in determining "illegal use" is based upon the same consistency and standards used in their concepts of justice and morality, then we are indeed in a state of market fluxation.

We have recognized some of the legal problems confronting the Review Appraiser concerning ownership, legal description of the estate to be appraised, the influences of the surrounding neighborhood and area upon the subject property, the definition of market value and some of the factors that can be used to determine the highest and best use of the property.

The conclusion regarding highest and best use cannot be reached except by a detailed examination and analysis of the land to be appraised. This requires the Appraiser to consider such factors as the size and shape of the tract, the type of soil, topography, vegetation, availability of utilities, roads or external access, internal accesibilities of one portion of the tract to another, encroachments, all types of encumbrances, the relationship of the tract to the area and neighborhood land patterns, the location of the tract in its economic environment and any type of use restriction.

In *Hubbard v. Harris County Flood Control District*, 286 S.W.2d 285 (Tex. Civ. App. — Galveston 1956, writ ref'd n.r.e.),[42] the Court held that the size, shape, location on the bayou and erosion limited the usefulness of the tract and that this "testimony bore directly on the question of value." The Court in this instance found that the tract, because of its physical features and location, was not adaptable to the building of improvements thereon and could not be valued the same as property which was adaptable to being improved.

Deed restrictions on the subject property are sometimes overlooked. In *Northern Natural Gas Company v. Johnson*, 278 S.W.2d 410 (Tex. Civ. App. — Amarillo 1954, writ ref'd n.r.e.),[43] there was a restriction by deed which prohibited the sale of an undivided one-half interest in the tract for a number of years. The Appraiser for the landowner testified that the best use of the property was for residential and commercial purposes. This testimony was admitted by the trial court. The appellate court overruled the trial court with regard to this testimony by pointing out that the landowner could not be a willing seller "regardless of how anxious they were to sell" — the restriction would have an adverse effect "upon any reasonable juror as to its value for residential, commercial or industrial" purposes.

Situations frequently arise where one appraisal witness believes that the topographical features of a tract render it virtually valueless. Another appraisal witness believes that the topography is not a prohibitive obstacle. The Court in *State v. Albright*, 337 S.W.2d 509 (Tex. Civ. App. — Dallas 1960, writ ref'd n.r.e),[44] allowed testimony regarding elevations and the amount of fill required, together with overlay exhibits prepared by an engineer or the witness, to show the physical feasibility of placing the improvements on the property. The Review Appraiser must exercise his judgment in determining the probable effect that prior court decisions will have upon the Appraiser's analysis of the adpatability of the site.

The rights of the dominant estate over the servient estate arises in cases where the fee is encumbered by an easement. In power line cases and pipe line cases, the contention is usually made that the use of the property is restricted, whether for farming purposes or development purposes, by the added burden on ingress and egress rights, the additional plottage problems, etc. Again, the Review Appraiser must require the Appraiser to furnish sufficient facts that will support his opinion. *Heddin v. Delhi Gas Pipeline Company*, 522 S.W.2d 886 (Tex. 1975).[45]

The courts have recognized that "traffic flow and the flow of business [are] such factors to influence value" and the need for a motel or restaurant to be located on a busy freeway "is contrasted to the location of a TV business which depends upon the travel of home folks between business and home". *See, State Ex Rel. City of Wichita Falls v. Wood*, 467 S.W.2d 648 (Tex. Civ. App. — Fort Worth 1971, writ dism'd);[46] *State Ex Rel. City of Wichita Falls v. Rust*, 468 S.W.2d 581 (Tex. Civ. App. — Fort Worth 1971, writ dism'd).[47]

These examples are given to highlight the importance of a careful analysis of the land that is to be valued. The Review Appraiser should require that the appraisal report describe in detail the influencing factors heretofore set out. Aerial and ground photos can constitute a comprehensive photographic description of the property and should be a part of the appraisal report. If they accurately represent the property as of the time of valuation, most courts will admit them as evidence. *See, State v. Albright, supra*;[48] *McConnico v. Texas Power & Light Company*, 335 S.W.2d 397 (Tex. Civ. App. — Beaumont 1960, writ ref'd n.r.e.).[49]

As a practical matter, tempers are less likely to explode if the Review Appraiser seeks answers to any questions regarding the analysis of the site prior to litigation, rather than letting it become the focal pont of opposing counsel in a jury trial.

Some of the most seriously contested valuation cases arise from problems involving improvements. If the Appraiser has relied upon the market data approach to valuation, the question arises as to the degree of similarity regarding the properties and it is within this area that the trial court has "exclusive discretion to rule." *Bruner v. State, supra.*[50] There are some instance where the land has improvements of such a nature that they add little, if any, value because of utility of use problems or like circumstances to the property and thus the courts have taken the position that it is in the discretion of the court to determine "whether real estate is actually improved or not." *Reynolds v. State,* 390 S.W.2d 493 (Tex. Civ. App. — Texarkana 1965, no writ;[51] *see, Stewart v. State,* 453 S.W.2d 524 (Tex. Civ. App. — Beaumont 1970, writ ref'd n.r.e.).[52]

When the reproduction cost method is used as the basis to support the Appraiser's opinion of value, the majority rule is that costs less depreciation is admissible in evidence "provided the adaptability of the improvement to the land is established and further, that the prices upon which the reproduction cost is calculated *are normal and are not inflated.*" (Emphasis added.) *Housing Authority of City of Galveston v. Henderson,* 267 S.W.2d 843 (Tex. Civ. App. — Galveston 1954, no writ).[53] In that instance, the Court held that it was proper for a building contractor to testify as a "replacement cost expert" to the items of costs when "other expert witnesses testified to depreciation."

In the situation where the income approach has been used as a basis of the Appraiser's opinion of market value, the courts have insisted that the improvements be of such a nature that they add value to the land. *Stewart v. State, supra.*[54] (The Court, in dicta, in the *Stewart* case cited a number of instances in which the above holding would apply, such as improvements that were overbuilt compared to the neighborhood improvements.) In *Johnson v. State,* 474 S.W.2d 327 (Tex. Civ. App. — Austin 1971, writ ref'd n.r.e.),[55] the appellate court held the trial court did not err in refusing to admit the landowner's expert witness' testimony regarding the income approach under the circumstances where the improvements had not been completed at the time of the take, holding that "the lease contracts represented a prospective income."

The instances cited above are used to call the Review Appraiser's attention to the importance of a sound improvement analysis regardless of which method is used as the basis to support the Appraiser's opinion of market value.

Johnson v. State, supra,[56] has caused me to take a harder look at the review appraisal process, particularly since my law firm represented the losing landowner. I now insist that the Appraiser complete a detailed improvement analysis along these lines:

Locate all improvements and draw to scale on survey plat; accurate floor plan of improvements; narrative description of architectural design, general condition and age of improvements; description of quality of construction; i.e., materials, equipment, workmanship, asthetic features, functionality or balance of utility in use of improvements; special purpose features and equipment; where possible, attach architectural drawings and specifications; otherwise, list visible component specifications; consideration of utility of land to improvements; i.e., landscaping, view, drainage, access, balance between land use and improvements of subject compared to that of neighborhood and area; depreciation factors; i.e., physical, economic and functional obsolescence.

In every proceeding involving valuation of improvements, the question regarding depreciation becomes a major issue. Usually the "trier of fact" can understand physical deterioration. The real problem arises in presenting economic obsolescence and functional obsolescence factors in a manner that can be readily understood and accepted as realistic. Some courts have expressed resistance to economic obsolescence. *In re United States Commission to Appraise Washington Market Co. Property,* 295 F. 950 (App. D.C. 1924), appeal dism'd 265 U.S. 598, 44 S.Ct. 634, 68 L.Ed. 1199 (1924);[57] *See, Bridges v. Aslaska Housing Authority,* 375 P.2d 696,[58] in which the court held that 21% economic depreciation was excessive, saying this was based upon speculation regarding the loss of future rental income.

The Review Appraiser would do well to follow the guideline stated by the Court in *Trustees of Grace & Hope Mission v. Providence Redevelopment Agency,* 100 R.I. 537, 217 A.2d 476,[59] to the effect that as a condition precedent to the admission of evidence regarding functional or physical depreciation, there should be a "showing, for example, that because the property . . . is becoming antiquated or out of date, it is not functioning efficiently in the use . . . to which it was dedicated at the time of the taking [valuation]." "Opinion evidence" without the "proper foundation becomes speculative and should not be admitted."

Demonstrative evidence can be of real value to the Reviewer. Not only can the physical condition and the adaptability of the improvement be shown, but other aspects regarding the character of the neighborhood and area can be depicted and attention directed to items of incurable or curable depreciation.

The discussion has thus far been directed to some of the legal concepts that confront the Reviewer regarding the elements or factors effecting valuation. The application of these elements or factors effecting valuation presents a different group of legal concepts when they are directed to the final determination of the issue of market value.

The majority of the judicial and quasi-judicial bodies take the position that it is the *final opinion of market value* of the expert that becomes direct evidence of compensation due the owner of the property; thus, the method that the expert uses is admissible only as a basis to support the final conclusion. *Hays v. State*, 342 S.W.2d 167 (Tex. Civ. App. — Dallas 1960, writ ref'd n.r.e.).[60]

In any event, the appraisal should clearly set out the qualifications of the Appraiser so his background can be shown, thereby qualifying him as an expert. Once the expert has shown his familiarity with the elements of valuation of the property to be valued, he will be permitted to state his opinion of market value. *Mitchell v. Texas Electric Service Company*, 299 S.W.2d 183 (Tex. Civ. App. — Fort Worth 1957, writ ref'd n.r.e.).[61] The credibility of the witness and the weight to be given to his testimony are for the trier. *Housing Authority of the City of Dallas v. Hubbard*, 274 S.W.2d 165 (Tex. Civ. App. — Dallas 1954, no writ).[62] *Hays v. State, supra.*[63] In order to determine the weight to be given the expert's opinion, it is proper to test his investigation, knowledge, experience and to require an account of the factual basis of his opinion. *Hays v. State, supra.*[64] Thus, it is the Reviewer's duty to keep in mind the tests regarding expertise when examining the appraisal report and to require the inclusion of the information needed to give weight and substance to the expert's opinion.

After the witness has shown that, because of his study, investigation and special knowledge, he has qualified as an "expert", he can proceed to give his opinion of market value. *Hays v. State, supra.*[65] In order to support his opinion of market value " . . . *voluntary* sales of *similar* property in the *vicinity*, made at or about the *same time* . . . " may be used. *United States v. 5139.5 Acres of Land, Etc.*, 200 F.2d 659 (4th Cir. 1952).[66] This process of making a determination of market value is the market data approach and is a " . . . reflection of state of mind of public with respect to property, . . . " *United States v. Smith*, 355 F.2d 807

(5th Cir. 1966).[67] As heretofore noted, the admission of sales in support of the Appraiser's opinion of value rests in the discretion of the court, however, " . . . should it appear that *reasonable minds* cannot differ from the conclusion that the evidence of another sale lacks probative force because of dissimilarities, remoteness in time and distance, or not being voluntary, then the trial court should exclude evidence of the details . . . " (Emphasis added.) *Hays v. State, supra* at p. 174.[68]

There appears to be no shortcut to the tests regarding the comparability of the sales to the subject property. Attention is called to some of the don'ts:

(1) Don't compare improved land to unimproved land. In *State v. Chavers*, 454 S.W.2d 395 (Tex. 1970),[69] the sale of improved property, where a substantial portion of the sales price was for improvements, was not admitted as being comparable to support the Appraiser's opinion as to unimproved land.

(2) Don't compare properties with obvious environmental differences. In *City of Houston v. Hendrix*, 374 S.W.2d 764 (Tex. Civ. App. — Austin 1964, writ ref'd n.r.e.),[70] the court took judicial knowledge that " . . . it is a matter of common knowledge that proximity to an airport, especially one of the dimensions of the Houston International Airport, depresses residential values . . . " The sales complained of were only a mile from the subject property; however, they were in close proximity of the airport and directly in the flight pattern.

(3) Don't compare properties with obvious physical differences in soil, elvations, usability, etc. Thus, in *Hubbard v. Harris County Flood Control District, supra*[71] where the subject tract was bounded by a bayou on the north and was considered to be located in the Shamrock Hotel, Presidential Building and Medical Center area of Houston, it was not error to admit sales located south of the bayou and leave out sales north of the bayou where, because of the *size, shape* and *erosion* problems affecting the subject, the purported comparable sales north of the bayou did not meet the test of similarity, as they were not affected by the physical problems of the subject property.

(4) Don't compare properties based upon proximity alone. The State's witness in *Creighton v. State, supra*,[72] admitted that the sales he used were dissimilar but were in close proximity to the subject property. The appellate court held their admission to be reversible error even though the witness had made adjustments for the dissimilarities.

(5) Don't compare properties where there has been a

material change in the market conditions. In *State v. Dickerson*, 370 S.W.2d 742 (Tex. Civ. App. — Houston 1963), no writ),[73] the court held that a sale eight years prior to the date of valuation was so remote in time that reasonable minds could not differ that such evidence lacked probative force. However, the court indicated that if there had been a showing in evidence of *no material changes in the market condition*, its inclusion would have been permitted.

(6) Don't fail to take into account the neighborhood and area characteristics, even though the uses are similar. The need for a motel to be located on a freeway available to the traveling public is contrasted to the location of a TV business which depends on local city traffic. *See, State Ex Rel. City of Wichita Falls v. Wood, supra.*[74]

(7) Don't fail to take into consideration the size of the tracts. In *Melton v. State, supra,*[75] the tract to be valued consisted of 7.891 acres. The trial court refused evidence of any comparable sale less than one acre in size. The appellate court affirmed the trial court's holding.

(8) Don't compare lot sales from a subdivision to raw acreage tracts. *State v. Willey, supra.*[76]

(9) Don't fail to confirm and make inquiry of the circumstances of the sales with the buyer or seller. Admissibility requires transactions between a willing buyer and a willing seller. *State v. Curtis*, 361 S.W.2d 448 (Tex. Civ. App. — San Antonio 1962, writ ref'd n.r.e.);[77] *Gomez Leon v. State*, 426 S.W.2d 562 (Tex. 1968).[78] Hearsay evidence is not admissible to show sale is a "distress sale" and a motion in limine would be a proper method to preserve objection to sale. *Austin v. Flink*, 454 S.W.2d 389 (Tex. 1970).[79]

(10) Don't ignore the test that if "reasonable minds" can differ as to time, distance, voluntariness and similarity, the sale should not be used. *Hays v. State, supra.*[80]

The above list of "don'ts" is incomplete but it does point out some things to which the Reviewer must remain alert when analyzing the appraisal report. The problems relating to comparativeness or similarities cannot be treated lightly, for these problems are presened throughout the appraisal process.

The replacement cost or reproduction cost *new* is not admissible *without depreciation* being shown in the record. *Housing Authority of City of Galveston v. Henderson, supra.*[81] However, the courts in some instances have allowed one expert to testify to the land value and another witness to testify to the improvements based on cost less depreciation. *State v. Adams,* 489 S.W.2d 398 (Tex. Civ. App. — San Antonio 1972, writ ref'd n.r.e.).[82] In the situation where the improvements are valued separately from the land, the judicial bodies require that it be made clear that the improvements have no separate value except as they enhance the land value. *State v. Adams, supra.*[83]

Many of the judicial bodies express reluctance in allowing the use of reproduction cost less depreciation method of determining value and hold to the effect that it must be shown that there is no market or that the buyers and sellers in the marketplace use this method to determine value before it becomes admissible. *City of Houston v. Lakewood Estats, Inc.,* 429 S.W.2d 938 (Tex. Civ. App. — Houston [1st Dist.] 1968, writ ref'd n.r.e.).[84] Thus, in the instance of special purpose improvements, unique improvements, historical sites, etc., the reproduction cost method may be the only feasible method to determine value. *People Ex Rel. New York Stock Exchange Building Co. v. Cantor,* 223 N.Y. 64, affirmed 248 N.Y. 533, 162 N.E. 514.[85]

Physical deterioration appears to cause the least problem in judicial proceedings. The trouble spots for the Appraiser arise in his justification for functional and economic obsolescence. The difficulty is compounded in the means used in the determination of depreciation rates because each judicial or quasi-judicial body seems to have its preference. This lack of uniformity requires the Reviewer to become acquainted with the decisions regarding valuation problems in tax cases, rate making hearings, hazard insurance, condemnation proceedings and the like. The Reviewer must determine the purpose of the appraisal and then apply the method used to determine the depreciation rate that is used in that particular market.

The courts, except in the valuation of a highly standardized improvement, will reject a rule of thumb cost approach based on the average cost per cubic foot multiplied by the total number of cubic feet. Thus, in *United States v. 5.77 Acres of Land, More or Less, Etc.,* 52 F. Supp. (E.D. N.Y. 1943),[86], the court struck the government's witnesses' testimony when it was found on cross-examination that they had based their opinion on costs charts and bulletins rather than upon a qualified builder's estimate of costs. The validity of the Appraiser's costs analysis rests upon the accuracy of the cost estimate. *See, In re United States Commission to Appraise Washington Market Co. Property, supra.*[87] With this warning of the courts in mind, in both review and pretrial procedure, the following information is sought from the Appraiser regarding his cost analysis and estimate basis: character of construction determined by design, materials, equipment, workmanship, etc.; availability of materials and their adaptability to local conditions; i.e., source, demand or desirability, soil conditions, climatic conditions, etc.; equipment necessary to provide the services and comfort required for the highest and best use; remaining use life; quality and type of building materials; functionality and utility of design; i.e., size, shape and location of rooms, utility areas, garages, special purpose areas, etc., any repairs and maintenance performed; any observed deferred repair or maintenance; indirect costs of improvements; i.e., financing costs, legal fees, design costs, supervision during construction, insurance, etc.; direct costs; i.e., labor, materials, etc.; depreciative factors and rates; market value conclusion based upon: land valuation + direct costs of improvements + indirect costs - accrued depreciation = market value.

[*Note*: In rate cases it appears that the courts will allow "going concern value" as bearing on the cost of reproduction.] *See, Valuation Under the Law of Eminent Domain*, 39 S194 (2nd Ed. 1953), also p. 67 S204.[88]]

Most economists accept, in principle, the theory that the value of wealth is based on a capitalization of the net income which it is expected to yield. This principle underlies the claim that income produced from a property is evidence of its value. *City of Dallas v. Shackelford*, 200 S.W.2d 869 (Tex. Civ. App. — Dallas 1946, writ ref'd n.r.e.).[89] The courts look with suspicion on potential or prospective income as evidence of the value of real property. *Johnson v. State, supra.*[90] This attitude is probably based on the ground that the "trier" is in no position to weigh the prospective earnings and to apply a proper rate of capitalization. The fact that there have been abuses in applying this method of valuation could also affect the courts and cause their reluctance to accept a method of valuation that is widely used in the business community.

When the owner of the property uses it himself, the amount of his profits from the business he conducts depends on skill and good management and furnishes no test as to market value of the land. *Texas Electric Service Company v. Linebery*, 344 S.W.2d 242 (Tex. Civ. App. — El Paso 1961), rev'd 162 Tex. 570, 349 S.W.2d 105 (1961);[91] *see also, State v. Zaruba*, 418 S.W.2d 499 (Tex. 1967),[92] to the effect that if "good will" or value as a "going concern" is included in the opinion, it will not be admitted, but it has been held that the volume of business may be admitted and that it has probative force bearing on value. *State v. Pecos Gin Company*, 434 S.W.2d 226 (Tex. Civ. App. — El Paso 1968, writ ref'd n.r.e.).[93]

In *Huckabee v. State*, 431 S.W.2d 927 (Tex. Civ. App. — Beaumont 1968, writ ref'd n.r.e.),[94] the appellate court held that the trial court had erred in striking the Appraiser's opinion based upon the income approach, saying that the income approach is approved in *State v. Zaruba, supra*.[95]

The Reviewer must be sure that the Appraiser did not take into consideration the "good will" of the business or value it as a "going concern" when the income approach is used.

The courts recognize the actual rents as being competent evidence of value in most instances, *City of Dallas v. Shackelford, supra*,[96] but that rent must represent the existing market conditions. For example, a lease that was executed 15 or 20 years prior to the date of valuation would not be indicative of the present economic rent. Generally, the same tests of comparabilityply to admission of sales apply to the admission of rents as the basis of an income approach.

The rate of capitalization is the area that presents the greatest danger to the witness on cross-examination. With this in mind, the Reviewer will render the Appraiser-witness a favor in questioning the capitalization rate if it appears out of line in any respect.

Burritt Mutual Savings Bank v. City of New Britain, 20 Conn. Sup. 476, 140 A.2d 324, rev'd on other grounds 146 Conn. 669, 154 A.2d 608,[97] sets out an excellent analysis of the capitalization of income. It is worth reading.

There are many questions that the courts leave unanswered regarding the income approach. For example, there is no real guideline given in the situation where the neighborhood or area is decaying, but the improvement still commands a fair rental income and, if it is capitalized, it evidences an abnormally high market value. The courts appear to be willing to leave the answers to situations of this kind to the Appraiser.

Will "reasonable minds" differ to the correlation and conclusion of values reached by the Appraiser? The Review Appraiser has the obligation to assure the judicial or quasi-judicial bodies that the answer to that question is a firm and honest, NO!

REFERENCES

List of Authorities

[1]Kamarth v. Bennett, 21 Tex. Sup. Ct. J. 315 (April 15, 1978)

[2]Jordan. Modern Texas Discovery (1st Ed. 1974)

[3]State v. Egger, 347 S.W.2d 630 (Tex. Civ. App. — Austin 1961, no writ)

[4]Wooten v. State, 142 Tex. 238, 177 S.W.2d 56 (1944)

[5]Miers v. Housing Authority of City of Dallas, 268 S.W.2d 325 (Tex. Civ. App. — El Plaso 1953, writ ref'd n.r.e.)

[6]State v. Nelson, 160 Tex. 515, 334 S.W.2d 788 (1960)

[7]Houston North Shore Ry. Co. v. Tyrell, 128 Tex. 248, 98 S.W.2d 786 (1936)

[8]Fort Worth and Denver Railway Company v. Judd, 4 S.W.2d 1032 (Tex. Civ. App. Amarillo 1928, writ dism'd)

[9]McGee Irrigating Ditch Co. v. Hudson, 85 Tex. 587, 22 S.W. 967 (1893)

[10]Brazos River C. and Reclamation District v. Adkisson, 173 S.W.2d 294 (Tex. Civ. App. — Eastland 1943, writ ref'd)

[11]Houston North Shore Ry. Co. v. Tyrell, 128 Tex. 248, 98 S.W.2d 786 (1936)

[12]Gossett v. State, 417 S.W.2d 730 (Tex. Civ. App. — Eastland 1967, writ ref'd n.r.e.)

[13]McLennan County v. Stanford, 350 S.W.2d 208 (Tex. Civ. App. — Waco 1961, no writ)

[14]Calvery v. City of Denton, 375 S.W.2d 522 (Tex. Civ. App. — Fort Worth 1964, wirt ref'd n.r.e.)

[15]State v. South Main Baptist Church, 361 S.W.2d 898 (Tex. Civ. App. — Houston 1962, writ ref'd n.r.e.)

[16]State v. Lock, 468 S.W.2d 560 (Tex. Civ. App. — Beaumont 1971, writ ref'd n.r.e.)

[17]Creighton v. State, 366 S.W.2d 840 (Tex. Civ. App. — Eastland 1963, writ ref'd n.r.e.)

[18]Urban Renewal Agency v. Trammel, 407 S.W.2d 773 (Tex. 1966)

[19]State v. Meyer, 403 S.W.2d 366 (Tex. 1966)

[20]Urban Renewal Agency v. Trammel, 407 S.W.2d 773 (Tex. 1966)

[21]South Texas Electric Cooperative, Inc. v. Ermis, 396 S.W.2d 955 (Tex. Civ. App. Corpus Christi 1955, no writ)

[22]Bruner v. State, 391 S.W.2d 149 (Tex. Civ. App. — Fort Worth 1965, writ ref'd n.r.e.)

[23]City of Austin v. Cannizzo, 153 Tex. 324, 267 S.W.2d 808 (1954)

[24]City of Abilene v. Blackburn, 447 S.W.2d 474 (Tex. Civ. App. — Eastland 1969, writ ref'd n.r.e.)

[25]City of Corpus Christi v. Polasek, 404 S.W.2d 826 (Tex. Civ. App. — Corpus Christi 1966, no writ)

[26]State v. Willey, 351 S.W.2d 900 (Tex. Civ. App. — Waco 1961, no writ)

[27]State v. Cartwright, 351 S.W.2d 905 (Tex. Civ. App. — Waco 1961, writ ref'd n.r.e.)

[28]Floyd County v. Clements, 150 S.W.2d 447 (Tex. Civ. App. — Amarillo 1941, writ dism'd jdgmt. cor.)

[29]City of Ft. Worth v. Charbonneau, 166 S.W. 387 (Tex. Civ. App. — Fort Worth 1914, writ dism'd)

[30]City of Austin v. Cannizzo, 153 Tex. 324, 267 S.W.2d 808 (1954)

[31]City of Tyler v. Ginn, 225 S.W.2d 997 (Tex. Civ. App. — Texarkana 1948, wirt dism'd w.o.j.), 148 Tex. 604, 227 S.W.2d 1022 (1950)

[32]City of Cushing v. Buckles, 134 Okla. 206, 273 Pac. 346 (1928)

[33]U. S. v. Phillips, 50 F. Supp. 454 (N.D. Ga. 1943)

[34]United States v. Certain Lands, Etc., 51 F. Supp. 66 (S.D. N.Y. 1943)

[35]Morton Butler Timber Co. v. U.S., 91 F.2d 884 (1937)

[36]Melton v. State, 395 S.W.2d 426 (Tex. Civ. App. — Tyler 1965, writ ref'd n.r.e.)

[37]A. D. Graham & Co. v. Pennsylvania Turnpike Comm., 347 Pa. 622, 33 Atl.2d 22 (1943)

[38]United States v. Rayno, 136 F.2d 376 (1st Cir. 1943)

[39]Brewer v. Blue Mountain Consolidated Water Co., 126 Pa. Super. 553, 191 Atl. 408 (1937)

[40]South Texas Electric Cooperative, Inc. v. Ermis, 396 S.W.2d 955 (Tex. Civ. App. Corpus Christi 1955, no writ)

[41]City of Austin v. Cannizzo, 153 Tex. 324, 267 S.W.2d 808 (1954)

[42]Hubbard v. Harris County Flood Control District, 286 S.W.2d 285 (Tex. Civ. App. Galveston 1956, writ ref'd n.r.e.)

[43]Northern Natural Gas Company v. Johnson, 278 S.W.2d 410 (Tex. Civ. App. — Amarillo 1954, writ ref'd n.r.e.)

[44]State v. Albright, 337 S.W.2d 509 (Tex. Civ. App. — Dallas 1960, writ ref'd n.r.e.)

[45]Heddin v. Delhi Gas Pipeline Company, 522 S.W.2d 886 (Tex. 1975)

[46]State Ex Rel. City of Wichita Falls v. Wood, 467 S.W.2d 648 (Tex. Civ. App. — Fort Worth 1971, writ dism'd)

[47]State Ex Rel. City of Wichita Falls v. Rust, 468 S.W.2d 581 (Tex. Civ. App. — Fort Worth 1971, writ dism'd)

[48]State v. Albright, 337 S.W.2d 509 (Tex. Civ. App. — Dallas 1960, writ ref'd n.r.e.)

[49]McConnico v. Texas Power & Light Company, 335 S.W.2d 397 (Tex. Civ. App. — Beaumont 1960, writ ref'd n.r.e.)

[50]Bruner v. State, 391 S.W.2d 149 (Tex. Civ. App. — Fort Worth 1965, writ ref'd n.r.e.)

[51]Reynolds v. State, 390 S.W.2d 493 (Tex. Civ. App. — Texarkana 1965, no writ)

[52]Stewart v. State, 453 S.W.2d 524 (Tex. Civ. App. — Beaumont 1970, writ ref'd n.r.e.)

[53]Housing Authority of City of Galveston v. Henderson, 267 S.W.2d 843 (Tex. Civ. App. — Galveston 1954, no writ)

[54]Stewart v. State, 453 S.W.2d 524 (Tex. Civ. App. — Beaumont 1970, writ ref'd n.r.e.)

[55]Johnson v. State, 474 S.W.2d 327 (Tex. Civ. App. — Austin 1971, writ ref'd n.r.e.)

[56]Johnson v. State, 474 S.W.2d 327 (Tex. Civ. App. — Austin 1971, writ ref'd n.r.e.)

[57]In re United States Commission to Appraise Washington Market Co. Property, 295 F. 950 (App. D.C. 1924), appeal dism'd 265 U.S. 598, 44 S.Ct. 634, 68 L.Ed. 1199 (1924)

[58]Bridges v. Alaska Housing Authority, 375 P.2d 696

[59]Trustees of Grace & Hope Mission v. Providence Redevelopment Agency, 100 R.I. 537, 217 A.2d 476

[60]Hays v. State, 342 S.W.2d 167 (Tex. Civ. App. — Dallas 1960, writ ref'd n.r.e.)

[61]Mitchell v. Texas Electric Service Company, 299 S.W.2d 183 (Tex. Civ. App. — Fort Worth 1957, writ ref'd n.r.e.)

[62]Housing Authority of the City of Dallas v. Hubbard, 274 S.W.2d 165 (Tex. Civ. App. — Dallas 1954, no writ)

[63][64][65]Hays v. State, 342 S.W.2d 167 (Tex. Civ. App. — Dallas 1960, writ ref'd n.r.e.)

[66]United States v. 5139.5 Acres of Land, Etc., 200 F.2d 659 (4th Cir. 1952)

[67]United States v. Smith, 355 F.2d 807 (5th Cir. 1966)

[68]*Hays v. State, 342 S.W.2d 167 (Tex. Civ. App. — Dallas 1960, writ ref'd n.r.e.)*

[69]State v. Chavers, 454 S.W.2d 395 (Tex. 1970)

[70]City of Houston v. Hendrix, 374 S.W.2d 764 (Tex. Civ. App. — Austin 1964, writ ref'd n.r.e.)

[71]Hubbard v. Harris County Flood Control District, 286 S.W.2d 285 (Tex. Civ. App. Galveston 1956, writ ref'd n.r.e.)

[72]Creighton v. State, 366 S.W.2d 840 (Tex. Civ. App. — Eastland 1963, writ ref'd n.r.e.)

[73]State v. Dickerson, 370 S.W.2d 742 (Tex. Civ. App. — Houston 1963, no writ)

[74]State Ex Rel. City of Wichita Falls v. Wood, 467 S.W.2d 648 (Tex. Civ. App. — Fort Worth 1971, writ dism'd)

[75]Melton v. State, 395 S.W.2d 426 (Tex. Civ. App. — Tyler 1965, writ ref'd n.r.e.)

[76]State v. Willey, 351 S.W.2d 900 (Tex. Civ. App. — Waco 1961, no writ)

[77]State v. Curtis, 361 S.W.2d 448 (Tex. Civ. App. — San Antonio 1962, wirt ref'd n.r.e.)

[78]Gomez Leon v. State, 426 S.W.2d 562 (Tex. 1968)

[79]Austin v. Flink, 454 S.W.2d 389 (Tex. 1970)

[80]Hays v. State, 342 S.W.2d 167 (Tex. Civ. App. — Eastland 1967, writ ref'd n.r.e.)

[81]Housing Authority of City of Galvestion v. Henderson, 267 S.W.2d 843 (Tex. Civ. App. — Galveston 1954, no writ)

[82][83]State v. Adams, 489 S.W.2d 398 (Tex. Civ. App. — San Antonio 1972, writ ref'd n.r.e.)

[84]City of Houston v. Lakewood Estates, Inc., 429 S.W.2d 938 (Tex. Civ. App. — Houston [1st Dist.] 1968, writ ref'd n.r.e.)

[85]People Ex Rel. New York Stock Exchange Building Co. v. Cantor, 223 N.Y. 64, affirmed 248 N.Y. 533, 162 N.E. 514

[86]United States v. 5.77 Acres of Land, More or Less, Etc., 52 F. Supp. (E.D. N.Y. 1943)

[87]In re United States Commission to Appraise Washington Market Co. Property, 295 F. 950 (App. D.C. 1924), appeal dism'd 265 U.S. 598, 44 S.Ct. 634, 68 L.Ed. 1199 (1924)

[88]2 Orgel, Valuation Under the Law of Eminent Domain, 39 §194 (2nd Ed. 1953), also p. 67 §204

[89]City of Dallas v. Shackelford, 200 S.W.2d 869 (Tex. Civ. App. — Dallas 1946, writ ref'd n.r.e.)

[90]Johnson v. State, 474 S.W.2d 327 (Tex. Civ. App. — Austin 1971, writ ref'd n.r.e.)

[91]Texas Electric Service Company v. Linebery, 344 S.W.2d 242 (Tex. Civ. App. — El Paso 19610, rev'd 162 Tex. 570, 349 S.W.2d 105 (1961)

[92]State v. Zaruba, 418 S.W.2d 499 (Tex. 1967)

[93]State v. Pecos Gin Company, 434 S.W.2d 226 (Tex. Civ. App. — El Paso 1968, writ ref'd n.r.e.)

[94]Huckabee v. State, 431 S.W.2d 927 (Tex. Civ. App. — Beaumont 1968, writ ref'd n.r.e.)

[95]State v. Zaruba, 418 S.W.2d 499 (Tex. 1967)

[96]City of Dallas v. Shackelford, 200 S.W.2d 869 (Tex. Civ. App. — Dallas 1946, writ ref'd n.r.e.)

[97]Burritt Mutual Savings Bank v. City of New Britain, 20 Conn. Sup. 476, 140 A.2d 324, rev'd on other grounds 146 Conn. 669, 154 A.2d 608

Annotations

2 A.L.R. 785

95 A.L.R. 1090

CHAPTER SIX

A Study On

Government Reviewing

CLAUDE R. MOORE, JR., CRA

Claude R. Moore, Jr., CRA, is a Real Estate Appraiser and Reviewer at the Real Estate Headquarters — Region 4 — of the General Services Administration, Atlanta, Georgia. Mr. Moore was recently with the U.S. Postal Service Real Estate Division. He received his education at Elon College in North Carolina, with a B.A. in Economics, Business Administration and Accounting.

In addition to holding the "Certified Review Appraiser" designation, Mr. Moore holds membership in the American Institute of Real Estate Appraisers and the American Society of Appraisers.

JAMES T. COE, CRA

James T. Coe, CRA, is Field Supervisor of Real Estate for the U.S. Postal Service in Atlanta, Georgia. He graduated with a B.A. in Real Estate and Urban Development from Georgia State University.

In addition to being a Senior Member of the National Association of Review Appraisers, Mr. Coe is a member of the Association of Federal Appraisers.

A Study On

Government Reviewing

INTRODUCTION

Governmental Reviewing

Historically, reviewing for institutions has been proforma and perhaps lacking, with much reliance placed on the judgment of the fee Appraiser. In one of the largest owners/lessees of property in our country, the United States Postal Service, professionalism in Reviewing is now expected along with professional appraising. The Postal Service requires review by professionally trained individuals with considerable expertise in Appraisal Review. This chapter deals with USPS/Institutional requirements for Appraisal Review and provides some examples of the Review process. This is required by the Real Estate and Buildings Department. Most of the formats were developed "in house" with suggestions adopted from NARA's professional seminar and other professional sources.

Acknowledgment

No dissertation of this scope is solely attributable to one person. This chapter became a reality due to the efforts of many persons who have contributed information and who were responsible for the review and editing of the material presented herein, which we believe includes the most contemporary thinking and appraisal review practices in use for Government Review.

We wish to thank the United States Postal Service for contributing appraisal review reports and other pertinent information which, when added to the information obtained from various published articles, resulted in the contents of this chapter.

We are especially indebted to the management of Southern Region, USPS, and Atlanta District for their encouragement and guidance. Last, but not least, was the help of many friends, who contributed in various ways to make this publication become a reality.

Claude R. Moore, Jr., CRA, MAI
James T. Coe, CRA

Communicating/Communicator

As many professional Appraisers have attested, the appraisal process is not simple. The professional Appraiser should be able to effectively inform the reader of his report of five important facets: 1. Purpose of the report. 2. What type of appraisal methods were utilized in the report. 3. How he plans to utilize the mentioned methods. 4. Why he should use those particular ones. 5. Why and how the Appraiser reached his final conclusions of value. This is also true of the professional Reviewer. The Reviewer must realize that a skillful communicator will prepare and present an appraisal review which should lead an intelligent reader through the logic and reasoning of the Appraiser, either to show the report holds merit or reflect how another opinion was derived.

One main key to becoming a successful Review Appraiser is organization. Like the Appraiser, the Reviewer must recognize the problem to be solved, analyze the presented data, and convey his judgments and decisions to his reader.

Basic grammar skills, organization of data and the ability to convey thoughts into comprehensible and easy to read review is one of the marks of the professional CRA Reviewer.

Professionalism

Obtaining credentials, schooling, experience, and recognition through designations are very important for the Appraiser or Review Appraiser. These are all important tools he needs in order to successfully perform his task.

Even with all of the previously mentioned skills, there is another requirement the Appraiser or Reviewer needs. It is an ingredient which makes him strive for excellence. This ingredient is Professionalism. According to Webster, Professionalism is defined as "conduct, aims, qualities characteristic of a profession". Professionalism for the Appraiser also embraces the concept of ethics. To be truly professional, the Appraiser/Reviewer must maintain strict objectivity. It can not be stressed to highly, for only be precticing professionalism, can the Appraiser and Reviewer gain the respect of his peers as well as the confidence of the public he serves.

In qualifications, the position of the Review Appraiser requires experience, education, sensitivity to market forces, knowledge of legal, engineering and appraisal principles and organizational policies. It also requires a high degree of common sense, analytical ability and the mature judgment commonly required in equivalent supervisory positions. Like the Appraiser, the professionally qualified Reviewer must keep abreast of developments in a wide variety of fields, such as real estate financing, construction methods, population trends, government activities, etc. This appears to be an impossible task, but if a Reviewer is to fulfill all the above requirements be must first be a thoroughly qualified and experienced real estate Appraiser with formal training in appraising and extensive experience in his field of appraisal activity. The Review Appraiser, unless adequately trained in appraisal previously, can not adequately adept to the Review job in absence of this most needed appraisal experience. The Reviewer must be cognizant of the many techniques required in arriving at conclusions of value and have the ability to adequately defend this position in written review.

Do not be an advacate or amateur or a "rubber stamper". Obtain the "art" of Appraisal Review by securing the experience, acquiring the qualification's and by promoting increased professionalism in the review process.

Management Control

Some schools of thought list two primary methods through which the review function may be accomplished.

Most Institutional Appraisal Reports are contract appraisals which pose different problems in that they require more time in review than staff work, as the Reviewer usually is not familiar with the outside professional Appraiser's capabilities and individualized report format.

The primary methods are altered due to this fact. The two methods are: (A) The Echelon Method; (B) The Single Method. The Echelon (or cummulative) method is whereby the appraisal is reviewed in whole or in part at several different levels or echelons, with final review being made by a Reviewer sometimes located remote from the project or property. The Single (or Terminal) Method is whereby the report is reviewed and approved by one individual. This individual may or may not be remote from the property.

In the postal service, the present procedure is to have a professional, experienced Reviewer, review the contract appraisal report and offer his opinion to higher echelon for approval. This method offers a very thorough review plus the expertise of very knowledgable individuals in management. The single method is seldom used because of the chance of error. Reviewing as well as Appraising is not an "Exact Science".

General Procedural Steps for the Review Appraiser

It is suggested that the following items should be considered and utilized in most normal appraisal reviews to the extent practical.

Timing
Appraisals should be logged in at the time they are received and marked to clearly indicate the date of receipt. Any supplements or revisions should be similarly marked at the time they are received. Usually target dates are known and adequate allowance should be made (lead time) for performances of functions. Wherever appropriate, the Review Appraiser should attempt to determine and obtain a reasonable time allowance for the satisfactory and adequate performance of his function.

A follow-up system should be instituted for any late appraisals or for requests for supplemental information or revisions. Any problems in complying with established schedules or target dates should be promptly communicated to management.

It is significant and essential that adequate time be permitted for the appraisal review function. Any undue curtailment of lead time in the Appraisal and Appraisal Review functions inevitably leads to (a) improper expenditures of funds, (b) deterioration of public relations, (c) increasing difficulties in negotiations and incidence of public and private complaints.

It is usually logical for the appraisal to be office reviewed for the purpose of discovering any errors or inadequacies before the field inspection is made.

Content

In virtually every organization, some sort of standards have been developed with respect to appraisal content requirements. Documentary requirements of appraisals naturally vary from jurisdiction to jurisdiction in accordance with state or local law and established procedures.

Requirements are spelled out in many forms, such as (a) approved appraisal forms, (b) appraisal contracts, (c) appraisal guidelines, (d) written standards or specifications, etc. The Reviewing Appraiser should check to assure necessary compliance with such requirements.

It is desirable that, at the time of receipt of the first appraisals on a project and prior thereto, the reviewing Appraiser check the project to determine any need for specialty appraisal work, legal opinions or any unusual appraisal problems that may be involved, including problems of unity of use or title, real-personal property distinctions, reasonableness of remaining access and compensability of construction features. If deemed necessary by the reviewing Appraiser, in unusual cases, he should accumulate or have accumulated for him any additional comparable sales, rentals or construction costs that he believes essential. The Reviewer should acquaint himself sufficiently with the area and become knowledgable of real estate trends and area econmic data.

The desk Reviewer should check the appraisal very carefully, and he should ascertain that the Appraiser incorporated all requirements of the contract. A check should be made to determine that the affidavit of the Appraiser has been properly completed, signed and notarized. The total area of the entire property should be compared with the approved plan and title. The site to be acquired, as shown in the appraisal, should be verified with the approved plan. The narrative description of the entire property should be compared with the plan to ascertain whether all improvements listed in the appraisal are actually shown on the plan. An investigation should be made to assure that the value to be estimated under this appraisal is the same value as specified in the contract with the Appraiser. The title upon which the value is to be estimated, such as fee simple should be examined against the interest to be acquired.

Also, at this time, it is appropraite for the Review Appraiser to consider and be cognizant of possible problems relating to lack of uniformity as between "interest owned" and "interest to be appraised." Quite often, appraisal specifications and procedures require the appraisement of the fee simple interest in the property. However, it may be that the owner of the real property does not possess a fee simple ownership and, accordingly, appraisal and settlement on a fee simple basis may well be inappropriate and excessive. This is frequently the case, particularly in public lands, railroad and utility lands and, in some cases, private lands, where uses may be restricted.

This should not be confused with separation of interests within the fee simple entity, such as lessor and and lessee of various easement conveyances, etc. Some jurisdictions require that separate values be placed on the separate interests. Unless the contract rent exceeds the economic rent, the sum of the separate interest valuations cannot exceed the whole (fee simple interest), and if this possibility occurs, the excess value may not be a compensable item under the laws of the particular jurisdiction.

The appraisal and certificate of title or abstract should be compared for sales of the subject property for a minimum of the last five years and, in any event, the last sale of the subject property should be examined for at least historical data and any possible relevancy. An examination should be made to see that all three approaches to value are used or, if one or more of these approaches is not used, that the Appraiser has given an adequate explanation of its omission. For example, the cost approach has very little validity as buildings grow older, except for special use properties, such as public buildings, churches, etc., where the cost approach is frequently the only available guide to valuation.

The correlation and conclusion as to value of the interest appraisal should convey the distinct impression a logical, sound determination has been reached based upon accepted appraisal interpretation of the data presented in the report.

The appraisal should be checked to assure that it contains a sketch or plat of the subject property, showing any subdivision in valued and the general location of any significant improvements. Review should also ascertain that a sufficient number of properly identified photographs, taken at several angles to show significant front, side and rear features of the property, especially any improvements, are attached to the appraisal.

Then comes the arduous task of auditing all computations contained in the appraisal. This check may include all calculations as to square feet, acreage, square and cubic feet of improvements and plus or minus adjustments of comparables. All computations used in the cost approach and income approach where tabulated data is presented should always receive particular attention.

The valuation of real property normally requires the use of arithmetic or mathematics in some form and the degree of use will vary considerably with the complexity of the appraisal problem.

For the purposes of appraisal review as discussed herein, a distinction should be made between arithmetic and mathematics. Arithmetic is considered as the art of computation of positive real numbers. Mathematics involves unknowns and the use of appraisal principles, theory and judgment.

Appraising involves the translation into real numbers (by substitution for unknowns in mathematics) a valuation figure based on critical judgment factors obtained from factual economic data. Once the substitutions are made, the mathematics of appraising becomes arithmetic. Hence, the more conclusive the judgment factors obtained from factual data, the sounder the evaluation.

At the desk review stage, the arithmetic of an evaluation can be checked for accuracy. This check can be performed by a Review Appraiser's assistant or the desk Reviewer (as can many other functions in the preliminary stages of review). It is principally a check on accuracy of arithmetic calculations. Errors in utilization or selection of principles, theories, techniques, etc., may or may not be discovered in this preliminary stage of the review, depending on the ability of the person doing this phase of the work; for instance, the Review Appraiser's assistant.

Theoretically and practically, the more acceptable approach is to adjust from a known number (the sale price of the comparable) to an unknown number (the value of the subject property). In other words, the adjustment should be made from the comparable to the subject. If the comparable is better than the subject, an appropriate deduction should be made; if poorer than the subject, an appropriate increase should be added; and if equal to the subject, of course, no adjustment is made.

Although not impossible, it is not considered good practice to make adjustments from the subject to the comparable. It is much better practice for the subject to remain fixed as the unknown value, and the known values of the comparables adjusted to compare the conditions of the subject to those of the sale property.

Also, if adjustments are made on a percentage basis, the reviewing Appraiser should assure himself that the mathematics and arithmetic are fundamentally sound and void of duplication. Generally, percentages should be converted to a single factor before application, rather than applied progressively; otherwise, there can be a compounding of adjustments which can result in an erroneous conclusion.

Whether these items are checked in the preliminary desk review depends on the capabilities of the individual. In any event, the calculations in the market approach relating to adjustments, viz., when comparable is better, deducting; when the comparable is poorer, adding should be accurate. If percentages are used, correspondingly correct adjustments should be used in checking the multiplication process.

The Reviewer examines each comparable sale against the appraisal of the subject property. In addition to checking all the mathematics and the basic theory of the cost approach, the desk Reviewer also assures himself that raw land values are based upon proper comparable sales, if available, specifically adjusted to support the land value arrived at in this approach for each type of land involved.

All unit costs of structures and significant improvements included in the cost approach should be supported by comparison to specific examples of current construction costs in the area or by a reliable cost service. If a cost service is used, he should check all unit costs and adjustments as shown in the appraisal, against official cost service books. He should satisfy himself that the cost service has been adjusted both to the current date of the appraisal and to the specific locale of the subject property. If the property is an income-producing property, or is a type which is subject to the use of the income approach to value, he should ascertain that not only all of the calculations are correct, but that the income approach has been properly applied and that there is adequate support for any pertinent items such as capitalization rate, interest rate, recovery rate and vacancy and credit allowance.

Field reviews are an integral part of the review process. Each completed appraisal should be reviewed in the field and the Reviewer should periodically review current work during the appraisal process to assure compliance with departmental policies, to examine specific controversial or unique parcels, and to advise the Appraiser on procedure in unique circumstances.

One of the purposes of the field review is to satisfy the Reviewer of the thoroughness of the Appraiser's investigation, into trends and conditions. The depth and extent of field review investigation will depend in large measure on the Reviewer's evaluation of the reliability of the Appraiser, the nature of the parcel, and the requirements for exercising necessary quality control. The following discussion contains a listing of many steps the Reviewer may select in assuring the Appraiser's compliance with his obligations.

Before making a field review, the Review Appraiser should make certain that he is familiar with the historical data pertaining to the property, the appraisal report and all available comparable data and other information supplied by the Appraiser or which is available through other sources. If there is more than one appraisal for a specific property, it is desirable to review all appraisals simultaneously in order to conserve time and permit easier comparison and for better recall of variations in arriving at a decision on an estimate of value.

The Reviewer should orient himself and analyze the general neighborhood data, the comparables listed in the appraisal reports and others of which he may have knowledge. The Appraiser's reasoning used to arrive at his estimate of value should also be examined for fallation logic. He should then inspect the subject property, and may inspect the interior of the improvements that are taken or substantially affected, if such inspection is deemed necessary. It is desirable that such inspection of improvements be made in the presence of an owner or with his knowledge when an interior inspection is involved. The date of inspection should be noted and recorded, together with the names of parties present or advised of the inspection.

The Reviewer should answer any questions that he properly can concerning procedure. A systematic, efficient and complete inspection of the property may help assure the owner that full and individual consideration is being given to him. Items not ordinarily considered real property, but included in the appraisal, must be carefully checked to assure that they meet all the requirements to become part of the real property.

During the initial appraisal, the Appraiser should have carefully inspected the construction details of the real property improvements, with attention given to any items of depreciation, functional or economic obsolescence. During the review, it may be reassuring to the owner and helpful to the review if the Reviewer asks him about any recent improvements, repairs or renovation he has made to the structures or land and his cost in making such improvements. This may be an appropriate time for the Reviewer to check details concerning income, operating expenses, vacancy and credit loss and, in the case of relatively new structures, details concerning original cost.

Unsupported and arbitrary adjustments in the appraisal process can produce almost any kind of valuation. They may or may not reflect fair market value. As a general rule, unsupported and arbitrary adjustments are considered unacceptable. Evidence of market recognition is deemed the most professional method of adjustment justification.

An excellent means of determining the adequacy and reasonableness of adjustments is by personally verifying them during the field review.

Some adjustments can be supported directly from available data. Others require development by reason, logic or judgment. In no case, however, should a significant adjustment be accepted without support or explanation.

At the time of the initial appraisal, an examination should be made of each room, noting construction, quality and materials. Arrangements of space should be considered for its functionality. Any special features should be noted. The interior inspection is not complete until the Reviewer has examined all rooms, including any special facilities, noting any inadequacies or any super-adequacies.

The Reviewer, while inspecting the property, may ask the property owner to point out any special items of construction or value that they feel should be considered. This may help assure the property owners that full consideration has been given to al items that they feel are important. A Reviewer may inspect the exterior land area of the property, including trees, shrubbery and other on-site improvements. Where necessary, he may have the owner confirm the location of gas, water and sewer lines to see that proper allowance has been given to these in the appraisal and in their representation on the plans.

He may verify with the property owner the conditions, terms and sale price of any transfers of the property when he purchased it and, also, any other data relative to sale, rental or lease of the subject property for at least the last five years, to the extent that the owner has first-hand knowledge of these facts.

In all cases, he should review present use of the property and determine its zoning, if any. He should analyze the highest and best use, as shown in the appraisal both before and after the taking, and satisfy himself that the conclusion of the Appraiser is correct and, if different from the existing use, that it is properly supported and sound.

He should check the Appraiser's sketch of any significant buildings taken or damaged against the actual buildings themselves and, where necessary, spot check the measurements of these buildings. He should verify that the pictures correctly represent the property and its features.

After completing his inspection of the subject property, he should personally field check and, if necessary, verify any comparable sales. It would be desirable for him or his assistant to personally inspect each one of the comparable sales and attempt to view the insider of any improved property(ies) which are cited by the Appraiser. The Appraiser should inquire about any improvements made to the comparables since the date of transfer. If other sales data is available to the reviewing Appraiser, which he feels may be pertinent to the subject appraisal, he should also evaluate and compare it with the subject to the extent he deems necessary. Where necessary, he or his assistant may verify the price, area, terms and condition of the sale of any comparable property with either the seller, buyer or broker or other acceptable reliable source.

The Review Appraiser should always give careful attention to the appraisals of nearby properties containing similar land or improvements to assure that consistent sales data and approaches are used for comparable types of land and improvements. Use of a summary table for similar adjacent properties is sometimes helpful.

The Reviewer should make additional checks if the cost or income approaches are used on the property. He should ascertain the reliability of the cost data used in the appraisal against current construction costs in the market or in the subject property. Checking with local builders or builders' supply firms provides data concerning current cost of comparable types of building materials. He should verify that the cost data used in the appraisal is for similar quality of structural components.

If the income approach is used, he should verify the economic rent on similar properties in the area and verify the interest rate of in the vicinity for income properties of the subject type. He may deem it advisable to attempt to find typical operating statements for this type of property in the area. In the land residual technique, careful consideration should have been given to the improvement cost, age, income and highest and best use. In the building residual technique, land value should have been well established in the market. If Gross Monthly Multiples have been ued in the income approach, he should check their reliability and effective range, as well as the rental sales used in computing these multiples.

Returning to his office, the Appraiser should then again review the appraisal or appraisals as an entity, determining whether the approaches that have been used are proper, whether the conclusion and correlation of the market data and the overall conclusions and correlations in the appraisal or appraisals are proper and whether or not the data actually fully supports and documents each of the Appraiser's conclusions and findings.

An arithmetical check was made in the preliminary review stage. That was principally for accuracy of positive real numbers that were used in the appraisal proper. Certain mathematical functions relating to adjustments in the market approach are perhaps more properly considered as a "mathematical check."

It now is necessary to determine whether proper mathematics were used in the application of numbers to the appraisal process and whether the transposition of unknown numbers from facts or theory to real numbers is supported and reasonable. This is a critical area in valuation and a severe test of the Review Appraiser's capabilities.

For Example:

(1) The Appraiser substituted 75 percent for unknown depreciation.

(2) The Appraiser substituted a $5,000 lump sum to sale price of comparable for "location" because comparable is in a better location than subject.

(3) The Appraiser substituted nothing for annual taxes in a stabilized expense statement.

(4) The Appraiser substituted three percent for an unknown capitalization rate in the income approach.

Items (1) and (4) appear to be unsupported by the Appraiser. Item (2) was adjusted in the wrong direction. Item (3) was in error by omission. All four items may have been supportable by more detailed market data analysis.

If market data is inconclusive or not acceptable, the adjustments must be based on sound reasoning.

Virtually any kind of value conclusion can be derived by manipulation of mathematics. Unless, however, the mathematics are founded on acurate market data or reasonable inferences and based on sound appraisal theory and principles, the product is of doubtful validity.

The practice of substituting unsupported numbers for unknown factors in the appraisal process is, in fact, a form of valuation by unsupported written opinion.

Unless that opinion is acceptably documented, it has little relevancy in today's real property acquisition programs.

Many examples or illustrations can be drawn relative to the use and application of mathematics to appraising. Arithmetic and mathematics are used in all three approaches to value. However, in essence, appraising is the science of developing positive real numbers (expressed in terms of dollars) from known and unknown factors. Mathematics are often utilized in the process. Once the substitution is made, mathematics becomes a simple arithmetical computation.

The dependability of the mathematical treatment is for the Reviewer to determine by testing and application of sound appraisal theory and techniques.

The Reviewer should carefully check any appraising by abstraction. The technique of determining the amount of an unknown quantity when certain other quantities are known is referred to in appraising or mathematics by "abstraction." Obtaining a given value by abstraction is a useful and accurate technique if used properly in the appraisal and appraisal review process. Its accuracy, however, is entirely dependent on the accuracy of the known quantities also used in the process.

There are a number of areas where the technique of abstraction is utilized in appraising and reviewing; for example, (a) in determining the contributing value of certain classes of industrial land, and (b) in determining the amount of benefits or severance damages in the allocation function. Abstraction should only be used in the absence of good comparable sales when other known quantities are properly supported.

The reviewing Appraiser should determine that all proper

elements of value, damages or benefits have been considered and that no improper items are included. If the reviewing Appraiser agrees with the appraisal and believes it is sound and adequately supported, he should so note it on the appraisal by showing the date on which he inspected the property, his findings of fair market value and signing the appraisal.

Governmental Review Techniques

Many types of forms, formats, etc. are utilized for the review process. Exhibit A is the United States Postal Service's format used as a guide for their narrative review. Exhibit B lists USPS specifications for the Appraiser. No matter what format, the Reviewer must first understand the reasons for, and the theories of comprehensive appraisal review. With this understanding, he can develop his individual review techniques and procedures for fulfilling his obligations.

Some appraisals can be accepted by the "minimum requirements basis." This is wherein a careful office check of the appraisal is accomplished only. No field review appears warranted to mangement. The most acceptable method is the "comprehensive review". Desk audits, field reviews, Appraiser conferences, all take place to accomplish this most "comprehensive review."

It is believed that it is not the Appraiser's function to disapprove, as such, but more to attempt to secure an approvable and justified valuation within measurable degree of the value probability for the property in question and which solves the intended purpose.

The following are examples of reviews acceptable to the USPS and it is hoped they will lend themselves to the purpose for which they are intended — to educate the professional Reviewer to some other acceptable methods of professional appraisal reviewing.

U.S. POSTAL SERVICE
REVIEWER'S APPRAISAL ANALYSIS
(For use by Staff Appraiser in Reviewing Appraisal Reports)

☐ ACQUISI-TION ☐ LEASING	P/A NO.	TIME ALLOWED	NAME AND ADDRESS OF PROPERTY
☐ TRANSFER ☐ DISPOSAL	CONTRACT DATE	DATE RECEIVED	
☐ OUT-LEASING ☐			

APPRAISER'S NAME AND ADDRESS	NAME AND ADDRESS OF OWNER

TELEPHONE NO.	FINANCE NO.	SUB-LOCATION NO.	TITLE OF PROPERTY

EFFECTIVE REPORT DATE	APPRAISED VALUE (FMV) $	APPROVED VALUE (Adj.) $	LAND VALUE (FMV) $	LEASEHOLD INTEREST $	LAND AREA (Sq. Ft.)
GROSS BLDG. AREA (Sq. Ft.)	CHRONOLOGICAL AGE (Yrs.)	EFFECTIVE AGE (Yrs.)	NEIGHBORHOOD TREND (+, =, −) ☐	FAIR ECONOMIC RENT $	CONTRACT RENT $
OPERATING EXPENSES	CAPITALIZATION RATE (Overall) %	FAIR ECONOMIC TAXES $	APPRAISAL FEE $	PROFESSIONAL DESIGNATIONS	

INSTRUCTIONS

Explain all negative answers on reverse.
Comment fully on inadequacies and recommendations.

E —Excellent - Meets or exceeds specifications.
A —Adequate - Meets minimum needs. Clarifications may be desirable.
I —Inadequate - Does not meet needs. Revision or clarification necessary.

ITEM	E	A	I	ITEM	E/YES	A	I/NO
I. FORM AND PRESENTATION				**MARKET APPROACH** Development of a gross rent multiplier.			
Conformance to USPS Specifications *(Section 2 Appraisal Contract).* Form, sequence and inclusion of significant items.				Contract rent.			
Historical background and acknowledgements.				Fair, economic rent by comparison.			
Area, city and neighborhood data.				Vacancy, collection or credit losses.			
Land and prop. descriptions—conditions and uses.				Fixed, operating and reserve expenses by comparison or historical information *(including administrative expense.)*			
Legal description included. (YES/NO)				Net annual income before recapture.			
Zoning, utilities easements, fair-economic assessed value, tax and insurance costs.				Method of capitalization.			
Certifications, plans, specifications, photos, maps, *(addenda inclusions)* dates and signature.				Capitalization rate - justified.			
II. DELIN. OF ASSIGN-MENT Purposes and function of appraisal.				Value indicated by income approach.			
Highest and best use appropriately analyzed and defined *(as applied to appraised property).*				Leased-fee interest properly analyzed.			
Statement of Limiting conditions.				Leasehold interest properly analyzed.			
III. ANALYSIS, TECHNIQUES AND DATA UTILIZED				Logical relationship to comparables.			
Adequate comparative transactions.				**IV. FAIR RENTAL** Does estimate reflect contemplated lease provisions?			
Individual description showing date and conditions of each comparative transaction.							
Differences adjusted to current market conditions for subject with each comparable.				**V.** Reasonableness of final value conclusion.			
Adjustment chart.				Is the appraisal problem clearly stated? (YES/NO)			
Correlation and logical conclusions.				Is supporting data factual, adequately and appropriately analyzed?			
Comparable location map.				Is supporting data accurate?			
Cost Estimates.				Is conclusion logically related to supporting data and the appraisal problem?			
Depreciation - physical, justified.				Are all essential items included?			
Depreciation - functional, justified.				As a basis for contemplated action?			
Depreciation - economic.				Without further clarification?			
Summation Value.				For fee payment?			
Individual description and analysis showing date and conditions of each comparative transaction.				As evidenced by this report, would you recommend this appraiser for other assignments?			
Differences adjusted to current market conditions for subject with each comparable.				Field Reviewed?			
Value indicated by market approach.				Conference with appraiser?			

REVIEWER'S SIGNATURE	DATE	CONTRACTING OFFICER'S SIGNATURE	DATE

PS Form 7404-F
May 1976   (Continue on reverse)

U.S. POSTAL SERVICE

SPECIFICATIONS FOR THE ANALYTICAL NARRATIVE APPRAISAL REPORT

Contract for Appraisal Report

GENERAL — In the preparation of this report, the Contractor shall follow current professional appraisal practices giving consideration to three approaches to value, namely, the Cost Less Depreciation, Income, and Comparative (or Market) approaches, unless otherwise specified in this contract. Should certain approaches or requirements covered in these specifications not be applicable to the assignment, the contractual obligation can be fulfilled by identifying that approach or requirement together with a brief explanation for its omission (i.e., an appraisal involving land valuation only). Of necessity, supplementary specifications will be furnished requiring additional data in the appraisal of highly specialized properties or under other unusual circumstances. The purpose and function of the appraisal report is to establish the applicable value defined and indicated in Part (V) hereof.

FORMAT — The report shall be bound, in book-fashion, in the left margin, in a durable cover with an identification of the property on the face thereof. The paper used shall be a good grade bond of size 8-½ by 11 inches. All pages shall be numbered consecutively, including all exhibit-, and each important heading shall be shown in the Table of Contents. To provide uniformity for files, the text shall be divided into four parts as outlined below.

PART I — INTRODUCTION

1. TITLE PAGE. This shall include (a) the name and street address of the property, (b) the name of the individual making the report, and (c) the effective date of the appraisal.

2. TABLE OF CONTENTS.

3. LETTER OF TRANSMITTAL.

4. PHOTOGRAPHS. .Pictures shall show at least the front elevation of the major improvements, plus any unusual features. There should also be views of the abutting properties on either side and that property directly opposite. When a large number of buildings are involved, including duplicates, one picture may be used for each type. Views of the best comparables should be included whenever possible. Except for the overall view, photographs may be bound as pages facing the discussion or description which the photographs concern. All graphic material shall include captions.

5. STATEMENT OF LIMITING CONDITIONS AND ASSUMPTIONS.

6. REFERENCES. If preferred, may be shown with applicable approach.

PART II — FACTUAL DATA

7. PURPOSE OF THE APPRAISAL. This shall include the reason for the appraisal, and a definition of all values required, and property rights appraised.

8. LEGAL DESCRIPTION. This description shall be so complete as to properly identify the property appraised. If lengthy, it should be referenced and included in Part IV. If furnished by Postal Service and would require lengthy reproduction, incorporate by reference only.

9. AREA, CITY AND NEIGHBORHOOD DATA. This data (mostly social and economic) should be kept to a minimum and should include only such information as directly affects the appraised property together with the appraiser's conclusions as to significant trends.

10. PROPERTY DATA —

   a. SITE - Describe the soil, topography, mineral deposits, easements, etc. A statement must be made concerning the existence or non-existence of mineral deposits having a commercial value.

   b. IMPROVEMENTS - This description may be by narrative or schedule form and shall include dimensions, cubic and/or square foot measurements, and where appropriate, a statement of the method of measurement used in determining rentable areas such as full floor, multitenancy, etc.

   c. EQUIPMENT - This shall be described by narrative or schedule form and shall include all items of equipment, including a statement of the type and purpose of the equipment and its state of cannibalization. The current physical condition and relative use and obsolescence shall be stated for each item or group appraised, and, whenever applicable, the repair or replacement requirements to bring the property to useable condition.

   Any related personalty or equipment, such as tenant trade fixtures, which are not attached or considered part of the realty, shall be separately inventoried. Where applicable, these detachable or individually owned items shall be separately valued.

   d. HISTORY - State briefly the purpose for which the improvements were designed, dates of original construction and major renovation and/or additions; include, for privately owned property, a five-year record as to each parcel, of all sales and, if possible, offers to buy or sell, and recent lease(s); if no sale in the past five years, include a report of the last sale.

   e. ASSESSED VALUE AND ANNUAL TAX LOAD. Include the current assessment and dollar amount of real estate taxes. If the property is not taxed, the appraiser shall estimate the assessment in case it is placed upon the tax roll, state the rate, and give the dollar amount of the tax estimate.

   f. INSURANCE - Give the estimated rate per thousand and the annual cost of adequate insurance coverage (not necessarily present coverage).

   g. ZONING - Describe the zoning for subject and comparable properties (where Government owned, state what the zoning probably will be under private ownership), and if rezoning is imminent, discuss further under item 11.

PART III — ANALYSES AND CONCLUSIONS

11. ANALYSIS OF HIGHEST AND BEST USE. The report shall state the highest and best use that can be made of the property (land and improvements and where applicable, machinery and equipment) for which there is a current market. Highest and best use is defined as the most profitable likely use, within the realm of reasonable probability, to which a property can be put or adopted, and for which there is a current market.

12. LAND VALUE. The appraiser's opinion of the value of the land shall be supported by confirmed sales of comparable, or nearly comparable lands having like optimum uses. Differences shall be weighed and explained to show how they indicate the value of the land being appraised.

13. VALUE ESTIMATE BY COST APPROACH. This section shall be in the form of computative data, arranged in sequence, beginning with reproduction or replacement cost, and shall state the source (book and page if a national service) of all figures used. The dollar amounts of physical deterioration and functional and economic obsolescence, or the omission of same, shall be explained in narrative form. This procedure may be omitted on improvements, both real and personal, for which only a salvage or scrap value is estimated.

14. VALUE ESTIMATE BY INCOME APPROACH. This shall include adequate factual data to support each figure and factor used and shall be arranged in detailed form to show at least (a) estimated gross economic rent or income; (b) allowance for vacancy and credit losses; (c) an itemized estimate of total expenses including reserves for replacements.

   Capitalization of net income shall be at the rate prevailing for this type of property and location. The capitalization technique, method and rate used shall be explained in narrative form supported by a statement of sources of rates and factors.

15. VALUE ESTIMATE BY COMPARATIVE (MARKET) APPROACH. All comparable sales used shall be confirmed by the buyer, seller, broker, or other person having knowledge of the price, terms and conditions of sale. Each comparable shall be weighed and explained in relation to the subject property to indicate the reasoning behind the appraiser's final value estimate from this approach.

16. INTERPRETATION AND CORRELATION OF ESTIMATES. The appraiser shall interpret the foregoing estimates and shall state his reasons why one or more of the conclusions reached in items (13), (14), and (15) are indicative of the market value of the property.

17. Certification of Appraisal. Part VI - Certification of Appraiser must be executed and included with the completed report indicating the date the appraiser personally inspected the premises, that the owner had been invited to accompany the appraiser on inspection, that the appraiser has no undisclosed interest in the property, etc.

U.S. POSTAL SERVICE
REVIEWER'S APPRAISAL ANALYSIS
(For use by Staff Appraiser in Reviewing Appraisal Reports)

☐ ACQUISI-TION ☐ LEASING	P/A NO.	TIME ALLOWED	NAME AND ADDRESS OF PROPERTY
☐ TRANSFER ☒ DISPOSAL		30 days	
OUT-☐ LEASING ☐	CONTRACT DATE March 30,78	DATE RECEIVED 5/24/78	

| APPRAISER'S NAME AND ADDRESS | NAME AND ADDRESS OF OWNER United States Postal Service |

TELEPHONE NO. 919/443-6028	FINANCE NO.	SUB-LOCATION NO.	TITLE OF PROPERTY Franklin Street Station Old MPO
EFFECTIVE REPORT DATE May 31, 1978	APPRAISED VALUE (FMV) $ 520,000	APPROVED VALUE (Adj.) $	LAND VALUE (FMV) $344,800	LEASEHOLD INTEREST $	LAND AREA (Sq. Ft.) 29,658
GROSS BLDG. AREA (Sq. Ft.) 16860	CHRONOLOGICAL AGE 41 (Yrs.)	EFFECTIVE AGE 40 (Yrs.)	NEIGHBORHOOD TREND (+, =, -) [=]	FAIR ECONOMIC RENT $48,322 net	CONTRACT RENT $ N/A
OPERATING EXPENSES $14,616	CAPITALIZATION RATE (Overall) 11.5 %	FAIR ECONOMIC TAXES $ 10,719	APPRAISAL FEE $ 1800.00	PROFESSIONAL DESIGNATIONS MAI

INSTRUCTIONS

Explain all negative answers on reverse.
Comment fully on inadequacies and recommendations.

E —Excellent - Meets or exceeds specifications.
A —Adequate - Meets minimum needs. Clarifications may be desirable.
I —Inadequate - Does not meet needs. Revision or clarification necessary.

ITEM	E	A	I		ITEM	E	A	I
Conformance to USPS Specifications		X			MARKET APPROACH (YES NO) Development of a gross rent multiplier.			X
Historical background and acknowledgements.		X			Contract rent.			
Area, city and neighborhood data.		X			Fair, economic rent by comparison.			
Land and prop. descriptions—conditions and uses.		X			Vacancy, collection or credit losses.			
Legal description included. (YES NO)			X		Fixed, operating and reserve expenses by comparison or historical information *see comments*			
Zoning, utilities easements, fair-economic assessed value, tax and insurance costs.		X			Net annual income before recapture.			
Certifications, plans, specifications, photos, maps, (addenda inclusions) dates and signature.		X			Method of capitalization.			
					Capitalization rate - justified.			
Purposes and function of appraisal.		X			Value indicated by income approach.			
Highest and best use appropriately analyzed and defined (as applied to appraised property).		X			Leased-fee interest properly analyzed.			
Statement of Limiting conditions.		X			Leasehold interest properly analyzed.			
Adequate comparative transactions.			X		Logical relationship to comparables.			
Individual description showing date and conditions of each comparative transaction.		X			Does estimate reflect contemplated lease provisions? (YES NO)			X
Differences adjusted to current market conditions for subject with each comparable.		X			Reasonableness of final value conclusion.			X
Adjustment chart.			X		Is the appraisal problem clearly stated? (YES NO)	X		
Correlation and logical conclusions.		X			Is supporting data factual, adequately and appropriately analyzed?	X		
Comparable location map.		X			Is supporting data accurate?	X		
Cost Estimates.					Is conclusion logically related to supporting data and the appraisal problem?			X
Depreciation - physical, justified. *see comments*					Are all essential items included?	X		
Depreciation - functional, justified.					As a basis for contemplated action?	X		
Depreciation - economic.					Without further clarification?	X		
Summation Value.					For fee payment?	X		
Individual description and analysis showing date and conditions of each comparative transaction.					As evidenced by this report, would you recommend this appraiser for other assignments?	X		
Differences adjusted to current market conditions for subject with each comparable. *see comments*					Field Reviewed?	X		
Value indicated by market approach.					Conference with appraiser?	X		

| REVIEWER'S SIGNATURE Carol K. Morey | DATE 6/12/78 | CONTRACTING OFFICER'S SIGNATURE James T. Co | DATE 6/27/78 |

PS Form 7404-F
May 1976

(Continue on reverse)

UNITED STATES POSTAL SERVICE
FIELD REAL ESTATE AND BUILDINGS OFFICE
Federal Annex Building, Room 418
Atlanta, GA 30304

OUR REF: 320B:CRM:11   **DATE:** June 21, 1978

SUBJECT: Appraisal Review - Disposal
Old Main Post Office

TO: •

        Memo to/James T. Coe
        Field Supervisor, Real Estate

The subject Disposal Appraisal, by   /MAI, has
been reviewed on-site with numerous review conferences held with
the appraiser. I have personally inspected the subject property
and all sales data on June 7, 8, and 9, 1978. Having previous
projects in the immediate area affords the reviewer with full
insight and knowledge of the market area.

An exhaustible 2 1/2 day search of courthouse records and "Door-
knocking" in subjects' area turned up nothing more than confirmation of the appraiser's data contained in the report. A few
additional sales were found which could be interpreted to read
something less than that indicated by the report. Namely, NCNB
to Belk Services in January, 1978, wherein Belk purchased a 14
story office building, 17 story office building, theatre and
parking deck - containing gross rentable area of 90,000/SF full
occupancy. The complex sold for $4.2 million - without a full
scale appraisal, land value apart from building value is impossible.
It does indicate that out there somewhere, investors do exist that
desire sites as large as the subject. This lends itself to the
possibility the highest and best use is not as stated in the report.

Mr.   has placed an estimated value of $520,000 (land and
improvements) on the subject. Consider this $520,000 + renovating
cost of $112,000 = $632,000 total investment - according to the
appraiser, a NIBR is approximately $48,322 (R) $50,000/year - not
taking into account any further expenses, 100% occupancy, etc; an
investor would only get 7.8% or 8% return. The market indicates
prudent investors demand at least 10% with some indications that
12% return is more applicable to the market. There may be some
non-prudent investors lurking in the shadows ready to invest, but
I firmly feel the likelihood is very, very thin. Therefore, as I
have demonstrated below, the appraiser's estimated value of land
and improvements are felt to be the upper limit and does not
represent present market.

Mr.   has presented a very professional report which is both
adequate and acceptable meeting all United States Postal Service
specifications. This review comments on each section of the report with final review recommendations regarding disposition.

Purpose of the Appraisal

Well presented and acceptable in present form.

Legal Description/Identification of Property

The report doesn't give a legal description but exhibit B is correct as to property dimensions. The remaining portions of this section appear adequate.

Area, City and Neighborhood

All area were adequately described by the appraiser wherein he placed a lot of emphasis on the downtown retail district with little parking along Franklin Street but having an enormous amount of "walk-in" traffic due to the current UNC enrollment of 20,000 students. This dependence upon pedestrian traffic has resulted in very dense land use such as specialty shops, retail stores and offices. There was some indications of vacanys, but very few along Franklin Street between Columbia and Henderson Streets.

The future, as stated by Mr.   , is good along the Franklin Street section of the downtown section due to the student population. The reviewer, being familiar with area, concurs.

Property Data (Site and Improvements)

The description of site and improvements are concise, correct and adequately presented.

It was the opinion of the appraiser that some functional inutility of the building existed; due mainly to large open spaces on 1st floor, high ceiling and general storage in basement.

I concur that subjects' location is excellent. In that no major adverse influence exist is incorrect due to the building being within a Historical District and the facade cannot be altered in any manner. This could lend itself to some possible adverse influence.

History of Property, Tax Data and Zoning

These sections appear to be adequately presented.

Highest and Best Use Estimate

The appraiser states highest and best use, as if vacant, should be divided into two lots and utilized for commercial purposes. The fact that very little parking exist for present business establishments along Franklin Street lends itself to an erroneous impression of the area - I concede that these businesses have little parking, but an analysis of the area reveals parking is provided along Rosemary Street by city and private parking lots. These businesses in fact do not need parking. I agree that the area needs more parking but could be accomplished by decks in lieu of surface parking.

The appraiser, on page 16, calls that portion along Rosemary Street office development but in the evaluation section calls it excess - He also states the building must be substantially renovated. He does not state if this is economical or if the theory of increasing/decreasing demands will support such a theory. The final determination by the appraiser is "if renovated" land and building would have highest and best use for commercial purposes. The reviewer concurs with this final analysis.

Estimates of Value

The Cost Approach indicated a land value of:

    a. 14,406/SF @$7.00/SF (Rosemary frontage) $100,800
    b. 15,252/SF @$16.00/SF (Franklin St. frontage) 244,000

Total Land Value $344,800

The appraiser utilized the theory that land use patterns indicated spliting the total site into two commercial sites. This is highly feasible except for two important facts. (1) A sale in late 1977, NCNB to Belk, wherein a site and improvements extending from Franklin to Rosemary took place. (2) Even though most businesses have no parking of their own, the city has almost 60% to 70% of Rosemary frontage tied up in Municipal parking. This lends itself to the theory that the complete site can be utilized as is.

After much consideration, I feel the following analysis of the appraiser's sales as well as some additional ones reflect a more logical indication of market conditions -

Land Sales Comparisons
Analysis

Subject 29,658/SF total

Sale No.	Date	Price	SF Area	SF Value	Adjusted SF Value	Percentage Adjustment
1	7/9/76	$60,000	7800	$7.69	$7.46	-3%
2	3/22/78	40,000	7000	5.71	6.91	+21%

Appraisers Indication <u>Rosemary Frontage</u>

14,404/SF @$7.00 = $100,800 (R)

The appraiser utilized only two sales half the size of this portion of subject. No size, location, motivation etc adjustments made. Also no consideration of sales along Columbia Street at $3.88/SF and 137E Rosemary, 38,948 @$3.85/SF. If all adjustments were properly made I feel appraisers $7.00/SF value should be reduced by 20%.

This $7.00 x .80 = $5.60/SF x 14406 = $80,674
Rounded $80,700

Sale No.	Date	Price	SF Area	SF Value	Adjusted SF Value	Percentage Adjustment
3	9/8/72	$155,000	25,760	$10.11	$14.15	+40%
4	1/15/75	59,000	3,655	22.43	16.82	-25%

Appraisers Indication Franklin Street Frontage

15,252/SF @ $16.00 = 244,000 (R)

The appraiser again utilized only two sales with no size, motivation nor locational adjustments made for these sales. The sales, located well do not represent any real market indications. Sales as indicated above plus others on W. Franklin at $5.90/SF; Stroff building on Franklin Street at $5.37/SF etc as well as sale No. 4 above was found to have sold for $45,000 in lieu of $59,000 lends itself to a more logical SF value in the range of $9 to $10/SF.

Considering the above, I feel a reduction of 40% of the appraisers
SF value reflects more of a market in subject's area. Thus:

$16 x 60% = $9.60/SF x 15,252 = $146,419
Rounded $146,500

Reviewer Comments:

In previous area projects, as well as recent market analysis afforded
this reviewer opportunities to study the market regarding land values.
Mr.   's land sales were thin but did give some indications of upper
limit values. If properly adjusted plus utilization of additional
sales, it is believed that land values would be substantially lower.
It is just not enough firm data to justify Mr.   's high land value.
Therefore, from a prudent investor's standpoint, a site 15,000/SF
would be fine if he had little to renovate. But as the highest and
best use indicated, the building is here to stay and the land should
be valued accordingly.

Therefore, I believe the following appropriate:

Appraisers analysis Site No. 1 15,252 @$16.00/SF = $244,000
                     Site No. 2 14,406 @$ 7.00/SF = 100,800

                     Total Land Value $344,800 (R)

Reviewers analysis   Site No. 1 15,252 @$9.60/SF = $146,500
                     Site No. 2 14,406 @$5.60/SF =   80,700

                     Total Land Value $227,200 (R)

Estimated Value of entire subject land $227,200

Cost Approach to Value of Improvements

The appraiser has well documented the RCN with the estimated depreciation
justified only by the age life method. Depreciation estimated by the age
life method indicated 67% of RCN. Considering previous PO sales, depreciation of 2.5% a year has been accepted as reasonable and logical. Effective age of 40 years indicates 100% depreciated improvement. However,
the appraiser states alternate usage, condition, etc. gives the building
20 years more life. I consider the building is actually 41 years and a
total life expectancy is 50 years in lieu of 60 years. Thus we have
a REL of only 10 years.

Considering age life - $\frac{40}{50}$ = 80% depreciation. Therefore, an effective
age of 40 years appears to be reasonable. Considering the condition,
etc.,depreciation at a rate of 2% a year equates to 80% depreciation.

Cost Approach (as applied)

Reproduction Cost New	$529,498
Estimated 80% Depreciation	423,598

	$105,900
Est. Depreciation Value Imp.	$105,900
Est. Total LV	227,200

Total Est. Value by Cost Approach $333,100

As further analysis:	Appraiser	Reviewer
Total Property Value	$519,500	$333,100
Less LV	344,800	227,200
Residual to Improvements	$174,700	$105,900

$$\frac{\$174,700}{8290/SF} = \$21.07/SF \qquad \frac{\$105,900}{8290/SF} = \$12.77/SF$$

The appraisers' estimate of depreciation cost is
$21.07

When related to RCN we have thus:

Appraiser $\dfrac{\$174,700}{529,498} = 32.9\%$

Complement 1.00 - .32.9 = 67% depreciation

Reviewer $\dfrac{\$105,900}{529,498} = 20\%$

Complement 1.00 - .20 = 80% depreciation

The total analysis reveals a depreciation range from 67% to 80%. In that this approach is highly subjective and the land value appears to be a big factor, I tend to lean towards my analysis as more reflective of the market. Therefore, I recommend the appraiser's cost approach be adjusted to read:

Land	$227,200
Improvements	105,900

Est. Total PV
by Cost Approach $333,100

Market Data Approach to Value
The appraiser's analysis indicates thus:

Date	Sale#	SP	Site SizeSF	Bldg SizeSF	Unit of Comparison	% Adj.	Adjusted SF LV-OA	Land/ Bldg Ratio
1976	5	$ 72,000	3120	3072	$23.08/SF	÷33%	$30.70	98%
1975	6	73,000	2745	4070	26.59/SF	+19%	31.64	74%
1978	7	75,000	3838	3575	19.54/SF	+30%	25.40	93%
1978	8	500,000	8749	11291	57.15/SF	-43%	32.57	78%

Those sales utilized by the appraiser are very thin in nature and one must stretch his imagination to think the above sales are anywhere comparable to the subject. Also the appraiser states there is 14,406/SF of "excess land". Other than the previous mentioned "Belk Sale", very few, if any, sales have occurred placing the burden on the above sales data.

Sales #5 and 7 are not comparable and deleted. Sale #6, located very close to subject has only 4070/SF of building area and 2747/SF of land. It was adjusted +19% yielding $31.64/SFLA. Only time, location, ratio of land to building and OA utility was adjusted. No size nor condition of building, etc, adjustments were made. Sale #8, after talking to Goforth Properties about the sale (the real owners) I found this sale to have some factors regarding its inception that lends itself to questionable indications of value.

Based on the above comments, the results of my own market analysis, I can only relate this approach to previous old post office sales to give some indication of value. Sale of old Ahoskie, North Carolina Post Office; Sale of the old Wallace, North Carolina Post Office indicated SF value of $10/SF. I realize these sales are a far cry from being comparable but I feel do give some market indications. Adjusting location, size, etc., I feel an adjusted SF value of $10 to $12/SF is more representative of the subject. Thus:

          Subject 29,658 (total land area) x $11/SF = $326,238
          Rounded $326,300

          Total Indicated Estimated Value by the
          Market Data Approach $326,300

Income Approach to Value

In my conversations with the appraiser, he stated the Income Approach was given least consideration due to renovation cost, substantial amount of risk to convert, etc. I tend to agree with his theory. Further down-grading of this approach lends itself to the rentals which are poor, the development of the OAR by the Mortgage Equity Method. In my market study, I found a typical holding period to be 20 years and loans were 75% to 80% with rates from 9%, also EDR started at 15%. The fact that the interest rates are current at 10% then adding recapture would give you a much higher rate than 11.5% as indicated by the report. My analysis developed 13.7% OAR indicating:

          NIBR $48,322 $\div$ .137 = $352,715

          Considering the renovation cost of $112,000
          plusing the "Excess land (reviews)   80,700

          Total Estimated Value of Subject
          by the Income Approach $321,400 (R)

          As further analysis:

          NIBR $ 48,322
          Less 10% land
          a. 344,800   -34,480

          Value "as is" $ 13,842

          Cap Shell   13,842

                            13.7% $101,037
          Less Conv. Cost   112,000
          Plus Land (total)   344,800

          Estimated Value $333,837

          SAY $333,900 (R)

The income approach yields a range of $321,400 to $333,900. From an investor standpoint, it is difficult to see how paying the appraiser's estimate of value can be justified.

Reconciliation and Final Estimate of Value	Appraiser	Reviewer
Indicated Value by Cost Approach	$519,500	$333,100
Indicated Value by Market Approach	$558,300	$326,300
Indicated Value by Income Approach	$409,000	$333,900

The cost approach, due to age of the building, is difficult to rely upon because of subjective nature of opinion of depreciation. However, due to land sales presented and their adjustments through review, a reasonable land value was estimated. Also, the depreciation was fairly well documented and it is felt it is reasonable.

Due to the fact that many other buildings in the immediate area are renovated older buildings adopted to some use, I feel this approach is felt to be reasonable in nature. The income approach is weak and due to difference in opinion of the OAR, little evidence is given this approach. The market data approach is based on sales in the area of what the reviewer felt to be non-comparable buildings due to size, condition, etc. Sales of old post office's in North Carolina were used as comparisons.

As stated in the opening paragraphs of this review a return of 7 to 8% was unreasonable, based on my review, we have a possible return of 11% to 12% ($333,000 + $112,000 ÷ $50,000) which I feel best represents the prudent investor in the area.

Therefore, giving credence to Mr.   's opinions of mini-mall usage, large amount of walk-in traffic, dense land use patterns, etc., reviewing the report and researching the market, it is my judgement that an Indicated Market Value range of $325,000 to $350,000 should be approved for disposition.

Claude R. Moore, Jr., MAI, CRA, ASA
Realty Management and Acquisition Specialist   Date: 6/23/78

Recommended for Approval by:

James T. Coe
Field Supervisor, Real Estate   Date: 6/27/78

U.S. POSTAL SERVICE
REVIEWER'S APPRAISAL ANALYSIS
(For use by Staff Appraiser in Reviewing Appraisal Reports)

| ☐ ACQUISI-TION ☐ LEASING | P/A NO. | TIME ALLOWED 30 days | NAME AND ADDRESS OF PROPERTY |
| ☐ TRANSFER ☒ DISPOSAL ☐ OUT-LEASING ☐ | CONTRACT DATE | DATE RECEIVED 4/3/78 | |

| APPRAISER'S NAME AND ADDRESS MAI | NAME AND ADDRESS OF OWNER U.S. Postal Service |

| TELEPHONE NO. 919/779-2190 | FINANCE NO. | SUB-LOCATION NO. | TITLE OF PROPERTY U.S. Postal Serv. Facility - Comm. |

EFFECTIVE REPORT DATE 3/10/78	APPRAISED VALUE (FMV) $40,000	APPROVED VALUE (Adj.) $	LAND VALUE (FMV) $28,350	LEASEHOLD INTEREST $	LAND AREA (Sq. Ft.) 10,500
GROSS BLDG. AREA (Sq.Ft.) 5164	CHRONOLOGICAL AGE 43 (Yrs.)	EFFECTIVE AGE (Yrs.)	NEIGHBORHOOD TREND (+, =, -) ±	FAIR ECONOMIC RENT $	CONTRACT RENT $
OPERATING EXPENSES 1791	CAPITALIZATION RATE (Overall) 12 %	FAIR ECONOMIC TAXES $720	APPRAISAL FEE $1100	PROFESSIONAL DESIGNATIONS MAI	

INSTRUCTIONS

Explain all negative answers on reverse.
Comment fully on inadequacies and recommendations.

E –Excellent - Meets or exceeds specifications.
A –Adequate - Meets minimum needs. Clarifications may be desirable.
I –Inadequate - Does not meet needs. Revision or clarification necessary.

ITEM	E	A	I		ITEM	E	A	I
Conformance to USPS Specifications *(Section 2 Appraisal Contract)*. Form, sequence and inclusion of significant items.		X			MARKET APPROACH Development of a gross rent multiplier. N/A	YES	NO	
Historical background and acknowledgements.		X			Contract rent.		X	
Area, city and neighborhood data.		X			Fair, economic rent by comparison.		X	
Land and prop. descriptions—conditions and uses.		X			Vacancy, collection or credit losses.		X	
Legal description included.	YES X	NO			Fixed, operating and reserve expenses by comparison or historical information *(including administrative expense.)*		X	
Zoning, utilities easements, fair-economic assessed value, tax and insurance costs.		X			Net annual income before recapture.		X	
					Method of capitalization.		X	
Certifications, plans, specifications, photos, maps, *(addenda inclusions)* dates and signature.		X			Capitalization rate - justified. see comments			
Purposes and function of appraisal.		X			Value indicated by income approach.			
Highest and best use appropriately analyzed and defined *(as applied to appraised property)*.		X			Leased-fee interest properly analyzed. N/A			
					Leasehold interest properly analyzed. N/A			
Statement of Limiting conditions.		X			Logical relationship to comparables.		X	
Adequate comparative transactions.		X				YES	NO	
Individual description showing date and conditions of each comparative transaction.		X			Does estimate reflect contemplated lease provisions? N/A			
Differences adjusted to current market conditions for subject with each comparable.		X			Reasonableness of final value conclusion.			
Adjustment chart.			X		Is the appraisal problem clearly stated?	YES X	NO	
Correlation and logical conclusions.		X			Is supporting data factual, adequately and appropriately analyzed.	X		
Comparable location map.		X			Is supporting data accurate?	X		
Cost Estimates.		X			Is conclusion logically related to supporting data and the appraisal problem?	X		
Depreciation - physical, justified.					Are all essential items included?		X	X
Depreciation - functional, justified. see comments					As a basis for contemplated action?		X	
Depreciation - economic.					Without further clarification?			X
Summation Value.					For fee payment?		X	
Individual description and analysis showing date and conditions of each comparative transaction.					As evidenced by this report, would you recommend this appraiser for other assignments?		X	
Differences adjusted to current market conditions for subject with each comparable. see comments					Field Reviewed?		X	
Value indicated by market approach.					Conference with appraiser?		X	

| REVIEWER'S SIGNATURE Claude R. Moore Jr. | DATE 5/15/78 | CONTRACTING OFFICER'S SIGNATURE J. T. Coc FS, R. | DATE 5/24/78 |

PS Form 9404-F
May 1976

(Continue on reverse)

320B:CRM:ll   May 26, 1978

Appraisal Review - Disposal
Main Post Office

        Memo to File: James T. Coe
                        Field Supervisor, Real Estate

The subject appraisal has been reviewed on site with review
conferences held with the appraiser for clarification of
various items. The appraiser resubmitted report corrections
on certain errors. Previous assignments in Graham area
affords the reviewer full insight and knowledge of area
market activities.

Mr.   , MAI, has presented a fairly professional
report which does meet minimum U.S. Postal Service specifications. Brief comments on each section of the report as
well as the final value conclusions of $40,000 follows:

        Purpose of the Appraisal

        The appraiser adequately delineated the purpose
        of the report.

        Analysis Techniques and Data Utilized

        A. Factual Data considered: The appraiser
            appears to have presented and considered
            the economics, general area, trends and
            environmental influences of the area and
            neighborhood.

                    , North Carolina, county seat of
                    County has a population of 9,500
            with the county population of 110,000.
            .   , North Carolina abutting to the
            northwest is the countys largest city.
            Mostly textile production preveals in
            Graham with land-use patterns primarily
            commercial activities.

            I agree with the appraisers judgement that
            the area neighborhood possesses qualities
            and requirements for continued growth and
            development.

            With the economic picture looking good,
            it can only be concluded that conversion
            and private usage of subject is highly
            probable at this time.

B. Factual Errors/Omissions: Several computa-
    tional and other errors were noted in the
    first report. On page 7, no mention of
    effective age of building; page 5 stated
    275/SF of loading dock but on page 13, cost
    approach, it was deleted in RCN. Also on
    page 7 paved parking was stated to be 2400/SF
    and in cost approach it listed it as 3300/SF.
    Various other math errors were noted but had
    no detrimental effect on reports value - the
    above errors were corrected in the resubmitted
    report.

C. Reasoning and Logic of Appraisal Process
    Utilized: The appraiser has utilized only
    the cost and income approaches which indi-
    cates:

Cost approach		$45,700
Income approach		
	M/E	37,300
	BRT	34,850

The cost approach is questionable due to
excessive and non-justified RCN as well as
depreciation. The income approach looses
credence due to thin rentals. No market data
approach was utilized in the report.

It is my considered opinion that the appraiser
rest upon "Thin Ice" as to his final determination of value even though it appears to be
within a logical "Market Value Range".

Reviewers Analysis:

Land Value - MDA: A large number of land
sales were utilized but only 5 reported.
A range of $2.36/SF to $2.78/SF was established. After careful consideration of
the subjects location, etc. $2.70/SF is
reasonable.

Cost Approach to Value: The building is
in rather good condition considering its
actual age of 43 years. No effective age
was given; however, my personal inspection
afforded the opinion that 38 years would
be a reasonable effective age due to previous maintenance. The appraisers depreciation equates to 1.9% per year with a
total of 83% listed for depreciation.
Because of opinion differences in RCN,
depreciation methods, etc., I offer the
following pro-forma cost approach:

COST APPROACH

RCN

Main Floor	3276	@$40.00	$131,040
Basement	1338	@ 22.00	29,436
Swing Area	550	@ 18.00	9,900
Loading Dock	275	@ 15.00	4,125
Paved Parking	3300	@ 1.00	3,300
Landscaping			1,000

Estimated Cost New $178,801

Depreciation from all causes
250% depreciation 1 year per attached sales
Effective age 38
Actual age 43
35 x 2.50 = 87.5% $156,451
Estimated Depreciation Value   22,350
Add: Est. Value of Land   28,350
Indicated Value - Cost approach

$ 50,700

Reviewer: Residual to Improvement $\frac{\$ 22,350}{\$178,801} = 12.5$

Complement 1.00 - 12.5 = 87.5%

Appraiser: Residual to Improvement $\frac{\$ 17,368}{\$184,300} = .094$

Complement 1.00 - .094 = 90.6%

The revised cost approach equates to 87.5%
depreciation was compared to 90.6% of the
appraiser. Appraisal conferences revealed a
certain level of agreement between appraiser
and reviewer in that due to his errors in the
first report in cost approach, he stated a
range of $50,000 to $54,000 was definitely
possible. Based on the above, I feel the cost
approach should be adjusted to $50,700, which
I feel is more indicative of value to any potential user.

Market Data Approach: The appraiser did not
utilize the MDA to value due to his opinion
of "lack of sufficiently comparable data".
He did state his familiazation with certain
U.S. Postal Service sales in North Carolina,
but said they loose credibility when he attempted to relate sales of special purpose
properties located in highly different economic areas. I disagree with the appraiser
for the following reasons: the MDA involves
a comparison of recent, comparable sales with
the subject. Two sales of comparable Post
Office buildings in Ahoshie and Wallace, NC,
on a price per gross/SF basis, equate directly with the subject property - adequate adjustments for dissimilarities project a gross
SF unit of comparison of $9/SF. Subject area
5164/SF x $9/SF = $46,476 SAY $46,500. There-
fore, the MDA should be placed in the final
reconciliation and value conclusion section.

Income Approach to Value: The greatest
weight was given (by the appraiser) to
this approach to value. The M/E technique
was utilized which I feel is not proper
(or way out in this case) because the required renovation cost to bring the building
to market standards would not equate to a
good investment. Therefore, 75% mortgage,
equity position, holding periods, etc just
are not applicable to this appraisal. Also,
the appraiser in the first report, failed
to deduct $21,350 for renovation from pro-
jected value of $56,200 equaling $34,850-
land value = $6,500. The "Shell" value as
listed below, indicates and affirms the
above judgement.

INCOME APPROACH TO VALUE

The income approach developed $34,850 by
BRT and $37,300 by M/E method - the rental
appears to reflect the market adequately.

The "Shell Value" of the building was
$27,858 accepting NIBR, the BRT indicates
shell thus:

NIBR	$ 6,178
Less increase to land	-2,835
Residual to Building	$ 3,343
$3,343	
12	$27,858
Less Remodeling to shell	-21,350
	$ 5,993
SAY	$ 6,000

Based on remodeling cost, the above affirms
the shell value does not bear any reasonable
relationship to remodeling cost due to necessary renovations.

Therefore, I feel the income approach
should be given the least amount of
consideration in this appraisal.

D. Reconciliation and Final Value Conclusions:
The appraiser was contacted as to errors and
omissions of which were answered/corrected by
attached letter. From the review and analysis,
the following values were reported:

	Appraiser	Reviewer
Cost Approach	$45,700	$50,700
Income "		
M/E	$37,300	not applicable
BRT	$34,850	$ 6,000
Market Data		
Approach	omitted	$46,500

The reviewer has given consideration to field appraisal review and analysis as well as data reported by the appraiser. From the appraisal as well as my analysis, I have considerable doubt in my mind as to the reliable indication of the income approach. The OAR is thin and without justification. The cost approach, in a building of this age, is highly subjective. The market approach as developed by the reviewer appears to strengthen the cost approach indications. The appraiser reported 90.6% depreciation wherein the reviewer reported 87.5%. Final values were within a reasonable range.

Analysis reveals a range of $46,500 to $59,300 as probable market value. It is my judgement, after a complete review that a range of $46,500 to $50,000 should be approved for disposition purposes.

Submitted by:

Claude R. Moore, Jr., MAI, CRA, ASA
Realty Management and Acquisition Analyst   Date: 5/18/78

Recommended for Approval by:

James T. Coe
Field Supervisor, Real Estate   Date: 5/28/78

UNITED STATES POSTAL SERVICE

FIELD REAL ESTATE AND BUILDINGS OFFICE
Federal Annex Building, Room 418
Atlanta, GA 30304

DATE: October 20, 1977

OUR REF: 320B:JTC:sr

SUBJECT: ACQUISITION - USPO -
Appraisal REVIEW

TO:
Memo to Record

Approval of the appraisal dated September 29, 1977, by
MAI, et al, in the amount of $230,000 is with the following comments:

1. In his cost approach, unit cost (RCN) of $13.00 per
   gross square foot is unacceptable. Appraiser should
   have used reproduction cost then cited functional
   obsolescence for any considered over-improvement.

2. The theory of appreciation of reversion is plausible,
   but unsupported. I could question the appraiser as to
   use of any figure other than present land value. (Reference
   Page 450, The Appraisal of Real Estate, 7th Edition AIREA).

3. Despite analysis of several improved sales, extraction was
   not used to develop an overall capitalization rate.

None of these comments prejudice the final value indication. This
appraisal is a good report, and above the average received.

James T. Coe
James T. Coe
Field Supervisor, Real Estate

(For use by Staff Appraiser in Reviewing Appraisal Reports)

ACQUISI-TION ☐ LEASING	P/A NO.	TIME ALLOWED	NAME AND ADDRESS OF PROPERTY
☐ TRANSFER ☐ DISPOSAL	CONTRACT DATE	DATE RECEIVED	U.S. Post Office
OUT-LEASING ☐			

APPRAISER'S NAME AND ADDRESS		NAME AND ADDRESS OF OWNER
		Leased

TELEPHONE NO.	FINANCE NO.	SUB-LOCATION NO.	TITLE OF PROPERTY
659-0099		Leased Fee	Commercial/Light Industrial/Special

EFFECTIVE REPORT DATE	APPRAISED VALUE (FMV)	APPROVED VALUE (Adj.)	LAND VALUE (FMV)	LEASEHOLD INTEREST	LAND AREA (Sq. Ft.)
Sept. 9, 1977	$ 279,000	$ 230,000	$ 71,400	$ 49,000	88,862.4

GROSS BLDG. AREA (Sq. Ft.)	CHRONOLOGICAL AGE	EFFECTIVE AGE	NEIGHBORHOOD TREND	FAIR ECONOMIC RENT	CONTRACT RENT
19,382	12 (Yrs.)	10 (Yrs.)	(+, =, -) =	$ 3,545.33/mo	$ 2,113.30 mo

OPERATING EXPENSES	CAPITALIZATION RATE	FAIR ECONOMIC TAXES	APPRAISAL FEE	PROFESSIONAL DESIGNATIONS
$11,730	(Overall) 9 3/4 %	$ 5,851.00	$ 1350	MAI

INSTRUCTIONS

Explain all negative answers on reverse.
Comment fully on inadequacies and recommendations.

E—Excellent - Meets or exceeds specifications.
A—Adequate - Meets minimum needs. Clarifications may be desirable.
I—Inadequate - Does not meet needs. Revision or clarification necessary.

ITEM	E	A	I
I. FORM AND PRESENTATION			
Conformance to USPS Specifications *(Section 2 Appraisal Contract)*. Form, sequence and inclusion of significant items.		X	
Historical background and acknowledgements.		X	
Area, city and neighborhood data.		X	
Land and prop. descriptions—conditions and uses.		X	
Legal description included.	YES: X / NO		
Zoning, utilities easements, fair-economic assessed value, tax and insurance costs.		X	
Certifications, plans, specifications, photos, maps, *(addenda inclusions)* dates and signature.		X	
II. DEFN. OF ASSIGNMENT			
Purposes and function of appraisal.		X	
Highest and best use appropriately analyzed and defined *(as applied to appraised property)*.		X	
Statement of Limiting conditions.		X	
III. ANALYSIS, TECHNIQUES AND DATA UTILIZED — Land Value By Comparison			
Adequate comparative transactions.		X	
Individual description showing date and conditions of each comparative transaction.		X	
Differences adjusted to current market conditions for subject with each comparable. See Comments			
Adjustment chart.			X
Correlation and logic. conclusion See Comments			
Cost Approach			
Comparable location map.		X	
Cost Estimates.		X	
Depreciation - physical, justified.			
Depreciation - functional, justified.			
Depreciation - economic. ⎫ See Comments			
Summation Value. ⎭			
Market Approach			
Individual description and analysis showing date and conditions of each comparative transaction.		X	
Differences adjusted to current market conditions for subject with each comparable.		X	
Value indicated by market approach.			X

ITEM	E	A	I
III. ANALYSIS, TECHNIQUES AND DATA UTILIZED (Continued) — Income Approach			
MARKET APPROACH	YES	NO	
Development of a gross rent multiplier.		X	
Contract rent.	X		
Fair, economic rent by comparison.	X		
Vacancy, collection or credit losses.	X		
Fixed, operating and reserve expenses by comparison or historical information *(including administrative expense.)*	X		
Net annual income before recapture.	X		
Method of capitalization.			
Capitalization rate - justified. See Comments			
Value Indicated by income approach.			
Leased-fee interest properly analyzed.	X		
Leasehold interest properly analyzed.	X		
Logical relationship to comparables.	X		
IV. FAIR RENTAL	YES	NO	
Does estimate reflect contemplated lease provisions?	X		
V. Reasonableness of final value conclusion.	X		
VI. OVERALL EFFECTIVENESS — Reviewer's Conclusion	YES	NO	
Is the appraisal problem clearly stated?	X		
Is supporting data factual, adequately and appropriately analyzed?	X		
Is supporting data accurate? See Comments			
Is conclusion logically related to supporting data and the appraisal problem?	X		
Are all essential items included? See Comments			
Is The Report Recommended?			
As a basis for contemplated action?	X		
Without further clarification?	X		
For fee payment?	X		
As evidenced by this report, would you recommend this appraiser for other assignments?	X		
Field Reviewed?	X		
Conference with appraiser?			

REVIEWER'S SIGNATURE	DATE	CONTRACTING OFFICER'S SIGNATURE	DATE
C. R. Moore, Jr., RMAAA	10/5/77	J. T. Coe, ES, PE	10/19/77

PS Form 7404-F
May 1976

(Continue on reverse)

APPRAISAL REVIEW
U.S. POST OFFICE BUILDING

BY

General Comments.

This review is based on my personal inspection of the subject property on
9/29/77 and 9/30/77, and knowledge of
real estate market by virtue of other Postal Service projects in the area.
Specific comments follow based on the format of the report which closely
relates to the Postal Service contract specifications.

Identification of Property.

This section of the appraisal report appears to be very adequate.

Purpose and Date of Appraisal.

Purpose is well stated in report and this section is adequate.

Area and Site Data.

The appraiser goes into an excellent description of area and adequately
states site data.

Description of Improvements.

The appraiser adequately describes all improvements.

Highest and Best Use.

The highest and best use as stated by the appraiser is reasonably probably
and physically possible and appropriately supported by my own market analysis.
The highest and best use of light industry is well supported and accepted by
the reviewer.

Valuation - Free and Clear Basis.

The appraiser utilized all three approaches to value. All appear to be well
organized and appropriately applied except as noted below.

Cost Approach.

Land Valuation. The appraiser utilized seven applicable sales which
established a per acre value of $35,000. The sales utilized were far
removed from the subjects area but trends and forces appear to be fairly
applicable. However, my market analysis revealed sales offerings from
$35,000 to $40,000/acre. The appraiser indicated these offerings were
considered but felt they set the upper limit to value. The appraiser
relied on Sales 3, 4 and 5, all three of which give a mean of $38,600 (R).
Consideration is given to location, size, etc. and it is felt the per acre
value should fall slightly above the value stated by the appraiser. Therefore, based on additional sales plus the appraiser's own evaluation, I feel
the per acre value should be $38,000 x 2.04 = $77,500 (R).

Improvement - RCN - Depreciation. The RCN is well documented and
justified. The appraiser used the age/life concept for lump sum depreciation. The cost to remodel is questionable but reasonable with market
findings. I agree with the valuation of the improvement by the cost
approach.

RCN	$294,770
Less Depreciation, 25%, all causes	73,693
Estimated Dep. Value	$221,077
Add Land (above)	77,500
	$298,577
Less Cost to Remodel	15,000
Value Indication by Cost Approach	$283,577
	$283,500 (R)

Income Approach.

Economic rent is well established and reasonable. The appraiser uses firm
market indications as well as good judgment in developing operating expense
and reserves. The projected NIBR is reasonable. An overall rate of 9 3/4%
was utilized. In my analysis of the market, I found no evidence that would
contradict any of the Income Approach Cash Flow Analysis nor its application.
Therefore, I accept the estimated value by the income approach of $279,000 as
reasonable and justified.

Market Approach.

The appraiser utilized three market sales to develop a per SF value of $14.
As a check and balance, I developed a GRM of 7 from my market data and also
utilizing the appraiser's three sales I developed an indicated value of
$297,500 as compared to the $283,000 as developed by the appraiser. It is
my judgment the appraiser's estimated value more readily reflects the market
trends and forces applicable to the subject property.

Reconciliation.

The indicated values from the three approaches utilized are as follow:

Cost Approach	$283,500 (Adjusted)
Income Approach	$279,000
Market Approach	$283,000
GRM	$297,500

The appraiser gave the greatest amount of emphasis on the income approach.
I would agree with this philosophy, if not for the close development of
estimates in the other two approaches to value. I realize in the cost
approach the difficulty of estimating replacement cost and depreciation.
However, the market approach, which includes the GRM develops a somewhat
higher value and these values are well supported in the market. Therefore,
I feel the market can support a somewhat higher market value and I recommend
the value on a free and clear basis be adjusted upward to $285,000.

Leased Fee Interest.

The appraiser developed leased fee interest on one premise only, that being
based on the reversion at the end of the final renewal term. If only the
basic term is utilized we have thus:

Present Worth of Income Stream	$ 98,759
Reversion $285,000 x .55832	159,121
Indicated Value - Leased Fee Interest	$257,880
	$258,000 (R)

In each case, the appraiser assumed reversion at a predetermined purchase price, but is well established by the contract. It is felt the leased fee analysis reveals certain influences inherent in the property and must be given credence in final judgment. With the improvements decreasing in REL, it is felt the prudent investor will not pay more than the estimated value leased fee in either case. Therefore, it is my judgment the leased fee estate in this property is valued between $230,000 to $250,000.

It is recommended this range be utilized in negotiations in the purchasing of this property.

Reviewed by:

Claude R. Moore, Jr. (Date)
Realty Management and
Acquisition Analyst

Approved by:

James T. Coe (Date) 10/19/77
Field Supervisor, Real Estate
(See Comments
dated 10/19/77)

U.S. POSTAL SERVICE
REVIEWER'S APPRAISAL ANALYSIS
(For use by Staff Appraiser in Reviewing Appraisal Reports)

☒ ACQUISI-TION ☐ LEASING	P/A NO.	TIME ALLOWED	NAME AND ADDRESS OF PROPERTY
☐ TRANSFER ☐ DISPOSAL	CONTRACT DATE	DATE RECEIVED	U.S. Post Office
OUT-LEASING ☐			
APPRAISER'S NAME AND ADDRESS			NAME AND ADDRESS OF OWNER
			Leased

TELEPHONE NO. 404/522-4264	FINANCE NO.	SUB-LOCATION NO.	TITLE OF PROPERTY Commercial/Special Purpose

EFFECTIVE REPORT DATE August 29, 1977	APPRAISED VALUE (FMV) $ 650,000	APPROVED VALUE (Adj.) $ 290,000	LAND VALUE (FMV) $ 100,000	LEASEHOLD INTEREST $ 350,000	LAND AREA (Sq. Ft.) 109,160
GROSS BLDG. AREA (Sq. Ft.) 24,833	CHRONOLOGICAL AGE 14 (Yrs.)	EFFECTIVE AGE 14 (Yrs.)	NEIGHBORHOOD TREND (+, -, =) ▣	FAIR ECONOMIC RENT $ 72,411	CONTRACT RENT $ 37,539
OPERATING EXPENSES 8,558.00	CAPITALIZATION RATE (Overall) 9.64 %	FAIR ECONOMIC TAXES $	APPRAISAL FEE $1200	PROFESSIONAL DESIGNATIONS MAI, SRPA	

INSTRUCTIONS

Explain all negative answers on reverse.
Comment fully on inadequacies and recommendations.

E –Excellent - Meets or exceeds specifications.
A –Adequate - Meets minimum needs. Clarifications may be desirable.
I –Inadequate - Does not meet needs. Revision or clarification necessary.

ITEM	E	A	I		ITEM	E	A	I
I. FORM AND PRESENTATION								
Conformance to USPS Specifications *(Section 2 Appraisal Contract).* Form, sequence and inclusion of significant items.		X			**MARKET APPROACH** Development of a gross rent multiplier.	YES	NO	
						X		
Historical background and acknowledgements.		X			Contract rent.			X
Area, city and neighborhood data.		X			Fair, economic rent by comparison.			X
Land and prop. descriptions—conditions and uses.		X			Vacancy, collection or credit losses. *See Comments*			
Legal description included.	YES X	NO			Fixed, operating and reserve expenses by comparison or historical information *(including administrative expense.)*			X
Zoning, utilities easements, fair-economic assessed value, tax and insurance costs.		X			Net annual income before recapture.			X
Certifications, plans, specifications, photos, maps, *(addenda inclusions)* dates and signature.		X			Method of capitalization.			
Purposes and function of appraisal.		X			Capitalization rate - justified.			
II. DELIN. OF ASSIGNMENT					Value indicated by income approach. *See Comments*			
Highest and best use appropriately analyzed and defined *(as applied to appraised property).* *See Comments*					Leased-fee interest properly analyzed.			
Statement of Limiting conditions.		X			Leasehold interest properly analyzed.			
					Logical relationship to comparables.			
III. ANALYSIS, TECHNIQUES AND DATA UTILIZED — Land Value By Comparison					**IV. FAIR RENTAL**	YES	NO	
Adequate comparative transactions.					Does estimate reflect contemplated lease provisions?	X		
Individual description showing date and conditions of each comparative transaction.								
Differences adjusted to current market conditions for subject with each comparable.					V. Reasonableness of final value conclusion.		X	
Adjustment chart. *Omitted*					**VI. OVERALL EFFECTIVENESS**	YES	NO	
Correlation and logical conclusions. *See Comments*					Is the appraisal problem clearly stated?	X		
Comparable location map.	X				Is supporting data factual, adequately and appropriately analyzed? *See Comments*			
Cost Approach Cost Estimates.					Is supporting data accurate? *See Comments*			
Depreciation - physical, justified.					Is conclusion logically related to supporting data and the appraisal problem? *See Comments*			
Depreciation - functional, justified. *See Comments*					Are all essential items included?			X
Depreciation - economic.					**Is The Report Recommended?** As a basis for contemplated action?	X		
Summation Value.					Without further clarification?	X		
Market Approach Individual description and analysis showing date and conditions of each comparative transaction.		X			For fee payment?	X		
Differences adjusted to current market conditions for subject with each comparable. *See Comments*					**Reviewer's Action** As evidenced by this report, would you recommend this appraiser for other assignments?	X		
					Field Reviewed?	X		
Value indicated by market approach.					Conference with appraiser?	X		

REVIEWER'S SIGNATURE C. R. Moore, JR., RMAAA	DATE 9/30/77	CONTRACTING OFFICER'S SIGNATURE J. T. COE, ES, RE	DATE 9/30/77

PS Form 7404-F
May 1976

(Continue on reverse)

APPRAISAL REVIEW
U.S. POST OFFICE BUILDING

BY

General Comments.

This review is based on personal inspection of the property on 9/23/77, and knowledge of _____ County real estate market by virtue of other Postal Service projects in the area. Specific comments follow based on the format of the report which closely relates to the Postal Service contract specifications.

Purpose of the Appraisal.

This section of the report is adequate. Purpose is to appraise on an unencumbered fee simple basis as well as lease interest.

Interest Defined.

The appraiser has adequately defined market value and leased fee interest.

Local and Specific Data.

The property was described adequately with the recorded "legal description". Neighborhood description briefly put forth required facts, with maps depicting local and site locations. The site description appeared to be adequate. Zoning and utilities comments are acceptable.

Highest and Best Use.

The appraiser's opinion of highest and best use is not very well supported.

In my search of the market in the subject's area, I found alternative uses that were reasonably probably and physically possible as well as appropriately supported by the market. These highest and best uses involved governmental uses, local commercial use, etc. The appraiser stated the highest and best use is its present use only.

This cannot be denied due to zoning, size, etc.; however, I feel to limit the use to this usage only would penalize the property unduly. Therefore, I feel the highest and best use should have been stated "As its present usage with a reasonable and probably chance for office/institutional and/or office/commercial usage".

Improvement Description.

The appraiser adequately described the improvements.

Cost Approach.

Site Valuation. The appraiser reports he considered many sales in the area and cites the five "most indicative" in his report. Detailed analysis was thin with no adjustment chart and very little comment on adjustments. During the review conference, the appraiser indicated he considered a 1973 sale between the Marietta Housing Authority to First National Bank for $183,000 with land valued at $40,000 and improvements at $143,000. Considerable renovation took place in the building. The land area was 36,000 square feet, indicating a square foot value of $1.11.

Sale No. 1 grantee was stated incorrectly and the sale price on Sale No. 2 was stated incorrectly; however, these errors made little difference in final value.

After considering the appraiser's sales, my own market analysis, I feel
Sale No. 3 and the 1973 Marietta Housing Authority Sale present a more
reasonable and realistic market picture; therefore, this reviewer concludes
a more reasonable conclusion would be a range of $1.11 to $1.53 with most
credence on the former. Thus: 109,160 SF @ $1.11/SF = $121,168
                                                    SAY $121,200

   Reproduction Cost New - Building. The building is 14 years old and the
appraiser used the age/life concept to develop overall depreciation. The
building has considerable deferred maintenance problems such as a leaky
roof, but was painted in 1973. The air conditioner is 13 years old and
should be replaced. The building is inadequately wired and ingress and
egress is questionable. It is felt the building's effective age is 16 to 17
years in lieu of the 14 years used by the appraiser.

Thus we have: RCN $943,654
               Effective Age 17
               REL 23
17/40 = 42.5% of $943,654 $401,053
Est. depreciated imp. value $542,601
+ land   121,200
Indicated Value by
Cost Approach $663,800 (R)

Income Approach.

The appraiser developed a reasonable and logical economic rent. Development
of operating statement was reasonable but to have no vacancy/credit and with
management at 2%, is beyond reasonable comprehension of the market. Thus, I
offer the following.

Estimated Gross Annual Income	$72,400
Less V & C 2%	1,448
Effective Gross Income	$70,952
Less Expenses - 12% (Inclusive)	8,514
NIBR	$62,438
Land Value $121,200 x *.096384	11,373
Residue Inc. to Building	$51,064
$51,064/*.153364	$332,959
Plus Land	$121,200
Estimated Value by Income Approach	$454,150 (R)

✻ *Loan .75 x .098657 (A/C)   =   .073993
   Equity .25 x .12   =   .030000
   Less Loan Ratio x P x SFF
   .75 x *.17806 x .05698   =   .007609
   Basic rate "r"   .096384
   Unload for land appreciation - None
   Load for building depreciation:
   1.00 x .05698   .05698
   Building capitalization rate   .153364

*2 $P = \dfrac{f - I}{fp- I} = \dfrac{.0987 - .0875}{.1504 - .0875} = \dfrac{.0112}{.0629} = .17806$

✻ DIFFERENCE IN CALCULATIONS DUE TO ROUNDING

Market Approach.

Due to the almost nonexistence of adequate market data, I feel the GRM
theory is incorrect and the market approach should not be utilized. Those
comparables used are much newer buildings and the GRM is distorted.

Reconciliation.

The values indicated by the appraiser are perhaps reasonable;however, I
believe the review analysis depicts a more realistic look at the market
area and the building as an economic factor.

Cost Approach	$663,800
Income Approach	$454,150
Market Approach (from Appraiser)	$650,000

The three approaches are reasonable, except the Income Approach, which depicts a more realistic reflection of income property. It is felt the market does in fact project fairly reasonable comparable income data and the cost approach, even with the difficulty of accurately estimating accrued depreciation, gives reasonable final estimates of value.

Therefore, it is this reviewer's judgment the estimated market value, free and clear is $500,000.

Leased Fee Interest.

The appraiser developed leased fee interest on three premises. The first premise is based on a reversion at the end of basic ten-year term (5/31/93). The proper present worth factors were utilized, indicating the

Present Worth of Income Stream	$206,545
Reverson Land and Building Purchase Option $350,000 x .2236 =	78,260
Estimated Lessor Interest (Reversion before Rent Reduction)	$284,805
SAY	$285,000

The second premise was based on the reversion at the end of the final renewal term with reversion of land only in that building will be totally depreciated in 35 years. The step-down analysis on page 30 of the report reflects accurately the:

Present Worth of Income Stream	$243,805
Plus reversion of land $100,000 x .0383	3,870
	$247,675
Estimated Lessor's Interest (Reversion End of Final Renewal)	$250,000 (R)

The Market Approach was the third premise utilized in the report. The appraiser used the GRM theory and a GRM of 9. This indicated a value of $300,000, which I feel is reasonable.

Reconciliation. (Final)

The three premises indicated the following for the present worth of income stream plus reversion.

Premise I	$285,000
Premise II	$250,000
Market Comparison	$300,000

Premises I and II assume reversion at a predetermined purchase price but is well established by the contract. It is felt the leased fee analysis reveals certain influences inherent in the property and must be given credence in final determination of value. With the improvements decreasing in REL, it is felt the prudent investor will not pay more than the estimated value of the land in either premise. Therefore, it is my judgment the leased fee estate in this property is valued at $290,000. It is recommended this figure be used as a basis for negotiation in purchase of this property.

Reviewed by: Approved by:

Claude R. Moore, Jr.   (Date)   James T. Coe   (Date)
Realty Management & Acquisition Analyst   Field Supervisor, Real Estate

		N/A		
☐ TRANSFER ☒ DISPOSAL		CONTRACT DATE	DATE RECEIVED	
OU☐ ☐ LEASING ☐				

APPRAISER'S NAME AND ADDRESS			NAME AND ADDRESS OF OWNER
MAI – SRPA			United States Postal Service

TELEPHONE NO. 704/377-3659	FINANCE NO.	SUB-LOCATION NO.	TYPE OF PROPERTY Old USPO and Courthouse			
EFFECTIVE REPORT DATE March 15, 1977	APPRAISED VALUE (FMV) $ 350,000	APPROVED VALUE (Adj.) $	LAND VALUE (FMV) $ 85,000	LEASEHOLD INTEREST $ N/A	LAND AREA (Sq. Ft.) 26,500	
GROSS BLDG. AREA (Sq. Ft.) 37,590	CHRONOLOGICAL AGE 70 (Yrs.)	EFFECTIVE AGE 70 (Yrs.)	NEIGHBORHOOD TREND (+, =, −) [+]	FAIR ECONOMIC RENT $ 108,060	CONTRACT RENT $ N/A	
OPERATING EXPENSES $44,600 (45%)	CAPITALIZATION RATE (Overall) .11370 %	FAIR ECONOMIC TAXES 4,802	APPRAISAL FEE $ 1250?	PROFESSIONAL DESIGNATIONS MAI – SRPA		

INSTRUCTIONS

Explain all negative answers on reverse.
Comment fully on inadequacies and recommendations.

E – Excellent - Meets or exceeds specifications.
A – Adequate - Meets minimum needs. Clarifications may be desirable.
I – Inadequate - Does not meet needs. Revision or clarification necessary.

ITEM	E	A	I
I. FORM AND PRESENTATION			
Conformance to USPS Specifications (Section 2 Appraisal Contract). Form, sequence and inclusion of significant items.			
Historical background and acknowledgements.	X		
Area, city and neighborhood data.	X		
Land and prop. descriptions –conditions and uses.			X
Legal description included.	YES	NO X	
Zoning, utilities easements, fair-economic assessed value, tax and insurance costs.	X		
Certifications, plans, specifications, photos, maps, (addenda inclusions) dates and signature.			X
Purposes and function of appraisal.		X	
II. DESIGN/DESCRIPTION/MENT			
Highest and best use appropriately analyzed and defined (as applied to appraised property).		X	
Statement of Limiting conditions.		X	
III. ANALYSIS, TECHNIQUES AND DATA UTILIZED			
Adequate comparative transactions.			X
Individual description showing date and conditions of each comparative transaction.		X	
Differences adjusted to current market conditions for subject with each comparable.		X	
Adjustment chart.			X
Correlation and logical conclusions. See Remarks			
Comparable location map.	X		
Cost Estimates.	X		
Depreciation - physical, justified. See Remarks			
Depreciation - functional, justified. See Remarks			
Depreciation - economic.	X		
Summation Value. See Remarks			
Individual description and analysis showing date and conditions of each comparative transaction.		X	
Differences adjusted to current market conditions for subject with each comparable.		X	
Value indicated by market approach. See Remarks			X

ITEM	E	A	I
MARKET APPROACH	YES		NO
Development of a gross rent multiplier.			X
Contract rent.	N/A		
Fair, economic rent by comparison.		X	
Vacancy, collection or credit losses.		X	
Fixed, operating and reserve expenses by comparison or historical information (including administrative expense.) See Remarks			
Net annual income before recapture.		X	
Method of capitalization.		X	
Capitalization rate - justified.		X	
Value indicated by income approach.		X	
Leased-fee interest properly analyzed.	N/A		
Leasehold interest properly analyzed.	N/A		
Logical relationship to comparables.		X	
IV. FAIR RENTAL	YES		NO
Does estimate reflect contemplated lease provisions?			X
V. Reasonableness of final value conclusion.	X		
VI. OVERALL EFFECTIVENESS	YES		NO
Is the appraisal problem clearly stated?	X		
Is supporting data factual, adequately and appropriately analyzed?	X		
Is supporting data accurate?	X		
Is conclusion logically related to supporting data and the appraisal problem?	X		
Are all essential items included?	X		
As a basis for contemplated action?			
Without further clarification?			
For fee payment?	X		
As evidenced by this report, would you recommend this appraiser for other assignments?	X		
Field Reviewed?	X		
Conference with appraiser? (Telephone)	X		

REVIEWER'S SIGNATURE J. T. Coe, FS, Real Estate	DATE 5/3/77	CONTRACTING OFFICER'S SIGNATURE J. T. Coe	DATE 5/3/77

PS Form 7404-F
May 1974

(Continue on reverse)

REVIEW COMMENTS - APPRAISAL
- USPO AND COURTHOUSE
APPRAISAL BY

General.

Review is based on personal inspection of the property on April 13, 1977,
and knowledge of Rowan County economics by virtue of several other Postal
Service projects in the area. Specific comments follow based on the format of the report which corresponds to the Postal Service contract specifications.

Part I - Introduction.

This section of the report is adequate. Property identification is proper
and an appropriate transmittal is provided. Assumptions and limiting conditions are not restrictive and are standard to the profession.

Part II - Factual Data.

The purpose of the appraisal (estimate fair market value) is appropriately
stated and an acceptable definition of "Market Value" is provided. Factual
data concerning site and building are accurate and clearly stated. Under
utilities, taxes, etc., clear factual data is presented, but is redundant
since it is also repeated under the cost approach expense analysis. Several
minor spelling, mathematical and other composition errors are noted in this
section but do not appear prejudicial.

Part III - Analysis and Conclusions.

Highest and Best Use: The appraiser apparently completed a thorough
analysis of demand in Salisbury. This was confirmed by the reviewer during
discussion with   County Manager, Mr. Murdock, on April 14, 1977.
Definite demand exists for multi-tenant office use, particularly by Rowan
County with whom we are currently negotiating for a substantial outlease.
The appraiser's conclusion is accepted as logically supported by the economic
demand and present zoning.

Site Valuation: The appraiser reports he considered ten sales and cites
the four "most indicative" in the report. Good detail is provided and adjustments are discussed although not tabulated. Sale 1 data reflects a slight
math error (SF price should be $3.97 not $4). The valuation could be slightly
high in the reviewer's opinion. Sale 1 involved allocation which can be a
highly subjective opinion. Sale 2 is an "add-on" purchase and could require
some motivation consideration. Sale 3 is good, requiring only time adjustment,

which the appraiser applied with moderation. Sale 4, his "best" comparable,
should have been adjusted for size. Based on the SF unit values of other
sales, a downward adjustment is suggested. Reviewer concludes Sales 2, 3
and 4, presenting a mean of $615, should project that FF value as being the
most reasonable conclusion; thus, 132.5 front feet @ $615 = $81,487.50,
say $81,500.

Cost Approach: Appraiser projects a very thorough and professional
approach to collection of cost data and his estimate. Depreciation schedules
precipitate some questions, however, particularly related to physical curable
(deferred maintenance). Reviewer agrees with the painting, elevators, and
restroom renovation estimates, but notes that heat is provided to the toilet
areas via steam radiators. Some of these would require repair which could
prove uneconomic, therefore the $30,000 is not unreasonable. The total of
the items upon which the appraiser and reviewer agree is $73,000. To this
reviewer, based on personal investigation and estimates from Design and Construction Branch, Atlanta FREBO, would add the following:

Roof (Entire Structure)	$18,000
Floor	12,360
Exterior Cleaning, Caulking and Painting of Masonry	15,000

The total physical deterioration-curable penalty should therefore be $118,360. Reviewer generally agrees with the other depreciation items. Simple age/life was used to measure physical-incurable. Two items of functional obsolescence were measured and by appropriate method. The appraiser did fail to reflect any penalty for excess cost of ownership due to the overimprovement, but due to the nature of the excess (elaborate facade), this would be of small consequence. Based on the above, the following restructure of the depreciation schedule is offered:

Total Reproduction Cost Less Depreciation: $2,716,420

Physical Curable	$ 118,360	
Physical Incurable	1,818,642	
Functional Obsolescence	479,580	
Economic Obsolescence	-0-	
Total		$2,416,582

Depreciated Value of Improvements	$ 299,838
Land Value	81,500
Gross Value	$ 381,338
Less Interior Rent Loss	54,030
Indicated Value	$ 327,308

(R) $325,000

Income Approach. Appraiser researched the market area very thoroughly. and cites five (5) comparables as a basis for his economic rental projection. With a range from $3 per SF to $7.29 per SF, there is wide latitude for judgment. Based on discussions with prospective tenants for the subject, $3.50 to $5 per SF "as is" is maximum. With the expenditure of the $118,360 for renovation the $4.75 might be obtained but is likely to warrant a higher vacancy and collection loss. To achieve 92.5% occupancy, the reviewer suggests $4.25 to be the maximum economic rental rate. The expense schedule appears well documented with the exception of electricity which was based on a period when this facility was operated 20 hours per day as a mail processing facility. The reviewer recommends the following reconstructed Income and Expense Statement.

Gross Income:

22,750 @ 4.25	$96,688
Less V&C Loss @ 7.5%	7,252
Effective Gross Income	$89,436

Less Expenses:

Taxes	$ 5,720	
Insurance	1,270	
Management @ 5%	4,472	
Janitorial	7,960	
Utilities:		
Gas	4,400	
Electricity	12,000	
Water		
Sewer	850	
Miscellaneous	2,000	
Reserves & Maint.	3,000	
TOTAL Expenses	(46% - $1.82 SF)	$41,612

Net Income Before Recapture $47,824

Utilizing the appraiser's overall capitalization rate (.11370) which appears plausible, the above represents the following valuation.

$47,827 (Net Income) ÷ .11370 (OAR) = $420,642
Less Deferred Maintenance   118,360
Less Rent Loss (Interior)   54,030
Indicated Value - Income Approach $248,252
                    (R) $250,000

Market Approach. The appraiser relied on one old USPO sale at High Point, North Carolina. Basically this is a reasonable comparison and is acceptable due to the low degree of reliance on this approach to value. Note, however, that two other USPO buildings at Wallace, NC and Ahoskie, NC, have recently sold, which although smaller could have been related to the subject by unit comparison. The appraiser should ha.e, in the reviewer's opinion, used a unit sales price to reflect his value for the

subject and ignored renovation or rent loss deduction, i.e.,

High Point $365,000   Adjusted Gross
           ÷ 54,040   SF
             $6.75   per GSF

Applied to Subject: 37,580 GSF
                    @ 6.75
                    $253,665

Summary and Conclusion.

Review indicated the following breakdown to be appropriate:

Cost Approach $325,000
Income Approach   250,000
Market Approach   253,665

The appraiser and reviewer are consistent in their reliance on the Income Approach primarily since the property is improved to highest and best use and this approach can be logically supported. The Cost Approach is secondary in reliability and the Market Approach is generally disregarded. Probability of reliance is weighted as follows:

Cost Approach $325,000 @ .15 = $48,750
Income Approach $250,000 @ .80 = $200,000
Market Approach $253,665 @ .05 = $12,683
                          100% $261,433

Based on this review, the appraisal, and consultation with the appraiser and other local sources of market data, $260,000 is recommended for a final disposal value.

James T. Coe
Field Supervisor, Real Estate
Field RE&B Office, Atlanta, GA

Date: May 2, 1977

CHAPTER SEVEN

Does the Appraisal

Report Unintentionally

Discriminate?

A Consideration

for the Reviewer

VIGDOR "VIC" GROSSMAN

Vigdor "Vic" Grossman is currently President of Equal Opportunity Associates, Minneapolis, Minnesota. He provides training and consultation to banks, savings and loan associations, corporations and Boards of REALTORS® in fair lending, fair housing and equal employment opportunity. He is also a Community Faculty Member of Metropolitan State University in the Affirmative Action Officers Training Program.

Mr. Grossman is a member of the Minnesota State Affirmative Action Association and an Associate Member of the American Association for Mortgage Underwriters. He also lectures and writes extensively on various equal opportunity topics.

Does the Appraisal

Report Unintentionally

Discriminate?

A Consideration

for the Reviewer

If you reviewed an appraisal report in which either a home with a minority family in it, or a predominantly minority neighborhood or an interracial one was treated differently from a comparable white home or neighborhood, you would probably say to yourself, "This appraisal is illegal because it is discriminatory," and, of course, you would be quite correct. However, there are other situations where, *in effect*, legal discrimination is present in the appraisal report—even though the Appraiser did not consciously intend to discriminate. You should, therefore, review each factor in the appraisal report that might be taken as evidence of:

(1) overt discrimination: e.g., reliance on factors relating to "social transition" or "changing neighborhoods";

(2) code words: e.g., use of vague and subjective phrases such as "pride of ownership" and

(3) unequal treatment: e.g., negative consideration of such factors as "traffic" or "commercialization" or "density" in certain areas but not others.

This article is based in part on: Warren Dennis, "Developing Policies and Procedures Under the Federal Home Loan Bank Board's Non Discrimination Regulations and Guidelines," Pottinger and Co., Washington, D.C., 1978. A shorter version of it appeared in the Appraisal Review Journal, Fall 1978.

You might assume that as long as an Appraiser treats comparables equally where one of these is white and the other is minority that no discrimination has occurred. This is not necessarily so.

This article will describe a type of equal treatment that the courts have found to be discriminatory. It is called either "disparate effect" or the "effects test" (to determine whether discrimination is present).

Disparate effect discrimination takes place when an appraisal policy, practice or procedure:

(1) is equally applied under the same circumstances; and
(2) is likely to eliminate, *in effect*, housing for a greater percentage of minorities than non-minorities, or *results* in a higher percentage of minorities receiving home loans on adverse terms, conditions, or rates (e.g., higher down payments, etc.) than comparable whites; and this
(3) cannot be justified in terms of risk.

An example of this is an Appraiser using as a rule of thumb that any residential property below "X" square feet is not marketable. This in turn results in lower appraisal values or negative narrative comments on such property where most minorities in a community live. At this point the financial institution for whom the appraisal is done would need to show a cause-effect relationship between the square footage of the property and marketability, and between marketability and mortgage risk. If such a relationship:

(1) did not exist at all; or
(2) was slight; or
(3) was short-term; or
(4) did not affect the security or utility of the property; or
(5) did not threaten the maintenance of the value at the level attained on the date of the loan,

then this rule of thumb on the nonmarketability of property below "X" square feet would be racially discriminatory.

Courts have recognized disparate effect discrimination under the Federal Fair Housing Act (Title VIII of the 1968 Civil Rights Act), as well as under the regulations of the Equal Credit Opportunity Act. Moreover, courts have ruled that the Federal Fair Housing Act specifically applies to the appraisal process.*

---

*William v. Matthews Co., 499 F. 2d 819, 826 (8th Cir.), cert. denied 419 U.S. 1027, 95 S. Ct. 507, 42 L. Ed. 2d 302 (1974); and United States v. AIREA, et al., 442 F. Supp. 1072, 1078-9 (N.O. Ill. 1977).

Since you, as the Review Appraiser, bear responsibility for the appraisal process, you, too, are considered a party to any discrimination charge filed against the Appraiser.

To avoid a *valid* charge of disparate effect discrimination, you should ask yourself: is any part of the appraisal report or the appraisal process:

(1) Likely to have a greater effect on minorities than non-minorities?

(2) Is this effect a negative one?

If the answer to both questions is "yes", then you should ask yourself:

(1) Is the appraisal based upon the characteristics of the structure being appraised?

(2) Is this appraisal unadjusted for neighborhood factors except as these can be specifically shown to affect the present or short-range future value of the security property (such as current market trends based on actual transactions involving comparable properties, or housing abandonment in the immediate area?

If the answers to either or both of these last two questions is "yes", then the appraisal policy, practice or procedure in question is not discriminatory EVEN IF MORE MINORITIES ARE ADVERSELY AFFECTED MORE THAN NONMINORITIES. This is because these last two questions asked whether or not sound appraisal principles were used in the appraisal process.

One of the likeliest indicators that disparate effect discrimination might be taking place is when the Appraiser indicates the property is either in a declining neighborhood or one that soon will be. If he/she bases that conclusion *even in part* on the following:

(1) the area has inadequate fire protection or street lighting;

(2) the area has a high percentage of welfare families;

(3) the area has low or moderate income residents;

(4) the minimum purchase price of the security property;

(5) the minimum loan amounts, and if any of these more likely pertain to minorities than nonminorities;

(6) the chronological age of the security property;

then disparate effect discrimination has taken place. This is because these factors disproportionately and adversely affect minorities (the first set of questions described above) and these factors are not valid appraisal considerations, since none of them are based upon the characteristics of the security property, or affect the present or short-range future value of the security property (the second set of questions just covered).

There are other factors which often influence a lender's willingness to loan in certain areas. These may or may not be actually related to marketability. They include:

(1) minimum lot sizes, width and room requirements;
(2) foreclosures in the area;
(3) abandonment in the area;
(4) arson and other crime rates in the area.

Some of these factors may affect marketability or property condition. *However, such factors should not automatically be assumed to have such a negative effect without evaluating their relationship to security, utility, value and marketability on a case-by-case basis.*

In order to validly report an area as either declining or soon to be declining, this conclusion should be thoroughly documented. This should be done through facts and figures. Photographs and field notes will enable the Appraiser to verify the facts in his/her analysis. Make sure your documentation of conditions is equally good in all neighborhoods, not just in areas where you are reluctant to lend.

Make sure that the appraisal report uses the following approach in dealing with the attributes of decline. Those factors relating to the physical condition of the property in question should be handled separately. These, of course, are the easiest to observe and document. Those factors pertaining to the site, such as observable street conditions, utilities, flooding, view, etc., should likewise be treated by themselves. Factors relating to marketability should also be handled separately. These will be more subjective. However, hard data is usually available with respect to time on market, documentable value trends, etc.

In determining how to evaluate whether or not the security property is in a declining neighborhood and how this affects the security, utility, value, and marketability of the security property, the following approach should be used:

(1) Emphasis should be placed on physical, observable and measurable factors with economic impact, such as the condition of the house. In short, deal with tangible factors.
(2) Do not include social or cultural considerations such as "the compatibility of people." Examine instead the PHYSICAL EVIDENCE of decline, such as abandonment, that is close to the property.
(3) To the extent possible, rely on factors that have a short-range impact (no more than five years) unless there is some factor

that has an obviously long-range consequence. This might be a projected 30-year private development or an urban renewal plan.

(4) Avoid standards that appear rigid, inflexible or dogmatic. Always be willing to consider moderating influences even if it is difficult to do so. Build this flexibility into your appraisal policy.

(5) Establish formal safeguards against underappraisal by requiring a special review when an appraisal comes in well below the selling price or when an Appraiser reports decline.

(6) Well reasoned and supported standards whose practices are well documented have the best chances of holding up to a complaint or examination. An attempt to justify or support a standard or its practice after an investigation has begun will not be nearly as effective as a defense made beforehand.

It is not enough to simply refer to "deferred maintenance" in the area. Instead, the appraisal report should state:

(1) Where deferred maintenance of abnormal deterioration exists (by listing *specific* properties having these adverse conditions) in relation to the security property.

(2) The nature and extent of these adverse conditions. (There is quite a difference between peeling paint and abandoned houses in the immediate vicinity of the property being appraised.)

(3) The length of time these negative conditions have been present.

(4) The reasons why these conditions affect the immediate or short-term future value of the property in question (e.g., has there been an observed trend of deterioration with no rehabilitation effort underway or a high rate of foreclosures close to the security property?).

There are other valid indicators of an area's decline. Among these are: excessive taxes, special assessments or zoning changes or other governmental actions. Perhaps the area is changing from residential to industrial and/or commercial land use, or there are other changes in the highest and best use of the land. Perhaps the area is exposed to flooding or to land faults. Again these factors should be documented in the appraisal report by indicating: their location in relation to the property being appraised, the nature and extent as well as the length of time each factor has existed, and the reason(s) these conditions have affected the value of the property being appraised.

On the other hand, whether or not any of these adverse conditions exist, there are other factors that indicate either a stabilizing or rejuvenated area. These include: amenities such as parks and playgrounds, rehabilitation programs, improvements in public services and facilities, capital improvements, affirmative home, consumer and small business lending programs by financial institutions, as well as citizen's community improvement organizations.

Sometimes the revitalization of an area is spearheaded by the partnership concept of the Neighborhood Housing Service (NHS) Program of the Urban Reinvestment Task Force. Under this concept, the following are brought together:

(1) financial institutions who agree to make loans in the area;
(2) local government to provide code enforcement and to provide, as needed, appropriate public facilities and services to the neighborhood;
(3) residents' organizations and, in the case of NHS,
(4) the federal government supporting and monitoring the local NHS staff.

Sometimes local communities or states have their own version of such a partnership.

However, as the American Institute of Real Estate Appraisers (hereafter the AIREA) states in its text, *The Appraisal of Real Estate,* "The rebirth of an older inner city neighborhood . . . may occur without a planned renewal program simply because of changing preferences and life styles."

The Appraiser should be aware of these factors that indicate either neighborhood preservation or rejuvenation. He/she should evaluate the impact of these efforts on the area and particularly upon the property being appraised. These items should also be adequately documented. The appraisal report should indicate:

(1) The location of these efforts in relation to the security property;
(2) the nature and extent of these efforts:
(3) the length of time these have existed; and
(4) how these activities have affected the immediate or future value of the property in question.

The next page shows a summary of those indicators of an area's decline as of an area's stability, and how to document these.

INDICATORS OF NEIGHBORHOOD CHANGE AND WHAT TO INCLUDE IN THEIR DOCUMENTATION

INDICATORS	DOCUMENTATION			
	Location in Relation to Property Being Appraised	Nature and Extent of This Condition	Length of Time This Condition Has Existed	Why These Conditions Have Affected the Present or Future Value of Property Being Appraised
Of Neighborhood Decline:				
1. Deferred maintenance				
2. Taxes				
3. Zoning				
4. Changing land use				
Of Neighborhood Stability:				
1. Amenities				
2. Rehabilitation				
3. Other public improvements				
4. Affirmative lending programs				
5. Citizens' groups				

In deciding whether an area is truly in decline, there are some further considerations to keep in mind in reviewing the appraisal report. The government examiners are going to look critically at traditional indicators of risk. The marketplace may not be influenced as much by these factors as has been asumed (or at all). For example, if an area has a "high" crime rate but houses continue to be sold at the same prices that they had before crime rate had risen, then the "high" crime rate is being discounted by the marketplace. If an Appraiser attempts to predict its future effect on value and on marketability, he or she is "double counting." As the AIREA states in its text, *The Appraisal of Real Estate* (see Appendix 9):

"...After complete neighborhood anaylsis, the appraiser delineates the neighborhood and obtains an indication of value based on recent prices received for similar properties in the same neighborhood. In such a case, it would be incorrect to adjust value for neighborhood influences, since it can be assumed that these market influences are reflected in the observed market prices."

When reviewing the appraisal report, you should make sure that when an area is reported to be in an advanced state of deterioration, this is actually the case. Sometimes an area is considered quite "far gone" when in fact it is only showing some of the traditional "early warning" signals, but it is not yet at the heavy abandonment or severe physical deterioration stage. These traditional early warning signals are not necessarily that accurate. Such deterioration may not continue and sometimes may be reversed.

If a lower appraisal is given to that and other properties in the area on the assumption the deterioration will continue, such an action IN ITSELF may create a "self-fulfilling prophesy." Thus such low appraisals, which would probably affect the marketability of the property, could in turn cause other nearby property owners to believe they had better sell as quickly and cheaply as possible before the market gets any lower. This, in turn, could prematurely depress the marketplace. Thus the initial appraisal which lead to this depressed market helped bring about the decline that it predicted would take place. It would indeed be ironic if the area's deterioration without this panic selling would have leveled out or even reversed itself.

There is another consideration about so-called "declining areas." Residential space per se is limited and finite. Low and moderate income individuals will always have housing needs.

Not every neighborhood can or should conform to a suburban model. This is particularly true in this period of increasingly tight money and high inflation. Modest neighborhoods often continue for very long periods in a stable condition. Some might mistakenly label such neighborhoods as "declining" by comparing them to developing suburban growth areas.

In spite of the suggestions just made, significant problems still persist in trying to appraise inner city property. Sometimes physical deterioration and related economic ills make it quite difficult to determine the current and future value of property. However, by following the guidelines in this article, you will be taking an important step as a Review Appraiser to ensure that the appraisal process and report is objective. This, in turn, will safeguard against underappraisals based upon improper appraisal procedures. In the process, you will not only comply with the equal opportunity requirements, but, equally important, you will be enhancing your most important asset, YOUR PROFESSIONAL INTEGRITY.

CHAPTER EIGHT

The Reviewer's

Final Decision

and Recommendation

WALTER S. HANNI, CRA, MAI

Walter S. Hanni, CRA, MAI, is a private Real Estate Appraisal Consultant in San Francisco, California. He has been Chief Appraiser and Chief Review Appraiser for the U.S. Army Corps of Engineers, San Francisco District, and was Chief of Real Estate for the Federal Public Housing Administration, San Francisco Regional Office, and Chief Real Property Officer, Department of Housing and Urban Development, San Francisco Regional Office, prior to retirement.

The Reviewer's

Final Decision

and Recommendation

INTRODUCTION

In the course of a formal review of any appraisal, the final step in the reviewing process is the Reviewer's final decision and recommendation, and his formal written report thereon; or other indication of his determination as a result of his review.

This determination may take several different forms or types; from that of merely a determination of approval or disapproval with the signature of the Reviewer, to that of the formal detailed narrative written review, or some form in between these two. This depends, to a great extent, upon the type of appraisal being reviewed and the organizational policy, requirements and regulations. However, generally these final decisions will all fall into certain specified classifications, which I will discuss herein.

Classification of Reviewing Decisions
or Recommendations

Approved or Approval Recommended
In this instance, the appraisal was found, by the Reviewer, to be acceptable in all respects; meeting contractual requirements, fully substantiated and justified of all factors and conclusions, as well as

meeting sound professional appraisal principles and practices. "Approval Recommended" is the term used where higher authority or other echelons of an organization may be the final approval authority. This may also be applicable in the case where a Reviewing Appraiser is working on a fee or contractual basis for a principal, and he is authorized, under his contract, to only make recommendations to his principal. An example of a detailed narrative approval is shown in Part III addenda exhibit 1.

Qualified Approval or Recommendation
In this instance, the appraisal report is not approved in its entirety; in other words, a qualified complete approval. This may be applicable in a case of an appraisal comprising numerous parcels involved in an acquisition. The total appraised value of all parcels in the acquisition may not be approved; however, certain parcels are approved, and certain parcels disapproved for justifiable reasons. Another instance may be that, in the Reviewers judgement, the appraisal is approved as an upper limit of value or a lower limit of value, which is a judgement determination by the Reviewer. The Reviewer may make a determination that the Appraiser has justified his valuation — to a reasonable degree, but there is some reasonable doubt in the Reviewer's mind as to fully substantiating and justifying his conclusions. I am a firm believer, and I am sure that I will have many professionals in the field disagree, that under certain economic circumstances, certain properties do not have a "value", but can only be valued on a "range of value" basis. In support of this theory, appraisal is not an exact science. Therefore, in some cases we can only resort to a "range" as being the closest proximity we can estimate.

Non-Approval — At This Time
In this instance, an appraisal report is highly questionable on being indictive of true fair market value for one of many reasons from the standpoint of the review and analysis by the Reviewer. In this event, the Reviewer can disapprove the appraisal "at this time", subject to:
   a. Securing additional justification and substantiation from the Appraiser to support his conclusions.
   b. Conditionally — subject to securing a second appraisal with a joint review of the two appraisals being made after the second appraisal is obtained.
   c. Supplementing his review with information, the Reviewer has obtained from either his own sources and/or field review

which tends to indicate a different conclusion than that the Appraiser has arrived at.

The conclusion on this classification can be resolved by:

a. Additional supplemental data from the Appraiser to adequately substantiate his conclusion.

b. Securing a second appraisal — in which event the final conclusion rests upon a joint review of both appraisal reports.

A qualified valuation from the Reviewer is based upon his determinations of the revised value he has estimated. In this case, he actually becomes the Appraiser and must be prepared to defend any changes he has made in the Appraiser's valuation conclusion, and be prepared to testify as the Appraiser, if litigation is involved.

Acceptable for Fee Only

Any appraisal may be acceptable as having met the contractual requirements; however, the conclusions may not have met the reviewing Appraiser's and/or organizational requirements as to what they expected. Although the Appraiser may have produced a product which was to the best of his ability, it may not have met his principal's full expectations. While he may have done a job which was to the best of his professional ability, there may have been some areas which could be questioned, which is the Reviewer's or principal's prerogative. If he has met his contractual requirements, he is entitled to his fee, no matter whether or not he has made an appraisal which is absolutely in agreement with what the Reviewer would have done or would have liked. He must be paid his fee, if he has met his contractual agreement.

Disapproval with Recommendations

An appraisal may be disapproved for any justifiable reason, by the Reviewer; however, these reasons must be justified and substantiated by the reviewer beyond any reasonable doubt, and must be based upon unquestionable facts which the Appraiser has not adequately justified and substantiated or where the Reviewer has information or factual data which will refute the appraiser's conclusions. In no way must the Reviewer disapprove any appraisal based solely upon his unsupported opinion or "seat of the pants" judgement. These recommendations on disapproval may include the following:

a. That a second contract or additional fee appraisal be obtained from an independent, unbiased appraiser on the same project property.

b. That a staff appraisal be obtained in addition to whatever has previously been done.

c. That the Reviewer prepare his own appraisal, in which case he becomes the Appraiser rather than the Reviewer. Also, he is no longer in the position of reviewing his appraisal or valuation.

An example of this type of disapproval is shown in Part III, Addenda Exhibit 2.

Disapproval Without Recommendations

In this instance, the appraisal report is recommended for disapproval in all respects. It has not met contractual requirements and therefore should not be accepted. Also, if not having met contractual requirements, the recommendation should be made that any fee not be paid. This classification is very rare, and should not be initiated unless the Appraiser has not unequivocably met his contractual requirements, and refuses to do so after the opportunity to rectify his deficiencies has been offered to him. Whatever the Reviewer may find wrong with an appraisal, in his opinion, the Appraiser should be offered the opportunity to correct it or refute the Reviewer's contention and questions. In no event should an appraisal be disapproved without offering the Appraiser an opportunity to correct or refute the Reviewer's determination. Also, the Reviewer must substantiate and justify his conclusion.

Disapproval with Reviewer's Adjustments

In this instance, the Reviewer generally agress with the Appraiser's findings to a limited extent. However, based upon his field review or other data available to him, he is not in full agreement with the Appraiser, and adjusts the Appraiser's conclusions according to his own justifiable factual data and judgement, which he must justify and substantiate and adequately explain. In this case, the Reviewer, as such, becomes, to a great degree, the Appraiser — since he has changed the Appraiser's conclusions. Therefore, the Reviewer must be in the position to defend his conclusions and, in the event of litigation, he must be willing to testify to his findings.

Alterations of Appraisal

It is a cardinal rule that in no event may a Reviewer ever alter, in any way, an appraisal made by another, without his permission — this permission should usually be in writing. In the case of minor changes, such as corrections of typographical errors, or other obvious errors, it is within the Reviewer's discretion to correct these, provided he has checked with the Appraiser and his determination is correct; however, he should always check with the Appraiser and secure verification for all such corrections. He should also note that it has been approved by the Appraiser.

Two Appraisal Reviews

In the course of the review of two independent appraisals on the same property, a major problem may often develop when two Appraisers, who are considered to be professionally qualified, arrive at widely differentiated opinions of value. From the Reviewer's approach, the initial step is to attempt to determine what is the major problem or difference of opinion. If it appears to be factual basis of difference, both Appraisers should be consulted for confirmation of the factual data submitted, in each report, and consider reanalysis of possible changes which may have resulted since their conclusion. Judgement differences, between any two Appraisers, are not usually reconsilable by re-analysis. Differences may result from different interpretaions of the purpose or other concepts upon which the property is being appraised. When such differences of opinion or judgement results, the Reviewer is faced with a "Solomon's Decision" of his and judgement. He must make a decision as to which Appraiser has best justified and substantiated his conclusions, in all respects, and which most reasonably evaluates the property under consideration. At this point, he must also make an evaluation of each Appraiser, as to their experience, capabilities on appraising such properties, and other professional factors. After his review and analysis, and determination of where the differences are, he should consult with each of the Appraisers, separately or jointly, and attempt to reconcile these differences and/or make his own determination as to which is most correct or what procedure should be followed at this point. Additional information and data may be required from each Appraiser to justify his conclusion. In the event the differences cannot be reconciled, the Reviewer must make a decision as to whether or not an additional appraisal is required, or make his own decision as to what his conclusion of value should be and must adequately justify and substantiate his conclusions. It has been normally accepted that a differential of ten percent (10%) between any two appraisals is reasonable; however, it is my opinion that this can vary somewhat, depending upon the type of property, market conditions, and the purpose of the appraisal. An "absolute" ten percent (10%) is not, in my opinion, "concrete" — it can vary one way or another from this figure.

Consolidated or Joint Reviewing Statement

Where two appraisals are obtained on a project or property, it is my recommended procedure to independently review each appraisal and prepare a report on each. Then, prepare a consolidated or joint review appraisal statement, which purpose is to reconcile the differences between the two and arrive at the Reviewer's conclusion of a justifiable valuation based upon the two appraisals, field review and whatever additional information is available to the Reviewer. The final conclusion or recommendation of the Reviewer may or may not be one or the other conclusion of each Appraiser. However, whatever conclusion the Reviewer arrives at, he must fully explain, substantiate and justify this conclusion. When one appraiser has more adequately substantiated his conclusions, the Reviewer will naturally tend to reach a conclusion or recommendation in the area of this valuation. However, when both have reasonably justified their conclusions, the Reviewer may tend to arrive at a conclusion somewhere between the two. Whatever decision he arrives at must be fully substantiated and justified. An example of a consolidated reviewing statement of two appraisals is shown in Part III, Addenda Exhibit 3.

Valuation Reported Different from the Appraiser
by the Reviewer
In some instances, the Reviewer's decision or valuation conclusion may differ from that as estimated by the Appraiser. In this event, the Reviewer, in effect then becomes the Appraiser and not the reviewing Appraiser. There may be some exceptional cases where a valuation is made up of say two or more separate elements — compensable items — value for governmental use vs. value for highest and best use. The Reviewer may approve one and not the other. However, whenever the Reviewer approves a valuation, substantially different from that concluded by the Appraiser, he must be able to substantiate and justify his

conclusion in all respects. Also, in the event of litigation, he must be prepared to testify to his conclusions.

Reviewer Not Only Dependent Upon Appraisal

In the course of his review, the Reviewer is not solely dependent upon the information contained in the appraisal report for his conclusion. Other information, which may be available to him from his "data plant", as well as his own experience and knowledge of values in the area, and of the property in question, should be utilized. This information should be set forth and substantiated in his review to justify his conclusions, especially if his conclusion of value differs from that of the Appraiser.

Disqualification of Reviewer

It has been said by some that a Reviewer should disqualify himself from reviewing an appraisal of a type which he has had limited or no experience. I do not agree with this entirely. It is my opinion that a Reviewer should mainly restrict himself to reviewing appraisals of properties that he is most familiar with and experienced in. This criteria will be applicable only if he is entirely without knowledge of the methods and procedures of appraising such a property. He may not have appraised such a property himself, but he may have versed himself (secured the necessary knowledge or consulted or associated himself with an expert in the field) to be adequately qualified to make such a determination. He therefore cannot be considered as being without knowledge and be disqualified from such a review.

SUMMARY

The end result, the total accomplishment, the completed work of th review Appraiser, then should be a report in which he has outlined his explanation of the steps the Appraiser did or did not do, or the work that he failed to perform or did incorrectly, or the conclusion which the Reviewer has arrived at independently. The report should set forth an explanation by the Reviewer, of why it is considered wrong and the effect this erroneous determination would have upon the conclusion reached by the Appraiser. The decision which the Reviewer decided to adopt will vary with the circumstances of each case, and it calls for excellent seasoned judgement by the Reviewer. At the final stage, the Review Appraiser should sit back and look at the appraisal, as a whole, to see if a sound, justified, logical result has been arrived at. This is the last major step where the reviewer reviews the appraisal in its totality, as against all information, his findings on the field review and supplemental data. At this point, the Reviewer must make a final decision as to the acceptability of the final appraisal product, and whether or not the Appraiser has complied with the contract terms, specifications and instructions, as well as accepted appraisal principles and practices. In some cases, the reviewer must make what is commonly called a "Solomon's Decision". A "nit picker" or an individual who becomes "lost" in methodology and theory (while these factors have their importance) will never make a good Reviewer. It takes a fully qualified individual who can comprehend reported data, interpret and understand its relationship to the appraised property, and who can re-verify and double check its validity, to be a good reviewing Appraiser and be classified as a "C.R.A." (Certified Review Appraiser). Appraising is classified as an "inexact science" and therefore must be reviewed as such by the Reviewer. The Reviewer's objective is to secure an approvable appraisal and not merely to act as a "disapprover" as such.

CHAPTER NINE

Common Errors

and Deficiencies

in Appraisal Reports

JULIUS A. GILLIAM, CRA

Julius A. Gilliam, CRA, has been involved in real estate sales, leasing, management, appraising and review appraising since 1946. Mr. Gilliam was formerly Senior Supervisory Appraiser/Federal Properties Resources Service for the General Services Administration in Washington, D.C. His appraisal experience has been primarily in commercial, industrial and special purpose properties for condemnation, acquisition or disposal. He has been involved in the review of commercial properties for acquisition and military housing, industrial properties, including machinery and equipment, and special purpose properties for disposal by the Federal Government.

In addition to being a Senior Member of the National Association of Review Appraisers, Mr. Gilliam is a member of the American Institute of Real Estate Appraisers and the National Government Affairs Committee.

Common Errors

and Deficiencies

in Appraisal Reports

The apostle Paul, in his letter to the Roman Christians (chap. 3:23) wrote, "For all have sinned and come short of the glory of God." Paraphrasing this, it can be said, "All Appraisers have erred and fallen short of the goal." But like Christians, some Appraisers diligently strive for perfection while others merely try to get by.

The following list of common errors and deficiencies has been compiled from personal experience and from other government Review Appraisers mostly with General Services Administration and the Justice Department.

Let us consider them under the following categories:
1. Contractural
2. Data
3. Premises and Techniques
4. Report Production

CONTRACTURAL

Appraisal Requests Not Clear, Complete, or Correct

The contracting officer or client may be inexperienced as to appraisal procedures or legal ramifications in complex appraisal cases and without professional help (appraisal and possibly legal) may ask for values which are not what they really want or the wording is ambiguous or data inaccurate.

Contract Specifications Not Followed

Too often appraisals are submitted that do not meet the specifications of the contract. This is due in part to the appraiser not carefully reading the contract while preparing the report.

Appraisers Not Accustomed to Client's Requirements or Procedures

Many Appraisers become accustomed to writing appraisal reports for one type of client and find it difficult to meet requirements of a client requiring a substantially different type report. An example might be a condemnation attorney wanting only a "bare-bones" report for trial purposes and General Services Administration which needs a fully documented report.

Appraisers Using Less Experienced Help Without Adequate Supervision or Review

Some appraisers because of their professional designations or wide reputation are solicited for appraisals in preference to less experienced Appraisers and the appraisal is then prepared by a staff member or other Appraiser with apparently little, if any, review or supervision from the contract Appraiser. As a result, the reports are often sub-standard for a well-qualified Appraiser and the client feels gyped.

The Appraiser's responsibility is to thoroughly understand the contract specifications, the client's requirements and furnish a professional appraisal report. The Reviewer's responsibility is to see that the contractural specifications have been substantially complied with in the report.

DATA

Material Not Related to the Appraisal Problem

Appraisals are often loaded with "Chamber of Commerce" type data that the appraiser fails to relate to the subject appraisal problem. If the material is pertinent, it should be related to the subject. If not, leave it out.

Inadequate History of the Subject Property

The historical background of a property is extremely helpful to a reader who is not familiar with the property. This background aids the reader greatly in understanding the Appraiser's value conclusions.

Errors in Land or Building Areas

Mistakes are frequently found in land or building areas. Care should be exercised by both Appraiser and Reviewer to insure the accuracy of the property areas. An example of a possible error would be of a high-rise building where the superstitious owner left out the 13th floor and the Appraiser did not thoroughly check the building or plans.

Lack of Adequate Market Research

Appraisers who are after the "fast buck" frequently fail to make a thorough search of the market for sales or leases. In an active market there is little excuse for not having good current sales or leases to support the value conclusions.

Using Un-Comparable Comparables

The extreme of using inadequate comparable data is the use of comparables that are so far different from the subject that large adjustments are necessary. This is particularly hazardous in court cases as this opens the gate to wild speculations by the opposing side. The sales may be cited as having been considered but not used.

Failure to Fully Analyse Comparable Data

Even though a large number of comparables have been listed in the report, this of little help to the Reviewer without a thorough analysis and comparison of each with the subject. As an example, 20 land sales from $150.00 per acre to $1,500.00 per acre without analysis and comparison with the subject.

Using Different Methods of Area Measurements Between Comparables and Subject

Consistency is the key word in comparing comparable areas and the subject area—gross to gross, net to net, full floor to full floor, net rentable to net rentable. Substantial errors may result if this rule is not followed and proper adjustment made.

Inconsistent Adjustment Patterns

It is not uncommon for an Appraiser to make an adjustment in one approach, say the cost approach, for some feature or lack of feature in the subject by possibly capitalizing loss of rent and completely ignore it in the other approaches used.

Failure to Follow Through in the Analysis on Data in the Factual Presentation

Again, consistency is the key. Be sure the analysis of data has been reflected in the value conclusions.

Making Unsupported Adjustments

Percentage or dollar adjustments without supportive evidence is not very convincing. If at all possible, adjustments should be supported for such items as time, easements, etc. with facts and figures. If this is not possible, then convincing rationale should be furnished.

PREMISES AND TECHNIQUES

Failure to Properly Consider Restrictions

Restrictions can greatly affect values and should not be ignored or taken for granted. Windfall profits have resulted from changes in zoning. The probability of zoning changes should be carefully considered and possibly value estimates given based on present as well as probable zoning.

Inadequate Discussion of "Highest and Best Use"

The Highest and Best Use is the very heart of the appraisal. Probably more and greater divergencies in value conclusions result from differences in the Highest and Best Use concepts than any other single factor in appraising.

The highest and best use of some typical properties is obvious. However, if the highest and best use is considered to be something other than its original intended use or present use, it is deserving of careful study and thorough discussion.

Inconsistencies Between the Approaches to Value

Frequently Appraisers are not consistent in the approaches used relating to such factors as economic life, depreciation, net returns, etc. This obviously damages the credibility of the report and the Appraiser and should be avoided.

Values Not Consistent With Highest and Best Use

Occasionally Appraisers will use approaches to value based on a use other than the stated highest and best use. This usually occurs where there is a change of use or conversion.

This should only be done as a back-up to the approach based on the highest and best use and not as a substitute.

Lack of Clarity or Explanation

Often the Reviewer does not understand the Appraiser's rationale or reasoning. When asked, the Appraiser often explains it very satisfactorily in a few words. Appraisers should bear in mind that the reader may know only what is read in the report and a few words or a short paragraph can clarify much in the reader's mind.

Unsupported Capitalization Rates

With the exception of the Highest and Best use, probably no other factor affects the value conclusion more than the capitalization rate in the Income Approach.

In these times of controlled economy and fluctuating interest rates, it is of the greatest importance that the capitalization rates used be supported by the market and sound reasoning.

Using Techniques and Procedures Not Applicable To Problem

Many techniques and procedures are great tools but are fitted for specific uses and when misused can produce rather sad results. An example might be multiple regression which, if used on 1,000 properties, might produce excellent results but if used on five, could be disaster.

Relying Too Heavily on Mathematical Exercises, Formulas

Many mathematical exercises, formulas, curves, etc. have and are being written about, taught, and expounded upon. Some are good, some have limited use, and some have questionable value.

These, when presented in lectures or publications, are sometimes grabbed onto and used by Appraisers who may not have a clear understanding of the technique or circumstances under which it should be used and end up with results that are far from sound.

There is no substitute for sound judgment based upon research and experience; otherwise, we can be replaced by the computer.

All untried theories and formulas should be tested in the fires of reason and good common sense.

Inconsistent Updatings

The update appraisal, whether a substantial change in value has occurred or not, should indicate to the Reviewer that the Appraiser is familiar with the current market and the current condition of the property. If there is a substantial change in value, it should be well supported. Negotiations may be in progress, the board of directors may have met and concurred in the original report, so any change must be convincing and defensible.

REPORT PRODUCTION

Typing, Grammatical, and Punctuation Errors

The appraisal report is the Appraiser's product and will be judged to a greater or lesser degree by its appearance. If the report is full of typographical, grammatical, and puncutation errors, the Appraiser loses credibility, especially in the eyes of a casual reader.

Mathematical Errors

Errors in math do frequently appear in the best of appraisals. If mathematical changes have been made after the rough draft has been prepared, the figures often appear throughout the report, making it difficult to correct all of them.

The Appraiser should be doubly careful to check all figures and the Reviewer should also check to insure no mistakes have been made.

Poorly Reproduced Copies

Reports that are poorly reproduced not only give a poor appearance but at times are difficult, if not impossible, to read. This is especially true of carbon copies. Care should be exercised by the Appraiser to have all copies neat and legible. Attractive covers are desirable but elaborate covers and logos do not hide a poor quality appraisal.

In large appraisals, more than one volume makes for easier handling by the reader.

Poor Format

Some agencies develop their own format and should be followed by the Appraiser. In narrative reports the one that leads the Reviewer step by step in the thought process to the conclusion is the ideal. Having to flip pages back and forth and search through the report in reviewing takes time.

Poor Exhibits

Exhibits such as maps, photos, etc. are sometimes of little value to the Reviewer because of the poor quality or because they are not relevant.

Maps should be prepared so the properties can be located without difficulty. Photos should be of a quality that the Reviewer can have a reasonably good idea of the type, construction, and condition of the subject and comparable properties.

Hopefully, these comments will assist the Appraiser in

preparing a more acceptable report and aid the Reviewer by pointing out some of the more common errors and deficiencies.

May we all, through better communication, understand each other's situation more clearly.

May we all diligently strive to upgrade our profession through our own experience and through continuing education.

Below is a summary of some of the more common "Errors and Deficiencies" previously mentioned.

1. Requests not clear, complete or correct.
2. Contract specifications not followed.
3. Typing, Grammatical, and Punctuation Errors.
4. Mathematical Errors.
5. Poorly reproduced copies.
6. Poor Exhibits — Quality & Relevance.
7. Poor Format.
8. Appraisers not accustomed to clients' requirements or procedures.
9. Loading appraisal with "Chamber of Commerce", Type Data without relating factual Data to subject.
10. Inadequate history of property.
11. Errors in land or building areas (no 13th floor).
12. Failure to properly consider zoning or potential zoning and other restrictions affecting value.
13. Inadequate discussion of "Highest & Best Use".
14. Not adequately searching market for sales and leases.
15. Using comparables too far afield in size & use, which in condemnation, can open gate to wild speculation.
16. Failure to fully analyze and adjust all comparable data.
17. Abundant sales or rental data with little or no discussion relating these to the "Subject".
18. Not using same methods of measurement between comparables and subject — method used should be clear and consistent.
19. Inconsistent Adjustment Patterns.
20. Relying on mathematical exercises, formulas, curves; i.e., regressions, Stanford learning curves, Dilmore depth curve, etc.
21. Failure to follow through in the analysis on data in the factual presentation.

22. Values derived on assumptions not consistent with the highest and best used statement.
23. Inconsistencies between cost, market, and income approaches relating to economic life, depreciation, net returns, etc.
24. Making unsupprted adjustments; i.e., time, for easements, etc.
25. Using techniques and procedures not appropriate to the problem.
26. Capitalization rates not current or adequately supported from market.
27. Lack of clarity or explanation of Appraiser's reasoning or procedures.
28. Appraisers using less experienced without adequate supervision or review.
29. Updatings inconsistent with original findings.
    a. Going through the motions of updating without making any changes.
    b. Making substantial changes with weak justification.

PART II

Appraisal Review

CHAPTER TEN

Clerical Review for

Quality Control of

Form Appraisal Reports

RUSSELL L. JOHNSON, CRA

Russell L. Johnson, CRA, currently serves as Manager/Residential Appraising for Alaska Valuation Services, Inc. in Anchorage, Alaska. His duties include the appraisal of single and multi-family residences, vacant lots and acreage, commercial and condemnation reports, and their review.

In addition to being a Senior Member of the National Association of Review Appraisers, Mr. Johnson is an Associate member of the Society of Real Estate Appraisers.

Clerical Review for

Quality Control of

Form Appraisal Reports

This presentation is in three parts. Part one is an introduction intended to acquaint you with the need for quality control and a basic understanding of how this type of review evolved. Part two is a seven page Appraisal Review Analysis Form which is coordinated to a sample FHLMC Form 70/FNMA Form 1004 (Rev 7/79). There are eight major sections identified on both the Review Form and the Appraisal Form. They are correlated by alpha-numeric references, allowing the Reviewer to cross-reference those sections of the Appraisal Form to the Review Form.

The Review Form performs a double function: As a check for appraisal report completion and also for compliance with established underwriting guidelines. Thereby the form is multi-functional in that it draws attention to each major section of the form requiring a Clerical Reviewer to check sub-areas for completeness and compliance.

Part three is an instruction guide based on the methodology that I use locally for completion of the Appraisal Review Analysis form. I stress local because some of the methodology that is contained herein may be contrary to preference or completely irrelevant to any particularly underwriting situation. I instruct workshops to local lending institutions in the same manner in which I am presenting this to you. I always stress that it is flexible and can be customized to any particular need. Therefore, if an item does not meet with your preference, appraisal practice or underwriting criteria, you can simply delete, modify or add those instructions as may be applicable to your situation.

Throughout this presentation I will stress that it is for clerical review: That is, designed to supplement an established quality control system. It is not designed to replace or delete the necessity for a qualified, experienced quality review. Many of the lenders with whom I have worked have indicated that they find this a useful training aid for new personnel. In my capacity as a Residential Appraisal Manager, supervising seven field Appraisers, I have found it invaluable for both training and internal quality control as well.

The following presentation will give you some of the basic points that I cover when instructing individuals that are not Appraisers, but are clerically involved in the review of appraisal reports. It may seem somewhat sterile in this approach because I am not trying to teach these individuals how to be Appraisers or Review Appraisers. As Clerical Reviewers, I anticipate they will be able to review a Guide Form Appraisal only for completion and compliance with established guidelines. The qualitative part of the process is necessarily referred to other appropriately trained personnel.

PART I

The Guide Form Appraisal — Review for Quality Control

Appraisal report review and review appraising constitute two markedly different concepts in the review process. The former requires limited exposure to appraisal theory and practice and can be accomplished by properly instructed administrative personnel. The latter requires a broader background in theory and practice and should be performed only by appropriately trained individuals.

Both review concepts will be presented with particular emphasis on their role in an effective Quality Control System (QCS). A QCS, as used here, refers to a systematic process for the continual monitoring of the accuracy and completeness of credit and property information. One possible question raised in terms of appraisal is "Why do we need quality control?" If, after all, Appraisers are required to demonstrate competence prior to lender approval and investor acceptance, why then, should these "proven experts" be subject to review? The answer is simple: Appraising is an art! Predicated on scientific techniques perhaps, but nonetheless an art. The appraisal process is the application of proper techniques, tempered by educated judgement, culminating in a conclusion of value which is the *opinion* of the Appraiser.

The review process, as an integral part of the QCS, must also respond to apparent abuses in appraisal reporting by unqualified individuals. This is evidenced by investor tightening of acceptance procedures for Appraisers. However, the review process is not employed only to "catch" technical inaccuracy or Appraiser incompetence, but also to recognize and respond to established investor guidelines. Thereby we come to the basics of any review, the tricky part: Read the report.

Take, for example, the situation where the investor rejects a loan submission with a note something to the effect that the property did not meet their criteria for acceptance. What really hurts is when you pull the loan submission file, read the report, and find out that, in addition to an excellent credit verification, you have an equally excellent appraisal describing in minute detail the last remaining single family residence in an industrial zone heavily built up with conforming industrial uses and an estimated remaining economic life for the subject of 5 years. . . and you've closed the loan on a 25 year mortgage. But not to worry, the loan will pay off in 7 or 8 years. . . maybe. All you've lost is a little liquidity, right? Not so; you've also lost a ton of investor confidence. A comprehensive quality control system will include an effective appraisal review process geared to check not only for accuracy and completeness, but also to respond to established investor criteria for property acceptance.

Of significant importance in today's real estate financing in-dustry is the influence of the Federal Home Loan Mortgage Corporation (FHLMC) and the Federal National Mortgage Associ-ation (FNMA). These organizations have standardized mortgage loan purchase programs on a national basis which allow lenders around the country to sell mortgages not only to FNMA and FHLMC, but with greater liquidity between each other as well. This has been accomplished by nearly full standard formatting in credit reporting *and* property appraising. In this regard, the FHLMC/FNMA guide form appraisal and instructions for completion have set a national standard.

I believe certain review functions can be delegated to

competent administrative personnel by providing them with a formatted clerical review procedures.

This presentation will not teach the reader how to be an Appraiser. It will, hopefully, achieve its ultimate goal of providing a systematically consistent review of appraisal reports as required by a comprehensive Quality Control System.

PART II

BRANCH _____

LOAN PROCESSOR _____

APPRAISAL REVIEW ANALYSIS

(Intended primarily for review analysis of the

FHLMC Form 70/FNMA Form 1004, Revised 7/79)

1. File Information

Customer (Buyer) _____ Seller _____

Property Address _____

Proposed_____ Under Construction _____ Existing(yr.Blt) _____

SFR_____ Other (Specify)_____ Type & Design _____

Zone_____ Lot Size_____ Rights Appraised_____

Appraised Subject to: _____

Sales Price _____ Em Date _____ Loan Term _____

Est. FMV $ _____ As of _____ Firm _____

Investor Code _____ Appraiser # _____ Appraiser _____

Est. closing costs to be paid by Seller $ _____

2. Report Analysis

Instructions: The following questions are intended to evaluate the completeness of the guide form appraisal submitted by the Appraiser and to identify any areas of potential investor concern. Questions progress logically from neighborhood to final reconciliation and conclusion of value. Each question requires a response. Responses "X"d are flag items. Coordinate all flag items and/or indications of inconsistent adjustments with the staff or Review Appraiser or quality control officer.

A.   *Neighborhood:* Has the Appraiser —

   1.   Indicated any condition as Rural: Under 25%; Slow; Declining; Over supply; or over 6 months?
Yes__**X**__No_____

   2.   Indicated present land use "total" of 100%?
Yes_____ No__**X**__

   3.   Indicated either "likely" or "taking place" (in "Change in Present Land Use") Yes__**X**__ No_____

   4.   Reflected the Subject within the ranges indicated for "Price" and "Age"? Yes_____ No__**X**__

   5.   Indicated in the Neighborhood (Grid) any rating as "Fair" or "Poor"? Yes__**X**__ No_____

   6.   Reflected in "Comments" references consistent with and/or supportive of observations above.
Yes_____ No__**X**__

B.   *Site:* Has the Appraiser —

   1.   Indicated conformance to present zoning and present/proposed highest and best use? Yes_____ No__**X**__

   2.   Identified all utilities as to source or type? Yes_____ No__**X**__

   3.   Reflected Road Maintenance as Public?
Yes_____ No__**X**__

4. Identified a drainage problem or flood hazard condition? Yes__X__ No_____

5. Reflected in "Comments" references consistent with and/or supportive of observations above? Yes_____ No__X__

C. *Improvements:* Has the Appraiser —

1. Reflected subject in an age range consistent with the neighborhood? Yes_____ No__X__ (Correlates to question A4)

2. Identified by style and material? Exterior walls, roofing gutters and downspouts, windows, insulation and foundation walls? Yes_____ No__X__

3. Specified the material used and degree of finish in the basement, for ceiling, walls, and floors? Yes_____ No__X__

4. Reflected in "Comments" references consistent with and/or supportive of observations above. Yes_____ No__X__

D. *Room List:*

1. Count the number of rooms *above* the basement. Do they equal the total reflected in "Finished Area Above Grade?" Yes_____ No__X__ (This should also correlate to section G2a)

2. Do the square foot areas reflected in this section correlate to the Cost (F1) and Market (G2a) Data Section? Yes_____ No__X__

E. *Interior Finish & Equipment:* Has the Appraiser —

1. Included a refrigerator, washer, dryer, and/or other non-realty items in Estimate of Fair Market Value? Yes__X__ No_____

2. Identified heat type, fuel and condition? Yes_____ No__X__

3. Indicated adequate car storage? Yes_____ No__**X**__

4. Reflected a fair or poor rating in the Property Rating (Grid) Yes__**X**__ No_____

5. Reflected a Remaining Economic Life at or *less* than probable loan term? Yes__**X**__ No_____

6. Made any comments regarding physical or functional inadequacies or repairs needed? Yes__**X**__ No_____ (This should correlate to Sections F2, G2b, and H2)

F. *Cost Approach:*

1. Check the "measurements" for correct math and consistency to the dimensions indicated on the sketch. Are they correct? Yes_____ No__**X**__ (This should correlate to Sections D2 and G2a)

2. Are there any comments or adjustments on functional or economic obsolescence? Yes__**X**__ No_____

3. Check the calculations on Estimated Reproduction Cost New. Has the Appraiser extended and added them correctly? Yes_____ No__**X**__

4. Divided Estimated Land Value by the *final* conclusion of value. (Reflect percentage in left margin.)

G. *Market Data Approach:*

1. The Adjustment Grid.

    a. Re-add all adjustments for each comparable. Are calculations accurate? Yes_____ No__**X**__

    b. Does the "Net Adj-Total" (NA) of any comparable exceed 25% of that comparable's sales price (SP)? (NA - SP) = %). Yes__**X**__ No_____

    c. Does any *single* adjustment exceed 10% of the sale price of the comparable? Yes__**X**__ No_____

(Tests for Consistency in Adjustments)

It is logical to anticipate that the Appraiser has adjusted certain comparison units on a consistent basis. For example: Date of sale at the same monthly or annual rate; size differences on the same dollar amount per square foot, etc. In sections G1-d,e,f and g, specific techniques are shown to test these comparison units assuming they are adjusted in two or more comparables. Inordinate variances between two comparables in the same comparison unit should be questioned and, if the judgement is mute or inadequate, referred back to the Appraiser for support and justification.

d. Time Adjustments: Divide each time adjustment by the *sale price* for that comparable. Divide the quotient by the number of months between the date of sale (for that comparable) and the date of appraisal. Multiply this quotient by twelve (12). The product is an indication (as an annually adjusted rate) of the market response to date of sale. Example: A six month old sale of a $75,000 house is adjusted $2,200 (plus): $2,200 ÷ $75,000 = .00293. (0293 - 6) x 12 = .0589 (say 6% per year annually adjusted)

Comp #1__% Comp #2__% Comp #3__% (py)

e. Age Adjustments: Divide each age adjustment by the number of years difference in age between the Subject and the comparable. The quotient is the indication (in dollars per year) of market response to age differences. Example: The Subject is effectively 5 years old, the comparable is 7 years and the adjustment is $1,000 (plus): 1,000 ÷ 2 = $500 per year. (Circle inconsistent indicators)

Comps #1_____ #2_____ #3$_____(py)

f.

Gross Livable Area Adjustments: Divided each comparables Gross Living Area (GLA) by the difference in square feet between the subject and the comparable. The quotient is the indication (in dollars per square foot) of market response to size differences. Example: The subject is 1,500 sq.ft., the Comparable is 1,400 sq.ft. and the adjustment is $1,500 (Plus): 1,500 sq. ft. - 1,400 sq. ft. = 100 sq.ft. $1,500 ÷100 sq. ft. = $15 per sq.ft.

Comp #1 $__psf Comp #2 $__psf Comp #3 $__

g. Basement Area Adjustments: Repeat procedure (in "f" above) for basement areas.
Comp #1 $____psf #2 $____psf #3 $____psf

2. Cross Check Adjustments for Consistency to other sections.

   a. Does the (subject) Living Area, Room Count and Total Gross Living Area (GLA); Basement and Basement Finished Rooms (area) correlate to the measurements in the Cost Approach (F1) and in the Room List, (D1)? Yes_____ No__**X**__

   b. Are there any adjustments for Functional Utility?: Yes__**X**__ No_____ (Correlate to F2 and E6)

   c. Is there adjustment for Energy Efficient Items? (E6) Yes__**X**__ No_____

   d. Are there any comments pertinent to adverse conditions or marketability? Yes__**X**__ No_____ (A6/B5/C4/E6)

H. *Reconciliation:*

   1. Has the appraiser made any requirements or conditions of the appraisal? Yes ___**X**___ No_____
   (if yes, tickle file for follow up)

   2. Has the Final Conclusion been weighted or other than that indicated by the Market Data Approach? Yes__**X**__ No_____
   (Refer to Quality Reviewer for verification of support).

3. Has the Appraiser indicated participation in a Home Warranty Program? Yes__**X**__ No_____
(If yes, you may need a copy of the warranty for the investor).

4. Has an Approved Appraiser dated and signed the report, attached a perimeter sketch (with pictures) and a location map; attached a signed/dated certification with Contingent and Limiting Conditions?
Yes_____ No__**X**__

ALASKA VALUATION SERVICE, INC.

550 WEST 54TH AVE. · ANCHORAGE, ALASKA 99502
(907) 278-3537 • 277-8675

RESIDENTIAL APPRAISAL REPORT

File No.

Borrower	Census Tract Map Reference
Property Address	Tax No.
City County	State Zip Code
Legal Description	
Sale Price $ Date of Sale Loan Term yrs	Property Rights Appraised ☐ Fee ☐ Leasehold ☐ DeMinimis PUD
Actual Real Estate Taxes $ (yr) Loan charges to be paid by seller $	Other sales concessions
Lender/Client	Address
Occupant Appraiser	Instructions to Appraiser (A-5)

To be completed by Lender

NEIGHBORHOOD

				Good Avg. Fair Poor
Location	☐ Urban	☐ Suburban	☑ Rural (A-1)	
Built Up	☐ Over 75%	☐ 25% to 75%	☐ Under 25%	Employment Stability ☐☐☐☐
Growth Rate ☐ Fully Dev.	☐ Rapid	☐ Steady	☐ Slow (A-1)	Convenience to Employment ☐☐☐☐
Property Values	☐ Increasing	☐ Stable	☐ Declining	Convenience to Shopping ☐☐☐☐
Demand/Supply	☐ Shortage	☐ In Balance	☐ Over Supply	Convenience to Schools ☐☐☐☐
Marketing Time	☐ Under 3 Mos.	☐ 4–6 Mos.	☐ Over 6 Mos.	Adequacy of Public Transportation ☐☐☐☐

(A-2)

Present Land Use ___% 1 Family ___% 2–4 Family ___% Apts. ___% Condo ___% Commercial — Recreational Facilities ☐☐☐☐
___% Industrial ___% Vacant ___% — Adequacy of Utilities ☐☐☐☐
Change in Present Land Use ☐ Not Likely ☐ Likely (*) ☑ Taking Place (*) (A-3) — Property Compatibility ☐☐☐☐
(*) From _____ To _____ — Protection from Detrimental Conditions ☐☐☐☐
Predominant Occupancy ☐ Owner ☐ Tenant ___% Vacant — Police and Fire Protection ☐☐☐☐
Single Family Price Range $ ___ to $ ___ Predominant Value $ ___ — General Appearance of Properties ☐☐☐☐
Single Family Age (A-4) ___ yrs to ___ yrs Predominant Age ___ yrs — Appeal to Market ☐☐☐☐

Note: FHLMC/FNMA do not consider race or the racial composition of the neighborhood to be reliable appraisal factors.
Comments including those factors, favorable or unfavorable, affecting marketability (e.g. public parks, schools, view, noise) _____

(A-6)

SITE

Dimensions (B-1) ___ = ___ Sq. Ft. or Acres ☐ Corner Lot
Zoning classification _____ Present improvements ☐ do ☐ do not conform to zoning regulations
Highest and best use: ☐ Present use ☐ Other (specify) _____

OFF SITE IMPROVEMENTS
Public Other (Describe)
Elec. ☐ — Street Access: ☐ Public ☐ Private (B-3) — Topo _____
Gas ☐ (B-2) — Surface _____ — Size _____
Water ☐ — Maintenance: ☐ Public ☐ Private — Shape _____
San.Sewer ☐ — ☐ Storm Sewer ☐ Curb/Gutter — View (B-4) _____
☐ Underground Elect. & Tel. ☐ Sidewalk ☐ Street Lights — Drainage _____
Is the property located in a HUD Identified Special Flood Hazard Area? ☐ No ☐ Yes
Comments (favorable or unfavorable including any apparent adverse easements, encroachments or other adverse conditions) _____

(B-5) (C-1)

IMPROVEMENTS

☐ Existing ☐ Proposed ☐ Under Constr. No. Units ___ Type (det, duplex, semi/det, etc.) Design (rambler, split level, etc.) Exterior Walls (C-2)
Yrs. Age: Actual ___ Effective ___ to ___ No. Stories ___
Roof Material (C-2) Gutters & Downspouts ☐ None Window (Type): (C-2) Insulation ☐ None ☐ Floor
☐ Storm Sash ☐ Screens ☐ Combination ☐ Ceiling ☐ Roof ☐ Walls
☐ Manufactured Housing ___% Basement ☐ Floor Drain Finished Ceiling _____
Foundation Walls (C-2) ☐ Outside Entrance ☐ Sump Pump Finished Walls _____
BSMT ☐ Concrete Floor ___% Finished (C-3) Finished Floor _____ (C-3)
☐ Slab on Grade ☐ Crawl Space Evidence of: ☐ Dampness ☐ Termites ☐ Settlement
Comments (C-4) _____

ROOM LIST

Room List	Foyer	Living	Dining	Kitchen	Den	Family Rm.	Rec. Rm.	Bedrooms	No. Baths	Laundry	Other
Basement											
1st Level (D-1)								(D-2)			
2nd Level											

(E-1)

Finished area above grade contains a total of ___ rooms ___ bedrooms ___ baths. Gross Living Area ___ sq.ft. Bsmt Area ___ sq.ft.

INTERIOR FINISH & EQUIPMENT

Kitchen Equipment: ☑ Refrigerator ☐ Range/Oven ☐ Disposal ☐ Dishwasher ☐ Fan/Hood ☐ Compactor ☐ Washer ☐ Dryer (E-4)
HEAT: Type ___ Fuel ___ Cond. ___ AIR COND: ☐ Central ☐ Other ___ ☐ Adequate ☐ Inadequate

			Good Avg. Fair Poor
Floors (E-2) ☐ Hardwood ☐ Carpet Over ☐	(E-1)		
Walls ☐ Drywall ☐ Plaster ☐	Quality of Construction (Materials & Finish)	☐☐☐☐
Trim/Finish ☐ Good ☐ Average ☐ Fair ☐ Poor	Condition of Improvements	☐☐☐☐
Bath Floor ☐ Ceramic ☐	Room sizes and layout	☐☐☐☐
Bath Wainscot ☐ Ceramic ☐	Closets and Storage	☐☐☐☐
Special Features (including energy efficient items) ___	Insulation—adequacy	☐☐☐☐

PROPERTY RATING

Plumbing—adequacy and condition ☐☐☐☐
Electrical—adequacy and condition ☐☐☐☐
Kitchen Cabinets—adequacy and condition ☐☐☐☐
ATTIC: ☐ Yes ☐ No ☐ Stairway ☐ Drop-stair ☐ Scuttle ☐ Floored — Compatibility to Neighborhood ☐☐☐☐
Finished (Describe) _____ ☐ Heated — Overall Livability ☐☐☐☐
CAR STORAGE: ☐ Garage ☐ Built-in ☐ Attached ☐ Detached ☐ Car Port — Appeal and Marketability (E-5) ☐☐☐☐
No. Cars ___ ☐ Adequate ☐ Inadequate Condition ___ — Yrs Est Remaining Economic Life ___ to ___ Explain if less than Loan Term

FIREPLACES, PATIOS, POOL, FENCES, etc. (describe) _____
(E-3)

COMMENTS (including functional or physical inadequacies, repairs needed, modernization, etc.) _____
(E-6)

FHLMC Form 70 Rev. 7/79   ATTACH DESCRIPTIVE PHOTOGRAPHS OF SUBJECT PROPERTY AND STREET SCENE   FNMA Form 1004 Rev. 7/79

VALUATION SECTION

Purpose of Appraisal is to estimate Market Value as defined in Certification & Statement of Limiting Conditions (FHLMC Form 439/FNMA Form 1004B). If submitted for FNMA, the appraiser must attach (1) sketch or map showing location of subject, street names, distance from nearest intersection, and any detrimental conditions and (2) exterior building sketch of improvements showing dimensions.

COST APPROACH

Measurements — No. Stories — Sq. Ft. *(F-1)*

ESTIMATED REPRODUCTION COST – NEW – OF IMPROVEMENTS:
Dwelling ___ Sq. Ft. @ $ ___ = $ *(F-3)*
Extras ___
Special Energy Efficient Items ___
Porches, Patios, etc. ___
Garage/Car Port ___ Sq. Ft. @ $ ___
Site Improvements (driveway, landscaping, etc.)
Total Estimated Cost New = $
Less Physical | Functional | Economic
Depreciation $ | $ | $ = $
Depreciated value of improvements *(F-2)* = $
ESTIMATED LAND VALUE = $ *(F-4)*
(If leasehold, show only leasehold value)
INDICATED VALUE BY COST APPROACH = $ *(F-3)*

Total Gross Living Area (List in Market Data Analysis below) ___
Comment on functional and economic obsolescence: ___ *(F-2)*

MARKET DATA ANALYSIS

The undersigned has recited three recent sales of properties most similar and proximate to subject and has considered these in the market analysis. The description includes a dollar adjustment, reflecting market reaction to those items of significant variation between the subject and comparable properties. If a significant item in the comparable property is superior to, or more favorable than, the subject property, a minus (-) adjustment is made, thus reducing the indicated value of subject; if a significant item in the comparable is inferior to, or less favorable than, the subject property, a plus (+) adjustment is made, thus increasing the indicated value of the subject.

ITEM	Subject Property	COMPARABLE NO. 1		COMPARABLE NO. 2		COMPARABLE NO. 3	
Address							
Proximity to Subj.							
Sales Price	$	$		$		$	
Price/Living area	$	$		$		$	
Data Source							
Date of Sale and Time Adjustment	DESCRIPTION	DESCRIPTION	Adjustment *(G1d)*	DESCRIPTION	Adjustment *(G1d)*	DESCRIPTION	Adjustment *(G1d)*
Location							
Site/View							
Design and Appeal							
Quality of Const.							
Age			*(G1e)*		*(G1e)*		*(G1e)*
Condition							
Living Area Room Count and Total	Total B-rms Baths	Total B-rms Baths *(G2a)*	*(G1f)*	Total B-rms Baths *(G2a)*	*(G1f)*	Total B-rms Baths *(G2a)*	*(G1f)*
Gross Living Area	Sq.Ft. *(G1c)*	Sq.Ft.	*(G1g)*	Sq.Ft.	*(G1g)*	Sq.Ft.	*(G1g)*
Basement & Bsmt. Finished Rooms		*(G2b)*		*(G2b)*		*(G2b)*	
Functional Utility							
Garage/Car Port							
Porches, Patio, Pools, etc.							
Special Energy Efficient Items			*(G2c)*		*(G2c)*		*(G2c)*
Other (e.g. fireplaces, kitchen equip., remodeling)							
Sales or Financing Concessions							
Net Adj. (Total)		☐ Plus; ☐ Minus $ *(G1ab)*		☐ Plus; ☐ Minus $ *(G1ab)*		☐ Plus; ☐ Minus $ *(G1ab)*	
Indicated Value of Subject		$		$		$	

Comments on Market Data *(G2d)*

INDICATED VALUE BY MARKET DATA APPROACH ___ $ *(H2)*
INDICATED VALUE BY INCOME APPROACH (If applicable) Economic Market Rent $ ___ /Mo. x Gross Rent Multiplier ___ = $ *(H2)*
This appraisal is made ☐ "as is" ☐ subject to the repairs, alterations, or conditions listed below ☐ completion per plans and specifications.
Comments and Conditions of Appraisal: *(H1)*

Final Reconciliation *(H2)* *(H3)*

Construction Warranty ☐ Yes ☐ No Name of Warranty Program ___ Warranty Coverage Expires ___
This appraisal is based upon the above requirements, the certification, contingent and limiting conditions, and Market Value definition that are stated in
☐ FHLMC Form 439 (Rev. 10/78)/FNMA Form 1004B (Rev. 10/78) filed with client ___ 19 ___ ☐ attached.
I ESTIMATE THE MARKET VALUE, AS DEFINED, OF SUBJECT PROPERTY AS OF *(H4)* 19 ___ to be $ ___

Appraiser(s) *(H4)* ___ Review Appraiser (If applicable) ___
☐ Did ☐ Did Not Physically Inspect Property

FHLMC Form 70 Rev. 7/79   REVERSE   FNMA Form 1004 Rev. 7/79

PART III

We'll start with page 1 of the Review Form. File Information: I believe this is relatively self-explanatory and can be customized to fit any particular underwriting or appraisal situation. Report Analysis: These are brief instructions on the completion of the Review Form. Pages 2-7 comprise 43 "questions", designed to draw the Clerical Reviewer's attention to each section of the appraisal report. Most questions provide for a circled or uncircled response. A yes or no answer circled may be of potential concern. It is not necessarily the Clerical Reviewer's job to determine if it's right or wrong, but to recognize that it exists and will require coordination to resolve it.

Section A — Neighborhood

Questions A-1 through A-6 perform the task of drawing the reader's attention to those areas of the neighborhood that must be completed. It is important to stress here that "flagged" responses do not automatically indicate an improper or unacceptable appraisal. The primary goal of this form is to evaluate it for two purposes: (1) completeness, and (2) investor acceptance (in an appraisal operation, it would be for internal quality control).

The Clerical Reviewer performs the important function of identifying potential problem areas. A Quality Reviewer will be responsible to determine if those areas require additional contact with the Appraiser or can be resolved internally.

Section B — Site Data

Questions B-1 through B-5 follow the same logic as the previous section. Completeness is the primary goal, compliance is the secondary goal. For example, if question B-3 is flagged "No", it indicates that either that section is incomplete or the Appraiser checked "Private" for road maintenance. This may entail (in all likelihood) a followup for determination of the method of road maintenance. Likewise, question B-4, on flood and drainage conditions, may be flagged "Yes". It may be necessary to obtain flood hazard insurance or require that proper drainage be provided. Question B-5, like question A-6 in neighborhood, is a summary analysis of the Appraiser's observations for Site Data.

Section C — Improvements

Questions C-1 through C-4. Following the same logic as presented in sections A and B, we now move to improvements analysis. The Clerical Reviewer will again check for completeness and compliance. I did not feel it necessary to flag every sub-area within a section in order to achieve the goal of a comprehensive review. In other underwriting situations, it may be advantageous or even mandatory that more specific information be required.

In the "Improvements Section", all the questions presumably should have a "yes" response. A "No" response indicates the Appraiser has either failed to complete the section or that the information is contrary to underwriting guidelines. For example: Question C-2 inquires as to the type and material of various components. Suppose that the Appraiser says "yes" in the appraisal block for "Exterior Wall". I suspect that this would be unacceptable to most underwriting situations because the object is to identify wall material. The Clerical Reviewer would likely be required to flag this in the review.

Section D — Room List

Questions D-1 through D-2. As we go through the Review Form, we now move to the first section that must correlate to other areas within the appraisal. A no response to either question indicates either incompletion or inconsistency. When this exists, it is necessary to coordinate with the Quality Reviewer.

Section E — Interior Finish & Equipment

Questions E-1 through E-6. This section deals with the Appraiser's observations as to the quality, condition and accuracy of descriptions of Interior Finish and Equipment. As in previous sections, not all flagged responses automatically presume an Appraiser error or an unacceptable report. The multi-functional nature of the Review Format presumes a qualitative analysis subsequent to the clerical review.

Section F — Cost Approach

Questions F-1 through F-4. The Clerical Reviewer will now perform a crosscheck of the math used by the Appraiser. It is not the Clerical Reviewer's responsibility to determine whether or not the Appraiser has used supportable cost data. Rather,the Clerical Reviewer is following the same premise established in the previous sections of checking for completion (and have the accuracy) of the data used by the Appraiser. I have identified throughout, those sub-sections that most frequently are in question and create the greatest amount of concern in my own situation. You may find additional information you wish to expand or cross-reference or even delete according to your own particular needs. For example, Question F-4 is important to us especially when land value is significantly disproportionate to whole property value. This, however, may be of no consequence in your geographic area or require more specific action.

Section G — Market Data Approach

Questions G-1-a through G-1-g. Let's take each of the following "questions" separately and see how it may or may not fit into your particular situation. Question G-1-a is relatively self-explanatory. It is a simple math process to determine accuracy. Question G-1-b provides a test whereby the Clerical Reviewer wil flag any comparable in which the net adjusted total exceeds 25% of that comparable's sale price. Again, it is not an automatic presumption of inaccuracy or error, but if one or more of the comparables are so adjusted (and not properly qualified by the Appraiser) it may raise questions as to the acceptable nature of that comparison. The problem is now for the Quality Reviewer to determine whether or not the Appraiser has qualified the adjustments and supported their extensions in this particular situation. Question G-1-c is similar to the G-1-b as to any single adjustment within the Market Data grid. Questions G-1-d,e,f & g are tests for consistency and because they are somewhat more complicated in clerical review than the previous information, the Review Form provides an explanation establishing the justification for their use and method of derivation. These methods are based on my own experiences and this may vary in application from one part of the country to another. For example, I desire to reduce time adjustments to an indicated percentage per year. In different geographic areas, an indication of a dollar amount per month or per year may be more appropriate. Concurrently, I have applied my own presumption to the extractions for age and gross living areas. I could fathom some disagreement or difference of opinion as to their application in the clerical review process. Again clerical review is only the first step in quality control. After the clerical review, a Quality Reviewer should be charged with responsibility for evaluating flag items and for qualifying acceptance in each particular underwriting situation. In a limited staff or high volume operation, the clerical review can greatly expedite the review process.

Section G-2 — Cross Check Adjustments for Consistency

Questions G-2-a, b, c, d are concerned with, again, identifying the completion of this information and its consistency with specific sub-areas in other sections.

Section H — Reconciliation

Questions H-1 through H-4. The logic employed throughout the Review Form is continued here. The Clerical Reviewer will verify completion of the sub-areas in this section and flag those items that may require correlation with the Quality Reviewer. The only question that needs perhaps a little more explanation is question H-2. This question asks if the final conclusion has been weighted on other than that indicated by the Market Data Approach. There are two other approaches typically used in the appraisal process: Cost and Income. It is not the Clerical Reviewer's responsibility to determine whether or not the Appraiser is justified in weighting other approaches, but the Clerical Reviewer should flag any comments pertinent to this indication. A determination will have to be made by the Quality Reviewer as to whether or not the Appraiser has justified any extensions of Cost or Income to a value conclusion.

CHAPTER ELEVEN

Reviewing the Single Family Residence

STEPHEN P. BYE, CRA

Stephen P. Bye, CRA, is an Appraiser/Reviewer for Coldwell Banker in Denver, Colorado. He received his B.B.A. from the University of Wisconsin in Real Estate and Urban Land Economics. He also received his M.B.A. from the University of Wisconsin in Real Estate Investment Analysis and Appraisal.

Mr. Bye is a Senior Member of the National Association of Review Appraisers and holds the "Certified Review Appraiser" designation.

Reviewing the

Single Family

Residence

Introduction

The estimate of value of a single family residence may be more difficult to predict with reasonable accuracy than estimating the value of a multi-million dollar commercial property due to the unpredictability of the market players. Single family purchasers and sellers are oftentimes unsophisticated,uninformed, and are occasionally forced to act under pressure. Therefore, many sales do not fall within the common definition of "market value". This, in turn, results in several judgements which a Review Appraiser must make.

Appraising is not an exact science and this is the most important concept that a Reviewer must keep in mind at all times. Pin-point judgement is not included in the duties of a Reviewer. Rather, the establishment of levels or probabilities of acceptance or of reasonableness should be the methodology used.

A Review Appraiser must recognize and must have shared common problems experienced by most field Appraisers to be objective in a judgement capacity. In addition, the Reviewer must be an expert in appraisal theory. The review process is analogous to a courtroom trial in several ways. First of all, the facts in any number of legal cases, or properties, will never be the same.

Second, the facts or the testimony is presented differently by each counsel, or Appraiser, as the case may be. Third, courtroom procedures, or the appraisal form, are used as the basis for the presentation of the facts of testimony. Fourth, case law, or appraisal theory, is used as the basis for the verdict. Finally, the judge or the Review Appraiser arrives at a final conclusion and acts on that decision. Therefore, for any appraisal, the Reviewer reads the appraisal facts, weighs the valuation procedures, consults "case law" on appraisal theory, and then arrives at a final conclusion of value.

In the remainder of this discussion, several rules of thumb or definitions are presented and may appear to be a set of rules or ultimate solutions to reviewing appraisals. However, my intentions are merely to provide my opinions based on several years of reviewing single family appraisals and to uncover some controversial issues. By no means should a Review Appraiser attempt to subscribe to a predetermined set of formulas. Rather, common sense should rule the review process.

Forms

Like an author, the duty of a field Appraiser is to lead a potential reader logically through the report. The final conclusion must be well supported and documented. First of all, an appraisal must contain a description section and a valuation section. The description should contain all neighborhood information, a detailed outline of the subject property in both quantitative and qualitative terms, and certain observations or judgements regarding its physical characteristics. The valuation section must contain market extracted support in the form f either comparable sales, a market related gross income multiplier analysis, and/or a cost approach. The Review Appraiser is either aided or handicapped by the detail and adaptability of the form to the type of property under appraisal.

FHLMC Form #70/FNMA Form #1004 is one appraisal form which is all-encompassing with provisions for a large amount of detailed information that is vital for a complete understanding of the property for any reader. Generally, it could be said that if the report is fully completed with detailed information, the Reviewer should be presented with a realistic synopsis of a property. However, I do not feel that all of the lines and boxes have to be filled out, as some items may not be applicable or may be inappropriate for the property in question. In such instances, the field Appraiser may wish to insert the words "not applicable".

Lenders, fee Appraisers, and other real estate oriented organizations often create their own appraisal forms to meet certain requirements or to collect information. The Review Appraiser should take an active part in the design of the form or should at least be aware of the reason behind the design of the form. Finally, Review Appraisers should encourage field Appraisers to add amendments to the appraisal form to elaborate on certain problems or unusual circumstances.

Appearance

Review Appraisers must demand a legible report which is professional in appearance. A Review Appraiser can sometimes assess the credibility of the field Appraiser if the report is filled with grammatical errors, punctuation mistakes, misspelled words, or smudges on the report pages.

A form report need not be typed, but should be neatly written or printed. Abbreviations should be avoided to avoid misinterpretation. Additional comments should not be squeezed into a predesignated section of the form when an addendum could be used.

Errors often occur, especially in the adjustment section of the market approach. Therefore, all calculations supplied by the field Appraiser should be carefully scrutinized.

Despite the argument that neat and legible appraisals may reflect the meticulousness of the field Appraiser, just having all of the "i's" dotted and the "t's" crossed does not mean that the appraisal is acceptable.

Photographs and Supporting Illustrations

Photographs are usually necessary since the Reviewer needs to establish a visual reference. Furthermore, a photo may verify the physical description contained in the report. Rear and side photos of the improvement may add a further visual reference, but typically are not necessary unless for unusual conditions. Street scenes are good, but an astute field Appraiser can select a camera angle which obscures an adjacent detrimental property. Oblique aerial photos are invaluable as they will give the reader a "bird's eye" view of the location in reference to the surrounding area and land uses. Aerial photos are typically not justified for a single family residential appraisal, however.

Site plans or plot plans are informative, but may not be necessary in platted or subdivided areas where lots are similar and conforming. Unusual properties involving such conditions as setback violations, shared driveways, high ground coverage, restrictive or adverse easements, etc., are situations where a site plan may be helpful. Subdivision or plat map requirements should be adhered to in similar situations. Area or city location maps, census tract maps, zip code maps, etc. may be helpful, especially if the Review Appraiser is not familiar with a particular community or neighborhood.

Supporting data and photos of comparables should be required in unusual circumstances and in cases where the accurate determination of value is extremely important. However, the photos and multiple listing information may not be as revealing as the field Appraiser's observations.

Plans and specifications on proposed dwellings may be important, especially where the structure has an unconventional architectural design. In the case of tract development, if the field Appraiser has inspected the model home, he or she should be qualified to value a proposed dwelling of the same design, despite the fact that there may be upgrades and minor alterations. In all cases, the Review Appraiser must be acquainted with the construction materials, design, finish items, site improvements, etc., with each locale as well as the costs. Field inspection trips and discussions with local building contractors are suggested as the most successful way to bridge this gap.

Quality Control Procedures

An astute Review Appraiser will quickly learn that reliance upon the field appraisal report may lead to inaccurate value conclusions. Field Appraisers have been known to produce false property information or to select a subset of inappropriate market comparables.

If an appraisal appears highly questionable, the Review Appraiser should consider a field inspection trip to analyze the situation first-hand. If a trend is detected in reference to a particular Appraiser, lending institution, geographic location, property type, or dwelling age, a personal inspection is certainly necessary. Meetings are suggested with field Appraisers in order to capture as much of their local real estate knowledge as possible, as well as to assess their professionalism. In addition, an inspection of the field Appraisers' offices and files may be enlightening.

Where field inspections and Appraiser contact are not possible, the use of spot check appraisals may aid in the review process. The selection of field Review Appraisers is vital to maintain a level of independence. The detail of a field review will vary depending upon the importance of the case. Drive-by inspections are sufficient where the purpose of the review is to verify the property description and location or to verify the existence of comparable sales that were presented by the field Appraiser. Where the establishment of value is important, each independent field Review Appraiser must fully inspect the property and must not consult with the original field Appraiser.

There are also a number of computer simulation models which may assist the Review Appraiser. One widely known program develops on-line cost information for every major city in the United States, which will be helpful in verifying cost figures used in a field appraisal. The most widely known market data model is the MULVAR system which is sponsored by the Society of Real Estate Appraisers, with data supplied through the SREA Market Data Center. Other programs such as Educare also involve the use of multiple regression and bring an entire new element into review appraising through the application of statistics.

Conditions and Pertinent Information

The Review Appraiser must be aware of the following assumptions, conditions and other vital information before the review can begin:
1. Property address and legal description
2. Property rights appraised (fee simple, leasehold, condo, etc.)
3. Effective date of the appraisal.
4. Date the property was inspected.
5. Contingent events or circumstance such as:
   a. subject to zoning change
   b. subject to repairs or alterations
   c. subject to completion in a workmanship manner according to plans and specifications
6. A copy of a statement of limiting conditions
7. Type of financing, if any
8. Definition of market value.

Location

The Review Appraiser is normally very interested in the property location information which ranges from the macro market to the micro market. Because real estate is fixed in location, value is largely determined by the impact of external market forces and, in particular, the forces of supply and demand. Both the field Appraiser and the Review Appraiser must identify the forces at work, measure the broad impact on the macro market, on the micro market, and, in particular, on the property being appraised. Although there are quantitative formulas available, the typical Appraiser will rely on mass media to evaluate these environmental, political, economic, or social factors. These determinants are difficult to measure, especially in advance. However, we are all familiar with examples of the following phenomena on the real estate market:

1. Gas rationing
2. Double digit inflation rates
3. Double digit interest rates
4. Smog, pollution, weather conditions
5. Taxes and public services
6. Industry strikes, layoffs, expansion
7. Population migration
8. Neighborhood revitalization
9. Recreational development

Not every area of the United States has experienced an inflation in residential values over the past decade. Why have some sections of the country witnessed an increase of residential property values of 20% while other areas have struggled through a decline? These are important factors which a Review Appraiser must be familiar with. National real estate publications, newspapers, and other periodicals are the most convenient method for the Review Appraiser to keep reasonably informed.

A Review Appraiser who may be reviewing local property appraisals certainly must be aware of all factors which would affect the local real estate market. Other Reviewers, however, may be hundreds or thousands of miles from the subject property. In such cases, it is suggested that the Review Appraiser keep in close contact with all forms of public media, conduct personal inspections, and consult with local experts.

Neighborhood Location

The questions of neighborhood description and definition have certainly come under close scrutiny over the past decade, especially in the residential sector, as outgrowths of various government legislation such as the Fair Housing Act of 1968, the Civil Rights Act of 1964, the Home Loan Disclosure Act, and the Equal Credit Opportunity Act. Unfortunately, discrimination has been and continues to be a reality in housing. Several court decisions such as Trifficante v. Metropolitan Life Insurance Company; Lauffman v. Oakley Building and Loan Company; Harrison v. Heinzeroth Mortgage Company; and Griggs v. Duke Power Company have concentrated on housing discrimination as related to the lending industry. The most recent cases have concentrated on the "effects test", or in other words, whether the actions of certain individuals or groups have discriminated against other minority groups, even though there was no expressed intent. The most recent case, United States v. AIREA, etal., represents the most contemporary view on discrimination from an appraisal standpoint. The significance of the case is that the suit filed by the Justice Department was dismissed against the Institute of Real Estate Appraisers and the Society of Real Estate Appraisers on the grounds that no evidence could be found that these organizations encouraged their members to treat race or national origin as a negative factor in determining the value of dwellings nor could it be determined that these groups instructed the members that dwellings in racially integrated areas have a substantially lower value than similarly located dwellings in racially homogenous areas. Finally, there was no proof that these organizations subscribed to the belief that the infiltration of blacks and other minorities into a geographic area was an important factor in lowering the value of homes of that area. The upshot of the suit was the acceptance of the Policy Statement issued by the Society of Real Estate Appraisers. This Appraiser, being a member of the Society of Real Estate Appraisers, subscribes to this Policy Statement and I am writing this article in the spirit of that Statement.

An Appraiser must objectively evaluate the economic, social, political, and physical forces of a neighborhood, as well as other significant determinants which have an impact on the valuation process. As indicated previously, real estate is a fixed asset with external forces continually influencing it. The Appraiser must recognize these factors and evalute the impact on the neighborhood. The recognition and evaluation, however, must be objective and must be unbiased with reference to race, color, religion, sex, national origin or other minority group. To quote the "Policy Statement: SREA Educational Professional Concepts Relating to Neighborhood Analysis and the Formation for an

Opinion of Value of Properties Located in Residential Settings"
which appeared in the March 21, 1979 issue of *Appraisal Briefs:*
"... neighborhood factors and forces, being in a
constant of change, must be observed, recorded and
analyzed with the recognition that some of those
factors and forces are not readily susceptible to
quantitative analysis. Extreme care must be taken in
articulating and considering any factor or force which
is not easily measured.

The responsible Appraiser must recognize that the
dynamic interplay of neighborhood forces and factors
directly affects the opinions and hence the behavior
of buyers and sellers of property within a neighborhood setting. These opinions, like the neighborhood
dynamics, are constantly changing."

One important point must be made here — racial, religious, or
ethnic composition may or may not have a relationship on value,
neighborhood stability, or compatibility. We subscribe to the
principle that there is no predetermined relationship of value
with race, religion, color, or national origin, etc. Any correlation
must be well documented or supported without bias. Similarly, a
property's convenience to shopping, adequacy of public
transportation, availability of public utilities, for example, may or
may not have a direct relationship with value, neighborhood
stability, or compatibility. Any statement suggesting that it did
must be supported with strong market data, and also without
bias.

How does one define a neighborhood? Traditional definitions
indicate that the neighborhood is defined by physical
boundaries, political boundaries, or land use. The "extent" of a
neighborhood, its size, or other measurements are the
judgement of the field Appraiser based on observations and
experience in the marketplace. For most Appraisers, the
definition of a neighborhood must be a homogeneous area and
therefore, somewhat limited in size. To others, it may encompass
a large geographic area composed of a variety of land uses.

The Review Appraiser must receive a clear definition of
neighborhood from the field Appraiser. Principally, the Review
Appraiser must be made aware of all supportable factors which
have a direct external influence on the subject property. Again, I
emphasize that such factors must be unbiased with respect to
minorities as discussed above. The State of California
Department of Savings and Loan has described proximity to the

subject property in consideration of "localized factor" (the neighborhood) in Subchapter 24, Chapter 2, Title 10, California Administration Code — "Guidelines Relating to Fair Lending" as "only those blocks and sides of blocks that are likely to most directly impact on the security property". The following exhibit, used in Subchapter of the "Code", illustrates the shaded areas as the subject property with the dashed lines representing those block sides which might most directly impact uon the subject property.

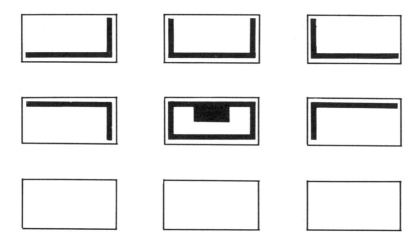

I would strongly suggest that the Review Appraiser emphasize to the field Appraiser that the Neighborhood be defined in the appraisal and that all comments stated indicate only those external forces which have a direct impact upon the subject property. I subscribe to the theory that the neighborhood be defined to as small a geographic area as possible and, hopefully, to the definition stated by the California Department of Savings and Loans.

The Review Appraiser is normally interested in locational factors which promote stability, compatibility, or other measurements of market acceptance. The FHLMC/FNMA form recognizes the following factors which appear to be categorized by physical or measurable descriptions:

1. Urban/suburban/rural
2. Percentage built up
3. Percent land use by type
4. Occupancy types
5. Marketing time
6. Value trends
7. Changes in land use
8. Single family age.

The several factors which follow are normally based on the Appraiser's judgement:

1. Growth rate
2. Demand/supply
3. Employment stability
4. Convenience to employment
5. Convenience to shopping
6. Convenience to schools
7. Adequacy of transportation
8. Recreation facilities
9. Adequacy of utilities
10. Protection from detrimental influences
11. Project compatibility
12. Police & fire protection
13. General appearance of property
14. Appeal to market.

In terms of the physical items, the Review Appraiser will be most interested in such items as present land use by type, marketing time, value trends, change in land use, and single family price range. Where a possible question arises from negative descriptions, the Review Appraiser will look to the judgement section in order to determine how the field Appraiser has interpreted this situation. If a problem is apparent, the field Appraiser must describe in appropriate detail the effect, if any, on the subject property. Furthermore, these problems should be treated consistently throughout the remainder of the report and supported with market evidence.

The Review Appraiser must be alert to the fact that the field Appraiser may have a certain bias or that the market information contained in the report may be inaccurate. Hence, questions related to the 14 items listed above under the judgemental category must be probed, if not properly defined or described in proper detail. Ultimately, the Review Appraiser should look to the last item, "appeal to market", as the field Appraiser may be somewhat concerned by isolated circumstances, but overall feels that the subject property evidences adequate marketability, or adequate security if it involves a mortgage.

For a proposed dwelling in a large residential project, the Review Appraiser must question the feasibility of the development in terms of location, price range, competition, potential demand, amenities, accessibility, etc. Many field Appraisers may be unprepared to make an accurate judgement in this area unless they have several years of experience upon which to base it. The period of the mid-1970's dramatically evidence this phenomenon. To properly evaluate the success of a proposed project, the resale market in the immediate vicinity must give unqualified evidence as to the strength of the demand/supply situation in terms of breadth and depth.

The Review Appraiser, in interpreting neighborhood factors, must always weigh the specific influence, if any, on the subject property. This is one area upon which the experience and judgement of the field Appraiser is most important. Confidence in the ability of the field Appraiser is generally the most effective way for the Review Appraiser to receive assurance that the neighborhood is properly defined.

The Site

The Review Appraiser must be supplied with the following information to objectively evaluate the subject site:
1. Lot dimensions and shape
2. Current, proposed, or probable future zoning
3. Public services and utilities
4. Off-site information
5. Topography, view, drainage
6. Easements or encroachments

The Review Appraiser must first analyze the site, as if vacant and available for any use, to determine its highest and best use. Then, the determination must be made if the present use is the same as the highest and best use. If the existing use is an under-utilization of the land, there should be concern and a further investigation is suggested. If an over-utilization is present, normally a potential problem exists and the Review Appraiser should look to the market analysis of the field Appraiser to determine its severity.

In terms of the six items listed above, the Review Appraiser must reference any unusual circumstance by its effect upon market value. A site, for example, may be shaped like a pretzel, but still have no loss in value, per unit of value cited, as evidenced by the market. Although there may be no detrimental conditions, the field Appraiser is obligated to complete in as sufficient detail as possible, all descriptions of site information.

Improvement Description

Review Appraisers must be given an adequate description of the dwelling unit and site improvements. Photos, as indicated, are vital in visualizing the improvement if the description is inadequate.

Normally, the field Appraiser will supply the following items:
   age of dwelling
   number of units
   type and design
   exterior wall and roof materials
   windows and door materials
   insulation
   foundation and basement description
   room — list
   gross living area
   equipment (built-in)
   mechanical items
   floor, wall, trim finish
   special features/finish/improvements or other items
   attics, porches, (enclosed areas not included in living area)
   garage or other on-site buildings
   on-site improvements (landscape, fence, patio, deck, pool, etc.

As listed on the FHLMC/FMMA Form, the following judgement factors will be the basis of the Review Appraiser's interpretation of the subject property as acceptable security as related to the market:
   quality of construction
   condition of improvements
   room size/layout
   closets and storage
   adequacy of insulation
   adequacy & condition of plumbing
   adequacy & condition of electrical
   adequacy of kitchen cabinets
   compatibility to neighborhood

overall livability
appeal and marketability
remaining economic life

The four items a Review Appraiser must concentrate on in reference to an overall evaluation are the following:

1. Compatibility to neighborhood
2. Overall livability
3. Appeal and marketability
4. Remaining years of economic life

All judgements of the field Appraiser must be supported by market evidence as discussed in the location section. The Review Appraiser reserves the right to challenge all such opinions. In addition, consistency must be recognized on the part of the field Appraiser throughout the report, including the valuation section.

In terms of "neighborhood compatibility", the Review Appraiser must be aware that potential problems exist where surrounding properties have a negative or detrimental influence on the subject. On the other hand, higher valued dwellings or proximate sites having a higher utilization may have a positive influence on the subject property despite the fact that compatibility is lacking.

The factor of "overall livability" generally pertains to the functional utility of the home in terms of market acceptance and current demand/supply determinants. The judgement of "appeal and marketability" is highly correlated with overall livability.

The remaining economic life of a dwelling may have a small correlation with actual physical age. Homes can be easily rehabilitated, remodeled, or renovated to provide a continuing basis for market acceptance and livability. Remaining economic life is often treated in relation to the properties located in the immediate neighborhood which exhibit a direct influence on the subject property. Abandonment, vandalism, deferred maintenance, etc. may have a detrimental effect on the subject. On the other hand, revitalization of a neighborhood may have the opposite effect and will prolong the economic life of a dwelling. In terms of a neighborhood definition in this regard, the State of California interpretation, as earlier alluded to in this article, appears to be most applicable. The traditional definition of neighborhood evolution (formation, equilibrium, and disintegration) is being questioned in terms of today's market.

The Review Appraiser must assume that the subject dwelling has been properly measured and the correct living area determined. Dwelling measurements cannot be verified unless another independent appraisal is conducted. The determination of living area is, however, an area of interpretation.

Typically, all areas above ground which are finished, enclosed, and heated can be treated as living area. Enclosed, but unheated porches and unfinished, but headed attics cannot be considered as living space. These areas could be given some contributory value, nonetheless, as supported in the market. Finished basements generally will not be recognized fully as living area due to degrees of disutility associated with below-ground space. Again, contributory value will be recognized if market determined. Split-level homes require special market segmentation since some below-ground space can be recognized as full living area.

When rooms are counted, again only above-ground finished areas should be included. A room can be defined as a distinctly separate space having a minimum of 80 to 100 square feet.

In defining living areas and room counts, the subject and the comparables must be dealth with on equal terms and assumptions.

The Cost Approach

The cost approach should normally be given little consideration in the support of the final value estimate unless the property is of a unique type, design, or construction. Many of the assumptions made in the cost approach, such as all forms of depreciation and the land value estimate, are subject to questionable assumptions. Furthermore, many of these assumptions are ultimately based on market information and observation which is contained in other sections of the report.

If the improvements involve unique construction materials or architectural design, it is suggested that local contractors be contacted as sources of cost information rather to rely upon cost manuals or modifiers. Even if the property is of a conventional design and cost manuals are utilized, the field Appraiser must be ultimately familiar with the cost manual specifications and utilize the current modifiers.

In terms of the land valuation, residential Appraisers infrequently search the market for vacant land sales except in developing areas. Normally, the land value is derived through a "back door" approach or through a residual, as typically in existing neighborhoods there are no comparable vacant land sales available.

Direct Sales Comparison Approach

The direct sales comparison approach employs the principle of substitution, or the substitution of alternative properties for the subject as the basis of the determination of value. The market is dependent upon the actions of buyers and sellers who are often irrational. But based on probabilities, and measured through experience and sound appraisal judgement, value can be determined within acceptable limits via statistical interpretation by the Review Appraiser.

The direct sales comparison approach begins with the selection of a relevant subset of similar properties. The subset may range from a subset of one to several hundred. The Review Appraiser will typically prefer at least three comparables to establish a statistical base of reference. Adjustments are then made, via market observation by comparing components of the selected market sales to the subject property. In cases where a value cannot be attached to a component by isolating market reaction, cost may be used as a limit.

The direct sales comparison approach is defined by the following steps:

1. The Review Appraiser must be given the specific location of each comparable sale (legal description or street address). In addition, listing identification numbers, public recording information, or other sale identification may be required by the Review Appraisr to verify each sale.

2. Proximity to the subject property is an important point in the selection of comparable properties. The Review Appraiser should select sales within the subject neighborhood in order to avoid adjustments for locational differences. Oftentimes, where appreciation is negligible, current sales outside of the subject neighborhood could be overlooked for the selection of older sales within the subject neighborhood. Where the Review Appraiser is unfamiliar with the specific property location, street maps should be obtained in order to pin-point the location of all comparables used. Field Appraisers have been known to select properties outside of the subject neighborhood to justify the sales price or inflate a property value.

3. The sale price of the comparables must be verified by the field Appraiser by contacting the principles of the transactions. Prices are normally reflected in dollars rounded off to the nearest hundred dollars. For example, sale prices reflecting such figures as $47,237 may not meet the criteria of a market transaction and should therefore be verified. Sale prices of the comparables should normally reflect a range slightly above and slightly below the final appraised value of the subject property. This is because another convenient method used to support a higher value for a property is to select higher valued properties as comparables than the subject. Negative adjustments are much more easily supported than larger positive adjustments and will arouse less suspicion.

4. Price per square foot of living area may be a good rule of thumb to select possible comparable sales, but will rarely be a means of arriving at a final value estimate. Value per square foot is generally inaccurate since it compares only living area and avoids amenity packages, condition, quality of construction, age, design, sales concessions and so on.

5. The date of sale is a vital piece of information, especially in contemporary markets where appreciation may be as much as 2% per month. First of all, all comparables should reflect a date of sale. The effective date should be the date the sale was negotiated rather than the date it was closed. This means that contracts could be accepted as reliable indications of value. Generally, however, the Review Appraiser will prefer to see transactions which have been closed. Nevertheless, contracts may be very reliable indicators of value in certain situations where closed sales are unavailable.

The adjustments for appreciation, or depreciation where appropriate, must be based on verifiable market evidence. Typically, real estate organizations publish area or regional statistics on appreciation rates which can be used as rules of thumb. Where field Appraisers are very active in a particular area, one can rely on their judgement. Normally, adjustments are based on percentages with the resulting dollar figure rounded to the nearest $100, $500, or $1,000, depending on the market. The comparables must be adjusted to the effective date of the appraisal. The Review Appraiser will find it necessary to check for consistency among these adjustments for each sale.

6. Location adjustments should not be necessary if the comparables are selected within the subject neighborhood. Never differences will exist and the Review Appraiser will normally not have a basis to evaluate the adjustment. The Reviewer may want to check the street map or aerial, if included, to locate possible sources of difference. In any event, the Review Appraiser should be suspicious if the location adjustment exceeds 5% of the sale price, especially if it is a positive adjustment, and should question the field appraisal.

7. The site adjustment should be nominal, especially if the comparables are located in the subject neighborhood. In areas of homogeneity such as an established subdivision, adjustments will be made on the basis of front footage. For irregular shaped parcels, adjustments can be based on square footage or some other market extracted basis. Site adjustments will be crucial on rural properties involving a large parcel or on properties which have a view amenity. In these cases, land sale comparables may be requested by the Reviewer.

8. Design and appeal adjustments are based solely upon the judgement of the field Appraiser. The Review Appriaser will be interested in the magnitude of such adjustments.

9. Quality of construction, age, and condition will also be based totally on the field Appraiser's opinions and experience. If the comparables are representatively selected, such adjustments will not be large. Normally, unless the field Appraiser has personally inspected each comparable, such adjustments will be token only. Unique features such as decorating probably should not be recognized since personal tastes between buyers and sellers are seldom similar. The field Appraiser should, therefore, reflect differences only where the subject or the comparable is definitely below market standards for condition or decorating. If a significant amount of repairs is required, the cost of such work will set the upper limit for the dollar adjustment.

10. Room count adjustments should be based only on rooms included in the living area of the dwelling, as previously discussed. Included, typically, are common areas such as a living room, kitchen, dining room, family room and den; bedrooms; and bathrooms (bathrooms should be rounded to the nearest ½ bath). Other areas such as finished basement rooms, dining nooks, ¼ baths, etc. should not be recognized fully as rooms or as full baths, respectively, and may be adjusted under a miscellaneous category. Comparables should typically reflect similar room counts, bedroom counts, and baths. Recognition of a room can usually be determined by size or by its utility.

Adjustments must be market determined. In some neighborhoods, demand can be distinguished between three and four bedroom homes, and so on. In subdivisions characterized by split-level homes or bi-level dwellings, lower-level finished rooms could be accepted as living area if demonstrated by the market.

11. Gross living area is an important criteria for comparable selection. Although prospective buyers normally do not physically measure a home, they typically make objective judgements concerning the size of the rooms. Unless the Appraiser is using comparables which have been actually measured, the living areas listed under multiple listing sale sheets must be questioned, especially where the comparable is irregular in shape or has some overlapping levels. Where the measurements of a comparable are questionable, the only alternative will be to actually measure the sales or to verify through public records.

Adjustments for differences in living area are also market determined. An adjustment based on construction costs per square foot is normally very unreliable, especially where the property is not new. The safest method is to select comparables of the same size range as the subject property.

12. Basements, porches, patios, pools, etc. will differ in approach, depending upon geographic location, climate, price range, and buyer preference. Basements, for example, are typically required in the midwest and in northern sections of the country. Homes without basements characteristically are difficult to sell in these areas, and a functional disutility will be attached in those locations evidencing market demand for basements.

Other site improvements such as pools, tennis courts, or other custom items are typically stratified by price range or location. For example, $300,000 homes in Phoenix will typically have pools. A $300,000 home without a pool, therefore, must be adjusted at a market determined rate which will approach the replacement cost as a limit. Adjustments between homes with and without pools in Minneapolis, for example, will probably be in the range of 50% of its replacement cost since the market is not well stratified for homes with pools in a northern climate.

Garages and carports are generally in demand in any price range and location. In the northern climates, the difference in value between a property with no garage and one with a garage will probably be greater than the difference in a southern climate location. In any event, the adjustment must be market determined and must not exceed cost.

13. Other improvements generally include such items as air conditioning, fireplaces, built-in appliances, energy features, etc. As previously discussed, adjustments for these items must be market determined.

14. Sales concessions and financing may be the most debatable section of adjustments. Specifically, how does one account for points paid by the seller for VA or FHA financing, for a land contract or other owner financed transaction, for chattel items included in the sale, for developers who provide favorable financing secured by points or fees paid to a lending institution, or for distressed projects offering sale concessions?

It is my opinion that in each of the above situations, the purchaser indirectly pays for each of these incentives. Therefore, the Appraiser must take into account concessions and financing involved in each of the comparable transactions and apply it to what is typical in the market. If the appraisal of the subject property is connected with a sale, the final valuation must be contingent upon the financing or concession utilized in that transaction, if not typical of the market. Furthermore, the Appraiser must explore the possibilities of another sale occurring under those same conditions. If the possibilities are remote, the Appraiser must adjust for the terms of the sale.

One such case which I have found most interesting is associated with a distressed project or a "work-out" situation. In such cases, developers or interim owners may be providing incentives in the form of reduced interest rates, homeowner fee waivers, no closing costs, promotional gifts, or cash rebates. In such cases, the Appraiser must evaluate whether the existing owner, or typical owner, would be able to provide the same incentives on a resale basis. If not, the following rules of thumb are suggested:

1. For interest rate subsidies, capitalize the difference between the market rate and the contract rate over the typical holding period of a residence.

2. For homeowner fees or other subsidies, take the present value of such amounts over the period of months or years applicable.

3. For rebates, points, or other promotional items, adjust for the actual dollars involved.

4. In particularly distressed markets, the Appraiser may make negative adjustments for the date of sale due to excessive holding costs.

The terms of a sale is an important item in the market comparison approach. A major error of many Appraisers is to consider each comparable as a conventional transaction. All comparable sales should be verified with the parties of the transaction or the realtors for these reasons.

The field Appraiser will normally rely on one or two sales as being most comparable to the subject and, therefore, most reliable as a prediction of value. These dates will typically be ones with the least number of adjustments, the most recent sales, the most proximate sales to the subject, and so on. The Review Appraiser can normally make this determination objectively by examining the comparable description and adjustments.

The comparables may not necessarily be within a narrow range of adjusted value when compared to the subject. To reiterate, one sale may be given the greatest consideration despite the fact that the other sale may be several thousand dollars different. However, the Review Appraiser is encouraged to challenge the field Appraiser when such differences occur.

The Income Approach

The income approach is a misnomer when applied to single family properties. First of all, even if rentals on single family residences are available, this approach is actually market determining the gross rent multiplier approach. GRM (Gross Rent Multiplier) may be applied either to a monthly market rent or to an annual rent, and is determined simply by dividing the sale price of a comparable by its monthly or annual rent.

Single family properties are typically not rented and, therefore, this entire approach may not even be applicable to most properties. However, in subidivions or areas characterized by rental occupancy and where residences are purchased as investment opportunities, the gross rent multiplier approach may be more valid than the direct sales comparison approach through adjustments.

This article has concentrated only on single family residences. Two to eight family dwellings are often categorized with single units. This author feels that the gross rent multiplier is an excellent indication of value for properties of this type and, in most instances, should be given the greatest weight in the final value determination.

Summary

In conclusion, I wish to reiterate my opening comments regarding the function of a Review Appraiser and to emphasize the objectivity which that position requires. Appraising is not an exact science and, therefore, review appraising is not an exact science. The Reviewer is obligated to exhibit knowledge of appraisal theory and to practice consistency in judgement. The Reviewer must rely upon wisdom, equity, and integrity in reaching the final conclusion.

CHAPTER TWELVE

Review of

Appraisals for

Partial Acquisition

ROBERT L. CLARK, CRA

Robert L. Clark, CRA, is an Appraiser for the Bureau of Land Management/Technical Services in Portland, Oregon. He received his B.A. in Civil Engineering from the University of California at Davis. Mr. Clark was recently an Appraiser for the U.S. Army Corps of Engineers.

Mr. Clark holds the "Certified Review Appraiser" designation and is a member of the American Society of Appraisers and the Association of Federal Appraisers.

Review of

Appraisals for

Partial Acquisition

A well prepared, complete appraisal for a partial taking is a work of art in the field of real estate. It can only be considered so when the continuity and order of the steps can be followed by the Reviewer who then arrives at the same conclusion as did the Appraiser.

Many articles have been prepared over the years which have discussed methods for the solution to the final value estimate. I do not intend to contradict the opinions of anyone, only to offer some ideas on the subject based on my own experience as an Appraiser and my observations as a Reviewer.

For whatever purpose the appraisal is to be used, whether it is the basis for acquisition of a right-of-way for an underground pipeline, a buried cable, a roadway, a reservoir site, a canal, an overhead transmission line, line of site or any other partial taking, the basic appraisal technique for partial takings is the same for all types of property.

It is imperative for the Reviewer to know the purpose of the proposed acquisition to permit him to intelligently support what effect the acquisition will have on the part not to be taken. The effect may be a detriment to, or it may substantially improve, the remainder.

In order for these conditions to be recognized in the appraisal report, the assigned Review Appraiser should have had actual appraisal experience in partial valuations to be qualified to make the technical review of the Appraiser's expertise which resulted in the final estimate of value. The Review Appraiser, before given the authority to review a particular report, should have demonstrated the ability to prepare such a report himself. Therefore, the Reviewer, as well as the Appraiser, should provide a "Statement of Qualifications" so that those who use the approved appraisal report can be made aware of the experience of each.

The Reviewer has the responsibility for assuring that the appraisal was based on acceptable valuation concepts and that the value conclusion was adequately supported. He must conduct an objective review in accordance with the complexity of the appraisal problem, which can be relied upon. Under these circumstances, only *one* technical review is necessary.

Three Appraisals — One Review

The appraisal for partial taking is the most sophisticated product in the field of Real Estate Valuation. It first requires all the Appraiser's expertise in justifying his conclusion as to the value of the property, clearly without the thought of threat of a partial taking.

Obviously, by the very nature of the problem, the value of the property, as the Appraiser first studies it, is only the *first* of three separate valuations he must make. Having omitted or taken lightly any one of the considerations pertinent to the whole problem, it would not be difficult to surmise that the final value estimate may *not* be in the best interest of all parties concerned.

The most important initial decision to be made in reviewing an appraisal for partial taking is whether or not the Appraiser has adequately supported the highest and best use of the property first appraised and the highest and best use, different if necessary, of the remaining parcel or parcels as indicated by the effect of the taking.

"Highest and best use" is well defined, but there are many variations in its interpretation, and herein lies one of the major reasons for such wide divergence in the text of partial taking appraisals and the valuation estimates contained therein.

Real estate is land plus the contributory value of any tangible permanent improvements. It has nothing whatever to do with the current owner or any of the other three agents in the production of income. Theoretically, if the operation is such that labor, management, the return of the investment, and the return on the investment consume all the income, then the land is worth nothing. The owner of the property may want the tax assessor and the Internal Revenue Service to believe this, but the proof is in the market and the market is always available to be searched.

In urban localities the highest and best use is generally quite obvious because of the attendant zoning. However, in suburban or rural areas where transition may or may not be a factor, the importance of highest and best use takes on added dimensions. I submit that land or soil will produce only vegetation or support improvements and that the method of obtaining income from the land or soil so used is purely a matter of management. As an example, while there are many crops which are grown for human consumption and obviously must be hand-picked or harvested by mechanical means, there are other crops which are "harvested" in place by animals. This leads to the theory that the owner and/or manager of a parcel of land may or may not like to work with animals. If he does, he is referred to as a "livestock man". If he does not, he may be called a "dirt farmer". All semantics perhaps, but nonetheless factual, leaving the Analyst with the proposition that the real estate produces *only* plants and that the method of harvesting the crop is purely a matter of management decided by the owner and based on his personal likes and dislikes tempered by his ability — or it may be that his likes or personal ability as a manager may not produce the greatest net return to the land.

The Appraiser is asked for the value of the legally described real estate, assuming it to be under competent management. There is nothing in the definition of an appraisal which even remotely indicates that the *owner* of the property is to be *evaluated*. In fact, the definition gives the owner the benefit of the doubt regarding his competency as a manager and, likewise, it does not provide for added compensation for superior managerial skills.

The proper conclusion as to the highest and best use is the *key* to the comparable sales which should be used as indicators of value.

The analysis of these sales should have lead to the reasonable "Before Value" of the property appraised.

This same analogy is appropriate in urban properties and even within certain legally zoned suburban and rural areas.

Up to this point in the assignment, the appraisal for partial acquisition is no different from any other professionally prepared real estate appraisal report and should be treated as such by both the Appraiser and the Reviewer.

Effect on the Remainder

The requirement for a portion of the "rights" in a particularly described parcel of real estate must be so clearly defined by the Appraiser that the reviewing Appraiser can readily relate to the problem as set out in the report being reviewed.

Once having clearly understood the physical requirements, the probable appearance of the finished project, the estate to be acquired — whether fee title or less, and the length of the term, if temporary — the Appraiser should logically discuss the anticipated condition of the part not to be taken. I say anticipated because this second appraisal is made only with the benefit of foresight and imagination. The Appraiser must, at this point, be capable of imaginary "tunnel vision" as far as the real estate is concerned. He must condition his mind to again start from the beginning, for it is an entirely new problem and it must be so treated even though this remainder is a part of that appraised the first time.

Of the seven cardinal aspects of value, size and shape have surely changed. Access, topography, soils, and water supply may or may not be different. The only aspect of value not affected in partial takings is physical location, because the remainder is still where it was before. This is not to say, however, that the proposed acquisition has not altered either or both the physical *use* or the economic desirability of the remainder. Any alteration, whether a detriment or an economic benefit, should be explained in the report in a separate statement of Highest and Best Use dealing with the remainder only.

I submit that it is the exception rather than the rule that the highest and best use of the remaining property will be the same as before, thus requiring a second group of sales data to substantiate the conclusions as to the value of the part or parts not to be taken.

Damages or Benefits

When the second or "After Value" estimate is completed, the Appraiser merely subtracts it from the first. This difference is his estimate of the value to the owner of all the rights to be acquired.

This figure is composed of the value of the part taken, based on the unit value shown in the "before" estimate. Obviously, if the value of the part taken is equal to the difference, there is neither severance damage nor benefits.

However, if the difference between the before and after estimates is greater than the value of the part taken, then the amount it takes to supplement the value of the part taken to equal the difference is referred to as *severance damage* or the diminution in the value of the remainder.

The reverse is true if the difference is less than the value of the part taken. In this case, the minus adjustment is referred to as *benefits to the remainder.*

History in this matter indicates that there is usually no severe dispute as to the unit value of the property as expressed in the report. But rather, the dispute generally arises over any damages and/or benefits applied to the remainder. Therefore, a thorough understanding of "damages" to rights of ownership is essential to all concerned.

In the case of severance damage there are occasions when it can be offset by an allowance for the cost to cure. This should not be considered until the previously discussed "Before and After Method" of appraisal has been completed — for it is not until then that the Appraiser has *proven* that there is severance damage, and without severance damage, a consideration of cost to cure is improper. It is likewise improper to suggest a cost to cure in an amount which exceeds the indicated severance damage.

Recommended Forms

Example 1 — Severance Damage & Cost-to-cure

Value Before Taking

20 ac. irrigated land @ $1,500	$30,000	
7 ac. wooded land @ $500	$3,500	
3 ac. riverwash @ $100	$300	
Improvements — single family dwelling	$20,000	
Sub Total		$53,800

Value After Taking (change in H & B)

16 ac. level dry land @ $1,000	$16,000	
3 ac. wooded land @ $500	$1,500	
3 ac. riverwash @ $100	$300	
Improvements — unchanged	$20,000	
Sub Total		$37,800
Difference Before and After		$16,000

Value of Part Taken

4 ac. irrigated land @ $1,500	$6,000	
4 ac. wooded land @ $500	$2,000	
Severance Damage (loss of well)	+$8,000*	
Value Estimate		$16,000

If at this point in the report, the Appraiser has stated that he has contacted a well driller and a pump dealer who have given bona-fide estimates for a new well and for pulling and resetting the existing pump, he should conclude as follows:

---

*A "cost-to-cure" item must be recommended if a new well can be produced for an estimated price not to exceed the amount shown as severance damage.

Cost-To-Cure Recommended

New Well	$4,000	
Pull & reinstall existing pump	$1,000	
Total "Cost-To-Cure"	$5,000	
Severance Damage	$8,000	
Less "Cost-To-Cure"	$5,000	
Deduct from Value Estimate above		$3,000
Final estimated fair market value		$13,000

Example 2 — Benefits

The property involved was a 240-acre parcel consisting of a quarter section (160 acres) plus a contiguous 80-acre parcel measuring in all one mile in length from north to south and one-half mile wide at the north end. It had no road frontage.

The "before" value was estimated, giving the property owner the benefit of the doubt in the amount of $300 per acre for a total of $72,000; even though the property neither had frontage on a public road nor any form of legal or physical access thereto (except perhaps a prescriptive right from a friendly neighbor).

This being the acquisition of one-half the total ownership, the effect of taking the east portion and the completion of the project in the proposed manner left a 120-acre remainder with more than one mile of frontage on a new first rate macadam surfaced public road. This fact left the Appraiser with the necessity of using a different set of sales, because in the 'after' condition he *must* prove benefits to the remainder. This was done and the remainder was found to be worth the "before value" on a unit basis, plus an amount attributable to the new legal access created. The "after" value was justified at $350 per acre or $42,000 for the 120-acre remainder.

It is obvious, then, that the difference between the "before" and "after" values was $30,000.

It is also obvious that if one divides the $30,000 by the 120 acres to be taken, the unit value is $250 per acre — but this is meaningless because of the benefits to the remainder.

The solution as to the value of the part taken is 120 acres times

$300 unit value before equals $36,000 minus $30,000 (difference) equals the $6,000 which must be claimed as benefits because of the construction of the new road and the creation of legal access.

The preceding narrative discussion of the Example 2 is accurate, but it *is* so *only* to the experienced and highly qualified Reviewer. However, the following summary sets out the facts so that it is more readily understandable to those who must "use" the report.

Before Value

240 ac. (no access) @ $300	$72,000	
Improvements — none		

After Value

120 ac. with one mile of public road frontage @ $350	$42,000	
Improvements — None		
Difference		$30,000

Value of Part Taken

120 ac. (no access) @ $300	$36,000	
Improvements — none		
Less Benefits to remainder	-6,000	
Final value estimate		$30,000*

Example 3 — A Minus Value

The Appraiser is not obligated to provide a final value estimate which will be acceptable to the property owner. In the case of "partial" valuations, many strange and unexpected things can occur which may frustrate all except the experiencd reviewing Appraiser. This example is such a case.

---

*The Final value estimate *must* equal the difference between the Before and After Values. This can only be accomplished by subtracting: in this case, $6,000 from the $36,000.

The subject property is in a transitional area between a suburban and a rural community. A right-of-way is being acquired for the location of a new, major highway. The design specifies the acquisition of 16 acres from the subject improved 20-acre semi-rural, single-family farm. The shape of the 4-acre remainder is rectangular, with 660 feet of accessible frontage on the new highway.

The appraisal report shows three "before" sales indicating $48,000, $50,000, and $51,000. Subject was purchased last month for $50,000.

Three recent sales of 4-acre parcels adjacent to a new highway in the general area indicate similar parcels being purchased and improved with restaurants, shops, motels and the like. The prices paid range from 40 to 50 cents per square foot.

The effect of the taking is the change of the highest and best use in the after condition to one for commercial development. That change has substantially increased the unit value of the land from $1,500 per acre (before) to $20,000 per acre (after).

The proof of the Final Value Estimate is demonstrated as follows:

Before Value

20 ac. farmland @ $1,500	$30,000	
Single family residence	20,000	
Before Value		$50,000

After Value

4 ac. commercial land @ $20,000	$80,000	
Improvements	---	
		$80,000
Difference	MINUS	$30,000

Value of Part Taken

16 ac. farmland @ $1,500	$24,000	
Single family residence	20,000	
	$44,000	
Benefits must be	-74,000	
Final Value Estimate	MINUS	$30,000

In this case, the *MINUS $30,000* is the *proper* Final Value Estimate, and the Reviewing Appraiser has *approved* the report.

This would indicate that the property owner owes $30,000 for the "economic favor".

Nonetheless, the Appraiser *and* the Reviewer have done their jobs correctly. And it now becomes the responsibility of another authority to deal fairly with the landowner.

Points of Review Importance

It is the responsibility of the person who makes the assignment to adequately inform the Appraiser of important facts so as to alleviate, to the greatest extent, all possibility of a certified appraisal report which might not be acceptable upon technical review.

The appraisal report must first be thoroughly checked and evaluated by its author. Secondly, it is *technically* analyzed by *one* qualified Reviewer.

If a Reviewer disagrees with a portion of a report, his reasons for disagreement should be verbally discussed *with the Appraiser,* followed by a written outline of the problem if necessary.

When approval of the report is not possible, the Reviewer should suggest alternatives for the Appraiser's consideration.

Under no circumstances should an Appraiser be coerced or directed to change his opinion of value.

A written review statement may expound on the Appraiser's rationale or provide additional facts justifying the Reviewer's approval or disapproval of the report.

CHAPTER THIRTEEN

Review of Easements

NORMAN G. SCHMUHL, CRA

Norman G. Schmuhl, CRA, is a Realty Specialist with the Northern Division, Naval Facilities Engineering Command in Philadelphia, Pennsylvania, which has jurisdiction in 24 states. He has received his B.S.C. from Temple University and his J.M. from Philadelphia College of Law. Mr. Schmuhl has been an appraiser since 1954.

Mr. Schmuhl holds the "C.R.A." designation (Certified Review Appraiser) and is a member of the Association of Federal Appraisers.

Review of

Easements

Easements are a contemporary appraisal problem. The problem multiplies as science expands the uses of the earth's surface, subsurface and the air space above its surface. An easement is a part of the "bundle of rights" that the owner of the land holds. For the purpose of considering appraisal review problems, the thoughts developed here will be directed to easements for which the owner of the land encumbered will receive value.

An easement is an encumbrance against the land. Easements put a burden on private and public property. That burden is a restriction or covenant to restrain, or the right to prevent the owner from making a specific use of the land. An easement confers an interest in land. The interest *may not be terminated* at the pleasure of the owner of the encumbered land. An easement is a right or privilege to use the real property of another for a limited specific purpose. The real estate which carries the burden of the easement is known as the *Servient Estate.* The right in the owner of one parcel of land, by reason of such ownership, to land of another for a specific purpose, is known as the *Dominant Estate.* An easement expressly granted in a deed is an *easement appurtenant* and runs with the land; thus it is a covenant which passes with the transfer or a disposition of an estate to the new owner. The benefits pass to subsequent grantees, whether mentioned in the deed or not.

The right or privilege may be created either by grant or agreement. It may be express or implied. Express easements are imposed by grant, and implied easements are created by operation of law where the easement is necessary and its prior use has been obvious.

Continuous adverse, open use for a specified time period (as required by law), can create an easement by prescription.

The Uniform Appraisal Standards for Federal Land Acquisitions states:

"A-19, Easements: An easement denotes ownership of limited real property rights; thus falling short of full fee simple estate ownership.

When an easement or servitude over land is condemned for the public use, the appraisal should be in the amount of the difference between the fair market value of the land before and the fair market value immediately after the imposition of the easement. Full consideration should be given to and due allowance made for the substantial enjoyment and beneficial ownership remaining to the owner subject only to the inter- ference occasioned by the taking and exercising of the easement."

It is essential that the Reviewer not only be a qualified Appraiser, but the Review Appraiser must have a keen, logical and analytical capability. The Reviewer must decide whether the conclusions presented are documented by the facts. Each appraisal report must stand on its own. It should require no additional documentation or explanation to support the value presented. Where there is an exercise of eminent domain that is accomplished either by purchase or condemnation, the Review Appraiser must decide whether the estimated conclusion as to value is fair and equitable and whether the appraisal report contains all the necessary facts and documentation. The Review Appraiser must ascertain whether all the allowances included are compensable.

The *value* of real property is not in the physical land and the improvements upon it, but *in the rights of ownership and use* attached to the land and improvements. The Appraiser cannot define the problem precisely unless the property rights are *involved* in the appraisal are clear and precise in the appraisal assignment.

Did the Appraiser solve the right problem? This is the question the Review Appraiser must be able to answer in the positive affirmative without any "gray area." Any appraisal assignment requires a clear definition of the problem, including a precise statement of the property right or rights that are to be appraised. The Appraiser must be given, and if not, acquire all the facts regarding the appraisal assignment. The Appraiser is valuing property rights when an assignment is accepted and is engaged in discovering the nature and extent of these rights.

It is not the Reviewer's obligation to make a reappraisal but to review the appraisal that has been submitted.

How does the Review Appraiser approach an appraisal that has been submitted for review?

The Review Appraiser should:

1. Review the legal descriptions presented.
2. Review the plans
3. View the property
4. View the comparables
5. Become knowledgable of laws and regulations
6. Make a judgement as to comparability.

At this point the appraisal report, per se, will be considered.

The legal description before and after are important documentation where there is a transfer of title. In the review of an easement appraisal report the plans should be reviewed at the site in order to make a better judgement of the before and after effects. The Review Appraiser must be able to view the problem in the overall. The Review Appraiser must see "the forest" and not just "the tree." The "forest" can have great effect on the "tree." When the Appraiser views the property and the comparables he must make a judgement as to whether the comparables are comparable.

There should be a description of the area and the property itself before the easement came into being. There should be a statement of all the factors that have an influence upon the property. In simple language a statement of those facts that affect the before and after value.

The Review Appraiser must be aware of the laws and regulations that are pertinent to the subject land and weigh whether the Appraiser has applied such laws and regulations and interpretations made thereof by the courts. Any questions the Reviewer has relative to legal questions involved should be referred to lawyers. The Review Appraiser is not a lawyer and even if trained in the law, the Review Appraiser cannot "wear two hats" without "court" trouble.

Does the appraisal reveal an understandable weighing of the factors? The Reviewer should not "reach" for a conclusion, but must be able to come to a clear understanding of the elements of damage involved. Are the correlations reasonable in the approaches to and the final estimate of value?

It is the Review Appraiser's duty to ascertain whether the appraisal was made in accordance with sound appraisal theories that will reflect just compensation to the owners of land whether it be by condemnation or purchase. It is the Appraiser's obligation to present the unbiased facts. The Appraiser or the Review Appraiser are not negotiators but present the facts, as a basis for negotiations.

The "bottom line" for the Review Appraiser should be: does the appraisal make sense and is it understandable? Have the accepted appraisal principles been followed therein? If so, the resultant valuation should be approved. To illustrate: when an easement over land is condemned for the public use, the appraisal should be in the amount of the difference between the fair market value of the land before and the fair market value immediately after the imposition of the easement. Full consideration should be given to and due allowance made for the substantial enjoyment and beneficial ownership remaining to the owner, subject only to the interference occasioned by the taking and exercising the easement.

The Review Appraiser must be able to determine from the appraisal submitted whether the highest and best use changed as a result of the taking.

Those parts of an appraisal that do not give the Review Appraiser a clear understanding should be brought to the attention of the Appraiser for explanation, clarification and the Appraiser's modification of the report.

The Review Appraiser must consider how the mathematics were employed in the appraisal. Were the mathematics the basis of the value or were they, as they should be, only as an aid to judgement? Mathematics do not make value, they only help to explain questions such as this: "Did the Appraiser appraise the "stick" in the "bundle" for which the value was sought? Did the Appraiser value the correct property rights? How did the Appraiser solve the problem for value? Is the application of the meaning of market value reflected in the appraisal? Is the valuation based on the principle that compensation is for the property taken upon the proposition to compensate the owner for that which the owner lost? Was it "just compensation" as interpreted by the courts?"

For the Review Appraiser to ascertain whether the Appraiser has presented a correct solution, the Appraiser must submit the facts in the appraisal. The "smallest" fact may be the one which changes the whole view of the "tree" out of the "forest", or the right stick out of the bundle of rights. As the expressions go: "Get the facts, man, get the facts".

The Review Appraiser will apply the idea of judicial knowledge which is defined in Black's Law Dictionary as, "Knowledge of that which is so notorious that everybody, including judges, knows it, and hence need not be proved." In this definition, if we substitute "including Review Appraisers" for "including Judges", the same principle will apply. The Appraiser will recognize the existence of facts having a bearing on property being appraised.

In summary, the title of "Review Appraiser" carries with it a significance that he is to be the judge of the evidence submitted to support a valuation submitted by a journeyman Appraiser. It does not mean that Review Appraiser is a "Reappraiser."

CHAPTER FOURTEEN

Case Study

on Easements

MARION E. EVERHART, CRA

Marion E. Everhart, CRA, is President of Everhart Appraisal Service, Inc., in Scottsdale, Arizona. He received his B.A. from Kansas State University and has been an Appraisal Review instructor in Chicago, New York, Los Angeles, and Houston.

Mr. Everhart is a Charter Member and Past International President of the National Association of Review Appraisers. He is also a member of the American Institute of Real Estate Appraisers, the American Society of Farm Managers and Rural Appraisers, and the American College of Real Estate Consultants.

Case Study

on Easements

Easements cover all land uses and involve all potential uses of property. Where property is in transition from one use to other higher and better uses, the appraisal of easements requires the valuation of all uses, present as well as future. There is no more difficult appraisal assignment than to value an easement across property in transition where the property consists of various land classes, uses, zones, vegetation, crops, and potential uses. The easement may enhance the property, have no apparent effect, or greatly reduce property values. Easements are of many types, but can generally be classified as: (a) Subsurface for pipelines, tunnels, etc., (b) Land surface for highways, canals, railroads, etc., and (c) Overhead for pole lines, electric transmission lines, avigation, etc. Many easements may include more than one classification, such as a pipeline and a road together. Easements create two distinct estates: The fee owner's remaining property rights, known as the underlying fee, which are permissive in nature. The second estate is the acquiring agency's property rights, or easement holder's property rights, known as the overlying fee. As to which has the dominant rights depends upon the nature of the easement.

Since this article is on review appraising, it is necessary that as much guidance be given as is possible on the subject. A review of literature on easements reveals that, although there have been many articles written on various types of easements, there have been only a few articles on the specifics of writing the appraisal report. Consequently, this writer has cited the specific author that discusses a pertinent topic that must be considered by an Appraiser and a Review Appraiser. Let me say on the outset that Appraisers and RA's (Review Appraisers) typically miss many of the pertinent factors that must be covered when appraising an easement. Electric transmission line easements have been selected to represent easements as a whole for an indepth study. Following the listing of authors that discuss pertinent topics, a model appraisal writeup of the valuation of the property "after the taking" is included.

A total of ten authors have been cited as providing some guidance on pertinent topics. The author's full name, article published, publication date, and pages involved is shown in the bibliography.

A. Introduction and Definitions:

1. Classification of easements
2. Distinct estates
3. Interests and rights conveyed or retained
4. Attitudes of Appraisers, right-of-way personnel, attorneys, and the courts concerning the current method of computation of the value of easement rights.

    Carll covers topics 1 through 4 on pages 333-4, 338-9, and 348.

B. Inventory and Classify Data

1. Inventory and classify agriculture land and value each use or class.

    Carll — page 343, Pilmer — page 43, Dunlap — page 249.
2. Classify land for nonagricultural uses

    Carll — page 343, Everhart — pages 32-36
3. Land in Transition

    Carll — page 343
4. Agricultural value computed using rural sales

    Carll — page 338
5. Agricultural value computed based on growth rings and remaining agricultural life.

    Carll — page 342, Campbell — page 43-6

6. Speculative value (nonagricultural value)
    Carll — page 333, Campbell — page 45

C. Valuation and Damages

1. Land Economic Studies
    Carll — pages 345-6, Campbell — pages 45-47, Derbes — page 375, Pilmer — page 33, Young — page 41, Patt — page 334
2. Paired sales (controls and encumbered)
    Carll — page 346, Campbell — pages 47-8, Derbes — page 377.
3. Damages are outside of right-of-way. How to compute.
    Carll — page 348, Campbell — page 48, Derbes — page 376.
4. Builders — Developers recognize full fee value as actual damages to right-of-way
    Kinnard — page 277
5. Studies divides sales into 4 categories
    Kinnard — page 272
6. Yields are reduced on agricultural lands. Examples cited
    Carll — pages 342-4, Campbell — page 46, Pilmer — page 36
7. Uses that can be made of the right-of-way
    Carll — page 343, Young — pages 41-2, Crawford — page 372
8. Agricultural value or right-of-way after the taking, how to compute using present worth factors, capitalization rates and reduced income.
    Carll — page 344, Campbell — page 46
9. Using percent of fee for value of easement not proper method.
    Carll — page 348, Clark — 16.
10. Salvage value sales used to determine nonagricultural value remaining in the right-of-way.
    Carll — page 344, Campbell — page 46.

The following model incorporates the cited authors concensus of factors to be included and procedures to be followed. This model modernizes the approach to the valuation of easements by eliminating certain suggested procedures that later authorities agree should be deleted. Appraisers and RA's should be familiar with the latest accepted procedures in appraisal literature and include a bibliography of such literature in each report as proof of this type of research. Easements have been a field of controversy for the past 30 years. It is hoped that the concensus of the cited authorities will provide the needed guidance.

VALUATION OF PART TAKEN AS A PART OF THE WHOLE PLUS DAMAGES TO THE REMAINDER *

Description of the Easement Taken

The easement to be granted is 330 feet in width upon which will be constructed two 500 KV Electric transmission lines. The lines will utilize self-supporting steel lattice towers with a normal span between towers of 1,650 feet. The height of the towers will average 132 feet, with a maximum height of 147 feet. The legal description of the part taken along with a drawing will be found in the addenda.

Rights Granted in the Easement

The easement rights to be granted are usable only to the acquiring organization, or their assignees. These rights are in the category of special uses and it is, therefore, difficult to form an opinion of value based on a consideration of the easements rights as a separate entity which will meet the definition of market value. Easement rights are not freely traded in the open market, and also because land use peculiar to the condemnee or to the condemnor are not to be considered. The property right remaining in the right-of-way area in the fee ownership have value by reason of the use to which the fee owner can devote the land. In some instances, such remaining rights have a present-day value for potential uses. While the remaining rights are servient rights, and in some instances have a useful life or period of profitable existence; nevertheless, they are all typical of the rights found in comparable properties and are actively traded in the open market. As such, they comply with the definition of market value.

---

*State of Arizona taking, therefore state laws apply.

Value of Rights Remaining to Fee Owner

Because the property rights within the right-of-way area remaining in the fee owner can be valued under the market value concept, the proper method of allocating the correct amounts of the market value of the full fee of the right-of-way area between the easement rights to be granted, and the remaining rights in the fee, is to render a valuation on the property rights remaining in the fee ownership. Some of the easement rights granted are:

1. The right to construct, reconstruct, operate, maintain, repair, and patrol one or more circuits of electric energy on conductors hung from steel towers.
2. The right to clear, remove, and keep clear the right-of-way area of all brush and tree growth more than a specified height.
3. The right to keep the right-of-way area free of any type of inflammable structure or materials.
4. The right to restrict the construction or place on any temporary or permanent structures or use said property for any use or purpose which will interfere with the rights staed under number 1.

The rights remaining are as follows:

1. There is reserved unto the parties having an interest therein the right of ingress and egress over and upon said real property, together with the right to use and occupy said easement for the following purposes: streets, alleys, sidewalks, fences, corrals, agricultural, irrigation ditches, pipelines for gas, water or electrical conduits, planting area for flowers and shrubs, parking area for cars, trucks and equipment, and such uses of similar nature which will not interfere with or endanger the construction operation, or maintenance of said transmission lines, towers, and poles, and related facilities.

Highest and Best Use

The highest and best use of the whole property outside of the right-of-way area remains the same. The highest and best use of the right-of-way area is for continued irrigated cropland during the agricultural life of the property. The operator may change his methods of farming and/or crops to mitigate damages. Examples would be to reduce the amount of row crops in the rotation, therefore mitigating the cost of watering and field operations. Another example would be to change row direction (occasionally this is possible) to reduce watering problems. After the agricultural life has ended and the land is ready for development, there are various choices for a feasible subdivision plan. See "Salvage Value", page *42*. Various uses are ancillary to residential, such as golf courses, parks, open areas, recreation, etc. Recent studies have shown that master planned communities devote a minimum of 22 percent to recreation, parks and similar uses.

Procedure

Your Appraiser made a study of the neighborhood, area, and region to locate tracts of land that were encumbered with a similar easement that had subsequently sold. An economic study was then made to show the effect this easement had on the sales price. Sales of tracts abutting the easement, but not encumbered, were included in the study to serve as controls. To make the study statistically significant, it was necessary to find and analyze a sufficient number of samples; therefore, the area of study was of necessity quite large. As many studies were made as time permitted.

The studies were divided into three categories:
   (a) Rural Lands
   (b) Suburban Lands
   (c) Urban Lands

Rural Lands involved the sale of lands in the rural area with a highest and best use for cropland, orchard and vineyard, ranching, desert tracts, rural industrial, or in transition from one of these uses to residential with a delay time exceeding 5 years. The usual buyers were farmers, ranchers, or land speculators.

Suburban Lands involved the sale of lands near the edge of towns or cities with a highest and best use for residential or commercial development within a 5 year period. The usual buyers were developers or investors.

Urban Lands involved the sale of subdivided lands within the city limits zoned for residential, industrial, or commercial uses. The usual buyers were people who planned to reside on these lands.

The economic studies indicated the following, shown by categories:
   (a) Rural lands — The easement area constituted a very

small percent of the whole property, usually less than 5 percent. Sales were unreliable indicators of diminution attributable to the easement area. Opinions of parties to the sale varied from no knowledge of th easement to an understanding of the restrictions imposed. It was apparent that the maximum diminution was no greater than 100 percent of the fee value of the easement area. (See schematic map.)

(b) Suburban lands — The easement area constituted from 3 to 10 percent of the whole property. Sales to *informed* developers indicated a diminution of the whole nearly equal to the full fee value of the easement area. No severance damages outside the easement area were indicated for residential subdivision had a use for parks, playgrounds, open space to provide more peace to the neighborhood, etc., and was an attractive item to help sell the abutting land. In the case of commercial use where 71 percent of the whole was needed for parking, the easement area did not present as much of a problem as in a residential subdivision. Subsequent development experience was the basis for this diminution.

(c) Urban lands — The easement area constituted from 10 to 100 percent of the whole property. Sales to *informed* potential residents indicated a diminution of square foot or front foot value according to the usable area remaining, angle of crossing, and whether already restricted by zoning. If the highest and best use changed, this either enhanced or lowered the value. No generalization can be made.

The following studies are cited for more complete analysis and reference and provide comparable sales:

Land Economic Studies

Study #1

The Prescott-Mesa and the Mesa-Coolidge *tower-supported* transmission lines in Maricopa County, Arizona, are 230 KV transmission lines which had been installed in 1950, 64 miles in length, and had normal right-of-way width of 125 feet, but in places had a width of 365 feet (3 lines parallel). There were 33 sales studied and, of this number, 23 were encumbered with the transmission line easement crossing at all angles. This line, starting from a point approximately 30 miles from urban development, extended to the city and beyond to a point approximately 20.0 miles on the other side. This line crossed cropland, noncropland, desert, and urban lands. This is a published study.

Study #2

The Mesa-Coolidge *tower-supported* transmission line in Pinal County, Arizona, from the Maricopa County line southeastward to the Gila Indian Reservation and from the reservation to the Coolidge Substation, a distance of 30 miles. This 230 KV line crossed cropland and noncropland.

Study #3

The Davis-Prescott 230 KV *tower-supported* transmission line in Mohave County, Arizona, which was installed in December, 1952. This line extends east and west across Mohave County, passing south of Kingman at a distance of 3 miles. This entire line, where studied, was across noncropland and covered a distance of 35 miles.

Study #4

The Mead-Liberty 345 KV *tower-supported* transmission line in Mohave County, Arizona, which had steel for the towers on the site in December, 1966, was erected by March, 1967. This entire line, where studied, was across noncropland and covered a distance of 80 miles.

Study #5

The Queen Creek-Blackwater *two-pole* 110 KV transmission line in Pinal County, Arizona, a distance of 4.5 miles. This line crossed noncropland.

Study #6

The ED-5 115 KV *two-pole* transmission line from the Coolidge Substation in Pinal County, Arizona, west and south covering 14 miles.

Study #7

The Coolidge-Oracle 115 KV *two-pole* transmission line from the Coolidge Substation, Pinal County, Arizona, eastward for a distance of 6.5 miles. A copy of the sales along with the easement area, as well as analysis tabes and discussion, are available but not included in this report.

Study #8
The Parker-Phoenix 116 KV *two-pole* transmission line in Maricopa County, Arizona. This line, which was installed in 1945, wed from Avondale to the Roosevelt Irrigation District Canal, a distance of 10 miles. Most of this line was across irrigated cropland.

Study #9
The Davis-Kingman 69 KV *two-pole* transmission line in Mohave County, Arizona. This line was across noncropland and covered a distance of 28 miles.

Study #10
The Parker-Bagdad 69 KV *two-pole* transmission line in Mohave County, Arizona. This line was across noncropland and covered a distance of 30 miles.

Study #11
The Davis-Las Vegas 69 KV *two-pole* transmission line in Clark County, Nevada. This line was across noncropland and covered 50 miles.

Study #12
The Boulder-Nellis Air Base 69 KV *two-pole* transmission line in Clark County, Nevada. The line crossed cropland, noncropland, mining, industrial and urban lands.

Study #13
The Peoria-Agua Fria-Pinnacle Peak Substation 230 KV *tower-supported* transmission line in Maricopa County, Arizona. This Salt River Project line was across cropland and noncropland, and covered a distance of 30 miles.

Studies #14 and #15
Your Appraiser made studies of the Lake Havasu City Development and the Salton City Development. The first abuts Lake Havasu, Arizona, and the latter abuts Salton Sea, California. Both of these developments were platted after being encumbered with an overhead electric transmission line with restrictions against permanent improvements on the easement area. Both of these developments resulted in a loss of residential lots in the easement area only. The developer indicated there was no reluctance on the part of buyers to purchase those lots

abutting the easement area. This agrees with many other studies (Ball's study for Salt River Project, Smith Associate's study for the Potomac Electric Power Company, West Trenton, New Jersey). The Havasu City and Salton City developments were not parallel to the easement area and resulted in curvilinear streets and lots; however, this type of platting is the accepted modern way and predominates even where there are no restrictive easements.

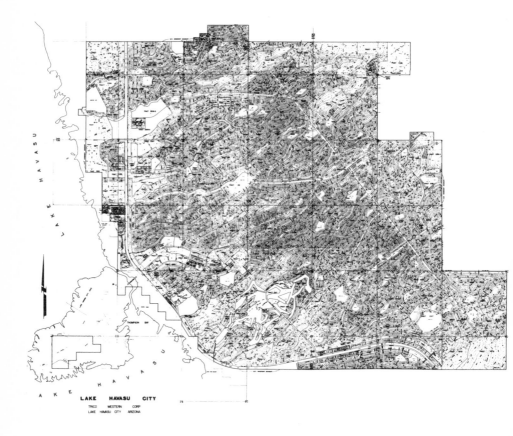

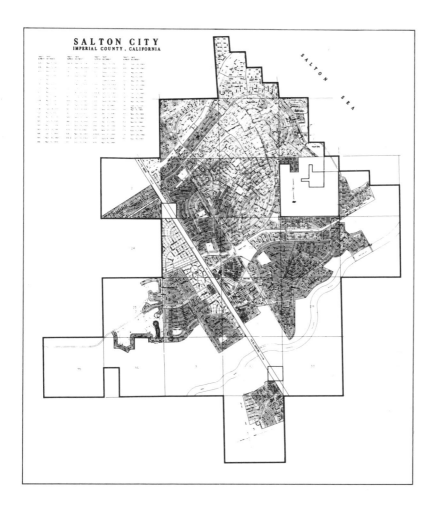

Study #30

The Mead-Liberty 345 KV *tower-supported* transmission line in Maricopa County, Arizona, was erected in March, 1967. (See Study #4.) The portion of this line that was studied lies north of the Roosevelt Irrigation District Canal and involved desert and rural residential land uses. This study was made in 1977.

Study #31
The Pinnacle Peak-Agus Fria 230 KV *tower-supported* transmission line in Maricopa County, Arizona extended from Scottsdale Road on the east to near the Agua Fria River, thence south to
Bell Road. This line crossed desert and rural residential land uses
(see Study #13). This study was made in 1977, while study #13
was made in 1968.

Study #32
The Prescott-Mesa 230 KV *tower-supported* transmission line in
Maricopa County, Arizona. This line was installed in 1950, and
this study was made in 1977. (See Study #1.) This study extended
from the Yavapai-Maricopa County line southeastward to the
north boundary of the Salt River Indian Reservation. This line
crossed desert and rural residential land uses.

The following conclusions were reached from these studies:

1. Transmission line easements crossing medium to large
desert tracts or farms constituted a very small portion of the
whole property, usually less than 5 percent; therefore, a minor
issue in the transaction. It was impossible to measure the exact
effect from a comparison of sales, while opinions of the parties to
the sale indicated that although they understood the restrictions
of the easement, the small amount of the diminution was within
the range of negotiations and not identified. Although
impossible to measure the exact diminution, it was apparent that
the maximum diminution (outer limits) was no greater than 100
percent of the fee value of the easement area.

2. Transmission line easements extending across rural
subdivision or abutting tracts (5-10 acres) that were not crossed
did not lower the lost values when sold; however, the buyers
were usually absentees who did not make a check visually or of
official records of the lots purchased. These buyers were
considered to be uninformed as to the easement restrictions. A
study was made of three units of Golden Valley Ranchos
Subdivision, located west of Kingman, Arizona. The Davis-
Prescott 230 KV transmission line crossed each of these three
units. A total of 262 lots were studied to determine: a. If
encumbered lots would sell and, if so, at what price. b. When
given a free choice of lots, would buyers prefer lots not in the
vicinity of the line — that is, lots at a distance of ¼ to ½ mile,
rather than lots near or abutting the line? The study revealed the
following: a. Those lots encumbered more than 5 percent were
not placed on the market, but were held for later sale. b. All lots

that were encumbered that were placed on the market sold as readily as any of the other lots and at the same price. c. Of the first 92 lots sold (out of a choice of 262) in the three units, 47 were close to the transmission line and 45 were away from the line (lots were divided equally with ½ being close and ½ being away). Of the first 24 lots sold, 14 were close to the line, with 4 out of the 14 actually abutting the line.

3. Transmission line easements extending across suburban-located potential subdivision tracts ready for development into lots with paved streets reduce the value of the land approximately the value of the full fee of the easement area. No severance damage outside of the easement area was found.

4. Irrigated farms, not ready for immediate development as subdivisions with lots and streets, have value in the present use(s). The extent of this value can be measured by the Income Approach, and is the present worth of the interim or transitional yearly income over this period of time prior to developments.

5. Study #8 included a sale of the fee interest to a 40-foot wide strip of land, 660 feet in length, under the transmission line and completely within the easement area. This sale was made for an acces road to land owned by a farmer who had other access, but desired additional access from the road on the west. The underlying fee interest sold for approximately 25 percent of the unencumbered fee of the surrounding land.

6. The Havasu City and Salton Sea Studies indicate that development can proceed on either side of an easement strip with no loss of saleable land outside the easement area.

A number of electric utility customers have made evaluations to determine the effect, if any, that electric transmission lines have on the value of adjacent lands. These evaluations take the form of Land Economic Studies, which are analyses of the *value* of encumbered lands vs. unencumbered lands in the same general area.

The committee on the Environment of the Edison Electric Institute, realizing the increasingly difficult problem of obtaining rights-of-way, requested that a library of Land Economic Studies be compiled. This is being done under the guidance of Mr. F.E. Manley, President of Fitchburg Gas & Electric Light Company, and a member of the Committee on Environment. Twenty-seven Land Economics Studies and nine additional materials have been accumulated thus far.

The studies indicated that an electric transmission line, in and of itself, does not affect the value of adjacent or nearby lands.

EDISON ELECTRIC INSTITUTE LIBRARY OF LAND ECONOMICS STUDIES

I. Studies Prepared by Electric Utility Company Personnel

Company	Title
Alabama Power Co.	Effect on Salability of Real Estate Caused by Imposition of Power Line Right-of-Way
Indiana & Michigan Electric Co.	A Study of Property Values Adjacent to Steel Tower Transmission Lines
New England Power Service Co.	A Study of the Effect of High Voltage Transmission Lines on Adjacent Real Estate Use and Values
Orange & Rockland Utilities, Inc.	Recreation Areas Affected by Transmission Lines, F.E. Manley
Pennsylvania Power & Light Co.	A Study of the Effects Which an Existing Transmission Line Has on the Development of the Immediate Area for Residential Housing, R.C. Zundel
Philadelphia Electric Co.	The Effect of "High Lines" on the Market Value of Abutting Properties — Let's Learn the Facts! R.P. Garbarino
Potomac Electric Power Co.	Land Economic Study — Cool Spring Heights Subdivision, Prince George's County, Maryland
Texas Power & Light Co.	Summary of a Study Made Concerning Values of Land Abutting Transmission Line Rights-of-Way
The Detroit Edison Co.	A Study of Land Values Adjacent to Steel Tower Transmission Line Easements, C.W. Layton

II. Studies Prepared by Independent Organizations or Individuals for Electric Utility Companies

Author	Title and Company
H.H. Gagnon	Analysis and Comments on a Land Economic Study — Fitchburg Gas & Electric Light Co.
R.B. Lamb	Appraisal of Conditions and Study of Effects of Electrical Transmission Lines on Adjacent Lands — Southern California Edison Co.
Two Real Estate Appraisers	A Report by Two Local Independent Appraisers — Duke Power Co.
C.W. Deremo	A Market Study of the Economic Effects of Steel Tower Transmission Line Easements Upon Dwelling Resales — The Detroit Edison Co.
P.F. Brennan	A Study of the Effect of Transmission Line Rights-of-Way on Adjacent Residential Properties —Southern California Edison Co.
Herbert H. Smith Associates	Electric Transmission Lines and Property Values — Potomac Electric Power Co.
E.B. Moffet	Market Values Along Transmission Line Easement, Friendly Hills — Menota Heights — Northern States Power Co.
G.A. Reeves, Jr. and R.E. Swan	The Effect of High Voltage Transmission Lines on the Value of Real Estate — Oklahoma Gas & Electric Co.
Institute of Urban Research, University of Connecticut	Transmission Line Rights-of-Way and Residential Values — The Connecticut Light & Power Co., Hartford Electric Light Co.

This is true whether the lands were utilized for residential, commercial, or industrial purposes. Further, electric transmission lines are compatible with adjacent land use. In all cases the evidence indicates that there are people willing to live, work, and play, near, around, or underneath electric transmission lines. These people constitute a segment of the market large enough to maintain the value of adjacent or nearby lands. In addition, several studies indicate that some people prefer to live on contiguous property due to the spaciousness the right-of-way affords.

Valuation and Discussion of Pertinent Approaches

The various economic studies previously discussed, along with the general conclusions that were reached from these studies, served as a basis for the valuation process. These studies furnished comparable sales for the Market Data Approach, the Income Approach on income producing properties, and the Anticipated Use method of the Cost Approach. Where the subject was a rural nonagricultural property and the Market Data Approach could not measure any diminution greater than the outer limits, it became necessary to use the Anticipated Use or Development Method of the Cost Approach. The Developmental Method of the Cost Approach is typically used in an area where market data is very limited. As used in this report, it serves to indicate the present worth of future diminution (or damage) arising from subdivision development. Subdivision potential is present in many rural lands and even though not imminent, it was considered in this method. The most likely future subdivision development plan was considered, as indicated by County Master Plans, or likely in the opinion of the Appraiser. The Anticipated Use or Developmental Method of the Cost Approach has been utilized through the process of measuring *salvage value* of the remainder property. To understand the thinking of developers and modern concepts of subdivision platting, Studies #14 and #15 were utilized in this approach.

The typical income producing property, wherein the Income Approach would be utilized, would be all types of agricultural lands with a future life exceeding 3 to 5 years. Properties that are in transition from agricultural to other higher and better uses would have value in the interim use, as well as a present value for other future uses. *Nonagricultural value* as used herein applies to all uses except agricultural. Nonagricultural use applies to rural desert lands held in speculation; suburban acreage developable, but not developed; and urban lots. Nonagricultural lands include all nonirrigable desert regardless of arability. At the time salvage value is determined the interim agricultural life has ended, so no agricultural value remains even though vegetable gardening, flower culture, fruit trees, citrus, dates, vineyard, and nut trees may be grown for home use. Such home use crops are grown at the risk of the operator.

Market Data Approach

The following sales were selected from the "Table of Sales" of the various studies as the *most comparable* to subject property:

Cropland Sales

Sale 1-15 (1N,6E) Maricopa County, Arizona. This sale property is similar to the subject with respect to present use, being in transition from cropland to other higher and better uses, location with respect to metropolitan Phoenix, roads, general size, utilities available, being in a water district, and encumbered with an electric transmission line that traverses the property. This sale property was included in economic study Number 1 (Prescott-Mesa 230 KV Line) on page 47.

Sale 3-24 (1N,3W) Maricopa County, Arizona. This sale property is similar to the subject with respect to present use, being in transition from cropland to other higher and better uses location with respect to metropolitan Phoenix, roads, general size, utilities available, being in a water district, and encumbered with an electric transmission line that traverses the property. This sale property was included in economic study Number 36 (Mead-Liberty 345 KV Line) on page 45.

Sale 1-28 (1N,2W) Maricopa County, Arizona. This sale property is similar to the subject with respect to present use, being in transition from cropland to other higher and better uses, location with respect to metropolitan Phoenix, roads, general size, utilities available, being in a water district, and encumbered with an electric transmission line that traverses the property in a diagonal similar to subject. This sale property was included in economic study Number 35 (Liberty-Estrella 230 KV Line) on page 4.

Sale 1-23 (1N,3W) Maricopa County, Arizona. This sale property is similar to the subject with respect to present use, being in transition from cropland to other higher and better uses, location with respect to metropolitan Phoenix, roads, general size, utilities available, being in a water district, and encumbered with an electric transmission line that traverses the property in a diagonal similar to subject. This sale property was included in economic study Number 8 (Parker-Phoenix 116 KV Line) on page 5.

The above cited sales were sufficiently large that the easement area constituted a small percent of the whole. It was apparent that the maximum diminution was no greater than 100 percent of the fee value of the easement area. These sales were unreliable indicators of diminution attributable to the easement area. Other approaches must be used for accurate calculation of diminution attributable to the easement.

VALUE INDICATED, MARKET
DATA APPROACH $ Not conclusive

Representation of transmission lines crossing cropland sales.

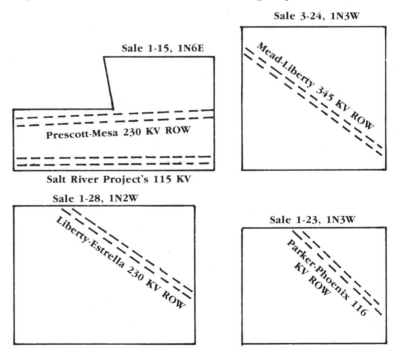

Sale 3-24, 1N3W

Sale 1-15, 1N6E

Mead-Liberty 345 KV ROW

Prescott-Mesa 230 KV ROW

Salt River Project's 115 KV

Sale 1-28, 1N2W

Liberty-Estrella 230 KV ROW

Sale 1-23, 1N3W

Parker-Phoenix 116 KV ROW

INCOME APPROACH

Irrigated farms, not ready for immediate development as subdivisions with lots and streets, have value in the present use(s). The extent of this value can be measured by the Income Approach, and is the present worth of the interim or transitional yearly income over this period of time prior to development.

Agricultural Life

The subject property is in transition from agricultural to other higher and better uses. The measure of agricultural life is through the analysis of urban growth in the neighborhood; also through a study of land values in the rural areas, suburban fringe, and current urbanized residential developments. This has been done and this analysis indicates an agricultural life of *10* years before the subject property has the potential for development as a residential subdivision, or a master planned community including various compatible uses.

Agricultural Value

The following sales were selected from the "Table of Sales" of the various studies as the *most comparable* to subject property:

> Sale 1-15 (1N,6E) Maricopa County, Arizona (Study No. 1, Prescott-Mesa, 230 KV Line) at page 47.
> Sale 1-23 (1N,3W) Maricopa County, Arizona (Study No. 8, Parker-Phoenix, 116 KV Line) at page 5.
> See Market Data Approach for items of comparability.

The structures holding the transmission lines occupy less than 3 percent of the easement area; however, the following increased production costs are attributable to the easement:

1. Compaction of the soil around the structures and between the structures during construction as the electric lines are laid is 1.15 acres at each structure location and 4.6 acres between the structures for a total of 5.75 acres; which is approximately 46 percent of the easement area (12.5 ac.). This area is considered to be compacted to the extent that extra costs of tillage will be required the *first year* of farming. This has been computed and is valued at *$15* per easement acre.

(Reference — Bulletin A-39, "Minimum Tillage in the Southwest," Agric. Exp. Station and the Cooperative addenda) Compaction, per acre $15

2. Extra labor will be required during all waterings to get the water past the structures. There will also be extra costs for land preparation, planting, and cultivation because of lost time at each structure. These have been computed and are valued as shown below. (Reference — Technical Bulletin 174, "Costs and Returns for Major Field Crops in Central Arizona," Agric. Exp. Station, College of Agriculture, the University of Arizona, Cooperative Extension Service and Agricultural Experiment Station.)

A. *Irrigation Operations — Before Easement*
Regular irrigation labor for a cotton crop has a value of $34.79 per acre. This involves 10.33 hours (620 minutes) of labor per acre with ten irrigations or 62 minutes per irrigation. Ten rows wide, ¼ mile long is 1 acre so the time is 6.2 minutes per row per irrigation.

B. *Irrigation Operations — After Easement*
The towers restrict the free flow of irrigation water and ditching must be done to allow the water to continue to flow down each row. The water must be channeled into one ditch to flow around the towers, then divided again into the appropriate and matching row on the other side of the tower. Labor is required to see that all of the water does not flow down the same row, but is spread out over as many as 13 rows. Every time field operations are undertaken the farm machinery knocks down some of the ridges between the rows. Computations were made to determine the average number of tower restrictions per easement acre and the extra time that was involved in labor. This was then expressed in hours per easement acre.
5.83 hrs. @ $3.36 per hr. = $19.59 .... use $19.60

C. *Field Operations — Before Easement*
Regular preharvest field operations labor for a cotton crop has a value of $14.67 per field acre. This involves 4.37 hours (262 minutes) of labor per acre involving 18 field operations, or 14.5 minutes per operation. Ten rows wide, one-fourth mile long is 1 acre, so the time is 1.45 minutes per row per operation.

D. *Field Operations — After Easement*

The towers restrict typical farming operations by requiring the operator to plant, cultivate, etc. to the tower location, stop his tractor, lift the equipment and pull around the tower, then back the tractor into the proper location, lower the equipment and proceed down the rows. This requires extra time which involves farm machinery costs and labor costs. Computations were made to determine the average number of rows that were restricted by the towers per easement acre and the extra time involved in field operations. This was then expressed in hours per easement acre.

5 hrs. x $3.36 per hr. = $16.93 .... use <u>$16.95</u>

3. Extra aerial spraying of herbicides, insecticides, and defoliants will be required in the easement area. This has been computed and is valued at $55.54 per easement acre when cotton is grown. Other farm crops such as alfalfa, barley or grain sorghum do not require as much aerial spraying. The cost of the aerial spraying for alfalfa is $26.78 per acre. The typical rotation is as follows:

Cotton 33 percent x $55.54 = $18.32
Alfalfa $\underline{67}$ percent x $26.78 = $\underline{17.94}$
100           $36.26 . . . use <u>$36.26</u>

4. There will be lost area around the structures. Structure locations have lost areas amounting to 0.29 acre per twin tower location. There is one twin tower location per 12.5 easement acres, therefore the lost area is 0.023 acre per easement acre, with a value of about $2.76, rounded to $3 per easement acre. (see page 39 — $120 per acre net income x 0.023 = $2.76)

Lost area, per acre ....use <u>$3.00</u>

Agricultural Value Computation, Before the Taking

Normal income (from page 39) is $120.00 per acre. Use 10 years, 4.0 percent rate of return (from page 52), present worth factor of 8.111.

$120.00 per acre x 8.111   = $973.32
rounded to   =   975

Agricultural Value Computation, After the Taking

1st year normal income (from page *39*) per acre $120.00
1. Compaction $15.00
2B. Irrigation operations 19.60
2D. Field operations 16.95
3. Aerial spraying 36.30
4. Lost areas 3.0
Extra Costs, per acre $90.85
Net Income, 1st year (not discounted)............$29.15
$29.15 per acre x present worth factor at 4% rate,
0.961 = ...$28.01

2nd through 10th year normal income (from page 39)
per acre $120.00

2B, 2D, 3, & 4 (all except No. 1)
Extra Costs, per acre $75.85
Net Income 2-10 year (not discounted).......$44.15
$44.15 per acre x present worth factor at 4% rate,
7.150 = ...$315.67

VALUE INDICATED —   Agricultural value $344 per acre
INCOME APPROACH

Anticipated Use or Developmental Method of the Cost Approach

Nonagricultural Value

Part A

The following sales are selected from the "Table of Sales" of the various studies as indicating *salvage value* when subdivision occurs. These sales are comparable to subject only with respect to measuring diminution at the end of the transition period.

1-14 (4N,4E) — Maricopa County, Arizona
1-14 (1N,6E) — Maricopa County, Arizona
1-16 (1N,7E) — Maricopa County, Arizona

Sale 1-14 (4N,4E) — Maricopa County, Arizona. This sale property is similar to subject with respect to angle of transmission line across the property, generally the same size, having a highest and best use for residential subdivision, location near the metropolitan Phoenix area, similar shape and access roads with some paved roads. Details of the sales are elsewhere in this report. This sale property was included in Economic Study Number 1 (Prescott-Mesa, 230 KV Line) on page 36.

Sale 1-14 (1N,6E) — Maricopa County, Arizona. This sale property is similar to subject with respect to having a transmission line across the property, nearly the same size, having a highest and best use at time of sale for residential subdivision later, it was developed as Dreamland Villa, located near the metropolitan Phoenix area, similar shape and access roads with some paved roads. Details of the sale are elsewhere in this report. This sale property was included in Economic Study Number 1 (Prescott-Mesa, 230 KV Line) at page 51.

Sale 1-16 (1N,7E) — Maricopa County, Arizona. This sale property is similar to subject with respect to angle of transmission line across the property, generally the same size, having a highest and best use for residential subdivision location was near the metropolitan Phoenix area, with similar shape and access roads with some paved roads. Details of the sale are elsewhere in this report. This sale property was included in Economic Study Number 1 (Prescott-Mesa, 230 KV Line) on page 62.

Part B

The following subdivisions are selected from the various studies as indicating damages, if present, when subdivision occurs. These subdivisions are comparable to subject only with respect to measuring the probable damages when subdivision occurs.

> Palm Gardens of Mesa Unit 1, 2, 3, and 4 — Maricopa County, Arizona
>
> Dreamland Villa 7 and 8, Mesa, Arizona — Maricopa County, Arizona
>
> > Tom Ball's Study, dated 3-27-64 of Mesa — Coolidge 230 KV Line at pages 18-39. (See reference to Ball's report under studies 14 and 15.)
>
> Francisco Park and Paradise Palms Subdivisions, Las Vegas, Nevada. Southern Nevada Power Co. 100 foot wide ROW.

Havasu City, near Lake Havasu, Mohave County, Arizona
    Study No. 15, Imperial Irrigation District, 100 ft. wide
    ROW, at pages 1-8.
The Riviera, Salton City, California
    Study No. 14, Davis-Parker No. 1, 230 KV Line, page 1-15.

Subdivision Plat of Francisco Park and Paradise Palms, Las Vegas, Nevada, showing
Southern Nevada Power Co. Transmission line through the subdivision.

Subdivision Plat of "The Riviera", Salton City, California showing The Imperial
Irrigation and Power District's Transmission line through the subdivision.

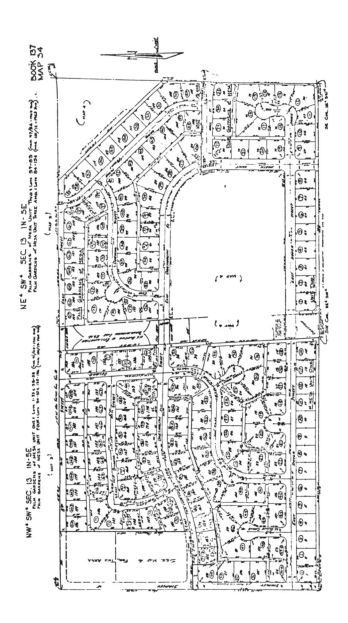

Subdivision Plats of Palm Gardens of Mesa Units 1, 2, 3, and 4, Mesa, Arizona showing Prescott-Mesa Transmission line through the subdivision.

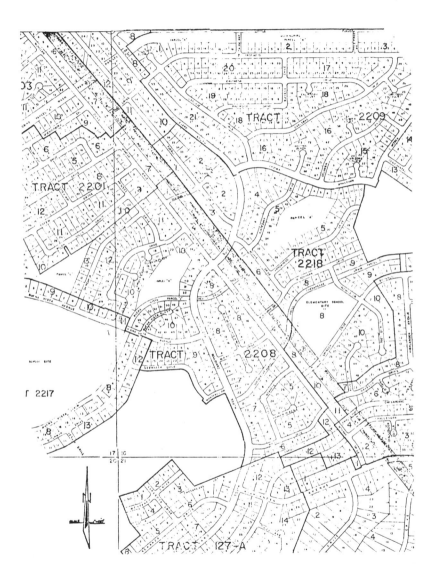

Subdivision Plat of Lake Havasu City, Arizona showing Parker-Davis Transmission line through the subdivision.

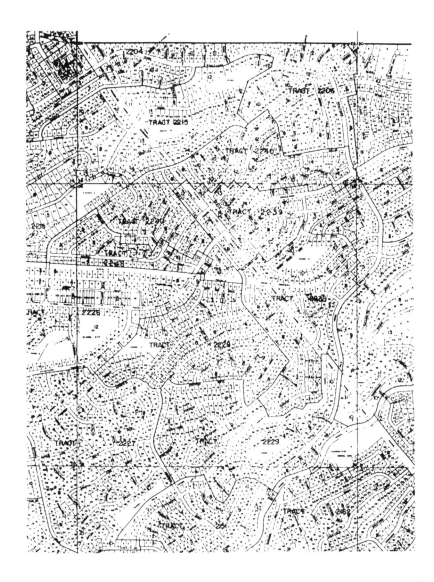

Subdivision Plat of Lake Havasu City, Arizona showing Parker-Davis Transmission line through the subdivision.

Salvage Value

Based on economic studies and especially the cited salvage value sales where installation of the transmission line preceded all sales by a period of from 5 to 20 years, the salvage value of the easement area, as determined by knowledgeable buyers and sellers, with *sufficient measurable sales to be statistically significant,* has little or no value when these rights are duly considered out in the open all parties have full knowledge of all the uses for which the easement area is adapted and for which it may be used.

When a housing developer undertakes the development of a tract of land that is encumbered with a restrictive easement, he considers the most practical and feasible subdivision plan, with thought being given to the following alternatives:

1. Using the easement area as a street (known as the street concept). The presence of power poles or towers on the easement area precludes full use of this area as a street; however, the center portion of the easement area may be used as a median between two streets. If this is done, the extra width of the two streets and the median means a loss of land that is usually equal to the full width of the easement area.

2. Using the easement area as the back portion of lots (known as the back-lot concept). If this is done, the center portion of the easement area on which is located the power poles or towers must be left open for a maintenance road, so this area is designated as an alley. This alley area which is outside of lot lines has a width of about 50 to 60 percent of the width of the easement area. Water, gas, electricity, and sewer lines, if located at the rear of the lots, must cross this easement area, thus increasing the developers' cost. Extra street paving, clearing, grading, surveying, curb and gutter costs are also incurred. The developer cannot charge more for the lots that abut the easement to defray this extra development cost, so this loss is charged against the proposed development. These development costs are approximately equal to the raw land cost of the easement in the alley; therefore, the total loss is approximately equal to the full value of the raw land costs of the entire easement area.

3. Do not develop the easement area, but use it as a utility corridor (known as the corridor concept). If this is done, the developer loses this land, but does not develop across it; therefore, does

not incur development costs on this land. The land on either side of the easement area is developed independent of the other.

At the end of the transition period (between speculator purchase and developer purchase), the easement area with structures will have little or no value, as shown by the studies indicated above. If the easement area with installed structures has only a small amount of value (say 3 or 4 percent) at the end of the transition period (salvage value), then the present worth of the nonagricultural value is a present worth factor times 3 or 4 percent which is approximately 2 percent.

Before Market Value (from prior pages)$3,000 per acre
    Less agricultural value of $975 per acre
    Nonagricultural Value $2,025 per acre

After Market Value
    $2,025 per acre x 2 percent   =   40.50 per acre
              rounded to   40.00 per acre

VALUE INDICATED — ANTICIPATED USE OR DEVELOP-MENTAL METHOD OF COST APPROACH
                    Nonagricultural value $40 per acre

Damages

There are two elements to be considered, severance and proximity damages.

An easement does not sever the property as does a fee taking. In a fee taking, the easement area can be fenced off, while damages do not necessarily result, the land is severed. In the case of an easement, the underlying fee retains the right to travel back and forth over the easement and use the area for any purpose that will not conflict with maintaining the facility for which the easement was acquired. In the case of the subject, there is sufficient land on each side of the easement area to be platted into streets and lots. The above cited subdivisions have similar types of easements crossing in a similar manner. A study of these subdivisions indicates there were no losses of platted lots outside the easement area. The highest and best use of the land outside the easement area remained the same as before the taking. The developer merely platted the subdivision to conform with the easement in the same manner as he would around washes, streambanks, cul-de-sacs; however, this is the accepted modern type of platting. The gridiron method of platting, which predominated 30 to 40 years ago, is now used only with curvilinear platting. This modern type of platting is necessary to control traffic and to provide a variety of lot shapes for a modern society.

Proximity damage is attributed to claims that people will not buy or be interested in properties adjacent to a transmission line. All economic studies have shown there was no reluctance on the part of the buyers to purchase lots abutting the easement area, nor was there any delay in the sale of these lots.

The taking of a perpetual easement usually results in no offsite residential damages, either severance or proximity, as discussed above.

A fee taking also results in no offsite residential damages, either severance or proximity, because the acquiring agency has no plans for fencing the right-of-way at mutually agreed upon areas.

Agricultural Damages

The taking for the right-of-way will leave a strip of land to the west 990 ft. in width, 2,460 feet in length consisting of 60 acres. The property plat (page 9) shows fields 14 and 15 are irrigated from head ditches that extend east to west, and the flow down the rows is to the south. If the right of way is acquired in the fee simple, it is assumed that the acquiring agency will allow the head ditch water to continue to flow to the west, and it is also assumed that the present owner operator will be allowed to enter into an agricultural lease to farm the ROW area. If the ROW is acquired as an easement, the present owner operator can level the land in the ROW area except immediately around the tower locations. This is a matter of concern to the present owners because they plan to level all the land in fields 14 and 15. The land lying west of the ROW (60 acres) can economically be farmed and will not be affected by the transmision line, therefore not increasing operation costs as shown on pages 52-54. These items are as follows: 2A & 2B Irrigation operations 2C & 2D field operations. 3. Aerial spraying, and 4. Lost areas.

In the event that the acquiring agency will not allow land leveling, or that the tower locations will require relocation of header ditches, additional damages will result and this Appraiser will amend this report.

COMPUTATION OF VALUE OF TAKING EASEMENT

Total market value of full fee, ROW area, per acre $3,000
Market value of property rights in ROW area
remaining with fee owner, land only:

    Agricultural rights, per acre $344

    Nonagricultural rights, per acre
    (value during transition period plus
    salvage value at end of transition
    period, discounted to present date) $40

Present value of fee owner's property rights, per acre $384

Market value of easement rights, per acre $2,616

EASEMENT

Value of part taken

10.0 acres easement x $2,616 per acre $26,160

Damages to remainder lands, caused by the taking of
the easement right of way, and/or by the construction
of the improvements in the manner as now proposed.

  None   acres x $ None   per acre $ None

Total market value of easement rights to be
acquired and damages to the remainder lands —
opinion of just compensation $26,160

FEE TAKING *

Value of part taken

10.0 acres fee x $3,000 per acre $30,000

Damages to remainder lands, caused by the taking of
the right-of-way, and/or by the construction of
the improvements in the manner as now proposed.[1].

  None   acres x $ None   per acre $ None

Total market value of fee taking and damages to
the remainder lands.
Opinion of just compensation. $30,000

---

[1] It is assumed that if fee taking is exercised, the access along the midsection
lines will not be affected.

* Acquiring agency requested valuation for a fee taking as well as easement. The
land owner is given a choice as to the taking.

BIBLIOGRAPHY

Campbell, Colin. Transmission Line Easements in Condemnation RIGHT OF WAY. Oct., 1963, p.45-52.

Carll, Cloice D. Valuation of Electric Transmission Line Easement Rights of Way. APPRAISAL JOURNAL. July, 1958, p. 332-348.
    Also printed in American Institute of Real Estate Appraisers. REAL ESTATE APPRAISAL PRACTICE. 1958, p. 591-614 and American Institute of Real Estate Appraisers. CONDEMNATION APPRAISAL PRACTICE. 1961. p. 251-274.

Carll, Cloice D. Valuation of a Power Line Right of Way. RIGHT OF WAY. Aug., 1965. p. 13-24.
    Also printed in APPRAISAL JOURNAL. Apr., 1956, p. 248-265.

Crawford, Claude O. Appraising Damages to Land From Power Line Easements, APPRAISAL JOURNAL. July, 1955, p. 367-378.

Derbes, Max J. Jr. Procedural Guidelines for Measurement of Proximity Damages. APPRAISAL JOURNAL. July, 1967, p. 374-379.

Dunlap, Donald C. Appraisal of Pipeline Rights of Way. APPRAISAL JOURNAL. July, 1951.
    Also printed in American Institute of Real Estate Appraisers. CONDEMNA-TION APPRAISAL PRACTICE. 1961, p. 243-250.

Everhart, Marion E. The Use of Suitability Classes in the Valuation of Nonagricultural Lands. THE REAL ESTATE APPRAISER, January-February, 1977, p. 32-36.

Kinnard, William N. Jr. Tower Lines and Residential Property Values. APPRAISAL JOURNAL. Apr., 1967, p. 269-284.

Patt, H.B. and W.B. Davis. Appraising of Damages to Farms by Power Line Easements. APPRAISAL JOURNAL. July, 1947, p. 330-338.
Pilmer, C.L. The Effect of Pipelines on the Farming Operation and on Farm Land Values in Webster County, Iowa. RIGHT OF WAY. Dec., 1969, p. 33-40.
Young, H.J. and R.S. Thorsell. Environment, Economics, and Electric Utility Right of Way. RIGHT OF WAY. Oct., 1970, p. 41-43.

CHAPTER FIFTEEN

Review for

Property Tax Purposes

MELVIN P. GRUENHAGEN, CRA

Melvin P. Gruenhagen, CRA, is an Associate Appraiser with the California State Board of Equalization in Sacramento, California. He received his B.A. in Business Administration from Sacramento State College and his M.A. in Real Estate Appraisal and Investment Analysis from the University of Wisconsin.

Mr. Gruenhagen holds the "Certified Review Appraiser" designation with the National Association of Review Appraisers and is a member of the Society of Real Estate Appraisers and the Society of Governmental Appraisers.

Review for

Property Tax Purposes

INTRODUCTION

Local governments nationwide rely upon ad valorem tax systems to provide a major portion of the monies needed to carry out operations. Equitable assessments, i.e., those based upon values that closely approximate fair market value as of assessment date, are a universally accepted standard for such systems.[1]

A reappraisal of property in the tax base area is necessary from time to time to maintain equity because market value changes do not affect all properties uniformly.

Many local governments maintain acceptable levels of equity by operating appraisal programs that annually cover a sizeable proportion of the whole. California, for example, passed legislation in 1976 requiring all county assessors to develop and file a plan by 1978 whereby each and every parcel of real property would be reappraised at least once within a five year period.[2]

Maintaining an equitable ad valorem tax base is a formidable task. Almost eight million real property parcels in California were taxed during the 1977-78 tax year, and an estimated 3.5 million of those values were changed from the prior year.[3] The 3.5 million value changes were made by some 2,100 real property Appraisers staffing 58 county assessor offices, and included lot splits, new construction, mass "trending", computer-assisted appraisals, conventional appraisals, and miscellaneous changes. Although similar data are not available on a nationwide basis, a scant moment's reflection is all that's needed to grasp the enormity of the appraisal task performed each year by the nation's tax assessment Appraisers. The appraisal review task is, of course, correspondingly large because, regardless of the type of value change, a review program is critically important to ensure that the appraisals are made thoughtfully and accurately.

Appraisals prepared for property tax purposes are reviewed to effect a level of quality control that produces an equitable tax base. Appraisal reviews can be performed by staff at several levels within the appraisal production unit and by Reviewers outside the production unit, including review by other-than-local levels of government. Because both the nature and size of the appraisal reviews rightfully vary with circumstance, this section will not attempt to treat all possible circumstances. Discussion will be limited to the California experience. The reader should not interpret this limitation to mean that the California experience is ideal, or even that it can be universally applied. However, because California's assessment program is generally recognized internationally as one of excellence, it will hopefully provide a useful guideline for others.

Ordinarily, appraisals for ad valorem tax purposes are produced in a mass appraisal system. Conventional appraisal techniques are applied in these systems, but unconventional techniques—such as EDP-produced multiple regression analysis or trending—may also be used. Reviewers should understand each technique in detail.

Appraisal Technique Defined

Conventional appraisal techniques are defined to include the three basic approaches to value: cost, income, and sales comparison. Depending on the circumstances, i.e., property use type, the availability of data, and the utility of each approach, one or more approaches will be processed. When more than one approach is processed, the several value indicators are reconciled into a final value estimate.

Unconventional appraisal techniques are defined to include the multiple regression analysis and trending techniques. In a step-wise multiple regression (MR) analysis, a sales price and property characteristics for each of a number of sold properties are processed by computer to develop a regression equation that provides the best fit between sale price and property characteristics. When an equation of acceptably high correlation is produced, it is applied via computer to develop, via property characteristics, an estimated selling price (value) for each subject of the population of properties.

Trending is an appraisal technique in which the differences between current selling prices for a class of property in a neighborhood and corresponding existing values are measured to develop sales ratios. These ratios are developed into adjustment factors which are applied to comparable sold and unsold properties in the neighborhood. This action produces an approximation of current fair market value. The process is fairly simple, but its effectiveness is directly related to the uniformity of ratios in the array from which the trend factors were developed.

Review Is A Multi-Level Process

In California, review of currently produced appraisals is performed by Appraisers from both line and staff divisions in assessors' offices and by Appraisers from the State Board of Equalization. The first level of appraisal review is performed by crew supervisors and others in the assessors' hierarchy of line management. A second level of review is performed by his standards section which is a staff division. A third level of appraisal review is conducted by the State Board of Equalization's Assessment Practices Survey crews. A fourth level of appraisal review is conducted by the Board's Office of Appraisal Appeals.

Figure 1 illustrates the several levels of appraisal review identified here, and several other levels that may also be involved from time to time.

An appraisal review evaluates how well an appraisal meets the profession's standards for technical competence.

APPRAISAL STANDARDS

Today, a number of organizations publish textbooks and journals, conduct educational programs, establish educational standards for professional designations, and enforce standards of ethical practice among their membership. Governmental-oriented organizations, and various state and local governmental

FIGURE 1
CHART OF ASSESSMENT
APPRAISAL REVIEWS
IN CALIFORNIA

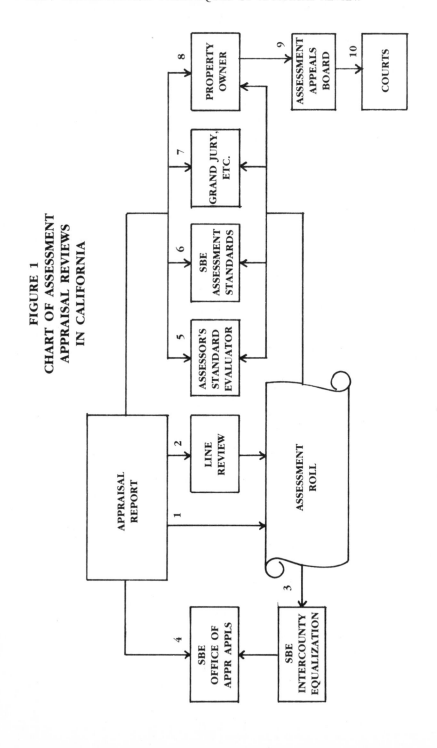

units, serve a somewhat similar function. The State Board of Equalization, for example, provides a very comprehensive program for establishing standards for California's county assessors. It publishes a series of manuals that are collectively called "The Assessors' Handbook." Although the Handbook is written specifically for use by California assessment personnel, it is entirely compatible with principles and theory accepted in the private sector. In addition, the Board, like the private-sector organizations, conducts appraisal training courses and seminars for property tax Appraisers. Moreover, Appraisers must be certificated before they are permitted to appraise property. Annual training credit must be maintained to keep an Appraiser's certificate active.

However thoroughly the principles and practices are treated in the industry's publications, training courses, journals, etc., not every detail likely to be encountered is, or could be, included. Like an appraisal itself, judgment is the keystone of success. Appraisal review, therefore, evaluates appraisals against both industry-established guidelines and standards and the Reviewer's judgment.

THE REVIEW

Highest and Best Use

Because the Appraisers' projections of highest and best use are the keystone upon which the appraisal rests, the Review

---

1 Many appraisals are enrolled without review
2 Line supervisors review appraisals before enrollment
3 State Board of Equalization, Intercounty Equalization Division (DIE) appraises randomly selected properties, and assessor reviews DIE appraisal
4 State Board of Equalization, Office of Appraisal Appeals resolves disputes between assessor's and DIE's appraisals
5 Assessor's standards unit reviews appraisals and other assessment procedures
6 State Board of Equalization, Assessment Standards Division, reviews appraisals and other assessment procedures
7 County Grand Jury, District Attorney, and other local government officials can review appraisals and other assessment procedures
8 Property owner may review the appraisal
9 Property may appeal the assessment for review by the county assessment appeal board (AAB)
10 Assessor or property owner may appeal AAB decision to court, but the courts usually refuse to review valuation questions

Appraiser evaluates this feature with great care. Its importance cannot be overemphasized, for it alone is the basis for selecting that set of market data that will be appropriate for processing into indicators of value. Moreover, each projection provides the necessary clues for determining whether the cost, income, or sales comparison approaches will, individually or in combination, best answer the appraisal question and solve the appraisal problem.

Highest and best use is generally considered to be that used for a particular property which at the time of appraisal is, in the minds of buyers and sellers that are representative of "the market", likely to produce the greatest net return over a period of time. Because a property's existing use is most often also its highest and best use, most projections pose little or no problem. On the other hand, properties which have a potential for higher and best uses that differ from existing uses inevitably pose more difficult problems.

The credibility of any projection of highest and best use is largely dependent upon how satisfactorily it meets the following criteria. The use must be legal, probable, the most profitable for the total property over a reasonable time, and based upon existing land ownership. Reviewers should be especially discriminating when evaluating the supporting basis for the "most profitable" criterion when the projection involves an undeveloped site or a property already developed for another use, because a feasibility analysis may be the only reasonable basis for supporting the projection. However, because feasibility studies require extensive, time-consuming research of a specialized nature, only the largest properties warrant such attention in a mass appraisal program.

The Cost Approach to Value

The cost approach to value can be applied to all improved properties by estimating land value, estimating cost new less depreciation, and summing the land and depreciated improvement values. The review should verify that cost factors applied in the replacement and reproduction cost methods are timely and appropriate for the improvement's quality classification, size, and locale, and that historical costs are properly established and, whenever necessary, trended to the effective appraisal date by timely trend factors. Land value estimates should be reviewed with respect to their bases which may be direct comparisons with comparable vacant land sales, abstractions from improved property sales, or land residual capitalization approaches postulating highest and best use improvements. The most closely comparable sales available should be applied in the direct comparison method; the improvements should be properly costed and depreciation estimates reasonable in the abstraction method; and the highest and best use projections, fair rent estimates, and capitalization rates should meet the test of credibility in the land residual capitalization method.

Because historical cost approach value indicators for newly constructed, high valued, commercial and industrial properties are often accorded a high credibility rating when reconciling several indicators into a final estimate of value, reviews should identify that all direct and indirect costs incurred by both the contractor and developer are properly accounted for.

Large construction projects frequently incur costs that require careful analysis to identify items and amounts includable from items and amounts excludable. Costs for temporary utilities, temporary by-pass sidewalks, contractor's fees, employee parking fees, builder's risk insurance, city business tax, and bonds are examples of direct, contractor-incurred costs that are normally included. Architect's fees, project administration, feasibility studies, soil and materials testing, and surveying are examples of direct, developer-incurred costs normally included. Real estate taxes covering both the site and partially complete structures for the construction period, insurance and interest on project costs, are examples of indirect developer-incurred costs also normally included. Excessive change order costs exemplify an excludable cost. The allowable and excessive amounts are based upon an evaluation of circumstances responsible for the orders.

Cost estimates for fully operational properties such as apartment complexes, offices, motels, shopping centers, and other multiple tenant properties should include costs for the "fill-up" or "start-up" period. Direct expenses incurred for leasing and promotional activities, as well as indirect costs for net income lost during the construction and business development period, are also includable costs.

The Income Approach to Value

Any method whereby income is converted into an estimate of value may be defined as the income approach to value.

Conversion may be accomplished by a capitalization process, in which a rate iteratively sums the present worth values for a series of incomes, or by a multiplier process in which income, by a multiple of itself, is expanded into an indicator of value.

The capitalization proces may convert perpetual or terminal incomes, each of which may be constant, inclining, declining, or in any combination, into indicators of value. The indicators may be produced directly by applying an overall rate to income imputed to the property or by a residual process whereby a portion of a property's income is imputed to the land, if the land value is known, or to both, if neither land or building value is known. Value indicators for the total property are obtained by adding the known land value to the capitalized building income value, building value to capitalized land value, and reversionary land value to capitalized land and building value. The multiplier process, on the other hand, may convert annual, monthly, or daily, gross or net, perpetual or terminal, incomes into indicators of value.

Whether an appraisal employs a capitalization or multiplier process, the income and conversion factor (rate or multipler) are two key items in a review of the income approach. Both items should be rooted in the most comparable market data available. Operating statements for the subject property, comparable properties, and rental studies contain basic information that Appraisers reconcile into the economic income projections that are subsequently converted into value indicators. An effective review must evaluate (1) the comparability of properties considered and resolutions for differences, (2) the reasonableness by which both earnings and expense trends and patterns are accommodated in the projected incomes, and (3) the discreteness by which each income and expense item on operating statements were evaluated.

Another key item in a review of the income approach to value is the estimate of remaining economic life. This item is also rooted in analyses of market behaviour that relates specifically to the appraisal problem. Although this estimate is rather subjective in nature, it should, nevertheless, be supported reasonably by market-based actions and attitudes.

The Comparative Sales Approach to Value

In the comparative sales approach to value, market data such as sales, listings, offers, options, and the opinions of realtors and people in the supply and demand sectors for both subject and comparable properties, are applied directly to the appraisal problem.

A review of the comparative sales approach evaluates the selection and processing of market data into an indicator of value. The selected sales should be the most comparable available at appraisal date and meet the criteria that qualifies them as reliable indicators of value. This criteria specifies that sales take place under open market conditions, the transacting parties have reasonable knowledge of the property's present and future uses, neither party takes advantage of the other's exigencies, a reasonable time is allowed to find a buyer, neither collusion nor love and affection influence the sale, and the sale is measured in terms of cash.

The selection of comparables can be evaluated by scanning the array of sales on a master list, or an analysis worksheet such as illustrated in Figure 4, identifying the set of comparables available, and comparing the selected sales to the unselected sales.

Reconciling Indicator Values into Value

In the reconciliation process, the Appraiser reviews, for each of the approaches to value included in an appraisal, the data selected and processed. He evaluates the manner in which each data item affects, positively, negatively, or neutrally, the several indicators' ability to predict actions of interested parties in the market. The strengths and weaknesses of each approach will, when considered in relationship to each other, indicate which direction within the range the value should fall. The Appraiser's opinion of value is the culminating judgment of the process.

Unless relevant data becomes available subsequent to original processing or was not originally included, value conclusions must fall within the indicated range. To reach a conclusion outside the range implies an incomplete or an inaccurate original processing.

Documentation, The Mass Appraisal's Report

An appraisal report provides the audit trail a Reviewer follows in order to evaluate an appraisal: its beginning—its middle—its end. As a rule, each appraisal prepared for other-than-ad valorem tax purposes will be documented by a report containing data

FIGURE 4
SALES ANALYSIS WORKSHEET

MULTI-FAMILY RESIDENTIAL PROPERTY
ANALYSIS WORKSHEET

Appraised By

Appraiser & Date

Parcel No.	No.	Sales Dates	Sale Price	Sq. Ft. Land	Zoning Units Allowed	No. Units	Sale Price Per Unit	Qty. Cl. Eff. Yr.	Total Sq. Ft.	Average Sq. Ft. Per Unit	Sale Price Per Sq. Ft.	Total Rooms	Sale Price P/Room	Gross Income	Vac. %	Exp. %	G.R.M.	Month Rent Per Sq. Ft.	O&R	No. Bedrooms 1 2 3 Stu.	Bath Per Unit	Actual Rents Monthly 1 2 3 Stu.	Utility Book	Garage or Carport	Built-Ins	Swimming Pool	Remarks
	1		$114,750	10,000	2	2	$9,373	1977	1,451	775	$12.09	8	$2,344	$2,760	.05	.35	6.8	$.11	9.3	2	1	110	No	No			
	2			13,220	3	2		1966	1,536	768		8		2,880	.10			.16		2	1	120	No	No			
	3			9,400	2	2		1977	2,150	1,075		8		3,840	.05			.15		2	2	160	Yes	Yes			
	4			10,120	2	2		1981	1,728	864		8		3,600	.03			.17		2	1	150	No	Yes			
	5		16,500	29,768	3	3	5,500	1925	1,558	519	10.59	9	1,833	2,700	.07	.40	6.1	.14	9.8	3	1	75	No	Yes			
	6			31,200	3	3		1948	2,618	873		12		4,920	.05			.16		3	1	116	Yes	Yes			
	7		26,000	31,640	3	3	15,333	1972	2,960	987	15.54	12	3,833	6,480	.04	.35	7.1	.18	9.2	3	2	140	No	Yes	I I		
	8			20,000	3	3		1972	2,828	943		12		8,100	.02			.24		3	2	225	No	Yes	I I I	I	
	9		23,650	38,928	4	4	5,913	1930	2,421	630	9.38	12	1,970	3,936	.08	.40	6.0	.13	10.0	4	1	82	No	No			
	10			40,320	4	4		1941	2,332	583		12		4,080	.03			.15		4	1	85	No	No			
	11			41,216	4	4		1942	2,710	678		12		4,800	.03			.13		4	1	100	No	Yes			
	12			49,665	4	4		1940	3,466	892		16		6,720	.07			.16		4	1	110	Yes	No			
	13		39,000	41,052	4	4	9,750	1962	2,912	728	13.39	16	2,438	5,760	.04	.35	6.8	.16	9.6	4	1	120	No	Yes	I I		I
	14			80,102	8	4		1971	3,922	981		16		11,340	.03			.24		4	2	236	Yes	Yes	I I I	I	I
	15		83,750	41,840	4	4	20,938	1974	3,922	981	21.35	16	5,234	11,160	.02	.37	7.5	.24	8.4	4	2	232	Yes	Yes	I I I	I	I

necessary to provide an audit trail through the data processed. Individual reports of this kind are not practical for tax appraisals, because the enormous task of maintaining current values for all properties within a jurisdiction is simply too time-consuming to be economic. Adequate documentation must, nevertheless, be provided. This is accomplished by shortcut methods which, in turn, become subject to evaluation by the Reviewer.

Documentation should be prepared in a manner whereby a Reviewer can readily identify the data applied; the development of data into usable units of comparison such as rates, multipliers, rents, economic lives, depreciation amounts, etc.; the considerations of the data such as the application of a capitalization rate to fair rent to develop capitalized earning ability, and the overall factors of influence on value such as those developed in the reconciliation process. In the sales comparison approach, for example, the comparables used should be noted, at least by an index number that references each to a master list, and indication of the comparable's overall comparability and the indicated subject property value that each comparable sale develops. While the Reviewer is unable to check each adjustment in this format, he will, nonetheless, be able to identify differences between sale and subject properties and evaluate the propriety of the overall adjustment.

Reviewers, Levels 1, 2, ---

The standards for, and features of, appraisal review discussed in this chapter provide a framework for review by the several levels of both local assessor and state review units. However, not all reviews are conducted in a like manner. For example, an assessor's first line supervisor, level one, ordinarily reviews such segments as the development of data into units of comparison, during, and upon completion of, development. Consequently, level one reviews are a part of the appraisal process and are largely complete by the time the data are ready for application. Other levels of line management, level two, also review segments upon completion of development, but they do it only from time to time and on a sample basis. More often, their reviews start with completed appraisals.

On the other hand, reviews conducted by standards divisions, e.g., local level three, and state level four, ordinarily start with completed appraisals and systematically follow through the appraisal process from beginning to end. Nevertheless, whether the review takes one form or the other, each level reviews the entire appraisal process.

A fifth level of review is conducted by the State Board's Office of Appraisal Appeals (OAA). Reviewers from this department concentrate on specific segments, or features, of appraisals that are prepared by the State Board's Division of Intercounty Equalization (DIE). These appraisals are prepared trienially for randomly selected properties in each county. An overall measurement of the assessment roll's relative closeness to current fair market value is obtained by comparing DIE and assessor's values for each selected property. If the assessor wishes to question a DIE value, he may appeal it to OAA for review. The basis for appeal, however, must be clearly stated, and the stated factors become the items for OAA review.

The following example illustrates an OAA review and report. California State Board of Equalization

Office of Appraisal Appeals . . .

PROPOSED FINDINGS

Summary

Classification	Intercounty Appraisal	County Request	RECOMMENDATION On Appeal
Land	$1,092,000	$868,000	$1,063,000

Property Description

The assessor requests a review and adjustment of land value for a 390.20 acre ranch located at the intersection of Bascom and Francisco Roads. The parcel is in that part of District A that is mostly farmed to rice. It is part of a larger farming operation.

Contentions

The assessor contends the Division of Intercounty Equalization's appraisal failed to (1) make all necessary cash equivalent adjustments, (2) adequately consider the better duck hunting potential of the comparable properties, and (3) adequately consider the fact that the property is a part of a larger holding.

Comment
We agree that certain cash equivalent adjustments should have been made. We do not believe that either the duck hunting or ownership factors were inadequately considered.

Analysis

Although each of Intercounty's four comparable sales had first and/or second trust deeds requiring cash equivalent adjustments because their interest rates were below locally indicated competitive levels, none were made by the Intercounty Appraiser. We made these adjustments. The Intercounty and OAA indicators are listed below.

Intercounty S/P	Per Acre	O.A.A. C/E	Per Acre
$559,000	$3,070	$552,500	$3,037
297,900	3,870	270,500	3,512
800,600	1,600	813,750	1,627
441,000	2,410	412,000	2,252
Estimated Subject	$2,890		$2,810

We agree with Intercounty's estimate of $260 per acre for the five acres of wasteland, but we convert our selling prices to cash equivalents yielding an indicator of $2,810 per acre. The recap is:

13 acres @ $260 =	$3,380
377.20 acres @ $2,810 =	1,059,900
	$1,063,280
(rounded)	$1,063,000

The Assessor believes two of the three comparable properties emphasized by Intercounty failed to adequately reflect recognizeable differences in the quality of duck hunting between the comparable and subject property locations. The comparable properties are in the northern part of District A, while the subject property is in the southern part. The Assessor believes the northern part has much better duck hunting.

We found the Intercounty Appraiser had considered the duck hunting factor in his appraisal, for it contained the following statement. "The subject is farmed to rice. It may have a little duck hunting influence, but I don't believe it has much hunting influence for it has County roads on two sides and a high voltage line on the other side." Intercounty valued the parcel at $2,800 per acre.

We reviewed Intercounty's comparable properties and the three supplemental comparable properties furnished us by the Assessor, but we could not isolate the duck hunting factor from the other variables that also required consideration. We researched the problem further by talking to two real estate brokers who were, from a long personal experience in the area, quite knowledgeable of the duck hunting and other characteristics of the comparable and subject properties. We also talked to a manager of a duck club situated near the comparable properties, a crop duster pilot who flies the area routinely in his work, an agricultural biologist who both works and hunts in the area, and a manager of a local sporting goods store. These people generally felt the subject property was a good hunting site which at times could be even better than sites in the northern part of the district. While this group seemed to feel the northern half has, as a rule, an edge over the southern half, it also felt the variables that must be evaluated in order to quantify the difference reliably was nearly impossible. We got the impression, nevertheless, that there was some, but not a great deal of, difference between the two locations.

We compared Intercounty Appraiser's estimate of $2,800 per acre for this sample with his $3,150 per acre value for another sample which is situated in the heart of the area the Assessor feels has the best duck hunting. Except for location, other characteristics are very comparable. We believe the $350 per acre spread between the good duck hunting location on the one hand and a fair to good location on the other adequately reflects the difference. The brokers we talked to each felt that, all other things being equal, good to very good duck hunting adds at least $775 per acre to the selling price of rice land.

Property value often varies, up to a point, by property size. We found neither sales data nor local real estate brokers' opinions, however, indicating a need to modify Intercounty's value for this characteristic. The subject property's 390 plus acres is sufficiently large that its being part of a larger holding does not warrant a different unit value.

Recommendation

We recommend the Board adopt a value of $1,063,000 for the property.

M.P. Hedge
Associate Property Appraiser

The foregoing OAA report illustrates the depth of research required for this type of review, but it also illustrates the type of review occasionally required when a property owner contests his assessment. In such cases, the Reviewer addresses his effort to the issues under contention by studying the available records, evaluating the arguments for each side, conducting the field research necessary to compile a complete set of data regarding the points of contention, and reaching a conclusion. The conclusion must, of course, be presented in a logical manner in order that each party may judiciously evaluate it.

The more common type of review, however, is a "desk job" where the Reviewer evaluates a sample of all appraisal reports without benefit of field review. While the number of properties in the sample tends to be a relatively small proportion of the population, the ordinary population's size, nevertheless, makes each sample large enough for such reviews to be classified as mini-mass projects. Consequently the Reviewer's evaluations, decisions, and conclusions regarding each feature reviewed will, like those of the Appraiser as he develops and processes data in a mass appraisal system, have an impact upon a vast expansion of the work. Therefore, this author proposes "careful attention to detail, however small," as the watchwords for Reviewers as they review appraisals for property tax purposes.

---

[1] Many jurisdictions apply selective assessment ratios to the market value estimates.
[2] California Revenue and Taxation Code, Section 405.6.
[3] All numerical data in this paragraph was developed from "Budgets & Workloads 1977-78", published by the California State Board of Equalization (letter to assessors No. 77/150.

CHAPTER SIXTEEN

Appraisal Review for Savings and Loan Associations

B. L. "BILL" DUNAWAY, CRA

B. L. "Bill" Dunaway, CRA, is Vice President of Ozarks Federal Savings & Loan Association in Farmington, Missouri. His primary duties include appraising of single family residences, agricultural properties, motel and commercial properties, and reviewing staff appraisals and outside fee appraisals.

In addition to being a Senior Member of the National Association of Review Appraisers, Mr. Dunaway holds membership in the American Institute of Real Estate Appraisers.

Appraisal Review

for Savings and

Loan Associations

The stated purpose of savings and loan associations, according to the Home Owners' Loan Act of 1933, is " . . . to provide local mutual thrift institutions in which people may invest their funds and. . .provide for the financing of homes." The philosophy of this purpose is generally stated "to promote thrift and home ownership", and while many changes in the savings and loan industry have occurred since 1933, the preoccupation with promotion of thrift and home ownership still exists. In recent years, however, savings and loan associations have become active in lending on real estate other than individual dwellings, and in the purchase and sale of loans in the secondary market.

Savings and loan associations are regulated by law as to the ratio of loan-to-value (appraisal) which may be made and this ratio may vary with the type of property and manner of loan repayment. Examiners of the Federal Home Loan Bank inspect the appraisals in an association's loan files and on occasion conduct sample tests of appraisals.

Because of stricter requirements of the regulatory authorities, expanded lending powers, and a general upgrading of appraisal requirements by the savings and loan industry, the demands made upon savings and loan association Appraisers and Reviewing Appraisers have increased in recent years. As loan-to-value ratios have increased so has the need for appraisal quality.

In the upgrading of appraisals the Review Appraiser plays a significant role.

As a primary requirement, a Review Appraiser should also be a competent Appraiser. Secondly, a Review Appraiser should have acquired special training in reviewing the appraisals of others by attending seminars offered by the National Association of Review Appraisers, the American Institute of Real Estate Appraisers, the Society of Real Estate Appraisers, or other profesional appraisal organizations. As in all of the appraisal processes, appraisal review is an ever-changing process and the Review Appraiser should keep his knowledge of techniques and procedures current. The *Appraisal Review Journal* and other publications of the National Association of Review Appraisers will greatly aid the Review Appraiser in keeping up to date.

As in the case of any Review Appraiser, the duty of the savings and loan Review Appraiser is to review the appraisal report and advise the underwriter/loan committee/board of directors, that the appraisal is or is not an adequate report upon which to base a loan approval or rejection. Ideally, the Review Appraiser is part of management but has no underwriting function. In practice, however, particularly in smaller associations, the Review Appraiser often functions as an underwriter, member of the loan committee, or board of directors, or may be the managing officer of an association. In such circumstances, the Review Appraiser is in the position of "wearing two hats" and must constantly strive for objectivity. The appraisal process must be kept free from being influenced by the underwriting process.

In circumstances where the appraisal review and the underwriting are to be done by the same person, objectivity is aided if the appraisal report is reviewed before any of the underwriting data are considered. Better still, if possible it is good practice to review the appraisal report before knowing the identity of the applicant or the size, term or interest rate of the requested loan.

Most savings and loan associations use the Terminal Type of review which is made after the appraisal report is completed and the Exception Type of review-recording wherein review records are kept only on the reports which require discussion with the Appraiser, or which may require action in the future. The exception record should be written in a complete manner so that, should questions about either the appraisal or the review arise in the future, all pertinent information will be available. Copies of correspondence or notes of conversations with the

Appraiser and copies of outside data supporting the Review Appraiser's position should be retained in the exception file.

As in appraising, in appraisal review one of the key words is "documentation". An appraisal report should lead the reader by logical process to the same conclusion as that arrived at by the Appraiser. If the Review Appraiser is not led by the appraisal report to the same conclusion as that of the Appraiser, it is fairly certain that no one else will be. Any variance in the appraisal report from the normal or typical should be justified and documented in order that it may later be demonstrated to be reasonable and pertinent. As one Federal Home Loan Bank Examiner put it, "It's all right (for the Appraiser) to know it, but it's only acceptable (to the examiners) if you show it."

In contrast to a seller who is interested in the value of a property only at the date of sale, the lender relies heavily upon the future prospects of a property which is being considered as collateral for a loan. The lender will probably live with that property in his portfolio for years and no one is more cognizant than a lender that value is generally regarded as the present worth of future benefits of ownership. Future appreciation, stability or depreciation of the property from any cause, will affect the soundness of the loan being secured by it. Because of this, any trend apparent at the time of appraisal which might affect the future property value should be clearly reported.

Similarly, when considering income-producing property as security for a loan, the potential income generated by the property is of vital interest to the lender, for usually it is upon that income that the lender will rely for repayment of the loan. Anything which would tend to affect that income should be fully discussed.

Most residential appraisals for savings and loan associations today utilize forms such as the FHLMC #70-FNMA #1004, in which data is recorded in an orderly check-list manner. These forms provide space for comments which should be used to explain any unusual circumstances or expand upon features of the property being appraised. Appraisers should be encouraged to attach such addenda or additional comments as are necessary to present a complete summation of the property and data processing.

There are many forms which will aid the Review Appraiser, most of which have been developed for particular review interests; e.g., mortgage loan, sale, condemnation, taxation, etc. One very good form which is so comprehensive as to be applicable for most appraisal purposes and functions, is reproduced in the article, "To Review an Appraisal Report", by Carl R. Trowbridge (*The Appraisal Review Journal*, Volume 1, Number 3, Fall 1978). A review form pertinent to the savings and loan industry which was developed after discussion with several Federal Home Loan Bank Examiners and others is reproduced at the end of this article. Used as a checklist, it is an aid to appraisal report review.

However, the best tools of a Review Appraiser are the Reviewer's own ability as an Appraiser, desire for personal competence and ability to communicate with the Appraiser on the one hand, and the underwriter on the other.

Most of the items on the appraisal review form are self-explanatory, but some require comment:

General

Item #2—An appraisal report should have a complete, even if brief, statement regarding the prospects for the future stability of the neighborhood. This is of great importance to a lender, not only in deciding whether or not a loan should be made, but also the term of the loan.

As an example, a long-term loan which would be feasible in a residential neighborhood with reasonable prospects for future stability, may not be desirable as long-term security if the area is being rapidly encroached upon by industrial installations or used-car sales lots. Any prospective changes in use or zoning of surrounding properties should be reported.

The Review Appraiser should be familiar with recent legislation, regulations and court decisions regarding equal-opportunity lending and the so-called "red-lining" of neighborhoods. No statement should be contained in an appraisal report which would be in conflict with these laws, regulations, or decisions.

Item #7—In the appraisal of existing properties, there appears to be a tendency to place little emphasis on the Cost Approach or to ignore it altogether. Generally, Market Data and Income Approaches, which usually are in the form of Gross Monthly Multipliers in residential properties, do offer the best value indicators. An exception to this, for which the Review Appraiser should be alert, occurs when an existing property is presented as having a greater value than the cost of a new, similar property. This may be feasible for individuals for personal reasons but the market place, in general, adheres to the Principle of Substitution which affirms that " . . . no rational person will pay more for a property than that amount by which he can obtain, by purchase of a site and construction of a building, without undue delay, a property of equal desirability and utility." (*The Appraisal of Real Estate*, Sixth Edition, American Institute of Real Estate Appraisers.)

In periods of rapid inflation or "boom" conditions in an active real estate market, it sometimes happens that buyers with limited knowledge will violate this generally accented principle. In such a case, if both the Appraiser and Review Appraiser totally ignore the Cost Approach as a check on the other two approaches, an erroneous appraisal could be passed on to underwriting as being adequate.

Conversely, it is not unusual that owner-occupants, particularly in residential properties, will invest more in their properties than the market place could support. Hence, the Market Data and Income Approaches serve as checks on the Cost Approach. Appraisals for mortgage loan purposes must adhere strictly to the market concept of the typical buyer rather than relying on atypical conditions.

Cost Approach

Item #3—If the Appraiser uses a cost data source other than a recognized standard cost manual, the Review Appraiser should be satisfied that the source is accurate and current.

Items #4 and #5—Depreciation estimates, especially those items which are incurable, are the product of the Appraiser's judgment, ability, experience, education, and endeavor.

Review Appraisers should make every effort to know the qualifications of the Appraiser and, if possible, to know the Appraiser. A sufficient amount of the Appraiser's work should be field-checked in order that the Review Appraiser will be able to assess the competence of the Appraiser. The Review Appraiser should not approach an appraisal review in the spirit of "picking it to pieces" but rather, merely to ascertain that the appraisal report represents factual data which has been correctly processed to a reasonable conclusion.

Market Data Approach

As in the estimation of depreciation, the assessment of an

Appraiser's ability to choose and correctly adjust comparable property sales as indicative data, can best be accomplished by a field-check of the appraisal. The Market Data Approach requires many judgment conclusions by the Appraiser.

The Income Approach

Items #3 and #4—When reviewing an Income Approach, particularly one upon which the Appraiser has placed primary reliance as a value indicator and where no previous income and expense statements are available, as in the case of a new business, the Review Appraiser should ascertain that the projections or pro forma statements are typical and reasonable.

Often this will involve consulting a trade organization or a similar enterprise to obtain typical operating data. Other good sources of information are Appraisers who specialize in the appraisal of particular types of income-producing properties.

Item #5—The Review Appraiser should keep in constant touch with the local market philosophy; e.g., current equity returns demanded by investors, current available financing terms and rates, current desirability of particular types of property to investors. This type information is readily obtained by being conversant with realtors, investors, personnel of financial institutions, and Appraisers.

Capitalization rates change frequently in response to fluctuations in interest rates and desired equity returns. Recapture of investment capital is usually unique to the property being appraised and should be given close attention by the Review Appraiser.

New Construction

Appraisals of proposed construction projects should be carefully considered to ascertain that the proposals are based upon reasonable, typical data. This is particularly important in considering the estimated absorption time for properties to be constructed as part of a subdivision complex. As an example, a proposed development of a large number of residences in a small town should clearly demonstrate the need for the residences. If it is contended that a need for many new dwellings has been created by a new industry moving into the area, grounds for this contention should be researched and verified.

Consideration should be given to the discounted cash flow of the development. Will it be sufficient to complete the project and service the debt?

The Review Appraiser should not hesitate to go to outside sources to obtain information from the market place if he questions the reasonableness of an Appraiser's data or the processing of that data. The best sources of information are those who routinely deal in the field of endeavor being considered: Private investors, developers, leasees, realtors, Appraisers, lenders, and trade organizations.

When reviewing appraisals of properties securing loans which are being considered for purchase and the Reviewer is unfamiliar with the Appraiser and/or the locality of the properties, field inspection of each of the properties is recommended as a normal part of the review process. The secondary market is a large industry within itself and like any large industry, contains some products which are inferior. Diligence at this point will result in a high quality portfolio of purchased loans.

Conclusion

Any discussion with the Appraiser regarding the appraisal being reviewed should be recorded on the review form and in the exception file. Any variances from normal or typical procedure should be resolved, or, if accepted without being changed in the appraisal report, the reasons for acceptance of the variance should be noted on the review form. All questions should be resolved before forwarding the appraisal to underwriting.

After the review has been completed, the Review Appraiser should forward the report and critique to underwriting. He should state clearly whether or not he considers the report to be adequate as the basis for a lending decision. He should be prepared to answer questions regarding the report to others in management.

Should an appraisal report be inadequate and the Review Appraiser not be able to effect a corrected or adequately amplified report, the Review Appraiser should recommend that the appraisal report not be accepted and that either another report be made by another Appraiser or that the loan be declined.

Is it seldom that an Appraiser is adamant about explaining a process or amplifying a report to a required degree of completeness. When this does occur it is the responsibility of the Review Appraiser to report to others in management that the appraisal report is not adequate for underwriting purposes and be prepared to explain the deficiencies.

Finally, the Review Appraiser should recognize that just as there are many skilled, capable undesignated Appraisers, there are some Appraisers who hold designations from professional appraisal organizations whose reports would not be suitable for mortgage loan underwriting purposes. The potential utility of an appraisal report will be reliant upon the report's content rather than the academic qualifications of the Appraiser or the amount of "boiler plate" material included.

APPRAISAL REVIEW FORM

RE: Application of _____Dated: _____

Property Address: _____

GENERAL	Adequate	Inadequate
1. Photo and plot of property.	_____	_____
2. Adequate description and identification of property as well as neighborhood environment.	_____	_____
3. Property rights appraised (including subrogation of leased fee).	_____	_____
4. Statement of inspection, independence and certification of appraised value.	_____	_____
5. A definition of value (fee simple; subjective, etc.)	_____	_____
6. Statement of premises and limiting conditions (such as rate of absorption study, market analysis, zoning, leases, proposed plans and specifications, etc.)	_____	_____
7. A minimum of two approaches to value and justification for not using the other.	_____	_____
8. Is flood hazard or lack of flood hazard noted (HUD-FHA Regulations)?	_____	_____
Other Comments:	_____	_____

	Adequate	Inadequate

COST APPROACH

1. Highest and best use of site and property. _____ _____

2. Market value estimate of site (must be supported by market comparable sales or lease data). _____ _____

3. Estimated replacement cost of the improvements by an acceptable cost manual or other reliable source data. _____ _____

4. Estimated total loss in accrued depreciation and method employed. _____ _____

5. Estimate of physical depreciation, functional and economic obsolescence, and justification thereof. _____ _____

6. The present worth of site improvements such as driveways, sidewalks, fences, or other increments affecting value. _____ _____

   Other Comments: _____ _____

MARKET DATA APPROACH

1. Is the Market Data Approach supported by market comparable sales? _____ _____

2. Were there a minimum of three comparables employed? _____ _____

3. Were the comparable sales reduced to common denominators and adjusted? _____ _____

4. Is the percentage range of net adjustments reasonable when considering units of comparison (a reasonable degree of compatibility is more important than the arithmetic range of adjustment)? _____ _____

5. Does the report show evidence of the purchase price by a copy of the sales contract? _____ _____

   Other comments: _____ _____

	Adequate	Inadequate

INCOME APPROACH TO VALUE

1. GRM was used as best indicator.   _____   _____

2. Have signed leases been included and considered in the appraisal report?   _____   _____

3. The report should include three to five year audited income and operating expense statements.   _____   _____

4. For purposes of appraisal, the actual income and operating statements (or projections in the case of new properties) have been reconstructed with appropriate justification and supporting comparisons.   _____   _____

5. Is the capitalization rate supported with regard to the mortgage and equity markets together with a justifiable provision for recapture?   _____   _____

6. Has the net income been processed into a final value estimate by a property method and technique?   _____   _____

Other comments: _____   _____

Adequate   Inadequate

NEW CONSTRUCTION

Note: Much of the preceding is applicable in new construction, including the following but not limited to
the same.

1. If an acquisition and development project:
   A. Is there an absorption period esti-
      mate?   _____   _____
   B. Is absorption period estimate sup-
      ported by a market analysis study?   _____   _____
   C. Is income stream for disposal period
      discounted?   _____   _____
   D. Are discount factors used reasonable?   _____   _____
   E. Is there a developer's plan?   _____   _____
   F. The above does not apply because this
      is construction on an individual tract.   _____   _____

2. Highest and best use.   _____   _____

3. Comments relative to zoning and building
   code compliance.   _____   _____

4. Does the report include complete plans
   and specifications of new construction?   _____   _____

5. Has a contractor's affidavit of total build-
   ing costs been included in the report?   _____   _____

6. Does the report include actual land acqui-   _____   _____
   sition costs?

                                                     _____   _____

Remarks:

Reviewing Appraiser: _____   Date: _____

The notes of any discussion regarding this report with Appraiser should be put on
the reverse side of this page.

CHAPTER SEVENTEEN

Appraisal Review

for Commercial Bank

Real Estate

Lending Purposes

HUBERT W. HITCHCOCK, CRA

Hubert W. Hitchcock, CRA, is currently Vice President of Wells Fargo Bank in San Francisco, California, and is the Chief Appraiser for the Wells Fargo Bank Real Estate Industries Group. He was formerly an Appraiser with New York Life and a Real Estate Specialist with the Wells Fargo Bank.

In addition to being a Senior Member of the National Association of Review Appraisers, Mr. Hitchcock holds membership in the Society of Real Estate Appraisers.

Appraisal Review

for Commercial Bank

Real Estate

Lending Purposes

Prudent lending practices dictate that Commercial Banks' Staff Appraisers, its Independent Fee Appraisers, and the Review Appraisers all be autonomous and separate from the Line Officers' functions. That is to say, the Appraiser should be under no pressure whatsoever to reach for a figure to support the loan requested in the application.

For long-term or permanent type loans, they should all strive for the ideal appraisal for the mortgage lender — one which tells the loan officer the maximum price that an *expert* buyer would offer for the subject of appraisal as of the date of appraisal, paying cash down to, and assuming, a portion of the purchase price financed at the loan-to-value ratio established by policy and legal requirements, with sufficient amortization to protect the margin of security against future depreciation from all causes, and with the interest rate that the lender is willing to offer at the time of appraisal.

This ideal appraisal may be a far cry from the amount a gullible buyer, acting under the influence of a high pressure salesman, might be willing to pay for the property offered as security. It will also differ with the price obtainable if the seller is willing to accept very favorable purchase money terms and, of course, will vary considerably from the amount obtainable from a buyer who is in dire need of the property for expansion purpose.

Many income producing properties today are being traded at highly inflated, indicated selling prices in order to hopefully influence the lenders to offer jumbo-type financing. Although the Appraiser should not be influenced by the mortgage loan application, they cannot, on the other hand, put themselves in an ivory tower, so to speak, and always appraise on such a conservative basis that the lender is simply unable to compete with his *fair competition*; I repeat, *fair competition.* They should always act in a professional manner and call the shots as they see them.

The Review Appraiser can be most helpful in properly underwriting the mortgage loan with his expertise and knowledge of values for various types of properties in the locale and current rental and operating expenses rates and ratios. The professional Review Appraiser will quickly spot any and all apraisals that are out, in line with the ideal lenders' report.

The Reviewer should know when other lenders are ignoring sound appraisal practices and underwriting principles as a result of heavy pressure to "get the money out" in times of ample credit supply, and he can caution the prudent lender accordingly, or assist him in gearing his amortization schedule to compensate for riskier positions.

During depressed real estate markets, the Reviewer will counsel the lender, advising him as to which properties have good future potential so as not to cause a panic and glut an already over-supplied real estate market. With a portfolio of properly documented real estate loans, the bank's earnings will be enhanced, and during periods of tight credit conditions, its real estate loans may be sold outright or through participations in the secondary market operations, thus increasing the bank's liquidity.

In a review of an appraisal report covering a property which is offered as security for a proposed loan, the Reviewer should, in all cases, be led along in a very logical and very convincing manner the same paths of reasoning which led the Appraiser to his final expressed opinion of value. All opinions should be supported by facts. Given a choice between a high figure based upon opinion and a low figure supported by facts, the Reviewer should favor the latter. The IRS has adopted a rule regarding property value, to wit: "opinion — expert or otherwise — is not admissible". This is a good axiom to place in the Review Appraiser's armamentarium.

The Appraiser's arithmetic should be carefully checked for accuracy and consistency since a serious error, such as incorrect building area calculation, may result in a major loss to the lender. There is always the possibility the lender may own the property at some future date.

After thoroughly checking all arithmetic and applying contemporary thumb rule guides to the Appraiser's estimated income and expense of income-producing properties, the Review Appraiser should then make an analysis at the rate of capitalization which the Appraiser has either: 1) abstracted from the market place or 2) constructed by the band of investment or other method in order to determine if the lender/clients' policies are being adhered to.

The Ellwood Technique or Ellwood Tables are very useful at this point for the Reviewer who has mastered their functions. For Reviewers who are not familiar with Ellwood and who prefer not to take up or go back to 9th grade algebra to utilize the technique, the following illustrations demonstrate a method which accomplishes the same purpose. This method was first published in the July, 1970 issue of the *Appraisal Journal of the American Institute of Real Estate Appraisers* authored by Charles Akerson, M.A.I., and Past President of the Institute, under the title "Ellwood Without Algebra". This method of analyzing and/or constructing the rate of capitalization requires only the use of two compound interest tables: 1) the annual sinking fund factors which show the amount requied to be deposited each year at varying interest rates to accumulate one dollar in various terms (please refer to Exhibit A); 2) loan constants or, namely, the required annual payment to interest and principal for level payment mortgage loans expressed as a percent of the original loan amount (please refer to Exhibit B).

Following are some illustrations demonstrating the use of this technique.

Illustration No. 1

At the time of writing this material, the markets for well located, properly designed apartment properties in the author's area of the San Francisco Bay Area indicate selling prices based upon gross annual income multipliers in the range of eight to ten and higher, even if conversion to condominium use is both feasible and possible.

Allowing 32½% to 37% for vacancies and operating expenses, which includes property taxes at 1% of selling price since Proposition No. 13 is applicable, the indicated range of overall cap rates is 7% to 7½% as follows:

Formula: $\qquad$ OAR $\quad \dfrac{(N.O.I.) \%}{GM}$

Wherein:

$$OAR = \text{Overall Cap Rate}$$
$$(N.O.I.)\% = \text{Net Annual Operating Income as a percent of Gross Income}$$
$$GM = \text{Gross Multiplier (Sales Price divided by Gross Annual Income)}$$

Lowest OAR $\quad = \qquad \dfrac{.63}{9} \quad = \quad .0700$

Highest OAR $\quad = \qquad \dfrac{.675}{9} \quad = \quad .0750$

Too many Appraisers attempt to justify this current apartment market by a modified bank of investment as follows:

Indicated Market OAR	=	.0725
*Mortgage Component .75 X .0966	=	.0725
Equity Component		-0-

(Assumes 75% for 30 years at 9% interest)

In many cases, the equity cash flow is actually negative.

Given a net annual income of $72,500., the indicated selling price would be $1,000,000. The above assumptions by the Appraisers ignore the fact that prudent long-term mortgage lenders insist upon a satisfactory cushion by requiring the Appraiser's estimated net annual income to cover debt service 1.2 to 1.3 times or more. This is for run-of-the-mill type properties and, naturally, given a long-term lease to financially responsible leasee with adequate escalation clauses, a one-to-one ratio may be in order (please refer to Exhibit C).

Capitalization Rate Structure for Long-Term Mortgage Loan Purposes:

Formula: CR =   M x f x c
                         CR   = Minimum Cap Rate
                         M   = Ratio of Loan to Loan Value
                         f   = Annual Loan Constant
                         c   = Debt Service Coverage Required

Substituting in the formula we find that 9.06% is the minimum cap rate which will provide for 1.25 Debt Service Coverage for a 75%, 30 year — 9% interest loan:

CR =   .75 x .0966 x 1.25 = .0906
Valuation: $72,500 ÷ .0906 = $800,220
                        75% = $600,165
                        SAY $600,000

As the case above illustrates, the maximum loan with debt service covered 1.25 times by present estimated net operating income is $600,000, or 60% of the indicated selling price as follows:

Illustration No. 2

Analyze the 7.25% Cap Rate in Illustration No. 1 to determine the 10th year property value required to yield 9% (The Mortgage Loan Interest Rate) on an assumed 40% equity investment subject to the 60% loan amortized over 30 years at 9% interest.

                Market OAR   .0725   .0725

Basic Capitalization Rate Structure (r):
        Mortgage Money 60% X .0966 = .0580
        Equity Money 40% X .09   = .0360
                                       .0940

Less Credit for Equity build up in the Mortgage Loan Plan:

Formula: E   = M x P x $1/s_n^7$

Wherein:

                E   = Equity Build Up During Holding
                           Period
                M   = Ratio Loan/Value
                P   = % Loan Amortized During Holding
                           Period

$$1/s_{n^7} \quad = \quad \text{The Sinking Fund Factor at Equity}$$
$$\text{Yield Rate for Holding Period}$$

Substituting:

$$E \quad = \quad .75 \times .1063 \times .0658 \quad = \quad -.0053$$

$$= \quad \text{Basic Cap Rate (r)} = \quad -.0887$$

$$\text{Difference} = \quad \text{OAR} \cdot r = \quad -.0162$$

Since OAR is smaller than Basic Cap Rate, appreciation in property value is required. The percent appreciation is found by dividing the .0162 difference in rates by $1/s_{n^7}$, or .0162 divided by .0658 = .2462.

Therefore, the property must appreciate 24.62% from $1 million to $1,246,200 over 10 years to yield 9% on the $400,000 equity investment.

Arithmetic Proof:

Assumed Distribution and Income

40 % Equity	$ 400,000	@	/0364	=	$14,540
60% Loan	600,000	@	.0966	=	57,960
Total	$1,000,000	@	.0725	=	$72,500

Re-sale (Value) 10th Year —
$1,000,000 x 1.2462 = $1,246,200

Less 10th year Loan Balance —
$600,000 x .8937 = $536,220
Tenth Year Equity (Reversion) $ 709,980

Present Worth Equity (10 Years — 9%)
Income $14,540 X 6.4177 = $ 93,313
Reversion 709.980 X 0.4224 = 299,896
$393,209

(Difference from $400,000 due to rounding)

Please refer to Exhibits D,E,F,G,H and I for additional examples of the use of "Ellwood Without Algebra".

The Built-To-Suit, Or Special-Purpose Problem

Very often the lender is requied to grant long-term, level payment mortgage loan plans secured by property under relatively short-term leases at premium rental rates, which include the amortization of leasee's special requirements (i.e., research and development office/warehouse buildings, etc.)

If the primary lease term is not extended and a new tenant is not available for the space on an "As Is" basis, considerable additional cost may be involved to redesign the building for releasing.

It, therefore, behooves the Review Appraiser to alert the lender to this eventuality if the Appraiser who prepared the report has not done so, and has simply accepted and capitalized the premium rent.

The lender can then require additional principal amortization to take advantage of the excess rent, for obvious reasons.

Following is one approach which the Reviewer may utilize, and with his knowledge and expertise, make the appropriate underwriting recommendation.

All he is doing is "standing in the shoes", so to speak, of an expert, well informed purchaser who would concern himself with the future threat of additional costs (Value is simply the Present Worth of all the benefits, less all disadvantages, accruing to ownership).

Example of the Special Purpose Problem:

1) Replacement Cost Estimate:

Land 20,000 Sq. Ft. @ $2.50 =		$50,000
Improvements:		
1) Basic Building Shell & Site Work		
10,000 Sq. Ft. @ $15 =	$150,000	
2) Tenant Interior Work		
10,000 Sq. Ft. @ $10 =	100,000	250,000
Total Build to Suit Cost Estimate		$300,000

2) Economic Analysis:
   Income(5 Yr. Lease With Landlord's responsibility limited to Maintenance of Roof and Exterior Walls only.)

10,000 Sq. Ft. @ $3.30 =	$33,000
Less 5% Vacancy Allowance =	1,650
Effective Gross Annual Income	$31,350

Expense Expectancy: ―

Management	$1,500	
Roof, Wall Reserves	800	$2,300
Net Annual Income Estimate		$29,050

Capitalization Rate Structure:

Mortgage Money — 75% — 30 Yrs @ 9% (.0966)	=	.0725
Equity Money — 25% @ 10%	=	.0250
Composite Rate		.0975

Valuation $29,050 divided by .0975 = $297,950

(Rounded to: $300,000)

Reviewer's Recommendation:

1) Basic Property Valuation Estimate

Income 10,000 Sq. Ft. @ $2.40	=	$24,000
Less 5% Vacancy	=	1,200
		$22,800

Expense:

Management	$1,000	
Contingencies	800	$ 1,800
Net Annual Income, Basic Property		$21,000

Capitalization Rate Structure, assuming 75% financing for 30 years at 9% interest and 1.30 Debt Service Coverage.

$$CR = .75 \times .0966 \times 1.30 = .0941$$

Basic Property Value

$21,000 divided by .0941   = $223,167

2) Additional value from 5 year lease

Premium Income 10,000 Sq. Ft. @ $.90   = $ 9,000

Capitalization Rate Structure assuming 75% financing for 10 years (5th year balance = 61%) @ 9% interest and 1.1 Debt Service Coverage.

$$CR = .75 \times .1521 \times 1.1 = .1254$$

Lease Value:

9,000 divided by .1245 = $ 71,770

Total Valuation $ 294,937

Although this technique does not change the value conclusion a great deal, it does provide a basis for stepped-up loan amortization as follows:

Item	Basic (Shell) Property	Lease Value	Total
Income	$24,000	$9,000	$33,000
Vacancy Allowance	1,200	-0-	1,200
Expenses	1,800	-0-	1,800
Net Operating Income	21,000	9,000	30,000
Overall Rate	.0941	.1254	.1017
Valuation	223,167	71,770	294,937
75% Loan	167,375	53,827	221,202
Loan Constant	.0966	.1521	.1101*
Debt Service	16,168	8,187	24,355
Coverage	1.30	1.10	1.23

* .1101 Annual Constant is 9% — 19 years

Risk — Rating The Quantity and Quality of Various Income Streams

Here is a technique which the Reviewer may utilize for analyzing and capitalizing into value the income from well leased shopping centers, office buildings, etc.

Net Annual Income Pro-Rata:

1) Major tenants long-term leases $298,875
2) Other tenants short-term leases $197,750

Assumed Available Financing and Capitalization Rate Structures:

1) Major tenants — 75% — 30 Years —9% (.0966) with 1.10 debt service coverage — C.R. = .75 x .0966 x 1.10 = .0797
2) Other tenants — 75% — 20 years — 10% (.1159) with 1.30 debt service coverage — C.R. = .75 x .1159 x 1.30

Valuation Estimate:

Item	Majors	Others	Total
Net Income	$298,875	$197,750	$496,625
Cap Rate	.0797	.1130	.0903
Value	$3,750,000	$1,750,000	$5,500,000
75% Loan	$2,812,500	$1,312,500	$4,125,000
Loan Constant	.0966	.1159	.1027*
Debt Service	$271,688	$152,119	$423,807
Coverage	$1.10	$1.30	$1.17

   * .1027 Annual Constant is 9½ — 28 Years +

Following are a few helpful guidelines to assist the Reviewer for mortgage loan clients:

1. Appraisal is not, and can never be, an exact science; neither is it an educated guess. It should be an opinion of value well supported by facts, and most competent professional Appraisers will arrive at a final value conclusion well within the range of reasonableness.

2. The Reviewer should not assume an adversary stance. Appraisers are only human and usually will accept constructive criticism when properly given.

3. The role of both the Appraiser and the Review Appraiser is to protect the lender/client's interest at all times. It is the Appraiser's task to prove his conclusions, and it is up to the Reviewer to recognize and challenge all evidence of incompetency in either technique or logic.

Summary

In reviewing appraisals for a Real Estate Lender, the Review Appraiser should stand in the shoes of an expert, fully informed buyer and be led along the same paths, logically, to the final value conclusion arrived at by the Appraiser.

He should be able to concur in the arithmetic used by the Appraiser and approaches to a valuation estimate.

The Rate of Capitalization should be analyzed to ascertain whether the lender/client's underwriting policies will be adhered to, and whether or not the future property value is likely to perform in accordance with the assumptions implied in the Cap Rate Structure.

The Reviewer can be very helpful to the lender/client in underwriting special purpose type property loans and in risk-rating the quantity, quality and duration of various income streams.

EXHIBIT A

ANNUAL SINKING FUND FACTORS

Table of Annual Payments which will grow to $1 in a given number of years, including the accumulation of interest compounded annually.

	INTEREST RATE								
YEARS	5	5¼	5½	5¾	6	6¼	6½	6¾	7
1	1.0000	1.0000	1.0000	1.0000	1.0000	1.0000	1.0000	1.0000	1.0000
2	.4878	.4872	.4866	.4860	.4854	.4848	.4843	.4837	.4831
3	.3172	.3164	.3157	.3149	.3141	.3133	.3126	.3118	.3111
4	.2320	.2312	.2303	.2294	.2286	.2277	.2269	.2261	.2252
5	.1810	.1801	.1792	.1783	.1774	.1765	.1756	.1748	.1739
6	.1470	.1461	.1452	.1443	.1434	.1425	.1416	.1407	.1398
7	.1228	.1219	.1210	.1200	.1191	.1182	.1173	.1164	.1156
8	.1047	.1038	.1029	.1019	.1010	.1001	.0992	.0983	.0975
9	.0907	.0898	.0888	.0879	.0870	.0861	.0852	.0844	.0835
10	.0795	.0786	.0777	.0768	.0759	.0750	.0741	.0732	.0724
11	.0704	.0695	.0686	.0677	.0668	.0659	.0651	.0642	.0634
12	.0628	.0619	.0610	.0601	.0593	.0584	.0576	.0567	.0559
13	.0565	.0556	.0547	.0538	.0530	.0521	.0513	.0505	.0497
14	.0510	.0501	.0493	.0484	.0476	.0468	.0459	.0451	.0443
15	.0463	.0455	.0446	.0438	.0430	.0422	.0414	.0406	.0398
16	.0423	.0414	.0406	.0398	.0390	.0382	.0374	.0366	.0359
17	.0387	.0379	.0370	.0362	.0354	.0347	.0339	.0332	.0324
18	.0355	.0347	.0339	.0331	.0324	.0316	.0309	.0301	.0294
19	.0327	.0319	.0312	.0304	.0296	.0289	.0282	.0274	.0268
20	.0302	.0295	.0287	.0279	.0272	.0265	.0258	.0251	.0244
21	.0280	.0272	.0265	.0257	.0250	.0243	.0236	.0229	.0223
22	.0260	.0252	.0245	.0237	.0230	.0224	.0217	.0210	.0204
23	.0241	.0234	.0227	.0220	.0213	.0206	.0200	.0193	.0187
24	.0225	.0217	.0210	.0203	.0197	.0190	.0184	.0178	.0172
25	.0210	.0202	.0195	.0189	.0182	.0176	.0170	.0164	.0158

	INTEREST RATE								
YEARS	7¼	7½	7¾	8	8¼	8½	8¾	9	9¼
1	1.0000	1.0000	1.0000	1.0000	1.0000	1.0000	1.0000	1.0000	1.0000
2	.4825	.4819	.4813	.4808	.4802	.4796	.4790	.4785	.4779
3	.3103	.3095	.3088	.3080	.3073	.3065	.3058	.3051	.3043
4	.2244	.2236	.2227	.2219	.2211	.2203	.2195	.2187	.2179
5	.1730	.1722	.1713	.1705	.1696	.1688	.1679	.1671	.1663
6	.1389	.1380	.1372	.1363	.1355	.1346	.1338	.1329	.1321
7	.1147	.1138	.1129	.1121	.1112	.1104	.1095	.1087	.1079
8	.0966	.0957	.0949	.0940	.0932	.0923	.0915	.0907	.0899
9	.0826	.0818	.0809	.0801	.0792	.0784	.0776	.0768	.0760
10	.0715	.0707	.0699	.0690	.0682	.0674	.0666	.0658	.0650
11	.0625	.0617	.0609	.0601	.0593	.0585	.0577	.0569	.0562
12	.0551	.0543	.0535	.0527	.0519	.0512	.0504	.0497	.0489
13	.0489	.0481	.0473	.0465	.0458	.0450	.0443	.0436	.0429
14	.0436	.0428	.0420	.0413	.0406	.0398	.0391	.0384	.0377
15	.0390	.0383	.0376	.0368	.0361	.0354	.0347	.0341	.0334
16	.0351	.0344	.0337	.0330	.0323	.0316	.0310	.0303	.0297
17	.0317	.0310	.0303	.0296	.0290	.0283	.0277	.0270	.0264
18	.0287	.0280	.0274	.0267	.0261	.0254	.0248	.0242	.0236
19	.0261	.0254	.0248	.0241	.0235	.0229	.0223	.0217	.0212
20	.0237	.0231	.0225	.0219	.0213	.0207	.0201	.0195	.0190
21	.0217	.0210	.0204	.0198	.0193	.0187	.0181	.0176	.0171
22	.0198	.0192	.0186	.0180	.0175	.0169	.0164	.0159	.0154
23	.0181	.0175	.0170	.0164	.0159	.0154	.0149	.0144	.0139
24	.0166	.0161	.0155	.0150	.0145	.0140	.0135	.0130	.0126
25	.0153	.0147	.0142	.0137	.0132	.0127	.0123	.0118	.0114

	INTEREST RATE								
YEARS	9½	9¾	10	10¼	10½	10¾	11	11¼	11½
1	1.0000	1.0000	1.0000	1.0000	1.0000	1.0000	1.0000	1.0000	1.0000
2	.4773	.4768	.4762	.4756	.4751	.4745	.4739	.4734	.4728
3	.3036	.3028	.3021	.3014	.3007	.2999	.2992	.2985	.2978
4	.2171	.2163	.2155	.2147	.2139	.2131	.2123	.2115	.2108
5	.1654	.1646	.1638	.1630	.1622	.1614	.1606	.1598	.1590
6	.1313	.1304	.1296	.1288	.1280	.1272	.1264	.1256	.1248
7	.1070	.1062	.1054	.1046	.1038	.1030	.1022	.1014	.1007
8	.0890	.0882	.0874	.0867	.0859	.0851	.0843	.0836	.0828
9	.0752	.0744	.0736	.0729	.0721	.0714	.0706	.0699	.0691
10	.0643	.0635	.0627	.0620	.0613	.0605	.0598	.0591	.0584
11	.0554	.0547	.0540	.0532	.0525	.0518	.0511	.0504	.0498
12	.0482	.0475	.0468	.0461	.0454	.0447	.0440	.0434	.0427
13	.0422	.0415	.0408	.0401	.0394	.0388	.0382	.0375	.0369
14	.0371	.0364	.0357	.0351	.0345	.0338	.0332	.0326	.0320
15	.0327	.0321	.0315	.0309	.0302	.0297	.0291	.0285	.0279
16	.0290	.0284	.0278	.0272	.0266	.0261	.0255	.0250	.0244
17	.0258	.0252	.0247	.0241	.0235	.0230	.0225	.0220	.0214
18	.0230	.0225	.0219	.0214	.0209	.0203	.0198	.0193	.0189
19	.0206	.0201	.0195	.0190	.0185	.0180	.0176	.0171	.0166
20	.0185	.0180	.0175	.0170	.0165	.0160	.0156	.0151	.0147
21	.0166	.0161	.0156	.0152	.0147	.0143	.0138	.0134	.0130
22	.0149	.0145	.0140	.0136	.0131	.0127	.0123	.0119	.0115
23	.0134	.0130	.0126	.0122	.0117	.0114	.0110	.0106	.0102
24	.0121	.0117	.0113	.0109	.0105	.0101	.0098	.0094	.0091
25	.0110	.0106	.0102	.0098	.0094	.0091	.0087	.0084	.0081

	INTEREST RATE								
YEARS	11¾	12	12¼	12½	12¾	13	13¼	13½	13¾
1	1.0000	1.0000	1.0000	1.0000	1.0000	1.0000	1.0000	1.0000	1.0000
2	.4723	.4717	.4711	.4706	.4700	.4695	.4689	.4684	.4678
3	.2971	.2963	.2956	.2949	.2942	.2935	.2928	.2921	.2914
4	.2100	.2092	.2085	.2077	.2069	.2062	.2054	.2047	.2039
5	.1582	.1574	.1566	.1559	.1551	.1543	.1536	.1528	.1520
6	.1240	.1232	.1225	.1217	.1209	.1202	.1194	.1186	.1179
7	.0999	.0991	.0984	.0976	.0969	.0961	.0954	.0946	.0939
8	.0820	.0813	.0806	.0798	.0791	.0784	.0777	.0770	.0763
9	.0684	.0677	.0670	.0663	.0656	.0649	.0642	.0635	.0628
10	.0577	.0570	.0563	.0556	.0550	.0543	.0536	.0530	.0523
11	.0491	.0484	.0478	.0471	.0465	.0458	.0452	.0446	.0440
12	.0421	.0414	.0408	.0402	.0396	.0390	.0384	.0378	.0372
13	.0363	.0357	.0351	.0345	.0339	.0334	.0328	.0322	.0317
14	.0314	.0309	.0303	.0298	.0292	.0287	.0281	.0276	.0271
15	.0274	.0268	.0263	.0258	.0252	.0247	.0242	.0238	.0233
16	.0239	.0234	.0229	.0224	.0219	.0214	.0210	.0205	.0201
17	.0209	.0205	.0200	.0195	.0191	.0186	.0182	.0177	.0173
18	.0184	.0179	.0175	.0170	.0166	.0162	.0158	.0154	.0150
19	.0162	.0158	.0153	.0149	.0145	.0141	.0138	.0134	.0130
20	.0143	.0139	.0135	.0131	.0127	.0124	.0120	.0117	.0113
21	.0126	.0122	.0119	.0115	.0112	.0108	.0105	.0102	.0098
22	.0112	.0108	.0105	.0101	.0098	.0095	.0092	.0089	.0086
23	.0099	.0096	.0092	.0089	.0086	.0083	.0080	.0078	.0075
24	.0088	.0085	.0082	.0079	.0076	.0073	.0070	.0068	.0065
25	.0078	.0075	.0072	.0069	.0067	.0064	.0062	.0059	.0057

	INTEREST RATE								
YEARS	14	14¼	14½	14¾	15	15¼	15½	15¾	16
1	1.0000	1.0000	1.0000	1.0000	1.0000	1.0000	1.0000	1.0000	1.0000
2	.4673	.4667	.4662	.4657	.4651	.4646	.4640	.4635	.4630
3	.2901	.2900	.2893	.2887	.2880	.2873	.2866	.2859	.2853
4	.2032	.2025	.2017	.2010	.2003	.1995	.1988	.1981	.1974
5	.1513	.1505	.1498	.1491	.1483	.1476	.1469	.1461	.1454
6	.1172	.1164	.1157	.1150	.1142	.1135	.1128	.1121	.1114
7	.0932	.0925	.0918	.0911	.0904	.0897	.0890	.0883	.0876
8	.0756	.0749	.0742	.0735	.0729	.0722	.0715	.0709	.0702
9	.0622	.0615	.0609	.0602	.0596	.0589	.0583	.0577	.0571
10	.0517	.0511	.0505	.0499	.0493	.0487	.0481	.0475	.0469
11	.0434	.0428	.0422	.0416	.0411	.0405	.0400	.0394	.0389
12	.0367	.0361	.0356	.0350	.0345	.0340	.0334	.0329	.0324
13	.0312	.0306	.0301	.0296	.0291	.0286	.0281	.0277	.0272
14	.0266	.0261	.0256	.0252	.0247	.0242	.0238	.0233	.0229
15	.0228	.0223	.0219	.0215	.0210	.0206	.0202	.0198	.0194
16	.0196	.0192	.0188	.0184	.0179	.0176	.0172	.0168	.0164
17	.0169	.0165	.0161	.0157	.0154	.0150	.0146	.0143	.0140
18	.0146	.0142	.0139	.0135	.0132	.0128	.0125	.0122	.0119
19	.0127	.0123	.0120	.0117	.0113	.0110	.0107	.0104	.0101
20	.0110	.0107	.0104	.0101	.0098	.0095	.0092	.0089	.0087
21	.0095	.0093	.0090	.0087	.0084	.0082	.0079	.0077	.0074
22	.0083	.0080	.0078	.0075	.0073	.0070	.0068	.0066	.0064
23	.0072	.0070	.0067	.0065	.0063	.0061	.0058	.0056	.0054
24	.0063	.0061	.0059	.0056	.0054	.0052	.0050	.0049	.0047
25	.0055	.0053	.0051	.0049	.0047	.0045	.0043	.0042	.0040

	INTEREST RATE								
YEARS	16¼	16½	16¾	17	17¼	17½	17¾	18	18¼
1	1.0000	1.0000	1.0000	1.0000	1.0000	1.0000	1.0000	1.0000	1.0000
2	.4624	.4619	.4614	.4608	.4603	.4598	.4592	.4587	.4582
3	.2846	.2839	.2832	.2826	.2819	.2812	.2806	.2799	.2793
4	.1967	.1959	.1952	.1945	.1938	.1931	.1924	.1917	.1910
5	.1447	.1440	.1433	.1426	.1419	.1412	.1405	.1398	.1391
6	.1107	.1100	.1093	.1086	.1079	.1073	.1066	.1059	.1052
7	.0869	.0863	.0856	.0849	.0843	.0836	.0830	.0824	.0817
8	.0696	.0689	.0683	.0677	.0671	.0665	.0658	.0652	.0646
9	.0565	.0559	.0553	.0547	.0541	.0535	.0530	.0524	.0518
10	.0463	.0458	.0452	.0447	.0441	.0436	.0430	.0425	.0420
11	.0383	.0378	.0373	.0368	.0363	.0358	.0353	.0348	.0343
12	.0319	.0314	.0309	.0305	.0300	.0295	.0291	.0286	.0282
13	.0267	.0263	.0258	.0254	.0249	.0245	.0241	.0237	.0233
14	.0225	.0220	.0216	.0212	.0208	.0204	.0201	.0197	.0193
15	.0190	.0186	.0182	.0178	.0175	.0171	.0167	.0164	.0161
16	.0160	.0157	.0153	.0150	.0147	.0143	.0140	.0137	.0134
17	.0136	.0133	.0130	.0127	.0124	.0121	.0118	.0115	.0112
18	.0116	.0113	.0110	.0107	.0104	.0102	.0099	.0096	.0094
19	.0099	.0096	.0093	.0091	.0088	.0086	.0083	.0081	.0079
20	.0084	.0082	.0079	.0077	.0075	.0072	.0070	.0068	.0066
21	.0072	.0070	.0067	.0065	.0063	.0061	.0059	.0057	.0056
22	.0061	.0059	.0057	.0056	.0054	.0052	.0050	.0048	.0047
23	.0053	.0051	.0049	.0047	.0046	.0044	.0042	.0041	.0039
24	.0045	.0043	.0042	.0040	.0039	.0037	.0036	.0035	.0033
25	.0039	.0037	.0036	.0034	.0033	.0032	.0030	.0029	.0028

EXHIBIT B

ANNUAL CONSTANT PERCENTAGES TO AMORTIZE A LOAN PRINCIPAL
TO CALCULATE MONTHLY PAYMENTS DIVIDE BY 12

RATE/YEARS	7	7 1/8	7 1/4	7 3/8	7 1/2	7 5/8	7 3/4	7 7/8	8	8 1/8	8 1/4	8 3/8	8 1/2	8 5/8	8 3/4	8 7/8	9	9 1/8	9 1/4	9 3/8	9 1/2	9 5/8	9 3/4	9 7/8	10	RATE/YEARS
5	23.77	23.84	23.91	23.98	24.05	24.12	24.19	24.26	24.34	24.41	24.48	24.55	24.62	24.68	24.77	24.84	24.92	24.99	25.06	25.13	25.21	25.28	25.35	25.43	25.50	5
6	20.46	20.54	20.61	20.68	20.75	20.83	20.90	20.98	21.04	21.12	21.19	21.27	21.34	21.41	21.49	21.56	21.64	21.71	21.78	21.86	21.93	22.01	22.09	22.16	22.24	6
7	18.12	18.19	18.26	18.34	18.41	18.49	18.56	18.63	18.71	18.78	18.86	18.93	19.01	19.08	19.16	19.24	19.31	19.39	19.46	19.54	19.62	19.69	19.77	19.85	19.93	7
8	16.37	16.45	16.52	16.59	16.67	16.74	16.82	16.89	16.97	17.05	17.12	17.20	17.28	17.35	17.43	17.51	17.57	17.66	17.74	17.82	17.90	17.98	18.06	18.13	18.21	8
9	15.01	15.09	15.16	15.24	15.32	15.39	15.47	15.55	15.63	15.71	15.78	15.86	15.94	16.02	16.10	16.18	16.26	16.34	16.42	16.50	16.58	16.66	16.74	16.82	16.90	9
10	13.94	14.02	14.09	14.17	14.25	14.33	14.41	14.49	14.56	14.64	14.72	14.80	14.88	14.96	15.04	15.13	15.21	15.29	15.37	15.45	15.53	15.61	15.70	15.78	15.86	10
11	13.07	13.14	13.22	13.30	13.38	13.46	13.54	13.62	13.70	13.78	13.87	13.95	14.03	14.11	14.19	14.28	14.36	14.44	14.52	14.61	14.69	14.78	14.86	14.94	15.03	11
12	12.35	12.43	12.51	12.59	12.67	12.75	12.83	12.91	12.99	13.08	13.16	13.24	13.33	13.41	13.50	13.58	13.66	13.75	13.83	13.92	14.00	14.09	14.17	14.26	14.35	12
13	11.74	11.82	11.91	11.99	12.07	12.15	12.24	12.32	12.40	12.49	12.57	12.65	12.74	12.82	12.91	13.00	13.08	13.17	13.25	13.34	13.43	13.52	13.60	13.69	13.78	13
14	11.23	11.31	11.40	11.48	11.56	11.65	11.73	11.82	11.90	11.99	12.07	12.16	12.24	12.33	12.42	12.50	12.59	12.68	12.77	12.85	12.95	13.03	13.12	13.21	13.30	14
15	10.79	10.87	10.96	11.04	11.13	11.21	11.30	11.39	11.47	11.56	11.65	11.73	11.82	11.91	12.00	12.09	12.18	12.27	12.36	12.45	12.54	12.63	12.72	12.81	12.90	15
16	10.41	10.50	10.59	10.67	10.75	10.84	10.93	11.02	11.10	11.19	11.28	11.37	11.46	11.55	11.64	11.73	11.82	11.91	12.00	12.09	12.18	12.28	12.37	12.46	12.56	16
17	10.08	10.17	10.25	10.34	10.43	10.52	10.61	10.70	10.78	10.87	10.96	11.06	11.15	11.24	11.33	11.43	11.52	11.60	11.70	11.79	11.89	11.98	12.08	12.16	12.26	17
18	9.79	9.88	9.97	10.06	10.15	10.23	10.32	10.42	10.51	10.60	10.69	10.78	10.87	10.96	11.06	11.15	11.24	11.34	11.43	11.53	11.62	11.72	11.81	11.91	12.00	18
19	9.54	9.62	9.71	9.80	9.89	9.98	10.08	10.17	10.26	10.35	10.45	10.54	10.63	10.73	10.82	10.91	11.01	11.10	11.20	11.30	11.39	11.49	11.58	11.68	11.78	19
20	9.31	9.40	9.49	9.58	9.67	9.76	9.86	9.95	10.04	10.14	10.23	10.32	10.42	10.51	10.61	10.71	10.80	10.90	11.00	11.09	11.19	11.29	11.39	11.49	11.59	20
21	9.11	9.20	9.29	9.38	9.47	9.57	9.66	9.76	9.85	9.94	10.04	10.14	10.23	10.33	10.43	10.52	10.62	10.72	10.82	10.92	11.01	11.11	11.21	11.31	11.41	21
22	8.93	9.02	9.11	9.21	9.30	9.40	9.49	9.58	9.68	9.78	9.87	9.97	10.07	10.16	10.26	10.36	10.46	10.56	10.66	10.76	10.86	10.96	11.06	11.16	11.26	22
23	8.76	8.86	8.95	9.05	9.14	9.24	9.33	9.43	9.53	9.62	9.72	9.82	9.92	10.02	10.12	10.22	10.32	10.42	10.52	10.62	10.72	10.82	10.93	11.01	11.13	23
24	8.62	8.71	8.81	8.90	9.00	9.10	9.19	9.29	9.39	9.49	9.59	9.69	9.79	9.89	9.99	10.09	10.19	10.29	10.39	10.50	10.60	10.70	10.80	10.91	11.01	24
25	8.49	8.58	8.68	8.78	8.87	8.97	9.07	9.17	9.27	9.37	9.47	9.57	9.67	9.77	9.87	9.97	10.08	10.18	10.28	10.39	10.49	10.59	10.70	10.80	10.91	25
26	8.37	8.46	8.56	8.66	8.76	8.86	8.96	9.06	9.16	9.26	9.36	9.46	9.56	9.66	9.77	9.87	9.97	10.08	10.18	10.29	10.39	10.50	10.60	10.71	10.82	26
27	8.26	8.36	8.46	8.55	8.65	8.75	8.85	8.96	9.06	9.16	9.26	9.36	9.47	9.57	9.67	9.78	9.88	9.99	10.09	10.20	10.31	10.41	10.52	10.63	10.73	27
28	8.16	8.26	8.36	8.46	8.56	8.66	8.76	8.86	8.96	9.06	9.17	9.27	9.38	9.48	9.59	9.69	9.80	9.91	10.01	10.12	10.23	10.34	10.44	10.55	10.66	28
29	8.07	8.17	8.27	8.37	8.47	8.57	8.68	8.78	8.88	8.98	9.09	9.19	9.30	9.41	9.51	9.62	9.73	9.83	9.94	10.05	10.16	10.27	10.38	10.48	10.59	29
30	7.99	8.09	8.19	8.29	8.40	8.50	8.60	8.71	8.81	8.92	9.02	9.13	9.23	9.34	9.45	9.55	9.66	9.77	9.88	9.99	10.10	10.20	10.31	10.43	10.54	30
31	7.91	8.02	8.12	8.22	8.32	8.43	8.53	8.64	8.74	8.85	8.95	9.06	9.17	9.28	9.38	9.49	9.60	9.71	9.82	9.93	10.04	10.15	10.26	10.37	10.48	31
32	7.85	7.95	8.05	8.16	8.26	8.36	8.47	8.58	8.68	8.79	8.90	9.00	9.11	9.22	9.32	9.43	9.54	9.66	9.77	9.88	9.99	10.10	10.21	10.32	10.44	32
33	7.78	7.89	7.99	8.09	8.20	8.31	8.41	8.52	8.63	8.73	8.84	8.95	9.06	9.17	9.28	9.38	9.49	9.60	9.72	9.83	9.94	10.05	10.17	10.27	10.39	33
34	7.73	7.83	7.93	8.04	8.15	8.25	8.36	8.47	8.57	8.68	8.79	8.90	9.01	9.12	9.23	9.34	9.45	9.56	9.68	9.79	9.90	10.02	10.13	10.24	10.36	34
35	7.67	7.78	7.88	7.99	8.10	8.20	8.31	8.42	8.53	8.64	8.75	8.86	8.97	9.08	9.19	9.30	9.41	9.52	9.64	9.75	9.86	9.98	10.09	10.21	10.32	35
36	7.62	7.73	7.84	7.94	8.05	8.16	8.27	8.38	8.49	8.60	8.71	8.82	8.93	9.04	9.15	9.26	9.38	9.49	9.60	9.72	9.83	9.94	10.06	10.17	10.29	36
37	7.58	7.68	7.79	7.90	8.01	8.12	8.23	8.34	8.45	8.56	8.67	8.78	8.89	9.00	9.11	9.23	9.34	9.46	9.57	9.68	9.80	9.92	10.03	10.15	10.26	37
38	7.54	7.65	7.75	7.86	7.97	8.08	8.19	8.30	8.41	8.52	8.63	8.75	8.86	8.97	9.08	9.20	9.31	9.42	9.54	9.65	9.77	9.88	10.00	10.12	10.24	38
39	7.50	7.61	7.72	7.82	7.93	8.05	8.16	8.27	8.38	8.49	8.60	8.71	8.83	8.94	9.06	9.17	9.29	9.40	9.51	9.63	9.74	9.86	9.98	10.10	10.21	39
40	7.46	7.57	7.68	7.79	7.90	8.01	8.12	8.24	8.35	8.46	8.57	8.69	8.80	8.92	9.03	9.15	9.26	9.38	9.49	9.61	9.73	9.84	9.96	10.08	10.19	40
41	7.43	7.54	7.65	7.76	7.87	7.98	8.10	8.21	8.32	8.43	8.55	8.66	8.78	8.89	9.01	9.12	9.24	9.35	9.47	9.59	9.71	9.82	9.94	10.06	10.18	41
42	7.40	7.51	7.62	7.73	7.84	7.96	8.07	8.18	8.30	8.41	8.52	8.64	8.75	8.87	8.99	9.10	9.22	9.33	9.45	9.57	9.69	9.80	9.92	10.04	10.16	42
43	7.37	7.48	7.59	7.71	7.82	7.93	8.05	8.16	8.27	8.39	8.50	8.62	8.73	8.85	8.97	9.08	9.20	9.32	9.43	9.55	9.67	9.79	9.91	10.03	10.15	43
44	7.35	7.46	7.57	7.68	7.80	7.91	8.02	8.14	8.25	8.37	8.48	8.60	8.71	8.83	8.95	9.07	9.18	9.30	9.42	9.54	9.66	9.77	9.89	10.01	10.13	44
45	7.32	7.43	7.55	7.66	7.78	7.89	8.00	8.12	8.23	8.35	8.46	8.58	8.70	8.81	8.93	9.05	9.17	9.29	9.40	9.52	9.64	9.76	9.88	10.00	10.12	45
46	7.30	7.41	7.53	7.64	7.75	7.87	7.98	8.10	8.21	8.33	8.45	8.56	8.68	8.80	8.92	9.03	9.15	9.27	9.39	9.51	9.63	9.75	9.87	9.99	10.11	46
47	7.28	7.39	7.51	7.62	7.74	7.85	7.97	8.08	8.20	8.31	8.43	8.55	8.67	8.78	8.90	9.02	9.14	9.26	9.38	9.50	9.62	9.74	9.86	9.98	10.10	47
48	7.26	7.38	7.49	7.60	7.72	7.83	7.95	8.07	8.18	8.30	8.42	8.54	8.65	8.77	8.89	9.01	9.13	9.25	9.37	9.49	9.61	9.73	9.85	9.97	10.09	48
49	7.24	7.36	7.47	7.59	7.70	7.82	7.94	8.05	8.17	8.29	8.40	8.52	8.64	8.76	8.88	9.00	9.12	9.24	9.36	9.48	9.60	9.72	9.84	9.96	10.08	49
50	7.23	7.34	7.46	7.57	7.69	7.80	7.92	8.04	8.16	8.27	8.39	8.51	8.63	8.75	8.87	8.99	9.11	9.23	9.35	9.47	9.59	9.71	9.83	9.95	10.07	50

EXHIBIT C

Debt Coverage Factors as Reflected by Loan Commitments of Major Insurance Companies** on Large Income Properties

	Conventional Elevator Apartments	Conventional Nonelevator Apartments	Shopping Centers (5 or more stores)	Retail Stores (less than 5 stores)	Office Bldgs.	Medical Office Bldgs.	Commercial Warehouses	Industrial Warehouses	Mfg. Plants	Motels
1968 IV	1.29	1.30	1.30	1.24	1.25	1.33	1.20	1.31	1.21	1.48
1969 I	1.26	1.29	1.37	1.20	1.23	—	1.17	1.32	1.30	1.56
II	1.39	1.27	1.40	1.32	1.33	1.27	1.23	1.23	1.19	1.57
III	1.30	1.29	1.31	1.27	1.22	1.16	1.30	1.21	1.22	1.51
IV	1.39	1.30	1.35	1.26	1.31	1.35	1.34	1.20	1.33	1.55
1970 I	1.31	1.33	1.29	1.29	1.34	1.21	1.26	1.22	1.24	1.95
II	1.37	1.44	1.41	1.29	1.35	1.22	1.23	1.29	1.47	—
III	1.28	1.31	1.50	1.29	1.31	1.19	1.44	1.26	1.38	—
IV	1.35	1.27	1.38	1.22	1.30	1.17	—	1.36	—	—
1971 I	1.29	1.29	1.36	1.28	1.32	1.35	1.43	1.26	1.31	1.48
II	1.28	1.26	1.38	1.37	1.24	1.28	1.24	1.24	1.25	1.69
III	1.26	1.28	1.31	1.32	1.25	1.25	1.23	1.22	1.25	1.47
IV	1.26	1.30	1.32	1.31	1.28	1.32	1.22	1.35	1.30	1.33
1972 I	1.29	1.29	1.30	1.30	1.25	1.36	1.23	1.28	1.54	1.90
II	1.28	1.29	1.32	1.10	1.30	1.34	1.24	1.31	1.43	1.49
III	1.35	1.30	1.32	1.33	1.28	1.28	1.21	1.29	1.27	1.75
IV	1.30	1.32	1.30	1.50	1.30	1.34	1.22	1.30	1.27	1.49

EXHIBIT C (Continued)

1973	I	1.28	1.29	1.33	1.40	1.31	1.31	1.26	1.35	1.30	1.48
	II	1.29	1.32	1.37	1.24	1.28	1.26	1.22	1.31	1.24	1.43
	III	1.27	1.31	1.28	1.29	1.26	1.25	1.19	1.26	1.32	1.34
	IV	1.27	1.27	1.24	1.22	1.25	1.24	1.21	1.27	1.33	1.30
1974	I	1.27	1.27	1.34	1.26	1.28	1.21	1.36	1.23	1.29	1.52
	II	1.21	1.31	1.37	1.30	1.28	1.34	1.26	1.23	1.24	1.77
	III	1.45	1.26	1.28	1.25	1.30	1.43	1.38	1.22	1.26	1.73
	IV	—	1.27	1.26	1.30	1.26	—	1.27	1.24	—	—
1975	I	—	1.34	1.25	1.35	1.28	1.35	1.29	1.35	—	1.68
	II	—	1.34	1.30	1.15	1.29	1.27	1.34	1.28	1.22	—
	III	1.34	1.30	1.29	1.22	1.35	1.35	1.33	1.25	—	1.93

*Source: Ongoing American Life Insurance Association study. "Survey of Mortgage Commitments on Nonresidential Properties Reported by 15 Life Insurance Companies."

**Notes: The 15 reporting companies account for over one-half of assets and over one-half of nonfarm mortgages held by all U.S. life insurance companies. Averages in the summary are weighted by number of loans committed. Very few commitments were made for loans on certain property types in certain quarters, and average interest rates were not reported.

EXHIBIT D

Utilizing The Mortgage/Equity Technique for Developing, or Analyzing Rates of Capitalization

Critical Assumptions to be Made:
1 — Available Financing Plan
2 — Acceptable Equity Yield Rate
3 — Income Projection Period
4 — Estimated Future Property Value Change

Example No. 1 — Construct a Cap Rate, assuming:
1 — Mortgage Financing: -75% of value for 30 years at 9½% interest
2 — Acceptable Equity Yield: — 10% of an assumed 25% investment
3 — Income Projection Period: — 10 years
4 — Estimated safe allowance for future depreciation: 10 years over next 10 years in constant dollars.

EXHIBIT E

Capitalization Rate Structure:

1 — Calculate "P", the percentage of loan amortized over 10 years.

$$P = \frac{f_{30} - i}{f_{10} - i} = \frac{.1010 - .095}{.1553 - .095} = \frac{.0060}{0603} = .0995$$

(f = loan constant, i = loan interest rate)

2 — Take out Sinking Fund Factor at 10% from table = .0627

3 — Build Basic Rate (r)

Mortgage money .75 x .101	=	.0758
Equity money .25 x .10	=	.0250
		.1008

Less credit for equity build-up

.75 x .0995 x .0627 =	=	-.0047
	r=	.0961

4 — Adjust for future value

Change .10 x .0627	=	+.0063
	R =	.1024

Valuation: A net annual income of $10,240 earns 10.24% on an investment of $100,000

Arithmetic Proof:

Distribution		Income
25% Equity $25,000 x .1066	=	$2,665
75% Loan 75,000 x .1010	=	7,575
Re-Sale (Value) 10th year	=	$90,000
Less loan balance		
$75,000 x (1-.0995)	=	67,538
Equity Reversion		$22,462
Present Worth Equity 10 years 10%		
Income $ 2,665 x 6.1446	=	$16,375
Reversion $22,462 x 0.38 =	=	8,659
		$25,034

$34 difference due to rounding.

EXHIBIT F

Example No. 2

An apartment complex recently sold for 7½ times its gross annual income. Net annual income is estimated at 60% after vacancy and operating expense.

Analyze this indicated rate of capitalization to show 10th year property value required to yield 9% on an assumed equity investment subject to a 75% loan for 30 years at 9% interest.

1 — Indicated Cap Rate = 0.6 ÷ 7.5 = .08
2 — Basic Cap Rate (r); i.e., the rate before adjustment for future depreciation/appreciation allowance

$$
\begin{aligned}
.75 \times .0966 &= .0725 \\
.25 \times .09 &= \underline{.0225} \\
& .0950
\end{aligned}
$$

$$
\begin{aligned}
\text{less } .75 \times .10628 \times .0658 &= \underline{.0052} \\
r &= .0898
\end{aligned}
$$

$$
R - r = .08 - .0898 \qquad = \text{ -}.0098
$$

Since R < r, appreciation is required.
Percentage appreciation = .0098 ÷ .0658 = 14.89%

Estimated Net Annual Income $80,000 next 10 years
Valuation: $80,000/.08 = $1,000,000.

Arithmetic Proof:

	Distribution		Income
Total	$1,000,000 x .0800	=	$80,000
75% Loan	750,000 x .0966	=	$72,450
25% Equity	250,000 x .0302	=	$ 7,550

Re-Sale (Value) 10th year:
 $1,000,000 x 1.1489 = $1,148,900
Less 10th year loan balance:

$750,000 x (1-.10628) =	=	670,290
10th year reversion	=	$478,610

Present Value Equity, 10 years @ 9%:

Income	=	$48,454
Reversion	=	202,165
Total		$250,619

($619 difference due to droping decimals)

EXHIBIT G

ANALYSIS OF 9.25% CAPITALIZATION RATE

Prospects for yield on equity investment assuming purchase at appraised value 75% financed by 30 year level monthly payment loan @ 9¼% interest per annum.

Yield curves below and above the central "Appraised Value" line indicate declines and increases in overall property value which would result in the equity yield (in terms of constant dollars) written on each curve.

EQUITY YIELD WILL BE:	IF IN 5 YEARS PROPERTY VALUE:	IF IN 10 YEARS PROPERTY VALUE:
6%	DECLINES 4.90%	DECLINES 12.12%
9%	DECLINES 0.53%	DECLINES 1.51%
12%	APPRECIATES 4.37%	APPRECIATES 12.63%

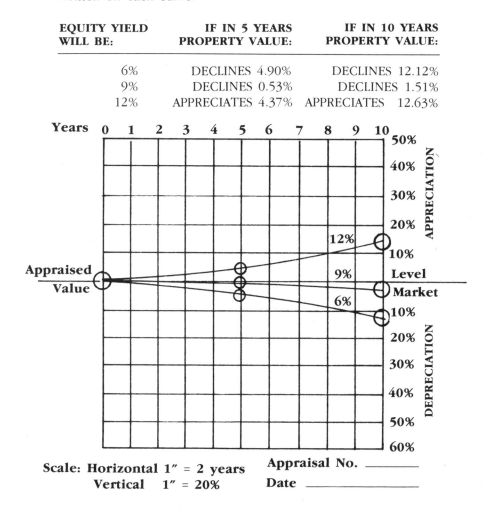

Scale: Horizontal 1" = 2 years
Vertical 1" = 20%

Appraisal No. _____
Date _____

EXHIBIT H

GRAPHIC ANALYSIS OF 9.25% CAPITALIZATION RATE
ASSUMING 75% FINANCED OVER 30 YEARS AT 9¼% INTEREST

Find 10th property value change required to yield 12% on an assumed 25% Equity Investment.

Step No. 1 — Calculate "P" (Percentage of loan amortized in the projected holding period "n", in this case 10 years).

Formula:

$$P = \frac{f_{30} - i}{f_{10} - i}$$

f_{30} = Loan Constant, full term
f_{10} = Loan Constant holding period   =   .0987
i = Annual Interest Rate = .0925   =   .1536

Substituting:

$$P = \frac{.0987 - .0925}{.1536 - .0925} = \frac{.0062}{.0611} = .1014$$

Step No. 2 — Calculate "r" at "Y", Equity Field Rate. (This is the basic rate of capitalization assuming a level market over holding period; i.e., before adjustment for future appreciation/depreciation allowances.)

Formula for "r" at 12% Equity Yield Rate ("Y")
$r = (mf) + [(1-m) Y] - (mp) 1/s_{n7}$
m = ratio mortgage to value = 75%
f = Annual Loan Constant, full term - .0987
Y = Equity Yield = 12%
$1/s_{n7}$ = Annual Sinking Fund Factor for n periods at "Y" rate = .0570

Substituting:
$r = (.75 \times .0987) + [(1-.75) .12] - (.75 \times .1014 \times .057)$
$r = .0997$

Step No. 3 — Determine percent future property value change over income projection period.

Formula:
APP/DEP % = (R - r) ÷ 1/s_{n7}
R = Capitalization rate =   .0925
r = Basic Rate   = -.0997
1/s_{n7} = Sinking Fund Factor   .0570

Rule:
If "r" is greater than "R" appreciation is required.
If "r" is less than "R" depreciation is required.

Substituting:
App % = (.0925 -.0997) ÷ .0570 = .1263
Therefore property value must appreciate 12.63% over next 10 years to yield 12% on the assumed equity position.

EXHIBIT I

Graphic analysis of 9.25% Capitalization Rate assuming 75% financed over 30 years at 9¼% interest.

Arithmetic Proof:

Assumed Captial Structure and Income Distribution
    25% Equity $297,049 @ .0738 = $21,952
    75% Loan   891,146 @ .0987 = 87,956

    Total $1,188,195 @ .0925 =$109,908
Estimated Re-Sale, (value) 10th year:
                $1,188,195 x (1 + .1263) = $1,338,264
    Less 10th year Loan Balance:
                891,146 x (1 -.1014) =   800,784
                10th year Equity Reversion $ 537,480
Present Worth Equity, 10 years @ 12%
    Income Stream $21,952 x 5.6502   = $124,033
    Reversion   537,480 x 0.3220   =   173,102
                                    Total $297,135

(Note — $53 error due to dropping decimals)

CHAPTER EIGHTEEN

Mortgage Equity

Analysis and the

Review Appraiser

MORGAN B. GILREATH, JR., CRA

*Morgan B. Gilreath, Jr., CRA, is Vice President of Gilreath &
Howard Property Consultants in Athens, Georgia, and is a
member of the faculty at the University of Georgia. He received
his M.A. in Real Estate from the University of Georgia.*

*Mr. Gilreath is a Senior Member of the National Association of
Review Appraisers and holds the "Certified Review Appraiser"
designation, and is a member of the International Association of
Assessing Officers.*

Mortgage Equity

Analysis and the

Review Appraiser

INTRODUCTION

Mortgage Equity valuation methods began to attract a significant amount of attention in the early 1960s and have continued to be viewed by some with awe ever since then. The Review Appraiser may anticipate the use of mortgage equity analysis in any income producing property appraisal report. In reviewing these reports, one should be able to identify the valuation technique utilized and accurately interpret its application to a given property. A more complete understanding of any valuation tool yields a higher degree of confidence and competence in a given area of the appraisal field.

As will be illustrated in this article, what is commonly referred to as the "Ellwood Method" is not the only approach to mortgage equity analysis. Leon W. Ellwood's formula and discussions beginning in the late 1950s did, however, signal the rise of some new and relevant methods of valuation.

Much of the rationale for utilization of the "income approach" is that the Appraiser is trying to view properties as the investor or purchaser would. The purchaser is basing his offering price on what he believes the property will produce him in terms of cold hard cash. The seller will only sell for a price which he is certain will support his own idea of the net returns from the property. In other words, the ultimate sales price (in a bonafide transaction considered the "best evidence of value") is determined by the ability of a given property to produce income. Therefore, when using the income approach, we are attempting to "simulate" the actions of buyers and sellers in estimating the income that properties will produce and also in estimating or making assumptions concerning the various rates of return which will accrue to the owners. Mortgage equity analysis probably offers one of the best opportunities for the Appraiser/Analyst to "simulate" market conditions. This might not be considered totally accurate under traditional mortgage equity methods, however, a preview of some new variations which may be utilized will provide sufficient evidence of applicability. These will be presented later in this chapter.

"Mortgage Equity" is a quite descriptive term. The process it implies does, in fact, separate a property (in terms of the dollar returns) into its mortgage and equity components. Mortgage equity concentrates on the position of the equity investor, since it is through his own perception of the productivity (in terms of income) of the property that he decides how much the property is worth. We then, as Appraiser/Analysts must also view the property from the perspective of the equity investor in order to arrive at our "best evidence of value", the worth of the property. The above statement might be expanded to include analysis for a specific equity investor or for the "typical" equity investor for a particular property type. For this reason, mortgage equity analysis does have universal application, both in terms of value to a specific individual client or in terms of the "market value" of the property.

Assumptions Involved in Mortgage Equity Analysis

Some of the assumptions involved in mortgage equity analysis are that, as stated above, the returns to the equity position and the mortgage position are specified and viewed separately. This is not true with traditional band-of-investment analysis which combined the mortgage interest rate and the equity dividened rates into a discount rate. NOI (net operating income), NIBR (net income before recapture), or NIBRT (net income before recapture and property taxes) was then capitalized or "discounted" at this discount rate via straight-line, sinking fund, or annuity capitalization with their respective techniques into an estimate of value. Mortgage equity analysis not only allows for analysis of the mortgage separately but allows for a build-up of the equity as the mortgage is paid off. It provides for the specific returns to the equity to be discounted at the equity yield rate, instead of the equity dividend rate. The difference between the two rates is that the equity dividend rate is a "cash-on-cash" rate and the equity yield rate allows for reinvestment of the equity returns at a specified rate of return which is compounded annually. Perhaps it would be of assistance at this point to view the returns to the debt and equity positions in a traditional band-of-investments type of valuation and in a mortgage equity problem in order to fully appreciate the differences. Since this is "putting the cart before the horse" in one sense (in terms of the orderly progression of this paper) all of the calculations involved will not be specified at this point but will be fully presented later in other exmaples.

Band-of-Investments Returns to Mortgage and Equity

> *Assume:* NIBR = $50,000
> Productive economic life = 20 years
> Land Value = $100,000
> Financing: 80% loan @ 9.5%
> Equity Dividend = 12%
> Resulting Value = $440,543

Returns to Captial Recovery:
$340,543 x .01746 = $ 5,946

Returns to Debt:
$440,543 x .076   = $33,481 ÷ $352,434 = .0950
(mortgage interest rate)

Returns to Equity:
$440,543 x .024   = $10,573 ÷ $88,109 = .1200
(equity dividend)

Total Return   = $50,000

The 12% equity dividend represents cash ($10,573) on the original equity investment ($88,109), hence the term "cash-on-cash."

Mortgage Equity Returns to Mortgage and Equity[1]

Assume: NIBR = $50,000
Holding Period = 10 years
Financing = 80% loan @ 9.5% for 20 years
Equity Yield = 12%
Appreciation in property value = 5% over holding
period
Resulting Value = $510,788

Mortgage @ 80% = $408,630 x .111856 = $45,708
Equity   @ 20% = 102,158 x .042014 =   4,292
Cash to Seller   = 510,788   NIBR = $50,000

Present Value of Property	$510,788
plus 5% appreciation	25,539
equals Property Reversion, deferred 10 years	$536,327

Original Mortgage   = $408,630
less amortization (x.279638) = 114,268
equals mortgage balance $294,362

Property Reversion less mortgage balance	$294,362
equals Equity Reversion	$241,965

Present value of equity income and equity reversion @ 12%
Equity Yield:

Equity income = $ 4,292 x 5.650223	=	$24,251
Equity Reversion = $241,965 x .321973	=	$77,906
Present Value of the Equity Position	=	$102,157
Original Equity Investment		$102,158

What may be evidenced by the two illustrations above is that the traditional band-of-investments method only provided for cash-on-cash return to the equity investor. In addition to that, capital recovery allowed for repayment of mortgage principal with the returns to debt representing repayment of mortgage interest. There was no evidence or opportunity to show a possible increase (or decrease) in the value of the property over the holding period. The holding period, in this instance, is equal to the productive economic life of the income stream (also an unlikely assumption). In addition, with the band-of-investments method, there was no opportunity to show any allowance for a build-up of the equity in the property as the mortgage was paid off over the holding period. As may be noted from the example, mortgage equity analysis provided for a specific holding period of 10 years (holding periods may be any given number of years); there was an allowance for capital appreciation of 5% over the holding period in the value of the property. Also, it should be noted that the returns to the equity position (both the income and the equity reversion) allowed for an annual compound return of 12.00% over the holding period, assuming reinvestment of equity capital. It might also be noted that the equity income was the "cash throw-off," the NIBR less mortgage payment. This is not the case with the band-of-investment method. In both instances, the income stream to the property was assumed to be level over the holding periods.

It should be clear by now that there are certain situations where the application of mortgage equity analysis will allow for simulating a number of the habits of investors. Mortgage equity provides for the expectation of returns which repay mortgage debt at the mortgage interest rate; it provides an allowance for equity return at an annual compound equity yield rate; it provides the opportunity for equity build-up over the holding period, and allows for possible capital gain or loss on the total value of the property over the holding period. The only desirable ingredient which is missing is a possibility of variable income streams which, as will be discussed later, may be incorporated in the Ellwood formula with the "J" factor, which allows for equal dollar increases or decreases in the income stream annually. Before and After-Cash Flow Analysis allow for annual increments of unequal amounts each year. This, as will be shown later, may provide a more realistic way of viewing variable income streams.

Methods of Arriving at Mortgage Equity Rates

There are several methods available to the Appraiser who wishes to develop a mortgage equity rate. Perhaps it should be stated at this point that this process of simulating the actions of the equity investor is accomplished through manipulations in the capitalization rate. The income to be capitalized is generally NOI less mortgage payments, "cash throw-off" or "before tax cash flow." At any rate (no pun intended) any valuation method which views the mortgage and equity positions separately should certainly be mentioned.

Band-of-Investments as Akerson Method

The first method discussed is often referred to as the "Akerson Method" or the "Band-of-Investments" method of mortgage equity analysis. It is probably one of the easiest to understand initially and is most likely the most often utilized for that reason. The method begins very much the same as the traditional BOI (band-of-investments) method with the exception that the "mortgage constant", is used in the place of mortgage interest rate. This is a simple but significant variation because it specifically places the entirety of the mortgage portion of the rate in one place. It might also be noted that the mortgage constant does represent the percentage payment on the mortgage annually, with monthly compounding, which is required to fully amortize the mortgage over the term of the loan. All calculations connected with this mortgage, as allowances for repayment of a portion of it and inclusion of the resulting equity build-up, are made at the mortgage interest rate, compounded monthly. All possible returns to the equity position are discounted at the equity yield rate, compounded on an annual basis. The assumption here is that mortgage payments are required on a monthly basis but investors usually think of returns on their invested capital annually.

The BOI method of mortgage equity analysis therefore begins with a melding or merging of the initial mortgage and equity requirements into a "weighted average." Most investors will hold investment properties for seven to twelve years, thus the need for the term "holding period" and for some allowance for the equity which they have accumulated as a result of repaying a portion of their mortgage indebtedness (hence the allowance for equity build-up). This allowance for equity build-up simply takes that portion of the property which is mortgaged and merges it with the percentage of the mortgage which has been paid off. This is then multiplied times the sinking fund factor at the equity yield rate to show that the funds accumulated will accrue to the equity investor at his desired rate of return. It might be useful, at this point, to view the entirety of the BOI method of mortgage equity rate composition and then view the component parts.

Mortgage-Equity Rate Composition:[2]

Loan Ratio x (Annual Constant) = Weighted Rate
Equity Ratio x Equity Yield Rate = Weighted Rate
_____
Weighted Average
Less credit for equity build-up:
Loan Ratio x Portion Paid Off x SFF =   (credit)
_____
Basic Rate "r"
Adjustment for dep. or app.:
Plus dep. (or minus app.) x SFF =   Adjustment
_____
Overall Rate "R"

The "weighted average" is, as indicated above, obtained much like in the traditional methods except that it does include provision for the entire mortgage in the annual mortgage constant. It might again be emphasized at this point that this mortgage constant is given as an annual figure but it is based on monthly compounding multiped by 12. The following set of assumptions will serve for illustrative purposes set of assumptions will serve for illustrative purposes through the presentation of the BOI method of mortgage equity analysis:

Assume: NOI = $125,000
          Financing = 75% loan @ 9% for 25 years
          Holding Period = 10 years
          Equity Yield = 10 years
          Appreciation = 10.00% over the holding period

Calculation of the Weighted Average:

.75 x (.008392 x 12 = .100704)	= .075528
.25 x .1250	= .031250
Weighted Average	= .106778

This weighted average is actually meaningless without some adjustment for equity build-up because some equity build-up will occur even if the holding period is one month or one year. Obviously, the longer the holding period, the more the mortgage is amortized and the more significant becomes the adjustment for equity build-up. In essence, it involves setting up a sinking fund at the equity yield rate for the amount of the mortgage which has been amortized up to the end of the holding period.

Once this adjustment has been made, we have a "basic rate" which makes allowances for returns covering mortgage payments, returns to the equity at 12.5% and the return of that equity which has been paid into the mortgage over the holding period. The "portion paid off" may be calculated several ways; one is to divide the sinking fund (compounded monthly at the mortgage interest rate) for the term of the mortgage by the sinking fund factor (SFF) for the holding period. This will provide for sufficient accuracy as long as one uses a calculator which will utilize 8 to 10 "significant digits." Another is to use the present worth of one per period (annuity factor= PW1/P) for the mortgage term and divide it into the PW1/P for the "remainder" of the mortgage to obtain the "unpaid balance." This may be subtracted from "one" to obtain the "portion paid off." Both of these will be calculated below (with equal significant digits) to illustrate that both will lead to the same conclusion as to the portion paid off.

Calculation of Portion Paid Off:

A. Using the SFF for the term divided by the SFF for the holding period. Mortgage interest is 9%, compounded monthly.

$$\frac{.00089196364}{.0051675774} = .172607698 \text{ (Portion Paid Off)}$$

B. Using the PW1/P for the "remainder" and dividing it by the PW1/P for the term. Mortgage interest is 9%, compounded montly.

$$\frac{98.59340884}{119.1616222} = .827392302 \text{ (Unpaid Balance)}$$

$$1 - .827392302 = .172607699 \text{ (Portion Paid Off)}$$

The allowance for equity build-up is then no more than multiplying the loan to value ratio (to reflect the portion of the property that is mortgaged) times the SFF at the equity yield rate (compounded annually). This then, as stated above, makes allowance for a fund (at the equity rate) to reflect the amount of the mortgage which has been amortized over the holding period.

Calculation of the Allowance for Equity Build-up:

$$.75 \times .172608 \times .055622 = .007201$$

Calculation of the Basic Rate "r":

Weighted Average	= .106778
less Allowance for Equity Build-up	= .007201
Basic Rate "r"	= .099577

The only remaining adjustment to be made to this basic rate is in the event of an anticipated increase or decrease in the value of the property over the holding period. This is expressed as a percentage which results from multiplying the anticipated appreciation (app.) or depreciation (dep.) times the sinking fund factor for the holding period at the equity yield rate. The equity yield rate is used because the investor will have anticipated his returns from any capital gain at his own desired rate of return (the equity yield rate). The remainder of the capitalization rate formulation may be accomplished as follows:

Calculation of the Overall Rate "R":

Basic rate "r"	= .099577
less Allowance for Appreciation	
.10 x .055662	= .005562
OVERALL RATE "R"	= .094015

It should be pointed out at this point that an allowance for appreciation is subtracted from the basic rate and an allowance for depreciation is added to the basic rate. The reasoning is simple, appreciation will increase captial value; to increase value requires a reduction in the rate. The opposite is true with depreciation, to provide for a decrease in the value, one must increase the rate.

Calculation of the Value Estimate:

$$\frac{\text{NOI}}{\text{OAR}} \quad \frac{\$125,000}{.094015} = \underline{\underline{\$1,329,575}}$$

Proof:

Mortgage @ 75% = $ 997,181 x .100704 = $100,420
Equity   @ 25% = $ 332,394 x .073948 = $ 24,580
Cash to Seller   = $ 1,329,575   BOI   = $125,000

Present Value of Property	$1,329,575
plus 10% Appreciation	132,958
equals Property Reversion, deferred 10 years	$1,462,533
Original Mortgage = $997,181	
less amortization (x .172608) = $172,121	
equals Mortgage Balance $825,060	
Property Reversion less Mortgage Balance	$ 825,060
equals Equity Reversion	$ 637,473

Present Value of Equity Position (equity income & equity reversion @ 12.5% equity yield):

Equity Income	= $ 24,580 x 5.536431	= $136,085
Equity Reversion	= $637,473 x .307946	= $196,307
Present Value of Equity Position		= $332,393
Original Equity Investment		= $332,394

Now that the entirety of the BOI or Akerson Method has been presented in segments, viewing its composite compilation might be beneficial to "tie things together" at this point.

Assume: NOI = $125,000
                Financing = 75% loan @ 9% for 25 years
                Holding Period = 10 years
                Equity Yield = 12.50%
                Apppreciation = 10.00% over the holding period

Calculation of the Weighted Average:

.75 x .100704 = .075528
.25 x .125000 = .031250

Weighted Average   = .106778

Calculation of the Equity Build-up

.75 x .172608 x .055622   = −.007201

Basic Rate "r"   = .0099557

Calculation for appreciation:

.10 x .055622   = −.005562

OVERALL RATE "R"   = .094015

The Ellwood Method

The second method of arriving at a mortgage equity rate is probably the most renown. In practice, however, it is perhaps the least used. This has been due to, in this author's opinion, a misunderstanding concerning the complexity of calculations involved in arriving at the ultimate Overall Rate (OAR) or "R" which is used in a direct capitalization of the appropriate income stream into an estimate of value for the property involved. Once understood, the Ellwood formula is no more difficult than the band-of-investments method of rate calculation (some might even consider it less cumbersome to work with). The Ellwood formula does have one distinct advantage over the band-of-investments method (this could be debated). That is, it offers a format which lends itself to "sensitivity analysis." Sensitivity analysis is simply holding all variables constant except one, and then varying it to see its effect on the equation. For example, one might want to see what would happen to the equity position or to the total value if mortgage loan-to-value ratios were varied from 60% to 90%. One might be interested in how the equity position would change if the mortgage interest rate were varied (as one would want to do when comparing potential mortgage loans). One might be interested to view the changes in values as equity rates were varied up and down, since all real estate projects do not always produce the desired yield on the equity investment. It might be advantageous to view the property returns with varying degrees of appreciation or depreciation over the anticipated holding period.

The best method of obtaining an understanding of anything is through either usage or the viewing of examples and illustrations. With that in mind, the basic Ellwood formula, accompanied with examples is shown below. At various points, further analysis and breakdown is provided for additional illustration of pertinent points.

$$R = r \begin{array}{c} +dep \\ -app \end{array} x \ 1/Sn^3$$

Where:

       $r = Y - MC$ = "basic rate"

       Y = Equity Yield Rate

       M = Mortgage Loan To Value Ratio

       $C = Y - P \ x \ 1/Sn - f$ = "mortgage coefficient"

       f = Annual/Mortgage Constant based on monthly
         compounding

   $1/Sn$ = Sinking Fund Factor (SFF) At Equity Yield Rate

       P = SFF for term divided by SFF fo r holding period = portion of mortgage paid off. Calculated with mortgage interest rate, monthly compounding.

$P \ x \ 1/Sn$ = Equity Build-up

$\begin{array}{c} + \ dep \\ -app \end{array}$ = % Change In Total Value Over Holding Period

It is perhaps this "formula-within-a-formula" type of forumla which has provided some of the "muddy water" around the Ellwood method over the years. For this reason, the basic forumla will be broken down several ways before an example is undertaken. The three formulas below are probably the most often presented ways of viewing the "Ellwood Method."

    1. $r = Y - MC$

    2. $C = Y + P \ x \ 1/Sn - f$

    3. $R = r \begin{array}{c} +dep \\ -app \end{array} x \ 1/Sn$

Even though symbols and letters in formulas are for purposes of simplification, sometimes it is still comforting to "do it the long way" and look at exactly what all of those "things" really mean. The above three formulations may be seen with less mystique as follows:

1. basic rate = equity yield rate – loan to value ratio x mortgage coefficient

2. Mortgage Coefficient = Equity yield rate plus portion of mortgage paid off times the SFF minus the mortgage constant
   = equity yield plus equity build-up minus mortgage constant.

3. Over-All Rate (OAR) = "R" = basic rate plus the % depreciation or minus the % appreciation x the SFF

There are two rates which are used throughout the formulation of an Ellwood OAR. The mortgage interest rate is used in calculating the portion paid off ("P") and also in calculating the mortgage constant ("f"). Any time the mortgage interest rate is used, montly compounding is assumed. The other rate is the equity yield rate which is used when calculating or looking up "1/Sn." The equity yield rate is based on annual compounding and is used in calculating the amount of equity build-up and the amount of appreciation or depreciation which might have accrued over the holding period. The overall formula might be viewed again as follows:

$$R = Y - M \times (Y + P \times 1/Sn - f) \, {{+dep} \atop {-app}} \times 1/Sn$$

Since (Y + P x 1/Sn – f) is actually the equity yield plus equity build-up minus mortgage constant and ($\frac{+dep}{-app}$ x 1/Sn) represents the captial gain/loss anticipated over the holding period, one more restatement of the basic formula may be in order at this time.

$$\text{Rate} = \underset{\downarrow}{\overset{\text{equity}}{\text{yield}}} - \underset{\downarrow}{\text{value ratio}}^{\text{Loan to}} \quad x \quad \underset{\downarrow}{\overset{\text{eq. yield}}{\overset{(+ \text{ eq. build-up})}{- \text{ mtge cons't}}}} + \underset{\downarrow}{\overset{\text{capital gain/loss}}{- \text{ over holding period}}}$$

$$R \;=\; T \;-\; M \quad x \quad C \quad \overset{+}{\underset{-}{}} \quad (\,\tfrac{\text{dep}}{\text{app}} \; x \; 1/\text{Sn}\,)$$

It should be evident by now that the same basic assumptions are made with the Ellwood formula that were seen with the band of investments method. The primary difference is that Ellwood rearranged the formula so as to be able to view the formulation from the standpoint of the mortgage lender who could readily see the effects of varying different component parts within the formula. The reason was probably to allow him to maximize his mortgage loans and also to enable him to view a large number of loan applications with maximum effectiveness. The same logic might be applied to the Review Appraiser who is attempting to view the property in light of its productivity to the mortgage and equity positions.

A set of assumptions for mortgage equity analysis is presented below. The over-all rate ("R") is calculated twice to show the formula broken down and also as one continuous calculation.

Assumptions:

NOI = $45,000
Financing: 75% loan @ 9% for 25 years
Yield to Equity: 12%
Holding Period: 10 years
Anticipated appreciation over holding period: 20%

1. $r = Y - MC$
   $r = .12 - .75\,(.029132)$
   $r = .12 - .021849$
   $r = .098151$

2. $C = Y + P \times 1/Sn - f$
   $C = .12 + .172608 \times .056984 - .100704$
   $C = .019276 + .009836$
   $C = .029132$

3. $R = r \begin{smallmatrix} +\text{dep} \\ -\text{app} \end{smallmatrix} \text{ x } 1/Sn$

    R = .098151 – .20 x .056984

    R = .098151 – .011397

    R = .086754

OR

    $R = Y - M (Y + P \text{ x } 1/Sn - f) \begin{smallmatrix} +\text{dep} \\ -\text{app} \end{smallmatrix} \text{ x } 1/Sn$

    R = .12 – .75(.12 + (.172608 x .056984) – .100704)

                                     – (.20 x .056984)

    R = .12 – .75(.12 + .009836 – .100704) – .011397

    R = .12 – .75(.029132) – .011397

    R = .12 – .021849 – .011397

    R = .086754

Valuation: $\dfrac{\text{NOI}}{\text{R}} = \text{Value}$

$$\frac{\$45,000}{.086754} = \$518,708$$

Proof of this as a valid estimate of value, given the above assumptions will be shown below three ways. The first will break the valuation down into the mortgage and equity components, calculating the equity income and the equity reversion and valuing these into an estimate of the present value of the equity position. The second will be to calculate the amount of equity dividend and average yearly rate of profit and calculate, through the iterative process, the internal rate of return to the equity position. This will have the effect of proving that the equity yield rate is, in fact, the internal rate of return. The third will value the present worth of the equity position using the annual equity divdend (instead of the equity income), the anticipated amount of capital gain and the deferred return of the original equity.

1. Present Value of the Equity Position Using Equity Income and Equity Reversion

Mortgage @ 75% = $389,031 x .100704	= $39,177
Equity @ 25% = $129,677 x .044904	= $ 5,823
Cash to Seller = $518,708	NOI = $45,000

Present Value of Property		$508,708
plus 20% Appreciation		103,742
equals Property Reversion, deferred 10 years		$622,450
Original Mortgage	$389,031	
less amortization (x .172608)	= 67,150	
equals Mortgage Balance	= $321,881	
Property Reversion less Mortgage Balance		$321,881
eqauls Equity Reversion		$300,569

Equity Income $ 5,823 x 5.650223 = $ 32,901	
Equity Reversion $300,569 x .321973 = $ 96,775	
Present Value of Equity Position = $129,676	
Original Equity Investment = $129,677	

2. Use of Equity Dividend to Prove the Internal Rate of Return (IRR)

$$Re = Y \frac{+dep}{-app} \times 1/Sn^4$$

Where: Re = Equity Dividend

Re = .12 − .80 (.056984)   Y = Equity Yield
Re = .12 − .045587   1/Sn = SFF @ Equity Yield Rate
Re = .074413
  (Equity Dividend) $\frac{+dep}{-app}$ = the app/dep expressed

Re = .74413 x original equity   as a percentage of
Re = .074413 x $129,677   original equity, not
Re = $9,649.65   total value

Value	$518,708
Original Investment	$129,677
Holding Period	10 years
Gain at Resale (in 10 years)	$103,742 (80.00% App.)
Annual Equity Dividend	$9,649.65
Annual Equity Dividend Rate	7.4413%
Total Profit	$200.239
Average Yearly Profit	$20,024
Average Rate of Profit	15.44%

A. Trial @ 15.00% IRR:

SFF @ 15.00% = .049252
Growth Rate = .80 x .049242 = .039402

Dividend Rate = .074413
Growth Rate   = .039402
Trail IRR   = .113815 (.036185 off of trial rate)

B. Trail @ 11.50% IRR:

SFF @ 11.50% = .058377
Growth Rate = .80 x .058377 = .046702

Dividend Rate = .074413
Growth Rate   = .046702
Trial IRR   = .121115 (.006115 off of trial rate)

C. Trail @ 12.00% IRR:

SFF @ 12.00% = .056984
Growth Rate = .80 x .056984 = .045587

Dividend Rate = .074413
Growth Rate   = .045587
Trial IRR   = .120000 (.000000 off trial rate = ACTUAL IRR)

3. Present Value of the Equity Position Using Equity Dividend

Net Operating Income (NOI)	$45,000.00
less Debt Service	$39,176.98
equals Equity Income	$ 5,823.02
plus Equity Build-up (annually .056984 x $67,150)	$ 3,826.48
equals Annual Equity Dividend	$ 9,649.50

(actually equals to $9,649.65, difference of $.15 due to use of only 5 significant digits in calculation)

Present Value of Equity Dividend = $ 9,649. 65 x 5.650223
                               = $ 54,523
plus Present Value of Appreciation = $103,742.00 x .321973
                               = $ 33,402
plus Present Value of Deferred Return of Original Equity
              = $129,677.00 x .321973 = $ 41,752
Present Value of Equity Position   = $129,677

Original Equity Investment   = $129,677

It should, at least, be evident that the Ellwood formulation does provide for a proper distribution of the returns to the mortgage and to the equity. The last illustration above shows that the equity dividend, said by some authors not to be present in mortgage equity analysis, is "alive and well." The equity dividend does, however, differ significantly from the "equity income." The equity income represents before tax cash flow (NOI less debt service) while the equity dividend incorporates equity build-up in its calculation. The basic difference is that the equity income (cash flow or cash throw-off) represents returns which are more tangible. Equity dividend includes all returns (including equity build-up) which might possibly accrue to the property on an annual basis. The reason that both equity income and equity dividend will provide the same present value of the equity position is two-fold. First, because there is only one present value of the equity position so any calculation that did not arrive at the original equity investment would be in error. Secondly, both methods used the same overall components from the Equity Reversion. The difference with the equity dividend is that the equity build-up is not shown as a sum to be received at the end of the holding period; it is shown as part of the annual return to the equity investment. The Equity Reversion is made of the following components:

Equity Reversion:

Capital Gain Over Holding Period (the % apprection)	$103,742
Equity Build-up over Holding Period	$ 67,150
Return of the Original Equity	$129,677
Equity Reversion	$300,569

Reference to example proof #1 above will confirm this amount as the proper equity reversion after allowance for payment of the balance owed on the mortgage at the end of the holding period.

One of the advantages stated earlier in utilizing the Ellwood formulazation was that it was easily adaptable for "sensitivity analysis." There are several of the basic assumptions which can be varied, holding the others constant, in order to view the effects of varying mortgage market or equity investor positions. These effects are viewed in terms of the value which will be

required to produce the desired returns to both the mortgage holder and the equity investor. The assumptions which will be varied below are:
1. Loan to Value Ratio
2. Mortgage Interest Rate
3. Equity Yield Rate
4. Increase or Decrease in Value
5. Holding Period

When viewing the entirely of the Ellwood formula, it is apparent that for each "sensitivity run," there are only one or two portions of the formula which will require adjustment. Other methods of mortgage equity analysis may not be quite so flexible in this regard.

$$R = Y - M \left(Y + (P \times 1/Sn) - f \right) \begin{smallmatrix} +dep \\ -app \end{smallmatrix} \times 1/Sn$$

1. Varying the Loan to Value Ratio — only "M" changes
  "M" = 75%
    R = .12 – .75(.029132) – .011397
    R = .086754
  "M" = 60%
    R = .108603 – .60(.029132)
    R = .091124
  "M" = 90%:
    R = .108603 – .90(.029132)
    R = .082384

Loan to Value	Value
60%	$493,833
75%	$518,708
90%	$546,233

2. Varying the Mortgage Interest Rate — "P" and "f" change
Mortgage Interest = 9%:
   R = .12 - .75(.12 + (.172608 x .056984) - .100704)

$$- .011397$$

   R = .086754
Mortgage Interest = 8.5%:
   R = .12 - .75(.12 + (.182294 x .056984) - .096627)

$$- .011397$$

   R = .083283
Mortgage Interest = 9.5%:
   R = .12 - .75(.12 + (.163306 x .056984) - .104844)

$$- .011397$$

   R = .090256

Mortgage Interest	Value
8.5%	$540,326
9.0%	$518,708
9.5%	$493,118

3. Varying the Equity Yield Rate — "Y" and "1/Sn" change
Equity Yield = 12%:
   R = .12 - .75(.12 + .172608 x .056984) - .100704)

$$- .20 \text{ x } .056984)$$

   R = .086754
Equity Yield = 10%:
   R = .10 - .75(.10 + (.172608 x .062745) - .100704)

$$- (.20 \text{ x } .062745)$$

   R = .079856
Equity Yield = 14%:
   R = .14 - .75(.14 + (.172608 x .051714) - .100704)

$$- (.20 \text{ x } .051714)$$

   R = .093490

Equity Yield	Value
10%	$563,514
12%	$518,708
14%	$481,335

4. *Varying the Anticipated Increase or Decrease in Value — only*
   "+dep" change
   –app
   20% Appreciation:
       R = .098151 – (.20 x .056984)
       R = .086754
   10% Appreciation:
       R = .098151 – (.10 x .056984)
       R = .092452
   0% Appreciation:
       R = .098151 – (0 x .056984)
       R = .098151 = basic "r"

Appreciation	Value
0%	$458,477
10%	$486,739
15%	$518,708

5. *Varying Holding Periods — "P" and "1/Sn" change*
   10 Year Holding Period:
       R = .12 – .75(.12 + (.172608 x .056984) – .100704)
                                              – (.20 x .056984)
       R = .086754
   5 Year Holding Period:
       R = .12 – .75(.12 + (.067276 x .157410) – .100704)
                                              – (.20 x .157410)
       R = .66103
   15 Year Holding Period:
       R = .12 – .75(.12 + (.337524 x .026824) – .100704)
                                              – (.20 x .026824)
       R = .093372

Holding Period	Value
5 years	$680,756
10 years	$518,708
15 years	$481,943

Using the example property as our "norm", the situation presented by the "sensitivity runs" may be analyzed.

1. Loan to Value Ratios:

A higher loan to value ratio would be desirable in terms of less original equity investment, but it would also require a larger mortgage and therefore larger debt service. The opposite is true as the loan to value ratio is lowered. In order to maintain the desired returns to the equity position, as the loan to value ratio increases, the property value must increase also to compensate.

2. Mortgage Interest Rate:

As would be expected, to provide the same stated returns to the equity position, increasing the mortgage interest rate would necessitate lowering the amount of value the mortgage would be paid from. A 12% return to equity may be maintained with a 9.5% mortgage (versus a 9.0% mortgage) if the amount of the mortgage is reduced. This methodology provides the precise amount of reduction or increase mat would be required in the mortgage position while not changing the returns to the equity position.

3. Equity Yield Rate:

Holding all other requirements stable, an increase in the desired equity yield rate must be accompanied by a decrease in the total mortgage and equity position. A lower equity investment against a less sensitive equity income will increase the return to that equity position.

4. Increase or Decrease in Value:

Increasing the anticipated amount of captial gain produces the obvious result, an increase in the value of the property. In terms of the equity position, this may be viewed as an increase in the Equity Reversion and Equity Income, in order to maintain a 12% return on the original equity. With increases in value, the "percent" return remains the same but it should be pointed out that the "dollar" returns will be increased.

5. Holding Period:

Because of the increased amount of income generated by increasing the holding period, the values must go down to maintain the 12% return to equity. Therefore, the shorter one anticipates holding an investment property, the more he must be willing to pay in order to achieve stated returns. Over time, the same returns may be achieved at a reduced purchase price.

The above is not intended to be an in-depth analysis of the

sensitivity analysis presented. It was merely designed to provide the reader with exposure and perhaps appreciation of the benefits which may be derived from such analysis. It is true that one may employ either the band-of-investments method or the Ellwood formula in any circumstance to arrive at precisely the same rate. The method ultimately employed by the Appraiser should be that which best suits the type of analysis undertaken.

One of the primary criticisms of the mortgage equity method of valuation is that it assumes a level income stream over the anticipated holding period. This is a legitimate criticism when evidence can be provided that projected income streams should be either declining or increasing. The Ellwood formulation does, however, allow for "constant" increases or decreases in the annual income stream through the use of the "J" Factor, as mentioned earlier. The "J" Factor only allows for equal increments and since, at the present time its use is not widespread, it will not be discussed in this article. Increases and decreases in the annual income stream (of equal or unequal increments) may be valued easily by using After Tax Cash Flow Analysis, as shown below. If the valuation desired is "Before-Tax", the formula below could still be utilized by changing the two numerators to "R_t" and "$P_n - UM$," respectively.

After-Tax Cash Flow Analysis

Another method of analyzing investment properties which separates the property into its mortgage and equity components is that of after-tax cash flow analysis. A detailed presentation of this method is beyond the scope of this chapter. Suffice it to say that after-tax cash flow analysis does lend itself more to "investment values" as specific assumptions are made concerning the income tax status of the particular investor. In the opinion of this author, the best reference and treatise on after-tax cash flows may be found in Paul F. Wendt's, *Real, Estate Apppraisal: Review and Outlook,* published by the University of Georgia Press (1974) and in his *Real Estate Investment Analysis and Taxation,* McGraw-Hill, 1969. Wendt's forumla for estimating the value of the equity position is as follows. It will accompany any type of varying income stream, holding period, or combination of financing arrangements.

$$V - D = E \sum_{t=1}^{n} \frac{R_t - I_t - A_t - T_t}{(1 + r)^t} + \frac{P_n - GT - UM^5}{(1 + r)^n}$$

Where:

V = Value of Property
R_t = Annual net income in period t
I_t = Interest paid on mortgage in period t
A_t = Mortgage amortization in period t
T_t = Income tax allowance in period t
P_n = Sales price or residual in period (t=n)
GT = Captial gains tax
UM = Unpaid mortgage
 r = Rate of return
 D = Mortgage debt

Instant Mortgage Equity Analysis

"Instant" mortgage equity analysis may be accomplished by using precomputed tables which provide a fast and efficient way of locating a mortgage equity rate. The books containing precomputed tables should be utilized as an appraisal "tool," not as an appraisal method. For this reason, listing instant mortgage equity anlaysis as the fourth method is somewhat erroneous. It is not a "method," it is a "place" where rates may be found.

The *Ellwood Tables for Real Estate Appraising and Financing* published by the American Institute of Real Estate Appraisers, contain both compound interest tables (from which precomputed tables are tabulated) and precomputed tables. The format, however, tends to be so cumbersome that many who aspire to enter the tables and emerge with a composite rate find themselves "up to their neck" in different sets of tables and left with the impression that perhaps "you just cannot get there from here." Irv Johnson's *The Instant Mortgage-Equity Technique,* published by Lexington Books, provides a much more understandable method of finding mortgage equity rates for varying situations with ease and comfort. One must still read the desired components carefully or find themselves on the wrong page or in the wrong column. However, if problems are encountered of that magnitude, perhaps the Appraiser should re-analyze his own capabilities.

This author would advise anyone to look at any "instant" anything with some degree of caution. It could be most disconcerting to be able to find something (like an overall rate) and not really understand the various components of it or exactly what it does. Instant mortgage equity techniques are highly recommended as an appraisal tool. Use of them however, should be put off until one feels completely confident that he could defend the rates in court. The comfort of knowing every portion of that overall rate makes the use of precomputed books a pleasure. The discomfort of using something not fully understood is indescribable. There are also times when the analyst has exactly the data needed to find the overall rate and that particular set of circumstances are not to be found in the precomputed tables.

Precomputed tables, are then, an excellent tool, given an understanding of how they are calculated. I find them a constant source of reference information but never use them as a substitute for the knowledge required for proficiency in mortgage equity valuation.

Mortgage Equity Analysis and the Review Appraiser

Mortgage Equity Analysis has univeral application to all types of income producing properties under a variety of assumptions. It provides an excellent mechanism for analyzing the particular desires of a given investor and for providing the investor with an "investment value" tailored to his equity requirements.

The Review Apprasier should be aware of these valuation techniques and their underlying assumptions which may be provided in any appraisal report concerning an income producing property. In his appraisal review of the techniques utilized in the Income Approach, he should check the throughness of the search for market (economic) rentals and analyze the various deductions which were made in arriving at the net operating income. Publications such as *The Dollars and Cents of Shopping Centers* (Urban Land Institute); *Income and Expense Analysis for Aprartments, Condominiums and Cooperatives* Institute of Real Estate Management); and the Business Owners and Operators Assoication's *BOMA* may be used to double check if income and expenses are "typical".

Mortgage terms utilized in the capitalization rate structure may be either verified and documented in the report with sales data or by data which was gathered from lending institutions on comparable properties which would represent "typical" terms for the subject property. The equity rates utilized in a report may be documented by market abstraction from sales data and as illustrated earlier in this article.

When a technique such as mortgage equity analysis is utilized, the mathematics within the report are more detailed and crucial (as they pertain to the capitalizations rate) to the resulting value estimate than with the other approaches to value. For this reason, the mathematics should be checked closely to insure that the intended inputs to the rate produce the correct estimate of value (given those assumptions).

In other words, the Review Appraiser should know the variations within each valuation method (i.e. the Income Approach and Mortgage Equity Analysis) as well as the Appraiser who utilized the technique in the report. His task of reviewing the accuracy and completeness of data presented in every report demands a high degree of technical expertise since he ultimately shares responsibility for the final value estimate.

FOOTNOTES

1. For format, see Leon W. Ellwood, *Ellwood Tables for Real Estate Appraising and Financing, Part I* (Chicago: American Institute of Real Estate Appraisers, 1970), p. 74.
2. Charles B. Akerson, *Capitalization Theory and Techniques* (Chicago: American Institute of Real Estate Appraisers, 1977), p. 87.
3. Ellwood, *op. cit.,* pp. 11-15.
4. Akerson, *op. cit.,* pp. 52, 65.
5. Paul F. Wendt, *Real Estate Appraisal: Review and Outlook* (Athens: University of Georgia Press, 1974), pp. 158-159.

REFERENCES

Akerson, C. B. "Ellwood Without Algerba." *The Appraisal Journal,* July 1970, pp. 325-335.

Akerson, C. B. *Capitalization Therory & Techniques.* Chicago: American Institute of Real Estate Appraisers, 1977.

American Institute of Real Estate Appraisers. *The Appraisal of Real Estate.* Chicago, 1977.

Babcock, F. W. *The Valuation of Real Estate.* New York: McGraw-Hill, 1932.

Bonbright, J. C. *The Valuation of Property.* Vol. I-II. New York: McGraw-Hill, 1937.

Ellwood, L. W. "Emphasis on Equity." *The Appraisal Journal,* July, 1964, pp. 332-334.

Ellwood, L. W. *Ellwood Tables for Real Estate Appraising and Financing.* Part I and Part II. Chicago: American Institute of Real Estate Appraisers, 1970.

Gilreath, Morgan B., Jr. "The Valuation of Partial Interest," *The Assessor's Journal,* June 1978, pp. 63-80.

Gilreath, Morgan B., Jr. "Perspectives On The Income Approach," *The Assessor's Journal,* March, 1979, pp. 35-48.

Kinnard, W. N. *Income Property Valuation.* Lexington, Mass.: Heath Lexington Books, 1971.

Messner, Stephen D.; Schreiber, Irving; and Lyon, Victor L. *Marketing Investment Real Estate, Finance Taxation Techniques.* Chicago: Realtors National Marketing Institute of the National Association of Realtors, 1975.

Morrison, D. J. "Cash Flow Valuation and Yield Valuation." *The Appraisal Journal,* January, 1972, pp. 83-95.

Ring, A. A. *The Valuations of Real Estate,* 2nd Ed. Englewood Cliffs, New Jersey: Prentice-Hall, 1970.

Wendt, Paul F. "Ellwood, Inwood, and the Internal Rate of Return." *The Appraisal Journal,* October, 1967, pp. 561-574.

Wendt, Paul F. *Real Estate Appraisal: Review and Outlook.* Athens: University of Georgia Press, 1974.

Wendt, Paul F. and Gilreath, Morgan B. "Apartment To Condominium Conversions," *The Real Estate Appraiser,* May-June, 1974, pp. 35-42.

The following exhibits were developed by Walter S. Hanni, CRA, MAI, Chairman of N.A.R.A.'s Education Committee. Mr. Hanni has drawn upon his extensive experience in Appraisal Review to provide examples that are comprehensive and clear to both the novice and the long-established professional. His talents and guidance in the preparation of "Principles and Techniques of Appraisal Review" have contributed immeasurably to the quality of the publication. The time and effort devoted by Mr. Hanni ensures this volume to be a most significant contribution to the Real Estate Industry.

PART III

Guidelines and Examples

EXHIBIT 1:

Detailed Appraisal

Review and Approval

EXAMPLE: DETAILED APPRAISAL REVIEW AND APPROVAL

Appraisal Review and Analysis

Mr. Joseph Nelson
General Manager
Real Estate Division

In compliance with your request, and in accordance with my authority, I have carefully reviewed the attached appraisal report which covers 109,798 square feet of vacant land situated on North Adams. Subject report as of: June 1, 1976, was prepared by: John Doe, an Associate Appraiser of Denver, Colorado.

I have reviewed the subject report from the standpoint of meeting established specifications and requirements, as well as conforming to acceptable professional appraisal practices and techniques; scope of the appraisal investigation; factual data considered; reasoning and logic of the appraisal process and reasonableness of the valuation conclusion of: $680,000.00.

FORM AND PRESENTATION:

This appraisal meets all Contract Requirements, as well as accepted appraisal standards for analytical narrative appraisal reports.

DELINEATION OF ASSIGNMENT:

The appraiser's have adequately delineated the purpose of the report; described the property; substantiated the highest and best use; and set forth limiting conditions and assumptions.

The following assumptions are recited as being of major importance in connection with the valuation:

(1)   That Rio Grande Drive will be properly graded and surfaced. Concrete curbs and gutter, will be installed by others.

(2)   That all required utilities will be provided to the site, at the cost of seller.

(3)   That the rear terraced portion and steep enbankment on the site is not usable.

(4)   A 15' sewer line traverses the site, which is not defined or a recorded easement, and it is assumed any such right of way to be fifteen feet in width.

(5)   That there is no adverse soil conditions.

ANALYSIS TECHNIQUES AND DATA UTILIZED

Factual Data Considered

The Appraiser's have adequately presented and considered the economics, general area, trends and environmental influences of the area and neighborhood.

Subject is situated in an outlying neighborhood which is mostly vacant land. Local governmental planning is attempting to shift governmental and commercial interests to this area, away from the downtown tourist oriented area.

The population has doubled in the past five years, and the local government re-wrote the zoning manual to control and limit the growth, which has affected development.

The energy crisis has also created a moritorium on natural gas hookups, which restricts developments.

The subject adjoins an existing sewer plant which is a detrimental influence. However, it is expected that the use of this plant will be phased out in the not-too-distant future.

Exhibit 1. Detailed Appraisal Review and Approval / 365

The existing zoning is for service, commercial and industrial use which is also a specially planned area.

The highest and best use determined by the Appaiser was to be for commercial usage in nature, which is concurred by the review.

The unusable rear area has been estimated by the Appraiser to be approximately 30,445 square feet, or approximately 28% of the total site area.

No mineral value was indicated.

Factual Errors or Omissions

No computational or other factual errors or omissions were noted.

Reasoning and Logic of Appraisal Process Utilized

The valuation of subject property has been based upon off site improvements installed at the cost of others. The Appraiser also went into the history of subject ownership, which indicated a sale at $2.45 per square foot on the total acquisition of 19.546 arces; a sale of 8.082 acres of the larger ownership at $5.43 per square foot in December of 1973; and another sale of 11.496 acres in September of 1973 at $3.49 per square foot.

The Appraisers have also taken congnizance of a pending sale of a corner parcel located adjacent to the subject for a super market, at a reported price of $8.25 per square foot, comprising of 2 acres.

The Appraisers have eliminated the cost and income approaches as being inapplicable, which is concurred in.

A diligent search of the market was made, and some 36 sales indices were utilized in the market approach to value.

These sales indicated a range of $2.45 to $22.67 per square foot in the period of 1970 to 1975 of site areas comprising .07 to 19.54 acres.

Because of location and size, it was their opinion that the subject tended toward the lower indicators.

After careful comparative analysis with the subject and after utilizing "bracketing procedures", the Appraiser narrowed this range to $2.45 to $8.93, and further to $5.43 to $8.50 per square foot. This analysis was carefully done and the conclusions are concurred in by the Reviewer.

The Appraiser segregated the site area into three categories:
A. — Level usable area.
B. — Steep upper terrace — unusable area.
C. — Sewer Main Right-of-Way area.

From the analysis they have made, the Appraisers concluded the following valuation, under their initial premise:

A. — $8.00 per square foot =		$592,824.00
B. — $2.00 per square foot =		$ 60,890.00
C. — $4.00 per square foot =		$ 21,000.00
	TOTAL	$674,714.00

A rationale under "C" was that the right-of-way area surface could be utilized for parking purposes.

A second premise was used whereby the cost of relocation of the sewer line was considered.

This indicated the following valuation:

Area's A & C at $8.00 per square foot	$634,824.00
Area B at $2.00 per square foot	$ 60,890.00
	$695,714.00
Less the estimated cost of relocating the sewer line	$ 10,000.00
	$685,714.00

The relocation cost of $10,000.00 was based upon an estimate obtained from a contractor and appears to be adequately justified.

In the final analysis, the Appraisers concluded a valuation of $680,000.00 for an average value of $6.19 per square foot.

Reconciliation and Reasonableness of Conclusion Reached

From my reviewing analysis, it is my considered judgement that the estimated valuation of $680,000.00 is a fair and reasonable estimate of the property's probable market value.

Adequacy of Report

It is my opinion that this appraisal is adequate for the purpose intended.

APPRAISERS QUALIFICATIONS

The Appraiser's are indicated to be well qualified and experi-

Exhibit 1. Detailed Appraisal Review and Approval / 367

enced in the appraisal of such properties in this area, and the quality of their report so indicated.

FIELD REVIEW

None made.

APPRAISER DISCUSSION (Conference)

None considered necessary.

OFFER TO SELL

The owners have offered the subject property at $800,000 which indicates an overall per square foot price of approximately $7.29.

REVIEWER'S CONCLUSIONS AND RECOMMENDATIONS

A. It is my recommendation that the appraised valuation of $680,000.00 be approved as being fair and just compensation for the subject property, including all off-site streets and utilities.
B. It is recommended that the Appraisers fee of $1,500 be paid as having satisfactorily met contract requirments.

CONTRACT DATA

1. Contract Number	06-9218-75-PT41
2. Date Of Contract	July 7th, 1975
3. Time Element	60 Days
4. Date Received	August 5th, 1975
5. Appraisal Fee	$1,500.00

BY: _____

Walter S. Hanni, C.R.A.
Reviewing Appraiser

EXHIBIT 2:

Detailed Appraisal

Review and Disapproval

with Attached

Field Representative

Review Form

EXAMPLE:
> Detailed Appraisal Review and Disapproval with Attached
> Field Representative Review Form

Bangor, Maine — Administrative Facility for Disposal
Appraisal Review and Analysis

Mr. James Smith, Director
Real Estate Division

In compliance with your request, and in accordance with my authority, I have carefully reviewed the attached appraisal report which covers 30,643 square feet of land area, and a two story building with a basement facility of approximately 26,379 square feet of floor area, situated on Main Street in Bangor, Maine.

Subject report as of March 15th, 1979, was prepared by John Doe, Appraiser, Boston, Massachusetts.

I have reviewed the subject report from the standpoint of meeting established specifications and requirements, as well as conforming to acceptable professional appraisal practices and techniques; scope of the appraisal investigation; factual data considered; reasoning and logic of the appraisal process and reasonableness of the valuation conclusion of $270,000.00.

FORM AND PRESENTATION

The appraisal meets contract requirements, as well as accepted standards for analytical narrative appraisal reports.

DATE: 4/24/75
SUBJECT: Field Appraisal Review & Analysis
PROJECT: Bangor, Maine — Exisiting Administrative Facility
CONTRACT APPRAISER: John Doe

1. I have reviewed the above referenced appraisal, and I will concur in the Appraiser's valuation estimate of: $_____ with the following comments: N/A
2. I have reviewed the above referenced appraisal and I do not concur in the Appraiser's valuation estimate of: $270,000.00 for the following reasons:

   The appraisal is well presented and convincing, except for the capitalization rate of 9½% which was used on the income approach. This is all-important, and I believe that no prudent investor would pay $270,000.00 for this marginal property in the hope of obtaining 9½% on his investment. I do not believe that properties such as warehouses, sold in Portland, have comparability to the subject. I also see little relationship of the subject to the office building in Bangor, located at 4th Avenue and 16th Street. It is clear that the greater risk involved in the subject should promise a greater return, say 12% to 16%.

3. It is recommended that the Appraiser's fee of: $2,500.00
   ☑ Be Paid

   ☐ Not be paid for at this time for the following reasons or subject to the following being submitted:

4. Other Remarks: Suggest contact with Appraiser regarding cap rate and his comments obtained prior to final estimate of value.

BY: _____
   Paul Jones
   Real Estate Representative

December 27th, 1974

Exhibit 2. Detailed Appraisal Review and Disapproval with Form / 371

DELINEATION OF ASSIGNMENT

The Appraisers have adequately delineated the purpose of the report; described the property; and set forth limiting conditions and assumptions. With respect to the Appraiser's conclusions concerning highest and best use, the Reviewer takes issue with the soundness of this conclusion which will later be discussed.

ANALYSIS TECHNIQUES AND DATA UTILIZED

Factual Data Considered

The Appraisers have presented and considered the economics, general area, trends and environmental influences of the area and neighborhood.

Bangor is supported mainly by an agricultural economy with the government being the largest employer in the County. The city has the highest per capita income in the State. Future growth is estimated to be steady, with good potential.

The subject is located in the old downtown area of Bangor, which has definitely and seriously been on the decline. Local efforts were made to revitalize the are with the "Bangor Mall" renovation project, to combat this downtown deterioration and the outflux of merchants. However, this has been unsuccessful. Some 27% of the stores were vacant in 1974, with numerous additional vacanies since then. The area South of the subject is a dilapidated residential area of which many buildings have been demolished. Business trends have been to the south. Demand for office space in this area is extremely limited, and with the increasing supply of convertable office space in vacant buildings, the market has been further affected. The Appraiser's have also indicated that it is highly improbable that the area will ever regain prominence, based upon the size of the City, rate of growth and the trend of growth.

With this economic picture, it can be concluded that conversion and private economic usage of the subject property is highly improbable at this time.

It is indicated that irrespective of its age, the facility is considered to be in excellent condition, including the installed equipment.

Factual Errors or Omissions

No computational or other factual errors or omissions were noted.

Reasoning and Logic of Appraisal Process Utilized

The Appraisers concluded that there is no economic need for the subject facility for private market useage. However, they indicated that it is highly improbable that this structure will be demolished within the next 40 years. This conclusion appears to be reasonable, based upon the factual data.

They have based their conclusion of highest and best usage and value concept upon the premise that the most likely user, and only tenancy capable of occupying the structure, will be some governmental type agency, desiring a large quanitity of office space and one who is politically motivated for this location.

The Reviewer has taken exception to this premise upon the basis of factual economic data presented for the area. Also, there was really no support presented — "Market-wise" for such usage.

The questionable premise was discussed with the Appraiser. His explanation, in effect, was that this was not based upon a market analysis, indicating a need by such agencies, as well as ability, to pay market value for such space. It was predicated mainly upon a subjective assumption that the city would endeavor to acquire this property for governmental usage in order to futher revitalize the "Bangor Mall" area.

While during the original concept of a new Administrative Facility, there was some interest in a "trade" of the subject for the proposed facility on City owned property. Such is apparently no longer being actively considered.

It is my considered opinion that the Appraiser's determination of usage is not adequately substantiated by factual market analysis, and therefore rests upon "Thin Ice". It is, therefore, not a very reasonable assumption.

In support of their value conclusion, the Appraiser's have considered the accepted the approaches to value, which will be separately commented upon by the Reviewer.

Land Value — Market Approach
The value of the subject site is directly related to surrounding

Exhibit 2. Detailed Appraisal Review and Disapproval with Form / 373

property values, and the ability to return a positive cash flow. The many properties vacated, and the poor likelihood of improvement has resulted in declining value of the remaining properties.

Some eleven (11) sales indices were utilized during a span of 1961 to 1973. These ranged in size from 1,520 to 117,000 square feet, and ranged in price from .36 to $4.41 per square foot. Of these sales, the Appraiser's concluded a "bracket" value of .42 per square foot on sales 2 and 3, to an upper limit of .69 under sale 6. From this, the Appraiser's concluded a valuation of .56 per square foot, or $17,200 being the median. They also indicated this to be a "speculators gamble" to some degree.

Upon the factual economic conditions of the area and trends, this estimate is concurred in as being reasonably indicative of the land's probable market value.

In the Site Planning Report, the valuation for land was estimated at $1.35 per square foot, or $43,000, which in my opinion, is quite high under the current conditions.

Cost Approach to Value
The structure is a reinforced concrete two story building with a full basement, constructed in 1933 and is in excellent physical condition. The first floor could be partitioned into office space without difficulty, and the second floor is already divided into offices. The Appraisers consider it improbable that the structure would be demolished within the next 40 years.

The Appraiser's eliminated the use of the cost approach as being an inappropriate technique for the subject property. The property being an over-improvement with substantial obsolescence, depreciation is difficult to estimate and can only be reflected in the income approach.

While the Reviewer is in agreement that the property is an over-improvement, construction-wise, and that there is substantial depreciation, I can not agree with their premise of non-use of this approach. Their income approach, as will be further discussed, is weak, and under these circumstances, the cost approach should have been utilized for further support. It is also my opinion that this technique, correctly executed, would show a valuation substantially below their value conclusion of $270,000.00. Also, for this type of property, and under the current circumstances, the remaining physical value of the structure would be most indicative of value to any potential user.

Market Approach — Overall Property
The Appraiser's presented some five sales, and one offering of a retail store property, which have taken place in the area from 1971 to 1973. Most of these were smaller properties and the range of price per square foot of the building indicated .50 to $6.11. The Appraisers discounted these sales as not being meaningful as indicators of the comparative value for the subject. Therefore, no value was indicated under this approach.

The Reviewer generally concurs with their conclusion concerning this approach. However, using even the upper limit of these indices, a valuation of $100,000 or more below the Appraiser's valualtion conclusion of $270,000 would be indicated.

Income Approach to Value
The approach to value was utilized as the Appraiser's *only* basis for market value.

The Appraiser's utilized some 19 leases of government and non-government space in various office buildings in Bangor. These ranged from approximately $2.00 to $6.60 per square foot, per year. From an analysis, and considering the location and quality, the Appraiser's estimated the economic rent as follows:

Basement: $2.25 per square foot per year
First Floor: $4.25 per square foot per year
1st Floor Mezzanine: $3.75 per squar foot per year
Second Floor: $3.75 per square foot per year

This resulted in a gross income of $69,759. If anything, in my opinion, this is probably on the high side, considering economic conditions of the area. In order to attract adequate occupancy, any rental rate would have to be quite low, possiblly lower than they have established.

The basis for the expenses appears to be adequately substantiated. The total expenses, approximating 59%, appears to be reasonable for such a property.

The estimated net operating income of $25,694.00 compares to $27,509, as estimated in the Site Report.

The Appraisers utilized a capitalization rate of 9.5%. This was based upon an indication of a Savings & Loan Company acquisition in Bangor, which indicated a 8.3%, and two J.C. Penney warehouses in Portland. The Reviewer takes exception to this rate, as being probably low for such a property. This matter was discussed with the Appraiser. He indicated that this rate was based on the assumption of governmental usage and predicated upon the City probably taking the property in its entirety. He also indi-

Exhibit 2. Detailed Appraisal Review and Disapproval with Form / 375

cated that if one were to assume multiple ownership under the general market, a much higher cap-rate would have to be used.

Some question is also raised by the Reviewer, as to the comparability of the cap-rate support properties to the subject property.

It is my considered opinion that to assume City acquistion of the subject property at such a price, is a precarious assumption.

Based upon this income approach, the Appraisers concluded a market valuation of $270,000.00. This compares with a valuation of $172,000.00 estimated in the site planning report.

From the analysis I have made of this approach, there is considerable doubt in my mind as to its being reliably indicative of the probable market value of the subject property for disposal purposes.

Correlation and Reasonableness of Conclusion Reached

From the review and analysis I have made, it is my considered judgement that the estimated valuation of $270,000.00 is probably quite high, and has not been substantiated and justified beyond a reasonable doubt.

In arriving at this conclusion, the Reviewer has given consideration to the field appraisal review and analysis, dated April 24th, 1975, prepared by Paul Jones, Real Estate Representative, which is attached herewith. I concur in his conclusions and recommendations. Mr. Jones prepared the previous valuation in the site report.

Adequacy of Report

It is my opinion that his report is adequate from the standpoint of being well presented and having satisfied the contract requirements; although I do not concur in the valuation conclusion reached. From this standpoint, it is not adequate for disposition purposes at this time. It is therfore recommended that a second appraisal be obtained prior to disposition of this property.

APPRAISER'S QUALIFICATIONS

Appraiser John Doe is known by the undersigned to be an extremely well qualified and experienced Appraiser in the New England Area.

FIELD REVIEW

None made by the Reviewer.

APPRAISER DISCUSSION (Conference)

As previously mentioned, certain factors were discussed with the Appraiser in the course of preparing this review.

SITE REPORT

Under the Site Selection Report, dated November 1974, prepared by Paul Jones, Real Estate Representative, the value for disposal purposes was estimated to be $172,000. Under review, dated December 9, 1974, the undersigned took some exception to this valuation conclusion; however, it is probably more indicative of value than that estimated by the appraisal.

OFFER TO SELL

No offer has been obtained in connection with the disposal of this property.

REVIEWER'S CONCLUSIONS AND RECOMMENDATIONS

A. It is my recommendation that the appraised valuation of $270,000.00 *not* be approved at this time, for disposal purposes.
B. It is further recommended that a second appraisal be obtained, from a well qualified Appraiser, prior to disposition of the subject property.
C. It is recommended that the Appraiser's fee of $2,500 be paid, as having satisfactorily met their contract requirements.

Exhibit 2. Detailed Appraisal Review and Disapproval with Form / 377

ADDITIONAL DATA

Appraisal Contract Number: #07-8742-67-Q-2C8T
Date of Contract: February 14th, 1975 (Transmittal February 24)
Time Allowed: 30 days
Date Received: April 22, 1975 (Note: Delay in submission was caused by a request from this office to defer this appraisal and complete another contract first).
Fee: $2,500.00

By _____

   Walter S. Hanni
   Reviewing Appraiser

Concurred _____

   Deborah S. Johnson
   Manager, Real Estate Section

COMMENTS:

The subject USPS - owned property is located in the old downtown area of Bangor, which has been in a serious economic decline. Righ now, 27% of the stores in the downtown area are presently vacant.

Demand for office space in the area is extemely limited, and there is no economic need for additional private market usage of office space. The Appraiser has based his highest and best usage and value conception upon the premise of Governmental type agency usage. His usage is not substantiated by factural market analysis. Therefore, I do not agree with his assumption, nor do I agree with his appraised value of $270,000, but should be at a market value substantially below this figure.

I concur with Walt Hanni, CRA, that the appraised value of $270,000 should not be approved and that a second appraisal be obtained prior to disposal of this property.

EXHIBIT 3:

Consolidated

Reviewing Statement

Two Appraisals

January 26,1976
EXAMPLE — Consolidated Reviewing Statement
Two Appraisals — Banner Property, Chicago, Illinois

Mr. Ralph Mason, Director
Real Estate Division

In connection with the above referenced project, attention is directed to the following:
1. Appraisal Report, dated September 27, 1974, prepared by Smith Associates, Chicago, Illinois, wherein the valuation of the subject property was estimated to be $10,000,000.
2. Appraisal Review and Analysis, dated November 12, 1974, prepared by Walter S. Hanni, CRA, Reviewing Appraiser on 1 above.
3. Joint Appraisal Report, dated December 19, 1974, prepared by Walter Grignon and Paul Bertrand (both of Chicago, Illinois) wherein the valuation of the subject property was estimated to be $11,250,000.
4. Appraisal Review and Analysis, dated January 22, 1975, prepared by Walter S. Hanni, CRA, Reviewing Appraiser on 3 above.

PURPOSE

The purpose of this reviewing statement is to make a comparative analysis of the two separate appraisals prepared on this project, and to arrive at certain resulting conclusions and recommendations.

We have had the benefit of valuation opinions from three well qualified, experienced Appraiser's on such properties in this area. The conclusions which they have reached should, in effect, indicate the probable market value of the subject property, beyond a reasonable doubt. In considering this, it is fully realized that appraising is not an exact science.

COMPARATIVE ANALYSIS

The Smith report basically utilized the cost approach to estimate the market value of the subject property. The Grignon-Bertrand report utilized all three accepted approaches, but places greatest reliance upon the income and market approaches to value.

The various individual factors or approaches will be separtely, comparatively analyzed.

DATE: 4/24/75
SUBJECT: Field Appraisal Review & Analysis
PROJECT: Bangor, Maine — Existing Administrative Facility
CONTRACT APPRAISER: John Doe

1. I have reviewed the above referenced appraisal, and I concur in the Appraiser's valuation estimate of: $ _____ with the following comments: N/A
2. I have reviewed the above referenced appraisal, and I do not concur in the Appraiser's valuation estimate of: $270,000.00 for the following reasons:

   The appraisal is well presented and convincing, except for the capitalization rate of 9½% which was used on the income approach. This is all important, and I believe that no prudent investor would pay $270,000 for this marginal property in the hope of obtaining 9½% on his investment. I do not believe that properties such as warehouses sold in Portland have comparability to the subject. Also, I see little relationship of the subject to the office building in Bangor at 4th Avenue and 16th Street. It is clear that the greater risk involved in the subject should promise a greater return, say 12% to 16%.
3. It is recommended that the Appraiser's fee of $2,500.00
   ☑ Be Paid
   ☐ Not Be paid, at this time For the following reasons, or subject to the following being submitted:
4. Other Remarks: Sugguest contact with Appraiser regarding: cap rate and his comments obtained prior to final estimate of value.

By _____

Paul Jones
Real Estate Representative
December 27, 1974

Exhibit 3. Consolidated Reviewing Statement — Two Appraisals / 381

Cost Approach to Value

Land Value: Smith concluded a land value of $3.67 per square foot, or $3,184,000, which compares to $5.02 per square foot or $4,350,000 estimated in the second appraisal. Mr. Smith utilized four (4) sales in the area, of which all except one was considered in the second report. The second report considered 14 sales, and as such, in my opinion, considered a broader spectrum of the market. In a conference with Mr. Smith on November 21st, 1974, in Chicago, he intimated that he probably could have gone higher on his land value. Giving consideration to the above, it is my considered opinion that the second appraisal estimate of $5.02 is better substantiated and justified, and is more realistically indicative of the probable market value.

Replacement Cost

The replacement cost, as estimated by Appraiser Smith, is $7,402,348 or $23.95 per square foot. However, this is without architectural fees and building changes. The second appraisal estimated replacement at $8,345,000 or $27.00 per sqaure foot including fees and charges. Deducting fees and charges of 10% of the cost estimate is $7,584,869 or $24.54 per square foot. The two appraisals basic costs therefore compare quite closely. These basic costs on the Smith appraisal were also previously checked by Mr. Grignon and Mr. Bertrand, and were considered to be reasonably indicative.

There is a difference in the two appraisals on architectural fees and building charges, which divergence was to some degree caused by the method used. Smith figured his costs after deducting over-improvement, and 7% was used versus 10% in the second appraisal.

Depreciation

Appraiser Smith used a 6% physical depreciation, or $429,544, as compared to the second appraisal of 6%, or $500,700. The difference, which is not excessive, results from the base used. Appraiser Smith estimated the amount of over-improvement to be $711,625. The second appraisal estimated functional obsolescene to be $751,050. While the two appraisals used different premise's, in effect, they are both functional obsolescene and are thus in quite close proximity and therefore can be considered realistic and acceptable.

Cost Approach Estimate

The final cost approach estimate of the Smith appraisal is $9,913,529, including land value, as compared to $11,450,000 in the second appraisal. The major difference is in the land value. Utilizing the higher land value of $4,350,000 of the second appraisal on Mr. Smith's depreciated replacement cost of $7,159,073, a valuation of $11,500,000 rounded, or vitually the same would be indicated.

It is therefore my considered opinion that a valuation of $11,500,000, under the cost approach, is a fair and reasonable indication of the "upper limit" of value for the subject property in both appraisals are compatable in this respect.

Market Approach

The Smith appraisal did not utilize the market approach; since in his opinion it was not indicative of market value on such a unique property. No comparative analysis can be made on this approach with the second appraisal. In my review of this report on November 22, 1974, I stressed that this was one of the weaknesses of Mr. Smith's appraisal.

The second appraisal estimated the valuation of the subject property under this approach to be $11,000,000 to $11,500,000, with a final conclusion of $11,250,000. My comments concerning this approach were covered in my review of the second appraisal, dated January 22, 1975. This valuation could be considered a value to a "market user" of the property as is.

Income Approach

The rentable area used in both reports were the same. The average rental value used by Smith was .27 per square foot, and in the second appraisal, .30 per square foot was used. This is relatively close, and in my opinion, an acceptable difference. Both appraisals utilized a 10% capitalization rate, which appears to be justifed and substantiated. Both appraisals considered the undeveloped vacant area as excess to the properties needs, and added the value to the income value. This is concurred in as being a reasonable premise. Apprasier Smith used a lesser value

Exhibit 3. Consolidated Reviewing Statement — Two Appraisals / 383

per square foot for this undeveloped parcel, which resulted in an approximately $96,800 lesser value.

Both Appraiser's in their initial submission, did not include any item for expenses, to which the Reviewer took exception. Mr. Smith submitted a revision which changed his original valuation of $10,081,600 to $8,889,600. No supplemental revision has yet been obtained on the second appraisal, which will be covered under supplemental review when received.

Adjusting Mr. Smith's income valuation upward for a higher land value on the vacant parcel would indicate a valuation of approximately $10,000,000. Reducing the second appraisal some, for an item of expenses would reduce the valuation to at least $11,200,000 or less.

From this analysis, it is my considered opinion that a fair and reasonable estimate of the property's probable market value is $10,000,000 to $11,000,000 under the income approach.

CONCLUSIONS

From the comparative analysis I have made, I have reached the following conclusions:

Three Valuation Approaches

From the three approaches used by both Appraiser's, I have concluded the following as being reasonable estimates:
1. Cost Approach $11,500,000
2. Market Approach $11,250,000
3. Income Approach $10,000,000 to $11,000,000

Correlation

These value estimates fall in the usually accepted theoretical indications of value, which are: under normal conditions, the cost approach indicates the upper limit of value and the income approach indicates the lower limit of value. From this, it could be concluded that the subject property has a range of market value of $10,000,000 to $11,500,000.

Other Factors of Consideration

1. The valuation of $11,250,000, as estimated in the second ap-

praisal, has basically been estimated on the highest and best use for a "market user", who would purchase, and be able to utilize the subject property, as it is presently developed and equipped, as a research and development facility. In effect, this is indicative of the "maximum value" the property would have on the market. Considering a wider spectrum of the market, its value could be somewhere below this amount.

2.   An appraisal, especially of a large, unique facility such as this, is an economic analysis under conditions of uncertainty and its findings can be expressed only in probablistic terms. No Appraiser is capable of making a predicition of probable selling price in the form of a precise figure. At best, he can define a range of prices within which the selling price would probably fall, and, in some cases, he may have sufficient data to express his judgement at various points within this range. The valuation of a property of this complex nature, in my opinion, cannot therefore be expressed as an "exact figure", as is theoretically desirable. In the case in question, it may not be the most practical or logical.

Owning to the many variable factors present, in my opinion, a "range of value" is probably more logical and realistic.

3.   Theoretically, an appraisal for "market value" is based upon the "highest and best use", which in this particular case has been determined to be a "market user" who could utilize the property to its "full activity", as is.

The purpose of an appraisal is to estimate the most probable selling price.

When considering the value to a "user" in the market, this can be a widely variable amount. The question in any purchaser's mind is not necessarily *what he may pay*, but more, *what he should pay*, when considering his own requirements, as well as the property itself, and to its fitting his needs. Therefore, while market value, theoretically may be one thing, value to a particular user may be something entirely different. This factor must be kept in retrospect especially considering the U.S. Postal Service's particular requirements and use, as to what the value may be to them.

RECOMMENDATIONS

Based upon the comparative review and analysis I have made, the following are my considered recommendations:

A.   The market value of the subject property lies within a range of $10,000,000 to $11,500,000 for negotiating purposes.

Exhibit 3. Consolidated Reviewing Statement — Two Appraisals / 385

B. Discretion should be used as to the actual amount, offered or paid, depending upon the "use value" of the subject facility.

By _____

Walter S. Hanni, CRA
Reviewing Appraiser

Concurred _____

Raymond Stone
Real Estate Director